Knowledge and Knowing in Library and Information Science

A Philosophical Framework

John M. Budd

To Lynnette

Best, John Budd

The Scarecrow Press, Inc.
Lanham, Maryland, and London
2001

SCARECROW PRESS, INC.

Published in the United States of America
by Scarecrow Press, Inc.
4720 Boston Way, Lanham, Maryland 20706
www.scarecrowpress.com

4 Pleydell Gardens, Folkestone
Kent CT20 2DN, England

British Library Cataloguing-in-Publication Information Available

Library of Congress Cataloging-in-Publication Data

Budd, John, 1953–
    Knowledge and knowing in library and information science : a philosophical
framework / John M. Budd.
        p. cm.
    Includes bibliographical references (p.) and index.
    ISBN 0-8108-4041-3 (alk. paper) — ISBN 0-8108-4025-1 (pbk. : alk. paper)
        1. Library science—Philosophy. 2. Information science—Philosophy. 3. Knowledge,
    Theory of. 4. Classification of sciences. I. Title.
    Z665 .B918 2001
    020'.1—dc21   2001020523

To the memory of my mother and father

Contents

Introduction   1

Chapter One: The Beginnings of Science:
    An Exploration into the Formulation
    of Scientific Thought   7

Chapter Two: A Continuation of the Genealogy
    of Thought   57

Chapter Three: What Is Real?:
    Science and Ideas of Reality   95

Chapter Four: False Starts and Dead Ends
    for Social Science and LIS   149

Chapter Five: Knowledge and Knowing in LIS   203

Chapter Six: Paths to Knowledge   243

Chapter Seven: Products and Possibilities in LIS   291

References   331

Index   353

About the Author   361

Introduction

Whenever I read a book I appreciate a succinct introduction that tells just what I'll be reading about. So, with this I hope to provide readers with something of a statement of purpose and a description of content. First, I want to recognize that, as a profession, librarianship has as its principal goal a set of actions that are both inwardly and outwardly directed. Simply stated, librarianship seeks to provide information and reading materials to people through the purposeful collection of books, periodicals, and other media, provision of access to information in various formats, the organization of information to enhance meaning, and the design of services that enable people to read, to learn, and to grow. These actions are at the heart of the profession, but they are grounded in ways of thinking and in conceptions of knowledge. Complex action, like the elements mentioned above, does not spring from intuition or tacit reliance on reaction to stimuli, but on that thinking and knowledge. It is the thought that is at the heart of librarianship that is the focus of this book.

The thinking that guides work in every profession and discipline, including library and information science (LIS), has a heritage, a genealogy. There may be aspects of the heritage of thought that some fields share; there may be some unique elements in each. The thought on which today's action is based, or of which it is a product, is a long line of conjectures, suggestions, evidence, refutation, and revision. Much of that heritage is hidden to those who practice in these fields, unless they purposely inquire into the past. It may be argued that practice proceeds and progresses just fine in ignorance of the heritage. I'd suggest that such a view mistakenly interprets continued action as progress. Genuine progress—which I'll define here as the development and offering of effective service to communities, fruitful inquiry into enduring questions that helps us understand the complexity of our world, and making decisions that are really informed (in the sense that fully allows for the most useful internal workings and external effect)—only occurs when there has been deep critical investigation into the workings of our field. Critical investigation, of necessity, relies on knowing where we came from and how we got here, as well as where we're going.

The purpose of this book is to provide our field of LIS with a critical examination of the thought that influences practice so that progress, as defined above, can be realized. Granted, this is a tall order, but it is essential, especially as technological and other changes prompt us to revisit practice. As we contemplate changes to services and, at the most fundamental level, to the way we help people become informed, we need to be wary of the received (from our intellectual heritage) ways of thinking.

Ultimately, and I probably cannot emphasize this frequently enough, the reason for studying the intellectual foundations of LIS is to ensure that we strive to design the most effective information systems, to create and offer the most useful services, to help people with their information and reading needs, and to enable information seekers to make sense of the sometimes overwhelming bulk of stuff that is available. No one in LIS would deny these goals, but some suggest that achieving the goals has no intellectual basis. Several years ago Peter Hernon and Cheryl Metoyer-Duran interviewed a number of librarians, asking them, among other things, to evaluate our literature. One respondent said, "We are not scholars; we are librarians! Theory is for LIS faculty and doctoral students, not for us" (Hernon and Metoyer-

Duran, 1992, 504). It may be that much of what is published in LIS has little utility for praxis (a term that will be defined in context later in the book), but a facile dismissal of the literature, especially because it may be grounded in some theory, is hardly productive. I sincerely hope that more than faculty and students are interested in theory that can inform practice. To be effective, practitioners should be reflexive, should examine and question what we do, how we do it, and why we make the choices we do. This kind of reflection is ineluctably bound to thought and, so, is related to our heritage of thought.

In 1933 Pierce Butler wrote that "The librarian stands alone in the simplicity of his [*sic*] pragmatism" (Butler, 1961 [1933], xii). Butler was not eschewing pragmatism as such; American pragmatists, such as William James, Charles Sanders Peirce, and John Dewey, have asked serious questions about the ways we think and act. In fact, we might go so far as to say that any profession should have a serious pragmatic element. Pragmatism, however, does not mean a dismissal of thought and reflection. Some philosophers, most notably Richard Rorty, claim that, effectively, pragmatism trumps epistemology, that there is no point to a theory of knowledge; what is important is discovering what works. The error in this claim is the assumption that epistemology cannot be pragmatic, that examining knowledge cannot help us find the most effective action. The thought and reflection in LIS contributes to effective praxis. Throughout this book I'll explore the essential relationship between thought and praxis.

At the outset it will be necessary to examine some intellectual history. A principal reason for historical treatment is the question of science in LIS. At various points in the twentieth century some have searched for the science in library and information science; others have stated that there is little or nothing scientific about LIS; still others have urged us to first study what science is to see if there is any fit for our field. These discussions are, in fact, common throughout the social sciences. Since such discussions have been so persistent, and since they continue today, some study of science and its beginnings is necessary. The first chapter will begin scrutiny of the origin of what I'll call "modern science."

A modern view of science frequently begins with the eighteenth century, with the Enlightenment. In chapter 1 I will accept arguments that the beginnings of the Enlightment, and the beginnings of modern science, are actually earlier. The starting point will be Francis Bacon.

Chapter 2 continues the investigation of our intellectual heritage, or genealogy, by focusing on the late eighteenth century and the nineteenth century. This is a pivotal period in the development of all of the social sciences, and the developments of that time influence thought and action to this day. It was at that time that "positivism" had its origins. What is commonly referred to as positivism now differs from the original conception, but some essential aspects were first articulated then. Perhaps more correctly the nineteenth century saw the rise of what was purported to be a science of society—that, it was envisioned, would rival the mature natural sciences in explanatory and predictive power. The second chapter eventually takes the genealogy into the twentieth century and adds the suggested contributions of logic and linguistic analysis to the nineteenth century idea of social science.

By the third chapter the attention turns to contemporary thought on science. Specifically, discussion centers on conceptions of reality. A variety of competing ideas are presented and examined critically in an effort to discover what positions have fruitful elements to offer and which create problems for LIS thinking today. One of the most problematic concepts presented is that of scientism—the misapplication of the methods, theories, and hypotheses of the natural sciences to fields where they don't fit. In particular, some assertions from LIS are examined in the context of certain propositions regarding the world we live in. The complex and conflicting stances of realism and relativism are explored here, and their efficacy assessed. Since these are challenging, but extremely important, propositions, they must be dealt with thoroughly so that our understanding of potentially helpful thought in LIS can be enhanced.

The genealogy of thought and contemporary ideas creates some dilemmas for all of the social sciences, including LIS. Chapter 4 details some specific positions that are seriously problematic, but quite influential in today's thought and practice. The examples employed are chosen *because* of the problems they present and *because* they are by no means simply obsolete ideas. We frequently learn a great deal from mistakes, if we are able to isolate precisely what went wrong. This chapter, then, is essentially a critique, but it is offered in the most positive vein. The problematic aspects enable us to comprehend what may constitute barriers to knowledge and position us so that we can explore what knowledge is and how it grows.

Chapter 5 explores what knowledge is, reviewing criteria for knowledge that have been suggested by several philosophers. It is here that the connection between pragmatism and epistemology becomes evident. One criterion for knowledge that is offered by philosophers is the reliability of practices. More particularly, reliable practices are identified as such by virtue of the fact that there is justification for believing the practices are reliable. This chapter also presents some challenges to epistemology (beyond Rorty's pragmatism); I use these arguments so that, I hope, the presentation on knowledge (1) makes more sense, and (2) can be evaluated as to its persuasiveness. One particular idea about knowledge receives considerable attention—social epistemology. The term was actually first introduced by Jesse Shera and was applied to work in LIS. His idea indirectly influenced later philosophers who have tried to develop the relationship between knowledge and social interaction. Social epistemology, I'll argue, holds potential for the development of thought and praxis in LIS. Applications of epistemology to the social sciences are also included here.

While the fifth chapter argues in favor of epistemology (and reasons why it is important to us in LIS), the sixth chapter suggests a way to reach the goal of knowledge. Technically (and I mean in philosophical terms), epistemology and phenomenology are not necessarily linked. I will, however, suggest that the key principles of phenomenology—including the exploration of the essence of a thing, that nature of being, the intentionality that guides our actions, and the recognition of the connection between self and other—offer us a way to achieve the goals of knowledge. The genuine end of a phenomenological approach is interpretation, which is integral to knowledge in all of the social sciences and certainly in LIS. While interpretation is sometimes taken to be quite subjective and variable, there are norms for interpretation that allow a more solid evaluation of both the process and product of interpretation. The focus on interpretation emphasizes that LIS and the other social sciences necessarily require a serious and critical examination of human action, including all human communication. As is the case with epistemology, there are some conflicting views regarding interpretation (hermeneutics). The major positions are reviewed, and a particular approach to interpretation is suggested.

The final chapter brings together the preceding arguments and propositions in order to look ahead. The entirety of the book is designed to present a conceptual framework that can lead to progress in LIS. Chapter 7 reviews some especially productive work in LIS that has helped us to understand some essential questions and has executed some research that is enlightening. These examples, I argue, are models for inquiry in our field. Future research and praxis can build upon this prior work, recognizing why that work is productive. Our future can also benefit from some well-developed and well-conceived suggestions by some writers outside of LIS. Those suggestions provide us with some ways of defining human action and structuring action that can assist that action.

I hope that, taken as a whole, the ideas presented in this book can enable discussion in classrooms, in libraries, and at professional conferences. The intent is for this presentation to offer something of a context so that we can look critically at our present and our future states, and for us to set our sights on progress. I'm taking my direction from Pierce Butler: "A professional philosophy would give to librarianship that directness of action which can spring only from a complete consciousness of purpose" (Butler, 1961 [1933], 103).

Chapter One

The Beginnings of Science:
An Exploration into the Formulation
of Scientific Thought

I should begin by asking the reader's forbearance. As I noted in the introduction, in order to understand fully the present state of library and information science (LIS) and to explore possibilities for future modes of thought, a considerable amount of background is needed. It is essential that I attempt to anticipate some questions that many readers may have at the outset of this project. The first question is: Given that library and information science is a practical profession, why is there any need for philosophical investigation of this field? It is certainly true that this, and other, professions are focused on action, and this focus is necessary. Even so, that action has foundations that are based in conceptions of the purpose of a library, the purpose and uses of information, the organization of information for use, and the behaviors of users. Our conceptions are influenced by a lengthy past, some of which may *seem* only tangentially related (at best) to the heart of library and information science. These influences affect the way we think about the work we do, the research we engage in, and the ways we teach others—both formally in LIS

7

education programs and less formally through in-house and association-related initiatives—to prepare them to enter or continue in the profession. Perhaps even more to the point, philosophical investigation of practice is not an abstract exercise, but is intrinsically connected to the nature of practice and is aimed at discovering how we act within our profession. A second question is: What does a particular mode of thought have to do with the working life of professionals in this field? Whether we are consciously aware of it at all times, our conceptions (which are likely to be rooted deep in the heritage of the discipline of LIS) guide our actions. The planning that leads to practice, the work that we do from day to day, are founded in a rich matrix of (usually tacit) ways of thinking about purpose and action. In order to understand the potential of LIS we should examine the ways we think; in order to examine that, we need to explore the sources of influence that have helped shape our thinking.

There is no denying that the influences that have worked to shape thinking and acting in LIS are many and varied. To take briefly just one example, a force that is readily apparent today is technology. Much of the information technology in use now in libraries and other agencies has been developed outside the realm of librarianship. This technology is then adapted and accepted for use by librarians and other information specialists for specific purposes. Technological development affects not only organizational functions, but also thinking. As new possibilities arise, we stretch our imaginations and explore the outcomes of our own deliberations. As will be explored later, the focus on technology, not just in libraries but in society at large, is an indicative characteristic of our age. This characteristic, and others of our time, will have to be explored at some length (and will be in a later chapter) in order to understand the factors influencing the structure of knowledge today. Before we reach the point of examining epistemology today, we must delve into the past in order to identify the roots of thought (and action) in library and information science. Just as we are influenced by activities in the world of information technology, so too have we been influenced in our thinking by other disciplines. If it can be accepted that LIS shares much with the social sciences, then there is a source (or series of sources) of influence, diverse though it may be. The social sciences, in turn, have been influenced by many factors. This is obvious since those fields usually grouped into the social sciences are relatively young and grew out of other, older, disciplines. To examine LIS requires examining the thought, work, and writings that have contributed to, and still influence, the social sciences. This, then, is a philosophical journey, a sojourn through a period of time that has seen the beginnings of what can be conceived as the modern age of science.

A Genealogical Approach

Foucault

The beginning of this project amounts to a genealogy of thought in LIS. I must be clear that by using the word *genealogy* I am not referring simply to examination of family histories. *Genealogy* was the term used by Nietzsche in *The Genealogy of Morals* to convey the idea that morals have descended to us through time, rather than having been immutable from the beginning of time. More specifically, I am borrowing Michel Foucault's usage of the word. He informs us that

> Genealogy does not resemble the evolution of a species and does not map the destiny of a people. On the contrary, to follow the complex course of descent is to maintain passing events in their proper dispersion; it is to identify the accidents, the minute deviations—or conversely, the complete reversals—the errors, the false appraisals, and the faulty calculations that gave birth to those things that continue to exist and have value for us; it is to discover that truth or being do not lie at the root of what we know and what we are, but the exteriority of accidents. (Foucault, 1977, 146)

I will admit that my use of "genealogy" does not match precisely the totality of Foucault's conception. He maintains that genealogy is not necessarily a search for origins, nor is it a pretense at creating a grand narrative that can explain history in all its detail.

In fact, as Hubert Dreyfus and Paul Rabinow interpret Foucault, genealogy avoids any search for depth and denies the existence of hidden meanings and truths (Dreyfus and Rabinow, 1983, 106-7). That is, it may be tempting for us to employ "genealogy" as referring to a complete description of lineage; this was not Foucault's usage, nor is it mine. Genealogy (and this is the aspect I find most attractive) illustrates the various branches from the main line, thus demonstrating the variability of thought. While Foucault did at times express hostility to the notion of a philosophy of first principles, such as truth, his hostility was not consistent. I am inclined to believe that there is truth (or are truths), but I will concur with Foucault on one point—any claim to truth is problematic in that it is articulated in a context of politics, economics, and history; the claim of truth should not automatically be equated with truth itself.

Because of the possibly problematic nature of truth claims, we have to heed Foucault's more consistent coexamination of power and knowledge. This study is not reducible to the banal "knowledge is power"; it is a serious investigation of the inescapable relationship between knowledge and power, and the influence each has on the other. As Foucault says, there is a "constant articulation . . . of power on knowledge and of knowledge on power. . . . The exercise of power perpetually creates knowledge and, conversely, knowledge constantly induces effects of power" (Foucault, 1980, 51-52). I prefer to adopt the generous assessment of Rudi Visker: "The power-knowledge concept neither indicates skepticism with regard to the possibility of (genuine) knowledge, nor a critique of actual knowledge (on the grounds, for example, that, because of its link with power, it is not real knowledge), but refers, rather, to a constitutive condition of knowledge and science in general" (Visker, 1995, 57). The relation of power and knowledge is evident if we follow Foucault in examining discursive practice—the language and the context in which things are said. He recognizes that discourse expresses a "will to knowledge" that is sustained in part through exclusion, which is unavoidably institutional: "it is both reinforced and accompanied by whole strata of practices such as pedagogy—naturally—the book-system, publishing, libraries [etc.]. . . . Finally, I believe that this will to knowledge, thus reliant upon institutional support and distribution, tends to exercise a sort of pressure, a power of constraint upon other forms of discourse" (Foucault, 1972, 219).

As I just noted, I prefer to adopt a particular interpretation of this idea of Foucault's. The first point to note is that power is not necessarily equated with something like Gramscian cultural hegemony. Power, as it may relate to knowledge, can be based on reason and logic, as well as on political and economic structures. The next point is that knowledge must be considered separately from claims; the latter may be grounded in hegemonic power. Knowledge, in the epistemic sense, must be based in a set of criteria that include some conceptions of truth, reliability, and justification. In this sense, knowledge is grounded in the power of these criteria. While I do recognize that a philosophy of library and information science has to come to grips with epistemics, I also recognize that such a philosophy must also recognize that claims are made. The claims, though, should be evaluated on epistemic grounds, which will allow the recognition of hegemonic power where it may exist. Claims can then be recognized as such, and the political, economic, and other forces at work can be examined. This book is fundamentally a study of knowledge in the social sciences and LIS, but it is also, in part, an analysis of discursive power and the exclusionary force it exerts.

This work is also an effort at coming to grips with the complexity of the genealogy. Since there certainly may be fits and starts as we move forward in time, and since the influences on the present are functions of the fits and starts (as well as the contradictions and confluences), it is incumbent upon any examiner of intellectual history to acknowledge that influence is not simple (which is one of Foucault's central points). To that end, I will admit that there is a great deal from the past that LIS and the social sciences benefit from. The realization that we are part of these disciplines is sufficient evidence that we see something worthwhile, or at the very least salvageable, in them. The emphasis through much of this book, though, will be on the wrong turns that the social sciences have taken through time. The rest of the book, which will be an analysis of knowledge and a strategy for increasing our knowledge, is a grateful acknowledgment of the fruitfulness of past thought. In a rather uneasy amalgamation, we are formed by all of the myriad intellectual forces that have coexisted and competed.

My acknowledgment of the productive tension that has both led us to this place and time and provided us with a path to the future owes a great deal to Stephen Jay Gould's observation that the study of thought necessarily embodies all thought; we do ourselves a disservice when we create disciplinary barriers that can become increasingly difficult to cross. He says we have made serious mistakes that result in a distrust of difference:

> The first bad habit—setting up dichotomies—may be deeply inbred into the mechanisms of cerebral divisions—good vs. evil, male vs. female, or culture vs. nature—and then, in a further unfortunate reflex, to rank or judge these alternatives. The second bad habit, making martial metaphors, represents an all-too-human potential for belligerence—a potential unfortunately realized in most cultural contexts. When we put the two themes together, we fall into simplistic readings of history as a set of battles between Light and Darkness. (Gould, 1998, 86)

The mistakes are tempting; I hope not to commit them (at least not too frequently). The genealogical approach, though perhaps not in the strictest Foucauldian sense, is one way to avoid the dichotomies existing in a state of warfare. All thought is part of the genealogy, and, while there may be competition or suppression, there is also the possibility to assess merit on the grounds of reason and intellectual soundness, as well as success.

In part, the present project does attempt to find at least some hint at origins of the current mode of thinking in LIS (which is shared, to a considerable extent, among all social sciences). On the other hand, as Foucault says, "[The genealogist] must be able to recognize the events of history, its jolts, its surprises, its unsteady victories and unpalatable defeats—the basis of all beginnings, atavisms, and heredities. Similarly, he must be able to diagnose the illnesses of the body, its conditions of weakness and strength, its breakdown and resistances, to be in a position to judge philosophical discourse" (Foucault, 1977, 144-45). This book is an effort at judging philosophical discourse both by way of description (the first few chapters will look at the uneven record of the past) and by way of suggesting a strategy for the evaluation of past and present thought and practice *and* a direction for the future. A search for influences will, assuredly, involve examination of the twists and turns that the course of human thought and action may take. The first part of the book will adopt a somewhat skeptical view of past discourse; the latter part will attempt to outline a means to genuine knowledge.

As is true in any genealogical search, there are occasional surprises and the path is only clear when all of the elements are in place. Another element of genealogical search is that there is seldom a neat, clean, straight line. With this particular genealogy we have to come to grips with a lineage that is wilfully, if not altogether consciously, produced. This means that the parentage of an idea is not necessarily a matter of subsequent thought being an absolute reflection of its antecedent. Rather, that predecessor's idea is interpreted—sometimes in ways not intended by the predecessor—by those who come after. The process of interpretation may be selective, or reactionary, or it may be obstructed by some other force. The outcome may be a lineage with a number of bends and breaks in it, but one that illustrates precursors, whether they be abstracted either purposely or accidentally. As is true of human genealogies, the offspring may have little or no awareness of parentage, but is nonetheless affected by what has gone before. Here is where we find ourselves in a present state that includes little consciousness of the past. The institutional memory, if you will, is a short one. The suggestion I make here is that this is a shortcoming of the field; this statement is accompanied by the realization that such a suggestion is not new. I would also add that the proposed remedy (the genealogy) that forms a substantial portion of this book is offered as a means of inviting discussion, not as a final word. The ultimate hope is that this genealogy contributes to what might be considered an examined life for LIS.

Claims of Positivism

theory of knowledge [handwritten annotation]

In any genealogy it is difficult to determine how far back to go. A first step is to turn to recent opinions on the intellectual grounding of LIS. Michael Harris states that positivism is the dominant epistemology and that it "now governs the thinking of most serious researchers in library science (and probably all who refer to themselves as 'information scientists')" (Harris, 1986, 220). He further writes that "research in library and information science has been characterized by an increasingly rigid commitment to a positivist epistemology that has led us to make a fetish of certain methodological approaches to our research and has blinded us to the right questions" (Harris, 1986, 217). Harris's claim is based on a rather convincing argument centering on the definition of positivism that he offers and manifestations of that positivism in the LIS literature.

Harris is not alone in his perception of the present mode of thinking in LIS. Gary Radford, for instance, observes that "The positivist approach aspires to discover the generalizable something else: systems of laws and rules that lie beyond the realm of the immediately observable. The objective is to describe the underlying schemes in which an individual event or observation fits and from which future events can be predicted" (Radford, 1992, 411). He then provides a link between his notion of positivism and our profession: "Like positivism, library science attempts to develop general and a priori rules with which to build systems that permit efficient and accurate access to knowledge" (Radford, 1992, 413). Radford further provides additional bibliographic evidence for his position and illustrates some effects of a positivist way of thinking on the work of librarianship. A. L. Dick also sees positivist underpinning to much of the writing on research in LIS. In reviewing some texts on research, he concludes that "The positivist insistence upon a stark either/or dichotomy, that is, either librarians employ the methodologies of experimentation and measurement to find universal relationships among library variables or much of research in librarianship is doomed to failure, is echoed in the argument that the choices for the library research community are 'science or nonscience'" (Dick,

1991, 233). After reviewing a number of discursive acts related to inquiry in this field, he states, "it is claimed by its proponents to be the only way of assuring the field of its scientific and hence professional status" (Dick, 1991, 233).

Positivism, however, is itself symptomatic of a way of thinking that predates the formal expression of the term and its acknowledged antecedents. The concept, of which positivism is one incarnation, might be referred to as deterministic scientism. This is not intended to appear to be the replacement of one bit of jargon for another; there are core differences between positivism and deterministic scientism. First, scientism is here defined as a belief that knowledge growth in all disciplines depends on the application of the methods of natural science. Tom Sorrel defines scientism as "the belief that science, especially natural science, is much the most valuable part of human learning—much the most valuable part because it is much the most authoritative, or serious, or beneficial" (Sorrel, 1991, 1). Sorrel outlines the essential theses of scientific empiricism: "(1) science is unified; (2) there are no limits to science; (3) science has been enormously successful at prediction, explanation and control; (4) the methods of science confer objectivity on scientific results; and (5) science has been beneficial for human beings" (Sorrel, 1991, 4). These theses are viewed by a number of writers as central to positivism; we will explore conceptions of the elements integral to positivism later. Sorrel then offers a reason for the subsumption of scientific empiricism and its theses within scientism. "What is crucial to scientism is not the identification of something as scientific or unscientific but the thought that the scientific is much more valuable than the non-scientific, or the thought that the non-scientific is of negligible value" (Sorrel, 1991, 9). When it comes to research, or to any structured inquiry for that matter, scientism purports to provide, not only *a* means of conduct, but *the* means of conduct. F. A. Hayek writes, "The scientistic as distinguished from the scientific view is *not* an unprejudiced but a very prejudiced approach which, before it has considered its subject, *claims to know what is the most appropriate way of investigating it* [emphasis added]" (Hayek, 1979, 24).

Many conceptions of knowledge could be classified as naturalistic; that is, they include at least some version of empiricism, frequently focusing on human cognition and some natural scientific ways of examining cognitive processes. Such naturalism does, and should, interest us in LIS and needs to be examined in its own right. However, according to Susan Haack, naturalism can deteriorate to scientism if the fundamental view of science becomes too firmly rooted in science and scientific method. In discussing the thought of W. V. O. Quine, Haack observes that the distinction between naturalism that admits empiricism and scientistic naturalism stems from a confusion with "the idea that epistemology is part of our whole web of empirical belief . . . and the idea that epistemology is internal to the sciences" (Haack, 1993, 122). In other words, scientism results from an appropriation by science of everything empirical, which leads to a claim that only science can provide answers to questions that are in any way dependent on empirical study. Much of the coming discussion will elaborate on how scientistic thinking stems from some conceptions of science. The question that naturally arises here is: What is meant by deterministic?   This question deserves a substantive answer, so we will take a brief detour here to explore what determinism means.

A Few Words on Determinism

Almost all of what follows in this book hinges on one key proposition. First, while library and information science should not be guilty of living an unexamined life, too much of our intellectual roots lie in a collective unconscious, as was noted earlier. Concepts that have evolved over the past few centuries are deeply ingrained in our behavior and thought as both a profession and a discipline. We share many of these concepts with, and indeed we inherited many of them from, the social sciences. They, in turn, have owed huge debts to the early articulations of scientific philosophy, purpose, and method. While these concepts are tenacious, they are not necessarily indomitable. Throughout the last century and a half there has been resistance to the prevalent construct, but the received view has shown a forceful resilience. The construct I speak of is at the center of this book's key proposition: through at least the period of professional librarianship—and from the beginnings of the social sciences—thought and action have been predicated upon deterministic scientism. We now have a short definition of scientism, but here I want to say a bit about determinism.

As is true of many false leads in science and in philosophy, determinism has proved a persistent idea because of its attractiveness. It has been a force for at least the last couple of millennia. As Jerome Zimmerman observes, "Perhaps the most enduring reformulation of the Aristotelian idea of efficient cause is that which is known as determinism. This reformulation states essentially that every phenomenon must have a cause and is predetermined" (Zimmerman, 1989, 54). If it were true that every phenomenon has a single cause and, conversely, that a single cause determines a phenomenon, then control over nature and humankind becomes not merely a wish, but a possibility. The motivation for control is irrelevant; the potentiality of control in any instance in the human realm is pernicious. This is why Colin Piele, whose discipline is social work, says, "It is the very belief in a deterministic, causal world that enables and justifies the dominance of one person over another and of people over the environment, regardless of whether that dominance or control has a benevolent or exploitive intention" (Piele, 1993, 129).

Before we consider in any greater detail the human effects of determinism, let us look a little closer at physical determinism. Perhaps the most explicit expression of determinism is that of Pierre Simon, Marquis de Laplace, written in 1814:

> An intelligence which, at a given instant, would know all the forces by which Nature is animated, and the respective situation of all the elements of which it is composed, if furthermore it were vast enough to submit all these data to analysis, would in the same formula encompass the motion of the largest bodies of the universe, and those of the most minute atom: nothing for it would be uncertain, and the future as well as the past would be present to its eyes. The human mind, in the

perfection that it has been able to give to astronomy, provides
a feeble semblance of this intelligence. (Laplace, 1814, 29)

The Laplacian notion of determinism had its grounding in
Newtonian (classical) mechanics, but it proved an impossible
doctrine to follow in early twentieth-century physics. First with
Max Planck's quantum hypothesis (the suggestion that light and
other waves are emitted in entities called quanta) and then with
Werner Heisenberg's formulation of his uncertainty principle
came a serious questioning of the strong determinism posited by
Laplace. Stephen Hawking says, "The uncertainty principle
signaled an end to Laplace's dream of a theory of science, a model
of the universe that would be completely deterministic: one
certainly cannot predict future events exactly if one cannot even
measure the present state of the universe precisely!" (Hawking,
1988, 55) I'm spending some time on these matters because there
are a number of people in LIS and the other social sciences who
turn to the physical sciences as a model for theory and practice.
Given the affinity for the natural sciences, we should understand
what has guided some work in those areas.

Even in the sphere of the physical sciences the negation of
strong determinism seemed unpalatable. Some very prominent
and brilliant scientists had to begin by relaxing their dependence
on the previous mode of thought, and then to examine critically
the possibility of a weaker determinism, one that may not be able
to explain causal links for all phenomena. A lengthy quote from
Ilya Prigogine and Isabelle Stengers indicates the transformation
in thought that occurred several decades ago:

> These consequences of quantum mechanics were unacceptable to
> many physicists, including Einstein; and many experiments were
> devised to demonstrate their absurdity. An attempt was also
> made to minimize the conceptual change involved. In particular,
> it was suggested that the foundation of quantum mechanics is in
> some way related to perturbations resulting from the process of
> observation. A system was thought to possess intrinsically well-
> defined mechanical parameters such as coordinates and momenta;
> but some of them would be made fuzzy by measurement, and

Heisenberg's uncertainty relation would only express the perturbation created by the measurement process. Classical realism thus would remain intact on the fundamental level, and we would simply have to add a positivistic qualification. This interpretation seems too narrow. It is not the quantum measurement process that disturbs the results. Far from it: Planck's constant forces us to revise our concepts of coordinates and momenta. This conclusion has been confirmed by recent experiments designed to test the assumption of local hidden variables that were introduced to restore classical determinism. The results of those experiments confirm the striking consequences of quantum mechanics. (Prigogine and Stengers, 1984, 224)

All of this does not mean that determinism is now absent from physical science. Rather, a reformulation of what constitutes determinism presently informs examination of physical bodies and systems. Theories based on chaos or, more appropriately, complexity, do not negate determinism, but do incorporate a realization that absolutely accurate predictions of the future are dependent on factors that are beyond the capabilities of researchers to measure or sometimes even to conceive. This point may be best illustrated by a hallmark concept of the theory of chaos or complexity—sensitive dependence on initial conditions. This means, in short, that for predictions to be accurate, we would have to know the exact properties and conditions of the physical state at the point of origin. Perhaps the best example of this dilemma is weather forecasting. In a landmark paper of almost forty years ago Edward Lorenz examined meteorological phenomena as deterministic nonperiodic flow. Lorenz began with a mathematical examination of meteorological patterns based on deterministic nonlinear equations that yielded "nonperiodic solutions, i. e., solutions which never repeat their past histories exactly and where all approximate repetitions are of finite duration" (Lorenz, 1963, 130). The influence of his work was extended to virtually every physical science and beyond. The research of this century has undoubtedly altered the definition of determinism and has led Zimmerman to conclude, "The precise observations required by classical determinism have given way to the conceptualization that every observation represents, in reality a probability distribution. Causality is then determined by observing the differences in probabilities at different times. Classical determinism may no longer be viewed as the most viable option for explaining most of the phenomena of subatomic physics, let alone human behavior" (Zimmerman, 1989, 55).

The implications of physical determinism extend beyond the physical. Strong determinism, such as that suggested by Laplace, carries a vision of the world that encompasses the mental, the philosophical, and the psychological. Karl Popper states, "I have called physical determinism a nightmare. It is a nightmare because it asserts that the whole world with everything in it is a huge automaton, and that we are nothing but little cog-wheels, or at best sub-automata, within it" (Popper, 1979, 222). Popper goes on to say that strong determinism destroys the idea of creativity, since composing a poem, painting on a canvas, or sculpting in clay, are all determined and could be recreated by anyone who could have enough data on the writer, etc., and the medium. In short, strong determinism, even as it extends into the mental and psychological realms, is reductionist. That is, all activity can be reduced to the physical. This, as we shall see in a later chapter, is central to the particular line of thought usually labeled positivism.

While there may, in extreme reductionism, be a temptation to impose strong physical determinism on psychological determinism, there is a paradox that has been created by the replacement of Newtonian mechanics with quantum mechanics. If, as the most rigid behaviorist might seek to do, one could hope for absolute precision with psychological "laws," one would have to, as Popper points out (Popper, 1979, 221), traverse behaviorism and move into physiology, and from there to physics. This would leave one in the hands of physical determinism and, as we have seen, the strong determinism has been destroyed. So some degree of indeterminacy would be a necessary element in psychological study. Moreover, the indeterminacy may be magnified as we regress (or progress) from the physical to the vagaries and potential contradictions of the psychological. Popper further says that the doctrine which we may call *philosophical* or *psychological* determinism is not only a very different affair from *physical* determinism, but it is also one which a physical determinist who understands this matter at all can hardly take seriously. For the thesis of philosophical determinism, that "Like effects have like causes" or that "Every event has a cause", is so vague that it is perfectly compatible with physical indeterminism [emphasis in original]. (Popper, 1979, 220)

Of primary importance in this discussion of determinism is a realization of its attractiveness. Such a realization connotes the necessity for a conscious awareness of the intellectual history we inherit. This history has not only been handed down over time, but has come to us from many and varied origins. An understanding of the history enables us to examine critically the current state of thought and practice in library and information science. Although Piele is writing about social work, we could appropriate his words; they apply equally well to our field:

Lack of attention to cosmological beliefs leaves social workers with a set of beliefs that operate sub rosa and as such are unavailable for analysis and further development. It is not surprising that social work appears to implicitly accept the dominant deterministic cosmology of our time, a cosmology that drew strength from the past successes of the physical sciences but that is being increasingly questioned within those sciences. (Piele, 1993, 127)

Of related interest and relevance is another version of determinism which will not be dealt with here, but will feature in later discussions of the current state of our field—technological determinism. In brief, technological determinism encompasses the possibility that a society's (or a discipline's) technology determines its social, political, intellectual, and cultural structure.

In a nutshell, then, by determinism I mean the thought that all occurrences are determined by a prior cause, and that cause usually emanates from natural science. In other words, there is a great deal of faith in a "scientific method," the existence of which will be questioned later, and that faith leads to the grasping for an ultimate cause for all phenomena, even behavioral ones. This deterministic scientism has as its foundation both the writings of some philosophers (and a few scientists) and, perhaps more importantly, interpretations, or readings, of those works. Also, it should be noted that both the scientism and the determinism can be seen as simplifications, not so much of the sources of knowledge and existence, but of explanation. Inherent in both is an effort to find a fundamental rationale that can be used both to explain phenomena and to provide a method that may be employed to achieve such explanation.

The Roots of the Genealogy

This book is, at its essence, a program aimed at (usurping Piele's terminology) bringing the sub-rosa thoughts and beliefs into the open so that they might be assessed critically. In order to accomplish this, I must begin with the origins of modernity (in the scientific and methodological sense) and examine:

- how the development of thought coalesced, over the centuries, into the all-too-frequently tacit basis for knowledge in library and information science;
- from there the power and influence of science must be examined, both as an epistemological foundation and as a set of knowledge structures, beliefs, and behaviors;
- then, the influence of current activity in the social sciences will provide an introduction to the resulting patterns of activity in our field;
- ultimately, an alternative epistemology will be presented, along with a strategy for the development of knowledge in the current social, political, and intellectual environment.

Admittedly, this is an ambitious goal and there is no pretense that what will be presented here in any way resembles the final word in this discourse. If this program works, then discussion will flourish in an atmosphere of inquiry. In time we will see if this comes about.

For the beginnings of the genealogy, especially as it relates to deterministic scientism, we can refer again to the work of Tom Sorrel. In looking for a genesis of scientism he writes,

> what I am calling scientism in philosophy is traceable to a number of related philosophical mistakes that were made by the early modern philosophers of science, figures such as Bacon, Descartes, and Locke. Tailoring their conception of the mind to what they believed suited the mind to science, these philosophers are supposed to have been attracted to foundationalism in epistemology, introspective theories of the mental in the philosophy of mind, and an exaggerated rationalism in the philosophy of science. Tailoring their conception of the mind to what science required, they put into circulation a deeply misleading metaphor for the mind, the metaphor of the mirror of nature. (Sorrel, 1991, 24)

A key element in this quotation from Sorrel is the identification of Bacon et al. as the important participants in a transformation of thought, because this places the particular idea of science as far back in time as the beginning of the seventeenth century. Equally key is his reference to them as "modern" philosophers of science. The terms modern, or modernism, or modernity have many referents today in writings on culture, art, literature, etc. I intend a particular usage for the term modernity here which is central to the foundation of this genealogy. Modernity, in ways that are very important to this genealogy, begins especially with Bacon, but it is certainly influenced by Copernicus, Kepler, Galileo, and others. With modernity there is a marked break with the past. Bacon and others did not simply reconstruct the scientific revolution into philosophical terms, they consciously and purposely negated a previous mode of thought and replaced it with something the world had not seen before. Specifically, the notion of teleology, defined as "purposive, or 'final' causality" (Durbin, 1988, 316) was rejected. A teleological view of causality is attributed to Aristotle, but the rejected version of teleology is that which dominated in the Middle Ages and propounded the idea that nature is the product of, and should be seen as, the glorification of, God, and that the ultimate cause of any phenom-

proposed

enon is divine. The stance of Bacon and others is that causality is mundane (in the sense of being of this world). Such a stance leads Susan Meyer to maintain that the opponents of Aristotle's theory of teleology are reductionist; "that is, they contend that they can explain simply by reference to the causal powers of the material elements all the phenomena that Aristotle claims must be explained teleologically" (Meyer, 1992, 794).

Francis Bacon

Bacon as the starting point of scientific modernity is not necessarily a matter of universal agreement; rather, it is a thesis I put forth here. Gerald Galgan, for one, posits that modernity really got its start with the rise of modern cosmology (what we may be tempted to call the Copernican Revolution, though the revolution was the product of more than just Copernicus) (Galgan, 1982). This revolution genuinely altered human vision—the conception of both cosmos and mundus. Prior to the revolution humans looked outward; knowledge was a product of an outside force, a deity, and was bestowed upon humans. This vision is evident in language, what Galgan calls the ancient logos. This language was focused outside of humans and knowledge of nature was the result of revelation from the divine. The new cosmology did not just alter (eventually) the received view of the physical universe; it provided a metaphor for the reconception of the logos. The modern logos is a product of humans; it is realized through active discovery, not revelation. This logos is a product of human construction and reflection and is connected to the humans who create it. The modern logos is probably best described by Georg Kühlewind, who says, "The word [logos] is the form of the idea through which there appears the word's relation to an I" (Kühlewind, 1986, 16). The Cartesian cogito is the epitome of the modern logos; it is the assertion that first knowledge is of one's own existence, and that knowledge is founded in one's own cognition, one's own thought. The modern logos represents a shift in the language employed in science and philosophy. While Galgan attributes the beginnings of maturation to Descartes, I would maintain that it found its beginnings in the discourse of Bacon. This position is bolstered by Bruce Mazlish, who states that "in spite of all his drawbacks and omissions he stands at the beginning of the sciences of Man. He elaborated a method of inquiry that would be later known as positivism" (Mazlish, 1998, 44). More particularly, it is the reception of Bacon—Baconianism—that designates both the philosophical and methodological beginning of modernity. The inward focus, as we shall see, is continued in empiricism, in which the most trustworthy source of knowledge (in the accounts of a long line of thinkers forming the present genealogy) is sensory perception. The language of empiricism is vastly different from premodern language; the former dependence upon imposition or revelation from the divine is greatly diminished, and sometimes vanishes altogether.

With this in mind, it seems most reasonable to begin with the writings of Francis Bacon. Lisa Jardine notes that Robert Hooke (a contemporary of Bacon) dubbed Bacon "the father of empiricism" (Jardine, 1990, 47). Bacon's own writings point to a reliance on science for knowledge. For instance, he states, "I mainly attribute the lame progress of knowledge hitherto to the neglect or the incidental study of the general sciences" (Bacon, 1899, 41). The method Bacon fixes on is induction. He describes this method in a primary opus of his Great Instauration (his plan for the restoration of scientific inquiry after a lengthy quiescent period), which appeared in 1620:

> There are and can exist but two ways of investigating and discovering truth. The one hurries on rapidly from the senses and particulars to the most general axioms, and from then, as principles, and their supposed indisputable truth, derives and discovers the intermediate axioms. This is the way now in use. The other constructs its axioms from the senses and particulars, by ascending continually and gradually, till it finally arrives at the most general axioms, which is the true but unattempted way. (Bacon, 1899, 316-17)

I. B. Cohen sums up Bacon's induction as it relates to its predecessors:

Bacon attacked the sterility of pure deductive logic, which never can increase knowledge. He also attacked the older induction by enumeration [as described immediately above], applicable only when the class of all things referred to is finite and accessible . . . . Bacon claimed that his new method of induction went beyond this kind of Aristotelian complete or perfect induction . . . because it led to generalizations about all things, not simply to some property shared by all members of a finite enumeration. (Cohen, 1985, 148)

For us to comprehend present-day views of science, we have to grasp how Bacon's work has been received over the years. The common understanding of Bacon's plan is articulated by Peter Urbach, who says, "the scientific method . . . starts out with a mass of factual data, either casually observed, or consciously sought by means of experiments, and from these, by employing a set of simple rules . . . , it builds up a complete body of knowledge, which is both certain and infallibly true" (Urbach, 1987, 17). It must be made clear that this is not necessarily what Bacon intended, but it is how his plan has been most commonly read over the years. The understanding Urbach speaks of has been the foundation of both adherence and criticism by later writers and in subsequent practice (research that is, or claims to be, scientific). In denial of the infallible-mechanical thesis of Baconianism (the customary interpretation of Bacon, whether intended or not), Max Horkheimer and Theodor Adorno interpret the thesis as follows: "The concordance between the mind of man and the nature of things that [Bacon] had in mind is patriarchal: the human mind, which overcomes superstition, is to hold sway over a disenchanted nature" (Horkheimer and Adorno, 1994, 4). Horkheimer and Adorno see the error of Baconianism as the establishment of an authoritarian relationship between humans and nature, with humans able to exert some kind of control over nature. While others suggest that there is error in Baconian thought, they disagree with the Horkheimer-Adorno reading. More typical is Karl Popper, who speaks of "the Baconian myth that all science starts from observation and then slowly and cautiously proceeds to theories" (Popper, 1989, 137). Popper does see an authority underlying Bacon's science, but it is the authority of the senses, and this authority is manifest through a very strong definition of "interpretation." This strong definition holds that interpretation is not so subjective or relative a thing, but is an act that results in a true reading, in this case, of nature. Thus, interpretation based on sensory observation is seen by Popper as the means by which an infallible truth can be arrived at in Baconianism.

Bacon's influence on his contemporaries was indeed pronounced. As Jardine points out, it seems clear to many of them "that Bacon devotes the major part of his intellectual energies in the *Novum Organum* to attempts at enlarging dramatically the possibilities for experimentally (or experientially) justifying the step-by-step ascent to Forms, and for experimentally cross-checking provisional results of that ascent" (Jardine, 1990, 60). "Form" for Bacon can be envisioned as both the necessary and sufficient causal condition of any phenomenon; in other words, form is a law in the sense that there is an infallible relationship between "the form and its manifestation, that is to say, the two are related as cause and effect" (Urbach, 1987, 62). Bacon himself provides the method for realizing the goal of discovering forms:

> We must not only search for, and procure a greater number of experiments, but also introduce a completely different method, order, and progress of continuing and promoting experience. For vague and arbitrary experience is . . . mere groping in the dark, and rather astonishes than instructs. But when experience shall proceed regularly and uninterruptedly by a determined rule, we may entertain better hopes of the sciences. (Bacon, 1899, 351)

This goal is shared by his contemporaries, but not all are convinced that Bacon's philosophy is sufficiently unified to attain this goal. Bacon writes of appeals to experience that are different in kind. According to Jardine, one appeal is based on experience expressed in terms of a set of preconceived and evaluative notions; the other appeal is founded on an effort at producing a set of rules and tentative explanations (Jardine, 1990, 61). Even today there is disagreement surrounding the central thrust of Bacon's plan, as is evident in Urbach's analysis of readings of Bacon (Urbach, 1987). Alvin Snider describes the lack of consensus best when he writes, "Although various interpretations of Bacon have prevailed, a palimpsestic quality clings to Bacon scholarship, a tendency to reinscribe variant readings within a single template" (Snider, 1991, 120-21). Some, for instance, focus attention on Bacon's adherence to induction, but, as is evident from a more careful reading of his plan, he was not opposed to the formulation and use of hypotheses in the process of theory building.

Why so much time spent on Bacon? For one thing, Bacon happened to have lived and written at a very fortuitous time, one in which he could be persuaded by some truly significant scientific work and in which he coalesces discovery into a perceived method that would lead to even more dramatic discovery. Less than a century before the appearance of *Novum Organum* Copernicus had published *De Revolutionibus Coelestium Orbium*. Further, Bacon was a contemporary of Galileo and Kepler. The "scientific revolution" was beginning to manifest effects in the practice of science and a philosophy of action was needed. More importantly, Bacon helped to form something of a bridge between the Renaissance and the Enlightenment; he did not completely reject the humanism of the Renaissance, but he helped pave the way for a much greater emphasis on rationalism. The next step, as Stephen Toulmin says, was for the seventeenth-century philosophers to develop new ways of thinking about nature and to employ rational methods to address problems of both nature and humankind (Toulmin, 1990, 9). Defining Enlightenment is, in some ways, as problematic as defining "modern." I agree with the assessment of Robert Kraynak, who says that

> The term "Enlightenment" is most often applied to the philoso-
> phers of the eighteenth century. But it should not be used so
> restrictively. For these philosophers are heirs to the founders of
> modernity—Bacon, Machiavelli, Descartes, Galileo, Hobbes,
> Spinoza, Locke—who in the sixteenth and seventeenth centu-
> ries sought to overthrow the Aristotelian-Scholastic tradition

in the universities and to redefine philosophy or science. (Kraynak, 1990, 97).

A characteristic of the modern philosophers of science is the increasing importance, in one way or another, of reason as a tool essential for the creation of knowledge. This means that knowledge must have a grounding that is more discernible than revelation. Kraynak further states that "The revolutionary aim of enlightenment science . . . is to build a theory of knowledge *without beginning from opinion* [emphasis in original]" (Kraynak, 1990, 101).

During the time between the Renaissance and the Enlightenment (as customarily identified) some very important political occurrences contributed to a galvanizing of support for the objectivity of science that was not entirely founded on purely scientific grounds. The seventeenth century saw a bloody civil war in England followed by the Restoration of the monarchy. Snider maintains, convincingly, that the pull of science melded effectively with a need for social and political stability.

> The turn towards scientific objectivism after 1660 formed part of a coordinated strategy to regulate involvement in public affairs and to defuse the threat of a resurgent radicalism. Since little could diminish Bacon's prestige or tarnish his reputation, the early supporters of the Royal Society moved to define Bacon according to their own program, transforming him into the prophetic father of royally sanctioned science. (Snider, 1991, 125-26)

The ramifications of the merger of science and society extended well beyond England. For one thing, France, under Louis XIV, was also beginning to experience some stability around 1660, in the aftermath of the domination of Cardinal Richelieu. It could be said that the Restoration (if we take the term as encompassing more than just England) stood on the brink of what we might call the modern period, a period which had a firm beginning in the Enlightenment of the eighteenth century.

[handwritten: Stating or appearing to be true, but not necessarily so.]

The first acknowledged scientific journal was published in France during this period of ostensible progress—*Journal des sçavans*. Its appearance was followed quickly by the publication of the *Philosophical Transactions* of the Royal Society of London. Perhaps not terribly noteworthy as such, the beginnings of these kinds of formal communications mark the impact and the extent of the influence of the kind of scientific action that Baconianism represents.

[handwritten: to take charge]

Snider points out that the political and ideological climate of the Restoration helped foster the usurpation of Bacon's writings as a validation for the rise of objectivism, something completely unanticipated by Bacon. This interpretation and use of Bacon provided a fundamental influence on interpretation to come. As Snider says, "The Restoration's use of Bacon as a token for its own passage into modernity, as both pre-text and agent of legitimation, forms a crucial part of the history of his reception" (Snider, 1991, 135). Bacon's influence may be seen to extend even beyond the Restoration era. Maurice Cranston points to the reach of Bacon's thought and to why it may have been so attractive:

> Bacon had died in 1626, but that did not mean that his message was out of date. On the contrary, it had a kind of actuality for eighteenth-century France which made him, to a greater extent even than Locke or Newton, a prophetic figure for the whole French Enlightenment. For Bacon was the first philosopher of science. It was not that Bacon made any scientific discoveries of his own; he simply proclaimed the doctrine that science could save us. (Cranston, 1985, 48)

This passage is a clear demonstration of the reception of Bacon both as interpreted during the period of the Enlightenment and in our own day. In fairness to Bacon, it should be noted that, as

Sorrel points out, "Scientism of a kind *is* [emphasis in original] to be found in Bacon, but it is much too muted to generate claims about the possibility of a scientific sort of salvation" (Sorrel, 1991, 35). It is the reading of Bacon, the appropriation of some of his ideas for reasons that may well be extrascientific, rather than the actual content of his writings, that affirm such a place of importance for him in this genealogy.

As an aside, I should say that I am not making the assertion that, with Bacon, science became a purely social construct. Nor am I claiming that there is an absolutist position in the opposite direction, that is, in favor of a purely objectivist approach. Bacon's writings come closer to the latter, since he claims the possibility of discerning infallible truth through observation. (The political and social effects of readings of Bacon are noted by Snider, and this context will be explored further in chapter 2.) I also do not want to state that Bacon alone led the charge that eventually manifests itself as deterministic scientism; such an eventuality, in fact, was not what Bacon had in mind. Readings of Bacon other than those of the Restoration (and later) are certainly possible and, in fact, are plentiful. It would be a gross inaccuracy, as well as a disservice to Bacon, to refer to him as a positivist in any pejorative sense. I want to emphasize that Bacon becomes a starting point in this genealogy because his voice, and especially his focus on method, was something heretofore unseen. While method formed a part of the body of writings at least as far back as Aristotle, Bacon's assertions regarding science and observation set discourse on a path that has continued to this day.

Discourse on Convergence: Descartes and Hobbes

Descartes

A furtherance of that path, the bridge between Renaissance and Enlightenment, is girded in the early seventeenth century by

René Descartes. Another aspect of modernism, and certainly of the Enlightenment, was a confidence in the power and efficacy of reason. This Descartes provided in the form of four laws on which the quest for knowledge can be founded:

> The *first* was never to accept anything for true which I did not clearly know to be such; that is to say, carefully to avoid precipitancy and prejudice, and to comprise nothing more in my judgment than what was presented to my mind so clearly and distinctly as to exclude all ground of doubt.
> The *second,* to divide each of the difficulties under examination into as many parts as possible, and as might be necessary for its adequate solution.
> The *third,* to conduct my thoughts in such order that, by commencing with objects the simplest and easiest to know, I might ascend by little and little, and, as it were, step by step, to the knowledge of the more complex; assigning in thought a certain order even to those objects which in their own nature do not stand in a relation of antecedence and sequence.
> And the *last,* in every case to make enumerations so complete, and reviews so general, that I might be assured that nothing was omitted. (Descartes, 1989, 21)

Descartes did not, as is the case of many later writings, entirely separate metaphysics from physics. What he did offer was the essential effort at explanation, something his predecessors of the more scholastic bent were less than successful at. The difference between the earlier thinkers and Descartes was that the former center their attention on description, especially in terms of form and quality of a thing, whereas Descartes looks to construct a hypothetical model aimed at indicating the cause of the phenomenon (Clarke, 1992). So Descartes shares with Bacon the distinction of helping to transform thought regarding science. There are, however, important differences between Bacon and Descartes. As Mazlish points out, "In one view of history of science, Bacon is taken to represent the 'empirical' and René Descartes the 'rationalist' basis of scientific thought . . . . (In fact, empiricism and rationalism. . . will later be joined in the unified methodology of positivism)" (Mazlish, 1998, 38). Further, J. D. Bernal states,

> The major difference . . . was that Descartes used his science to construct a *system* of the world, a system which, though now almost forgotten, was able in its time completely to supersede that of the medieval schoolmen, Bacon put forward no system of his own but was content to propose an *organization* to act as a collective builder of new systems. His function as he saw it was only to provide the builders with the new tool—the logic of the *Novum Organum*–with which to do it [emphasis in original]. (Bernal, 1965, 441-42)

In other words, many, in time, rejected Descartes's system, but few rejected Bacon's tool.

Descartes in particular embodies the old way coexisting somewhat with the new. This identifies him as a product of the time, which is the source of the ambiguity in his straddling the two eras. As Desmond Clarke says, "the 1630s and 1640s were a time of transition from the science of forms and qualities to what we describe now as modern science. One finds features of both of these philosophies of science in Descartes" (Clarke, 1992, 282). Further, while Descartes firmly articulated an authority in his philosophy based on reason (a strong link with the coming Enlightenment), his own scientific practice revealed him to be an empiricist as well. The ambiguities in Descartes prevent assessment of him as a definitive link between two periods, but reveal him to be encamped, to varying degrees, in both times at once. Descartes's influence probably has been greater on later writers than on those of the seventeenth and eighteenth centuries. His legacy, in those terms, lies in his notions of dualism (the distinctiveness of the mind and the body).

As we will see, empiricism in the nineteenth and, especially, twentieth century frequently includes a rejection of metaphysics. Knowledge, to many writers of those times, is ineluctably connected to sensory observation, to the point that everything may be reducible to the physical. (Many of us have been taught that empiricism is almost synonymous with science; this teaching may be a bit difficult to shake.) Inherent in this brand of empiricism is either a separation of mind and body, or a reduction of the mental to the physical. Descartes, though probably

Determinism— for every event, there are conditions that could cause No other event.

34 "Cause +Effect" *Chapter One*

unintentionally, provides those individuals with a legitimation of their ideas. In his Sixth Meditation, "Of the Existence of the Real Distinction between the Mind and Body of Man," he writes,

> it was not without reason that I thought I perceived certain objects wholly different from my thought, namely, bodies from which those ideas proceeded; for I was conscious that the ideas were presented to me without my consent being required, so that I could perceive any object, however desirous I might be, unless it were present to the organ of sense; and it was wholly out of my power not to perceive it when it was thus present. And because the ideas I perceived by the sense were much more lively and clear, and even, in their own way, more distinct than any of those I could of myself frame by meditation, or which I found impressed on my memory, it seemed that they could not have proceeded from myself, and must therefore have been caused in me by some other objects: and as of those objects I had no knowledge beyond what the ideas themselves gave me, nothing was so likely to occur to my mind as the supposition that the objects were similar to the ideas which they caused. And because I recollected also that I had formerly trusted to the senses, rather than to reason, and that the ideas which I myself formed were not so clear as those I perceived by sense, and that they were even for the most part composed of parts of the latter, I was readily persuaded that I had no idea in my intellect which had not formerly passed through the senses. (Descartes, 1989, 113)

As is the case with Bacon, the consequences of Descartes's thought could not have been foreseen by him; the uses to which it has been put rest with those who have incorporated, however imperfectly, the writings of Descartes into their own programs.

Nonetheless, Descartes's influence on following thinkers and writers is assuredly present. And, while not as immediately central to deterministic scientism as the readings, begun in about 1660, of Bacon, Cartesian thought is certainly important to any concept of modernism. And, I would maintain, deterministic scientism is a product of modernity. The attention paid to the source of knowledge as an inward-looking phenomenon leads, in the cases of these philosophers and those to follow, to a focus on nature and, more particularly, on the senses. Thus springs a faith

justifies the truth or falsity of a claim!

in natural science as the wellspring of knowledge and of this science as superior to other epistemological origins. Inherent in this scientism is the search for causality in nature.

Hobbes

A contemporary of Descartes was Thomas Hobbes. Hobbes fits better in a direct lineage begun by Bacon; there is more shared between the two than either shared with Descartes. This is not to say that there are no shared areas, however, between Descartes and Hobbes. For one thing, Hobbes was also an empiricist. He wrote in 1651 in *Leviathan* that "there is no conception in a mans mind, which hath not at first, totally, or by parts, been begotten upon the organs of Sense" (Hobbes, 1968, 85). Further, he stated, "The cause of Sense is the Externall Body, or Object, which presseth the organ proper to each Sense, either immediately, as in Tast and Touch; or mediately, as in Seeing, Hearing, and Smelling" (Hobbes, 1968, 85). While much of Hobbes's writing centered on society and politics, his philosophy had a grounding that was passed on, overtly or tacitly, to later thinkers. In some ways, for instance, he anticipated Hume in defining experience as a complex of things, not one simple reaction at a single time: "Much memory, or memory of many things is called *Experience* [emphasis in original]" (Hobbes, 1968, 89). In his concept of science, Hobbes fits as an enlightenment (in the broader sense) philosopher in his linking of science and reason. Reason, he said,

> is not as Sense, and Memory, borne within us; nor gotten by Experience onely; as Prudence is; but attayned by Industry; first in apt imposing of Names; and secondly by getting a good and orderly Method in proceeding from the Elements, which are Names, to Assertions made by Connexion of one of them to another; and so to Syllogismes, which are the Connexions of one Assertion to another. (Hobbes, 1968, 115)

Then he further defined science: "And whereas Sense and Memory are but knowledge of Fact, which is a thing past, and irrevocable; *Science* [emphasis in original] is the knowledge of Consequences, and dependence of one fact upon another" (Hobbes, 1968, 115).

Hobbes was also one of the early moderns; his thought was a distinct departure from classical tradition. In medieval teleological thought final cause was related to an ontological ascendancy, an order of being, based on differences of matter. Animals were seen as materially different from (and inferior to) humans and humans materially different from (and likewise inferior to) angels. Hobbes did not accept such material differences as meaningful; instead he viewed animals and humans as sharing many qualities, especially those related to the senses (Hobbes, 1968, 149). Martin Bertman states that Hobbes's reductionist stance (the negation of the ascendancy just mentioned) is "in great opposition to those who, from Plato onward, have been guided by a maxim of the ontological gradation of being" (Bertman, 1991, 25). More particularly, according to Bertman, Hobbes's thought is an embodiment of nominalism; that is, the exclusion from language of names for abstract ideas, such as that of classes of being. This simplified categorization, or nominalism, is combined in Hobbes with a mechanistic view which asserts that "everything can be reduced to a fundamental idea of matter and motion" (Bertman, 1991, 211). These decidedly modern characteristics in Hobbes are substantive influences for other manifestations to come of deterministic scientism. The contribution to modernity is pointed out by Robert Kraynak: "The Enlightenment philosophers as a whole, and Hobbes perhaps more than any other, aim at a historic change that eradicates the fundamental attitude or general cast of mind underlying all traditional modes of reasoning" (Kraynak, 1990, 100).

I stated earlier that Hobbes's thought is more closely related to Bacon than to Descartes; there are some important areas of disagreement between Hobbes and Descartes. Richard Tuck says that "From the point of view of many modern readers, the structure which Hobbes erected . . . is much more to their task, and houses more fittingly their ontological assumptions, than the one which Descartes built" (Tuck, 1988, 41). I would assert that Hobbes's structure had earlier roots and would be further built upon in the coming century, but the distinctions between Cartesian thought and his should be noted (Sorrel, 1988). One key point of disagreement is that of the accessibility of the sciences. Descartes sought to establish precepts, which, if followed, could lead to knowledge and understanding on the part of any rational person. Hobbes maintained that science is not intuitive, but acquired, and one had to work hard to reach an understanding of science's method of reasoning. A second area of disagreement is the completability of science. Descartes believed that experimentation could be applied to competing hypotheses to show which are correct; permanently open questions are unlikely. Hobbes thought that natural phenomena could have more than one possible origin; physics is unable to "reconstruct a course of events so that a unique operation is revealed as generating a particular effect" (Sorrel, 1988, 519). A third point of dispute regards the unity of science. Descartes uses metaphors to illustrate connections among the sciences; he thought the principles of the most basic sciences are linked to those of the most derivative. Hobbes agrees on the existence of a unity of science, but does not admit that the sciences are serial, one necessarily derived from, and understood by, its fundamental predecessor. On this last point, writers to come, especially in the nineteenth century, have more affinity with Descartes than with Hobbes. A primary distinction between the two philosophers is articulated by Sorrel:

> In Hobbes's scheme science or philosophy as a whole is composed of the sciences of natural bodies and the sciences of artificial bodies. In Descartes the two chief parts of philosophy concern material things (physics, mechanics) and immaterial things (metaphysics). Certain subjects that Descartes claimed were in the province of metaphysics and therefore outside natural science Hobbes located squarely within physics. (Sorrel, 1988, 515)

Metaphysics = a traditional branch of philosophy concerned c explaining the fundamental nature of being & the world that encompasses it. (The physical world)

Physics = the natural science that involves the study of matter & its motion through space & time, along c related concepts such as energy & force.

The British Empiricists:
Locke, Berkeley, and Hume

Locke

The continuance of the path begun by Bacon, Hobbes, and, to an extent, Descartes, was taken up by John Locke. I should emphasize that this path, in keeping with the Foucauldian concept of genealogy, is not a clean, unbroken road, nor is it a pure extension of the thought of Bacon. As I mentioned earlier, Bacon initiated a new line of discourse centering on a suggested method of study. Descartes, Locke, and others to come add to this general discourse, while maintaining at least some of the elements of method that Bacon proposed. More importantly, response to Bacon began an interpretive approach that is essential to the genealogy of thought in the social sciences and in LIS. An implication of interpretation is that the influence of a precursor on a successor, in any individual instance, may well be a subtle, suggestive insinuation of thought rather than an explicit intellectual debt. Locke's *Essay Concerning Human Understanding* was published in 1690 and the key to his empiricism can be summed up in one brief passage:

> How comes [the mind] to be furnished? Whence comes it by that vast store which the busy and boundless fancy of man has painted on it with an almost endless variety? Whence has it all the *materials* [emphasis in original] of reason and knowledge? To this I answer, in one word, from EXPERIENCE. In all that our knowledge is founded; and from that it ultimately derives itself. (Locke, 1974, 10)

This sounds attractively simple; in fact, its *simplicity* has formed the foundation of conceptions of experience, as related to knowledge, for most of the three centuries subsequent to its articulation. The foundation has proved persistent to an unbroken line of writers, as well as in the practice of some in the sciences and, eventually, to many in the social sciences and humanities.

Locke's vision of epistemology is not quite so simple, though. Knowledge is not just a matter of having an experience; knowledge depends on the reception and transformation of experience into something knowable. The physicality of experience then must be linked to the intellectual powers of the mind. Locke expresses the interaction of the mental and the physical: "Thus the first capacity of human intellect is,—that the mind is fitted to receive the impressions made on it; either through the senses by outward objects, or by its own operations when it reflects on them" (Locke, 1974, 15). The reflective aspect is operationalized, at least in the opinion of Alexander Koyré, in the process of experiment. He writes,

> We must not forget that observation and experience, in the sense of brute, common-sense experience, did not play a major role—or, if it did, it was a negative one, the role of obstacle—in the foundation of modern science. . . . It is not "experience" but "experiment" which played . . . a great positive role. Experimentation is the methodical interrogation of nature, an interrogation which presupposes and implies a *language* [emphasis in original] in which to formulate questions, and a dictionary which enables us to read and to interpret the answers. (Koyré, 1968, 18-19)

Observation, then, is active; and a possible reading of Locke is that experience is not merely an openness to physical sensation, but a structured inquiry into the objects of sensation, with understanding as the intended end. There are differences between this definition of experience and some which follow, even into the twentieth century.

The interaction between the physical and the mental, for Locke, is an explicit thing; that is, the linking of experience and knowledge has a decidedly physical element. Locke begins his *Essay* with an affirmation of the Cartesian cogito (I think, therefore I am). Descartes maintained that thinking is the essence of existence, that thinking is inseparable from being (Descartes, 1989, 80). Locke acknowledges that every human is conscious of thought, and that thought is signified by the *ideas* held in each person's mind. For Locke, "idea" has a specific denotation, that being the *object* of understanding. As an object, an idea is classified in one of two ways: "*External objects* furnish the mind with the ideas of sensible qualities, which are all those different perceptions they produce in us; and *the mind* furnishes the understanding with ideas of its own operation [emphasis in original]" (Locke, 1974, 11). The link of the physical and the mental, pervasive in Locke's *Essay*, leads R. B. Macleod to assess Locke's thinking in terms of the material or elemental notion of thought. He writes,

> [Locke] was led to the conception of the mind as composed of particles (the ideas) which exist in space and time and which are fused, amalgamated or chained by forces outside themselves. According to Locke we can have a science of mind analogous to the science of physical nature. This involved the assumption of *mental* [emphasis in original] elements analogous to physical particles, and the assumption that to explain anything is to break it down into its elements. (Macleod, 1970, 209)

In Locke, however, there is a paradox, and a purposeful one at that. At once his thinking led him to certainty that knowledge is possible in the ideal, but elusive in the actual. As Dunn says, Locke's search for truth operates "in two different ways. The first is to show how the human understanding works successfully: how it is capable of knowledge and of rational belief, what human beings can know and what they cannot. The second is to explain why on the whole in practice it works so badly" (Dunn, 1992, 92). (The former is, of course, a hallmark of the thrust of the Enlightenment.) What Locke is left with is assurance that any human being can attain knowledge of his or her own existence, but no other knowledge can be so perfect. Rather, the knowledge that is possible of all other things is more probabilistic than certain, so his epistemology is tinged with at least some skepticism.

If knowledge is grounded in sensory experience, and if there is a hint of skepticism regarding the certainty of human knowledge, then is there room in Locke's thinking for anything but a material and elemental path to knowledge? Locke's scheme was not intended to be a simplistic one, and it assuredly was not intended to be fatalistic. Ideas, the objects of understanding, are subject to testing by the intellect. The intellect, in turn, is guided by reason. For instance, Locke maintained that reason was the mechanism by which ideas could be ordered so that connections among them could be discerned and analyzed. Examination of connection—determination of the degree of agreement or disagreement between ideas—works to extend the boundaries of knowledge. The operation of reason as a mediating force of the mind, to which all sensation and subsequent thought could be subjected, provided a hallmark for the Enlightenment. It was through reason that order could be discovered and maintained. Further, the order most discernible (and the order at the root of human understanding) was seen to be a natural order. Locke, as Carl Becker observes, provided the eighteenth century with the rationale it most desired, the belief that, "since man and the mind of man were shaped by that nature which God had created, it was possible for men . . . to bring their ideas and their conduct, and hence the institutions by which they lived, into harmony with the natural order" (Becker, 1932, 65).

The desired rationale was, most assuredly, a product of the time. Shortly before Locke's *Essay* appeared, Isaac Newton published his *Principia* (*De Philosophiae Naturalis Principia Mathematica*, 1687). The effects of this work were felt beyond the realm of science; it represented a major step towards a new cosmology. J. D. Bernal writes:

> Newton's theory of gravitation and his contribution to astronomy mark the final stage of the transformation of the Aristotelian world-picture begun by Copernicus. For a vision of spheres, operated by a first mover or by the angels on God's order, Newton had effectively substituted that of a mechanism operating according to a simple natural law, requiring no continuous application of force, and only needing divine intervention to create it and set it in motion. (Bernal, 1965 487)

As Bernal says, Newtonianism is part of a shift in world view, and this shift permeated all aspects of society in the eighteenth century. Henry Guerlac writes that the thinkers during the Enlightenment

> saw in the *method* [emphasis in original] of science—and it is here that Newton exerted his greatest influence—an analytical instrument that could be extended into other intellectual spheres, to extinguish superstition and emancipate the human mind from traditional error . . . . Above all, perhaps, they saw in the great forward strides taken by science, the strongest argument for their belief in a law of human progress. (Guerlac, 1958, 19-20)

In no small measure, this marks a continuance of Baconianism, illustrating the breadth and depth that readings of Bacon have had. Further, the connection with Locke, as interpreted by Becker, is obvious. What these writings strongly indicate is that a popular notion of a deterministic scientism is taking hold more and more strongly. Further, this deterministic conception of human nature and human progress is becoming explicit in the writings of very influential philosophers. As the linkages of thought become clearer, the genealogy is added to; my proposition that there is a line of thought that extends from Bacon can, I hope, gain credence.

Berkeley

Continuing the genealogy in this manner, the next influential thinker in turn is George Berkeley. In some important respects, Berkeley represents a departure from his predecessors, both in the actual basis of his thinking and in the reception down through the years of his thought. While he held Newton in great esteem, he was opposed to the mechanistic structure of matter which, in the early eighteenth century, was most popularly propounded as corpuscularian philosophy. This mode of thought preceded Newton and can be traced formally to Peter Gassendi, who worked and wrote in the first half of the seventeenth century. The theory was picked up by Robert Boyle, who wrote that "the world is made up of an innumerable multitude of singly insensible corpuscles endowed with their own sizes, shapes and motions," and that these corpuscles, devoid of such properties as heat or color, come into contact with human sense organs and the contact and its subsequent excitation of the brain leads to sensations which seem to imbue the corpuscles with the properties sensed (quoted in Urmson, 1992, 100-1). This corpuscular philosophy was eventually adopted (substantially) by Newton and Locke. The Newtonian cosmology sees the universe as a mechanical system governed by mechanical laws.

Herein is a primary disagreement between Locke and Berkeley. Specifically, Berkeley rejected the corpuscular theory of matter. One reason for Berkeley's opinion is his skepticism of the notion of causation which is part of the mechanical-corpuscular theory. For instance, there is no indication in this construction, according to Berkeley, why the impact of corpuscles with sense organs leads to particular sensory experiences in a person. Such impact and agitation is neither sufficiently regular nor sufficiently predictable to result in any assertion of causation. In other words, there is no way to tell if something as mechanical as corpuscles striking a sense organ will lead to one sensory perception regarding color or another perception regarding size, for instance. For Berkeley, causation is the connection of one thing or event *making* another thing or event occur. In nature, one even precedes another; if it does so frequently and with regularity, the occurrence of the first event is a strong *indication* that the second event will occur. In his disagreement with corpuscular philosophy, however, Berkeley is willing to impart to the indications of regularity a nomological quality. By nomological I mean a confidence in the existence of universal laws which are closely tied to empiricism (the belief that sensory observation is the most valid grounding for knowledge). Berkeley himself said that natural philosophers' knowledge of the world around them "consists not in an exacter knowledge of the *efficient cause* that produces them—for *that* can be no other than the *will of a spirit*—but only in a greater largeness of comprehension ˙ ⸱⸱⸱hv analogies, harmonies, and agreements are discovered in of nature, and the particular effects explained, that is, *reduced to general rules* [emphases in original]" (Berkeley, 1986, 117).

Berkeley is in strong agreement with Locke on one key point, though. Their agreement lies in the essential character of ideas. Ideas, for both, are the object of the mind. Moreover, ideas, for both, are the product of experience. Berkeley's position on this point is made clear in the very first sentence of his *Treatise Concerning the Principles of Human Knowledge*, published in 1710:

> It is evident to anyone who takes a survey of the objects of human knowledge, that they are either *ideas* actually imprinted on the senses; or else such as are perceived by attending to the passions and operations of the mind; or lastly, *ideas* formed by help of memory and imagination—either compounding, dividing, or barely representing those originally perceived in the aforesaid ways [emphasis in original]. (Berkeley, 1986, 65)

The difference between Berkeley and Locke lies in Berkeley's unwillingness to impart to the sources of ideas a mechanical impetus, an unwillingness to accept that matter (as corpuscles) is imperceptible, is substance without tangible properties. This object of disagreement leads Berkeley to reject Locke's proposed abstract ideas—the ability of the mind to form ideas without any sensory stimulus. Berkeley, then, is even more purely empiricist than Locke. He goes so far as to say, "Foolish in men to despise the senses. If it were not for them the mind could have no knowledge, no thought at all" (Urmson, 1992, 110). His empiricism embraces reductionism, that is, the equation of the mental with the physical. He claims, as J. O. Urmson notes, that ideas can count as experiences of reality, that to be real and to be a product of the mind can be one and the same (Urmson, 130). In this, and in certain other aspects of his thought, Berkeley has a greater influence than his predecessors on a particular philosophical strain of the twentieth century—logical positivism. Some propositions (selected here among all of the propositions) set forth by Berkeley clearly anticipate tenets central to logical positivism:

Tenets of Logical Positivism

> 1 All significant words stand for ideas. . . .
> 3 All ideas come from within or from without.
> 4 If from without it must be by the senses, and they are called sensations.
> 5 If from within they are the operations of the mind, and are called thoughts. (Urmson, 1992, 110)

The last two of these propositions indicate Berkeley's temporal place in the Enlightenment. Sensory perception and reason are the only two phenomena that can lead to knowledge.

Hume

We continue our journey in time with David Hume. Hume, along with Locke and Berkeley, are not infrequently grouped together under the appellation "the British Empiricists." Hume in many ways provides a culmination of some lines of thought, and responses to a common set of questions. The primary question, asked by Locke and taken up by Berkeley, is: What is the source (foundation) of knowledge? Make no mistake about it, Hume is an epistemologist; the basis of knowledge is the foremost matter in his deliberations. Where does he fall in his thinking? What is his place in this genealogy? First, he had the good fortune to succeed Locke and, especially, Berkeley. I say good fortune because the writings of his predecessors helped him to frame some important questions regarding knowledge. I say especially Berkeley because he reacted directly to some of the thought of the bishop. This is not to say that he was not cognizant of, and did not respond (directly or indirectly) to Locke's philosophy. Hume, in fact, may have had a more profound influence on subsequent branches of this philosophical family tree than did his fellow empiricists. Josep Llobera says that Hume "was the man who got closer to becoming the Newton of the human sciences" than anyone else, and that "Hume's aim was to introduce the experimental method of reasoning into the so-called moral sciences. . . . Furthermore, he thought that his science could reach the same degree of certainty achieved by physics"

(Llobera, 1979, 151). This last may be a bit of an overstatement on Llobera's part, but it is a goal we will see revisited at a later time.

In a very real sense, though, Hume is an extension of the empiricist tradition. For one thing, all three—Locke, Berkeley, and Hume—mark a break with a substantial basis of classical philosophy. The empiricists, and their predecessors (Bacon, Hobbes, etc.), do not necessarily negate the place of metaphysics in epistemology and the conception of truth, but they do separate metaphysics from the science of the natural. Farhang Zabeeh maintains that "The polemic of . . . empiricists against scholastic and rationalistic metaphysics was an endeavor to prove that the only avenue to the kingdom of knowledge is sensory experience" (Zabeeh, 1960, 6). Zabeeh's statement may not apply absolutely in each instance, but a belief in knowledge based on experience is how the empiricists got that name.

At this point the reader may begin to tire of the continuous refrain of sensory perception being the road to knowledge. I apologize for this repetitive strain, but I also ask your indulgence. The reason this notion recurs with such frequency here is both the frequency of its occurrence in this genealogy of thought and its centrality to the major program of the set of thinkers dealt with in the early stages of this book.

There is evidence in Hume's own writing that sensory experience is primary. Early in his *Enquiry concerning Human Understanding*, published in 1748, Hume said, "The most lively thought is still inferior to the dullest sensation" (Hume, 1988, 63). He further stated, "If it happen, from a defect of the organ, that a man is not susceptible of any species of sensation, we always find that he is as little susceptible of the correspondent ideas" (Hume, 1988, 65).

While these passages seem perfectly straightforward, Hume presents us with a problem of interpretation. There is no doubt that he invested sensory perception with an importance that cannot be denied. He did, however, own up to some skepticism regarding the senses. The most vital caution he urged was to avoid mistaking an impression—which he defined as lively perceptions, such as sight, hearing, touch, etc.—with the object itself. He wrote in *A Treatise of Human Nature* (which predated the *Enquiry*), that

> The only defect of our senses is, that they give us disproportion'd images of things, and represent as minute and uncompounded what is really great and compos'd of a vast number of parts. This mistake we are not sensible of; but taking the impressions of those minute objects, which appear to the senses, to be equal or nearly equal to the objects, and finding by reason, that there are other objects, vastly more minute, we too hastily conclude, that these are inferior to any idea of our imagination or impression of our senses. (Hume, 1969, 77)

He reiterated this notion in the *Enquiry* and added that "nothing can ever be present to the mind but an image or perception, and that the senses are only the inlets, through which these images are conveyed, without being able to produce any immediate intercourse between the mind and the object" (Hume, 1988, 183). The problem created by this paradox, according to John Danford at least, is one of understanding. Understanding, particularly self-understanding, is a problem that not only is difficult to resolve, but is, by and large, separate from science in that the problem is one of "disjunction between reason and the senses" (Danford, 1990, 65). Hume expressed the problem of separation as it affects understanding as discontinuity between, for instance, mathematics, whose ideas are unfailingly clear and defined and "the finer sentiments of the mind, the operations of understanding, the various agitations of the passions, [which] though really in themselves distinct, easily escape us, when surveyed by reflection; nor is it in our power to recal [sic] the original object, as often as we have occasion to contemplate it" (Hume, 1988, 101).

Now we come to the actual importance of Hume in the line of thought that began with Bacon. If he does express some skepticism regarding senses, what is at the heart of this skepticism and in what way does it manifest itself? Answers to these questions center on the notion of causation. As I noted earlier, Hume is an epistemologist. For Hume, the essence of knowledge does not lie in an ability to apprehend matters of fact (that is, the mere description of physical properties or events), but in a wherewithal to explain. As Hume said, "All reasonings concerning matter of fact seem to be founded on the relation of *Cause and Effect* [emphasis in original]. By means of that relation alone we can go beyond the evidence of our memory and senses" (Hume, 1988, 72). The difficulty comes in trying to ascribe causes to particular effects. It had to be recognized, but Hume realized that it was scarcely adequate to explain that causes precede effects temporally. Danford examines Hume's thinking on causation in some depth and notes that, since precedence is not, in itself, sufficient to explain, a further step had to be taken. This step, for Hume, was one not merely of temporal relation, but something that went deeper—constant conjunction (Danford, 1990, 65-66).

> We remember to have had frequent instances of the existence of one species of objects; and also remember, that the individuals of another species of objects have always attended them, and have existed in a regular order of contiguity and succession with regard to them. . . . We likewise call to mind their constant conjunction in all past instances. Without any farther ceremony, we call the one *cause* and the other *effect*, and infer the existence of the one from that of the other [emphasis in original]. (Hume, 1969, 135)

This realization, however, does not succeed in advancing us along the road to knowledge. In the end, Hume admitted that there must be a subjective base to an understanding of causation. He stated that the foundation of any inference regarding phenomena is "the necessary connexion betwixt causes and effects," but he added that "Upon the whole, necessity is something that exists in the mind, not in objects" (Hume, 1969, 216). Still, Hume's writings on causation amounts to an homage to determinism. He comes dangerously close to a reduction of thought and behavior to the purely physical. One thing this line of thought makes possible is the offering of physical influences as causes for behavior or human attributes. For example, this clears a path for hypothesizing environmental or hereditary causes for intelligence.

What we seem to have in Hume is an aporia, a problem stemming from opposing views on the same matter. While the ultimate understanding that can lead to knowledge is, to some extent, subjective, causation, to Hume, rests in the objects. He defined causation as a product of experience: "as the power, by which one object produces another, is never discoverable merely from their idea, 'tis evident *cause* and *effect* are relations, of which we receive information from experience, and not from any abstract reasoning or reflection [emphasis in original]" (Hume, 1969, 117). So we see that the determination of causation lies beyond the abilities of reason alone. To add a further twist, causation cannot be determined solely by sensory perception either. "There is no single phaenomenon, even the most simple, which can be accounted for from the qualities of the objects as they appear to us; or which we cou'd foresee without the help of our memory and experience" (Hume, 1969, 117-18). The bottom line, at least according to my own interpretation of Hume, is that the accumulation of sensory perceptions and the reasonings to which they are subjected together form experience. While I can see no other interpretations, I must admit that Hume attempted to sever experience from both mere sensation and pure reasoning. This very separation is the basis for my conclusion that it is only the two combined that produce experience; no other resolution to the aporia created by his writings in the *Treatise* and the *Enquiry* is apparent to me.

What remains is examination of what, from Hume's philosophy, appears to have been extracted and adopted into deterministic scientism. Even though Hume's writings are problematic, there are elements that can be taken (as has been the case with all of the philosophers considered here) to present some assumed unity of thought. For instance, there is no doubt that Hume is an empiricist, that he places enormous import on sensory perception. This much has already been demonstrated; we need not delve

further into it. Next is the centrality of causation. Regardless of
the difficulties presented by Hume himself in determining cause
and effect, he offered general rules on which to base causation:

> (1) The cause and effect must be contiguous in space and time.
> (2) The cause must be prior to the effect.
> (3) There must be a constant union betwixt the cause and
> effect. 'Tis chiefly this quality, that constitutes the relation.
> (4) The same cause always produces the same effect, and the
> same effect never arises but from the same cause. (Hume, 1969,
> 223)

These two concepts (his empiricism and his structure of causation) can be incorporated into a model of thinking that looks for
certainty in the parts that can be extended to the whole. This is
so despite Hume's own recognition that induction is the victim
of an unresolvable dilemma—that dilemma being the absence of
any logical link between the existence of something in the past
and its assured existence in the future. The aim of determinism
is again aided by Hume's hedging. He did indeed state what has
since been termed the Problem of Induction, but he recognized
that inductive reasoning (although he doesn't use the word
induction) can be helpful in epistemology. As James Force says,

> For Hume and for Newton it is perfectly acceptable to reason
> from the part to the whole so long as the scientist or design
> theorist recognizes that such reasoning is fallible and corrigible
> and has the ontological status of a regulative hypothesis
> adopted as a methodological assumption only and which is
> always subject to the checks and revisions of future experience.
> (Force, 1990, 189-90)

What this seems to be saying is that induction can be a tool
employed in the process of deduction; that generalizing from the
parts to the whole can be used in forming theoretical statements,
which then can be tested. This is a logical problem that is
extremely difficult to resolve but which may, in fact, provide a
foundation for praxis (the practice of any discipline or field of
study, including library and information science).

What we see in Hume is an opportunity for a selective interpretation. Remember that both scientism and determinism are, in some important respects, simplifications. Hume's work can be simplified to an empiricism that stresses sensory perception above all, to a determinism that demands the search for effects and their causes, and to an emphasis on reason as a binding force (this last fixes him firmly in the Enlightenment and as a modern). One passage from his writings, perhaps more than any other, can be lifted and employed by later writers whose particular focus is positivistic. He concluded the *Enquiry* with the following state- ments which clearly do not summarize his thinking in general, but do express his thought on a particular kind of metaphysical reliance; these have provided a center of attention for some to come: "If we take in our hand any volume; of divinity or school metaphysics, for instance; let us ask, *Does it contain any abstract reasoning concerning quantity or number?* No. *Does it contain any experimental reasoning concerning matter of fact and existence?* No. Commit it then to the flames: for it can contain nothing but sophistry and illusion [emphasis in original]" (Hume, 1988, 195).

A Different Voice: Kant

The last of the philosophers to be dealt with in this first chapter is Immanuel Kant. For the present, treatment of Kant will be limited; only his thought that bears on the topic at hand will be considered. Some statements by Kant can be seen to support the line running through most of the thinkers discussed so far. In 1781, near the end of the period customarily labeled the Enlightenment, Kant wrote in his *Critique of Pure Reason*, "That all our knowledge begins with experience there can be no doubt. . . . In respect of time, therefore, no knowledge of ours is anteced- ent to experience, but begins with it" (Kant, 1990, 1). On the face of it, if we limit perusal of Kant to such a cursory glance, it seems as though he follows directly in the tradition begun with Bacon. Such is not the case, though. In fact, Kant is treated here as an example of something of a departure from that tradition.

from Bacon

Some writers before Kant had endeavored to incorporate reason into the scheme of the production of knowledge, particularly scientific knowledge. None of these go as far as Kant or treat reason in exactly the same way as Kant. For instance, Kant explicitly attempted to answer Hume's problem of causality in the *Prolegomena to Any Future Metaphysics* (1783):

> Hume started chiefly from a single but important concept in metaphysics, namely, that of the connection of cause and effect (including its derivatives force and action, and so on). He challenged reason, which pretends to have given birth to this concept of herself, to answer him by what right she thinks anything could be so constituted that if that thing be posited, something else also must necessarily be posited; for this is the meaning of the concept of cause. He demonstrated irrefutably that it was perfectly impossible for reason to think *a priori* and by means of concepts such a combination, for it implies necessity. We cannot at all see why, in consequence of the existence of one thing, another must necessarily exist or how the concept of such a combination can arise *a priori*. . . . I . . . soon found that the concept of the connection of cause and effect was by no means the only concept by which the understanding thinks the connection of things *a priori*, but rather that metaphysics consists altogether of such concepts. . . . I proceeded to the deduction of these concepts, which I was now certain were not derived from experience, as Hume had attempted to derive them, but sprang from the pure understanding. (Kant, 1950, 5, 8)

Michael Friedman addresses the difficulty of the adequacy of experience to explain the universality of a causal relationship:

> To say that even A causes event B is to say, first, that there is a universal rule or law of the form: Events of type A are followed by events of type B. Yet, because experience alone can never show that such a rule or law is *strictly* [emphasis in original] universal, the judgment that A causes B must be grounded, additionally, in an *a priori* source or faculty of knowledge. The latter is of course the understanding, with its *a priori* conditions of objective judgment in a possible experience. (Friedman, 1992, 163)

Kant offered a demonstrably different assessment of causation—one that admits the insufficiency of purely empirical means to arrive at universal statements. "An empirical judgment never exhibits strict and absolute, but only assumed and comparative universality (by induction); therefore the most we can say is . . . there is no exception to this or that rule. If, on the other hand, a judgment carries with it strict and absolute universality . . . it is not derived from experience, but is valid absolutely *a priori*" (Kant, 1990, 2-3). All of this illustrates the complexity of Kant and his use of reason in setting forth a structure upon which knowledge can be based. Thomas Wartenberg suggests that reason is used by Kant in a regulative, rather than a constitutive, manner.

> That is, in characterizing the use of reason as regulative rather than constitutive, Kant is making reference to the relation of this use of reason to empirical objects, phenomena. Kant is claiming that this use of reason is not constitutive of such objects. . . . By making this distinction, however, Kant is not claiming that the transcendental knowledge supplied by reason is not essential to understanding the nature of our knowledge, only that reason's contribution to the framework does not involve the actual constitution of the objects that we know. (Wartenberg, 1992, 237-38)

Kant presents "a picture of scientific practice that is at odds with the dominant empiricist view of science according to which science proceeds by means of the simple collection of observed regularities in experience" (Wartenberg, 1992, 242-43).

So, near the end of an acknowledged era of thought and the beginning of a new age, Kant presented a dilemma for philosophers to come. Do they accept and incorporate his vision of reason into a philosophy of science, or do they ignore him and proceed with a faith in empiricism that strengthens deterministic scientism? Certainly at the time Kant was producing his major work the older line of thought was dominant in much of the Western world.

The empiricism that seems to be persistent also appears to be materialist, that is, grounded in the physical. There are connotations of the materialist stance that are related to this intellectual genealogy, but affect the intellectual aspects in particular political and economic ways. The burgeoning of thought that characterizes the Enlightenment period owes a debt to the Renaissance, since the earlier age created the opportunity for intellectual growth. To a substantial extent, the intellectual growth accompanied material growth. Lisa Jardine argues (convincingly, I think) that the cultural developments of the Renaissance were closely linked to material developments, specifically the creation of wealth and the growth of markets (Jardine, 1996). During the period culture was valued not solely for aesthetic and intellectual reasons, but also because the products of culture were also commodities. One effect of the concentration on the material and the rational was a transformation in the consideration of what constitutes knowledge and how we achieve knowledge. Toulmin expresses the shift most clearly: "In four fundamental ways, however, 17th-century philosophers set aside the long-standing preoccupations of Renaissance humanism. In particular, they disclaimed any serious interest in four different kinds of practical knowledge: the oral, the particular, the local, and the timely" (Toulmin, 1990, 30).

The material side of the Renaissance was extended into later periods, including the Enlightenment and, indeed, all of modernity. The intellectual and cultural debts are indubitable, as Ernst Cassirer points out in his book that praises most aspects of the Enlightenment: "Enlightenment philosophy simply fell heir to the heritage of [previous] centuries; it ordered, sifted, developed, and clarified this heritage rather than contributed and gave currency to new and original ideas" (Cassirer, 1951, vi). The Enlightenment owed more to the previous age, though. The material influence, evident in the Renaissance, continued to have an impact on thought in the eighteenth century. The continuance of influence had both material and intellectual sides—in both periods there was a serious questioning of the assumptions and givens that had limited social and intellectual growth. The questioning was partly rooted in the development of markets and the commodification of cultural products. As Peter Gay says, "The spirit of capitalism questioned customary ways, despised tradition, and thus . . . helped to change the general way of thinking and to point it, if not directly toward humanitarianism, at least toward a rationalization of life" (Gay, 1969, 45). In fact, during the Enlightenment capitalism spread to just about every part of life—commerce, agriculture, banking, etc.—and affected the ideas in political, as well as intellectual, spheres (see Im Hof, 1994, 191-95). In addition to its roots in materialism, the capitalism that grew during the Enlightenment was also connected to the rationalism that also characterized the period. Also, this capitalism was peculiar to the Western world and firmly grounded in the religious, cultural, and intellectual (as well as material) aspects of society (see Weber, 1992 [1930]). The present book is an examination of the intellectual foundations and intellectual potential of the social sciences and LIS, but I will not be able to, nor should I, ignore the attendant cultural and material influences on the intellectual life. This is a theme that will recur in each chapter, but will be addressed at some length near the end of the book.

Douglas Adair offers a summation that serves well to conclude this chapter: "Bacon, Newton, and Locke were the famed trinity of representative great philosophers for Americans and all educated inhabitants of Western Europe in 1783. . . . By the middle of the eighteenth century, a multitude of researchers in all the countries of Europe were seeking, in Newtonian style, to advance the bounds of knowledge in politics, economics, law, and sociology" (Adair, 1976, 405). In the next chapter we will explore the state of philosophy of science in the nineteenth and twentieth centuries.

Chapter Two

A Continuation of the Genealogy of Thought

As the period traditionally referred to as the Enlightenment drew to a close, a couple of cataclysmic events affected the course of history. One of these events was of lesser importance to the genealogy of thought. The American Revolution certainly was significant in many senses, but its impact on the line of thinking that is of concern here was not great. In the cause of independence the shapers of thought and action in the newly formed United States were, in some ways, reactive. The quote from Douglas Adair which ended the first chapter gives an indication of the reaction of American writers to what had gone before in the world of science.

Of much greater significance to the topic at hand was the French Revolution. That Revolution differed enough in cause, means, and outcome from the American Revolution that the two cannot be considered as part of any single, coordinated movement. The French Revolution, including the few years immediately prior to revolutionary action, marks a branching of the genealogy. The roots remain the same—Baconian and Newtonian premises constitute the core of thinking throughout this period.

(It should be noted, again, that neither Baconianism nor Newtonianism are necessarily the literal expressions of Bacon or Newton, but may be the transmutations by successors.) If anything, the writings emanating from certain Frenchmen in the late eighteenth and early nineteenth centuries were more openly scientistic than any before. The French Revolution itself (and its causes and aftermath) influenced thinking. One line of both pre- and post-Revolutionary thought remained constant—there must be a means of achieving the perfectibility of society. Whether through a liberal or a conservative approach, this goal, at its most fundamental, remained the same. Further, perfectibility depended upon a scientific approach, not only to the problems, but to the very structure, of society. A particular kind of scientism, which attained prominence in the nineteenth century and continues through our own, was given the name positivism. It has been convenient, especially in recent years, to lump all deterministic scientism into the catch-all category of positivism, but there is no such single convenient, narrowly defined category. There have been different philosophies that have taken the name positivism, and many more have been saddled with this appellation, usually meant in a pejorative sense. Before we start throwing the positivist label around, we must continue through this genealogy to see how thought has developed.

Condorcet

A key figure (though one who is frequently ignored) is Marie-Jean-Antoine-Nicolas Caritat, marquis de Condorcet. Condorcet's background was in mathematics, but his interest in social and political problems led him to suggest that the same method could be applied with equal effectiveness to the social as to the physical. F. A. Hayek relates one of Condorcet's early articulations of this suggestion.

> As early as 1783, in the oration at his reception into the academy, [Condorcet] gave expression to what was to become a favorite idea of positivist sociology, that of an observer to

whom physical and social phenomena would appear in the same
light, because, "a stranger to our race, he would study human
society as we study those of the beavers and bees." And
although he admits that this is an unattainable ideal because
"the observer is himself part of human society," he repeatedly
exhorts the scholars "to introduce into the moral sciences the
philosophy and the method of the natural sciences." (passages
by Condorcet quoted in Hayek, 1979, 191-92)

Condorcet hoped for the establishment of a genuine social
science—one based on discoverable truths, rather than supposi-
tions. In one of his later written works, *Sketch for a Historical
Picture of the Progress of the Human Mind* (1793), Condorcet stated
that "All error in politics and morals are based on philosophical
errors and these in turn are connected with scientific errors"
(Condorcet, 1976, 250). He did not have the opportunity to
develop his thoughts further; as an ally of the Brissotins he was
imprisoned by the Jacobins on March 27, 1784. He was found
dead two days later. An earlier essay of his, the *Essay on the
Application of Mathematics to the Theory of Decision-Making* (1785),
included both an acknowledgment of an intellectual debt and the
strongest statement of his scientism: "A great man, Monsieur
[Anne-Robert-Jacques] Turgot, . . . was convinced that the truths
of the moral and political sciences are susceptible of the same
certainty as those forming the system of the physical sciences,
even those branches like astronomy which seem to approach
mathematical certainty" (Condorcet, 1976, 33). In this essay
Condorcet put forth his theory of rational choice, which could be
(and has been) applied to the political and economic spheres, and
beyond.

Lest the reader get the wrong impression, at no point in time
has deterministic scientism been an absolutely dominant way of
thinking; it had its challengers. This is also true at the time of the
French Revolution. Though the term scientism had not yet been
coined in the late eighteenth century, Edmund Burke recognized
the tenets of such thinking and urged all who read his work to
avoid what he saw as the intellectual, social, and moral pitfalls of
scientistic belief. Burke wrote, "The lines of morality are not like

the ideal lines in mathematics. They are broad and deep as well
as long. They admit of exception; they admit of modification"
(Burke, 1898, 16). Burke's warning was aimed in particular at
that group of French writers known as the *philosophes*. The
philosophes, and Condorcet was notable among them, espoused a
materialism that was strongly opposed to traditional religion,
both as a belief and as an institution. Maurice Crosland notes
that "On the European front [Burke] was attacking above all a
mentality, one which had come to the fore in the revolutionary
period and which believed in reductionism and social engineer-
ing" (Crosland, 1987, 306). Reductionism means, in one sense
that I've mentioned previously, the equation of the social or
mental with the physical. A reductionist belief implies that
humans behave in the same way as other elements of the physical
world. This is a pervasive aspect of deterministic scientism from
the late eighteenth century onward. In the *philosophes*, and for our
purposes in Condorcet, we have a definite application of reductionism, to be managed (politically, socially, and in most ways)
through the rational application of scientific methods.

It may be said that, in the *philosophes*, we have the culmination of the Enlightenment. In a sense, this is true. By 1800 the
faith in reason was not as dominant as it had been throughout
the century. Challenges to a firm confidence in reason and
rationality came from many quarters, but most of the challenges
centered on a reaction against any such confidence and a call to
grasp once again emotion and sentiment, which could supplant
reason and intellect. The strong reaction, usually seen as the
beginning of the Romantic period, swept over all of Europe, and
included the United States as well. Notable expressions of
Romanticism came in literature, art, and music. While this was
indeed a strong reaction, the genealogy we deal with here did not
come to an end. Its continuance is a clear flow from the seventeenth century and through (in France at least) Condorcet. W.
Jay Reedy observes, "It could be argued that Condorcet is a good
candidate to be considered one of the 'grandfathers' of French
social science. His *Equisse d'un tableau historique des progrés de
l'esprit humain* mixes scientism with its 'philosophical history' in
a manner at least as utopian (or dystopian) at the syntheses

created by [later writers]" (Reedy, 1994, 20-21). In this respect Condorcet may be taken as the epitome of the modern, with his empiricist insistence on the efficacy of mathematical application to all, including social, problems, and his reliance on reason. The quest for a science of society continued unabated, though altered in some important ways, in post-Revolutionary France.

Saint-Simon

As is true of the time covered in chapter 1, at this point many individuals could be mentioned, but it is more fruitful to concentrate on some key figures who continue the path begun by Bacon. In picking up the influence of Condorcet on successors the next step is Henri de Saint-Simon. Saint-Simon openly acknowledged his debt to Condorcet in his early writings; as Georg Iggers says, he "saw the perfection of scientific methodology as the basis of human progress" (Iggers, 1958, xxi). The drive to achieve progress was a deliberate reaction to the time. The Revolution, along with the Terror and Napoleon's reign, resulted in a tremendous amount of social, as well as personal, upheaval. As Reedy notes, "social scientism (i.e., the application of the assumptions and methods of natural science to studying society) were also products of that period of insecurity" (Reedy, 1994, 2). Saint-Simon was attempting to move beyond both the *philosophes* and the Jacobins in thought and practice. Even the valuable vestiges of the eighteenth century—that which could be deemed worthy as a contribution to progress—was insufficient in Saint-Simon's eyes. "The eighteenth century, Saint-Simon was fond of saying, had attempted to construct a positive system of society without being able to raise the new one in its place" (Simon, 1956, 314). His answer was to try to build a positive philosophy on which progress could be based. "Positive" had two meanings: the opposite of negative, or embodying a focus on progress and perfectibility of the human condition; and the opposite of speculative, or the employment of facts to increase knowledge and certainty. The facts to be employed were, of course, scientific facts. Saint-Simon's own words illustrate his scientism as used in his positive philosophy: "It is because science provides the means of making predictions that makes it useful, and that scientists are superior to all other men. All known phenomena have been divided into different classes. Here is one classification which has been adopted: astronomical, physical, chemical, and physiological phenomena" (Saint-Simon, 1975, 74).

As an aside, it is interesting to note that the scientistic pronouncements of the likes of Saint-Simon were finding their way into the literature of the day. In Mary Shelley's *Frankenstein, or the Modern Prometheus* (and the subtitle is genuinely enlightening of what could only be considered a popular view of the science of the day), Professor Waldman says that modern scientists "penetrate into the recesses of nature, and show how she works in her hiding places. They ascend into the heavens: they have discovered how the blood circulates, and the nature of the air we breathe. They have acquired new and almost unlimited powers; they can command the thunders of heaven, mimic the earthquake, and even mock the invisible world with its own shadows" (Shelley, 1993, 40). Of course it is the unknowable, according to Shelley, that results in the downfall of those espousing such scientistic hubris.

It must be made clear that Saint-Simon's aim was to reconstruct society, to bring about a new social order that would ensure stability and eradicate insecurity. Peyton Lyon states this clearly in his assessment of Saint-Simon's purpose: he "was obsessed with the need to re-establish social order on a new basis which would prevent the recurrence of such catastrophic upheavals as the French Revolution" (Lyon, 1961, 55). As is evident from Saint-Simon's writings, quoted above, the ability to predict is key. One means of predicting for Saint-Simon was to analyze historical progression in an effort to discover laws. These laws could then be used to predict the future. The search for laws of history on which to base prediction is known as historicism. Historicism is a form of determinism since, as Walter Simon points out, "A certain line of development, once started, could continue in one direction and one direction only" (Simon, 1956, 319). Historicism is a flawed principle, as is scientism, because, for one thing, there is no admission that there may not exist immutable laws that govern the course of history; for another, even if such laws might exist, that it would be impossible to know enough about the past to formulate the laws completely and unerringly; and for a third, that the past is not open to one, and only one, interpretation.

Historicism, of course, has other definitions. In a general sense it can mean the situating of any statement in its historical context, but it can also encompass the biases or interests of the period from which the statement emanates (see Hamilton, 1996). In literary study there has in the past few decades been a resurgence of historicism under the appellation New Historicism. This way of thinking is a reaction against the New Critical insistence that we look only at the text; New Historicism places that text in history (see Thomas, 1991). These uses of the term can be applicable to LIS; the more complete historical context of thought and action is important to us.

Saint-Simon's project was to alter the line of development so that a course of human progress could be followed. Historicism, in addition to being deterministic, is also strongly nomological; the purpose is to discern inherent laws and then to use the knowledge of those laws to predict what will happen. Saint-Simon fell victim to the fallacy of historicism; as Simon says, "Saint-Simon evidently changed the rules of the game by postulating what was going to happen because he wanted it to happen, and then used history to show why it was going to happen; but in this process he lost the hindsight which is the saving grace of the ordinary historian" (Simon, 1956, 321). Saint-Simon, in effect, changed a hermeneutic or interpretive process into a deterministic one. Even he had to admit that the events of 1789 were clear only in retrospect, only after they had played themselves out and could be examined by looking backward.

Ultimately Saint-Simon proposed disestablishing traditional religion and replacing it with a human religion. He saw physiological phenomena as one in a progression of sciences and human progress as governed by these phenomena. By the time he died in 1825 his project was not scientific (using his way of thinking), but ideological. The ideology, based on scientism and historicism, was put forth as the culmination of an evolutionary process. The ideology he was proposing he named physicism (based on physiological phenomena), and it was to be the new religion, to replace any sort of theistic religion. It was, actually, to be the third stage in the evolution of religion which progressed through polytheism and monotheism to physicism. Saint-Simon himself was able to lay down the precepts of this new religion. It remained for his followers and successors to pick up the program, but the Saint-Simonians diverged from their namesake in their efforts to establish a society governed centrally by an elite who would exercise complete control of all aspects of life. It is not the purpose here to critique in depth the political philosophy of the Saint-Simonians, but the next individual to be considered was foremost among their number and was vocal in articulating a science of society.

Comte

In 1817 Auguste Comte was hired by Saint-Simon to be his secretary. Comte, only nineteen at the time, had just been removed from the Ecole Polytechnique for allegedly becoming involved in a plot aimed at insurrection. Before beginning his alliance with Saint-Simon, Comte had been engaged in reading a number of philosophers from the seventeenth century through Condorcet and had been taught by the mathematicians Joseph Louis Lagrange and Gaspard Monge. It may have been Condorcet who had the most profound influence on the young Comte; he acknowledged Condorcet's notion of the perfectibility of humans and was attracted to a view of history that would find a future of individuals who were rational, free, and unfettered by the mastery of religious or tyrannical secular rule. As Mary Pickering points

out, "The acceptance of the limitations of the mind, the relationship of all knowledge to man, and the utility of science to the
human condition were aspects of Enlightenment humanism that
were fervently embraced by Condorcet. These ideas would also
have a great impact on Comte" (Mary Pickering, 1993, 50). Even
in his early development, Comte was exhibiting a denial of the
metaphysical as a basis for knowledge and a modified empiricism
(not so strong as to place all import in the object and not nearly
so rationalistic as to overemphasize the subject). Comte, then, is
a successor to the thinkers discussed thus far.

The foregoing statement may seem to be a rationalization,
made in order to fit individuals in this genealogy so that it
appears to be an unbroken line. First, the lineage of intellectual
debt can be made clear, as has been demonstrated to this point,
by an examination of the writings of the philosophers considered.
While other individuals could surely be added to the genealogy,
the principal proponents of the kind of deterministic scientism
that has been defined here are the ones included. Further, in the
case of Comte, direct homage is not infrequently paid to those
who most deeply affected the evolution of his thought. Pickering
notes some of those debts:

> The seventeenth-century sources of positive philosophy are, in
> fact, evident, and it is not surprising that Comte would later call
> Bacon and Descartes two of his main "predecessors." Bacon
> was at the origin of his empirical idea that all scientific princi-
> ples must be based on observed facts, and Descartes helped
> form Comte's rationalism, that is, his tendency to go from
> principles to facts. Descartes was responsible for the even more
> important idea that the unity of the sciences comes from unity
> of method. (Mary Pickering, 1993, 162)

Pickering also says that Comte made special mention of Kant as
"the 'last eminent thinker' who had preceded him" and "the one
'closest to the positive philosophy'" (Mary Pickering, 1993, 296).
Pickering adds, though, that Comte substantially misunderstood
Kant and at times attributed ideas to Kant erroneously.

Many of these influences on Comte's thinking were enhanced
during the time he worked with Saint-Simon. This is in part due

to Saint-Simon's active encouragement of Comte's reading while
in his employ. Of greater importance, in all likelihood, was
Comte's own maturation throughout those years. It was a
formative period in Comte's intellectual life. The combination of
forces led, initially, to Comte's assistance with much of Saint-
Simon's late writings. The articulation of a positive philosophy
was a shared goal of the elder and junior men. At times the
articulations of the two are so similar that it is difficult to tell
who might be responsible for particular ideas. Hayek suggests, for
instance, that Comte's *System of Positive Policy*, while not fully
developed, was essentially a restatement of Saint-Simon's own
doctrine. Further, Hayek wonders how much that is taken to be
Saint-Simon's work might have been more properly attributable
to Comte (Hayek, 1979, 253). It does seem clear that Comte was
not merely Saint-Simon's amanuensis, that he was more than a
scribe making note of the master's dictation.

Comte wrote profusely on positive philosophy, so some look
at his writings as essential. In fact, it was Comte who coined the
words "positivism" and "sociology." As has been previously
stated, positivism in Comte's philosophy, as it was in Saint-
Simon's, refers primarily to the antithesis of speculation. In order
to achieve a grounding based more on the definite than the
conditional, therefore, some empiricist elements must comprise
a part of positivism. Comte, however, was not a strict empiricist,
nor did he adhere strictly to induction as the only means to
knowledge. He recognized shortcomings in both induction and
deduction and says they must be supplemented by "the rational
construction and scientific use of *hypotheses* [emphasis in original],
regarded as a powerful and indispensable auxiliary to our study
of nature. . . . Neither [induction nor deduction] would help us,
even in regard to the simplest phenomena, if we did not begin by
anticipating the results, by making a provisional supposition,
altogether conjectural in the first instance, with regard to some of
the very notions that are the object of the inquiry. Hence the
necessary introduction of hypotheses into natural philosophy"
(Comte, 1975, 146). Comte in many ways anticipated the later
research approach by linking both theory and evidence (observation) as key components. Moreover, as Larry Laudan states,

Comte's departure from the likes of Bacon (in this regard) centers on his negation of induction as the sole source of theory (Laudan, 1996, 213-14). Comte is departing in an important way from the roots of deterministic scientism. A question that arises is: Does he depart in other ways?

On the face of it, there is another significant departure from the lineage. Mathematics holds an extremely important place in Comte's philosophy and a training in mathematics is vital if any researcher would pretend to understand the logic of theory, method, and positive confirmation of hypotheses. In the organic sciences (and social physics, or sociology, is the most complex of these) it is the logic of mathematics, and only the logic, that has a fundamental place. At least that is what Comte says in one instance: "As for any application of number and of a mathematical law to sociological problems, if such a method is inadmissible in biology, it must be yet more decisively so here" (Comte, 1975, 258). When writing of biology, however, Comte appeared to be more willing to give mathematics a more prominent place:

> In the phenomena of living bodies, as in all others, every action proceeds according to precise—that is, mathematical—laws, which we should ascertain if we could study each phenomenon by itself. The phenomena of the inorganic world are, for the most part, simple enough to be calculable; those of the organic world are too complex for our management. But this has nothing to do with any difference in their nature. (Comte, 1975, 176-77)

There is a departure from the past in Comte's rhetoric. but the rhetorical diversion with regard to mathematics is neither entirely consistent nor methodologically grounded in reasons for the inadequacy of the application of statistics in sociology. I do not mean this, necessarily, as a defense of such application, but as an illustration that some of Comte's ideas are less than fully developed.

In some respects Comte's positivism does seem to be begotten of his predecessors. For instance, he claimed that "the first characteristic of the positive philosophy is that it regards all phenomena as subjected to invariable natural *laws* [emphasis in

original]" (Comte, 1975, 75). The means for success in the quest
for laws is science based on positive philosophy. And this science
depends on progressing beyond our speculative past since no
amount of speculation can be fruitful in discerning laws. This
means, as Condorcet and Saint-Simon (and Hume before them)
urged, moving past theology and metaphysics, whose

> attributes are the same, consisting, in regard to method, in the
> preponderance of imagination over observation, and, in regard
> to doctrine, in the exclusive investigation of absolute ideas, the
> result of both of which is an inevitable tendency to exercise an
> arbitrary and indefinite action over phenomena that are not
> regarded as subject to invariable natural laws. (Comte, 1975,
> 219)

The nomological aspect (the grounding in laws) is not a new
feature in this genealogy; belief in the existence of natural laws is
a part of its determinism. The entirety of physical phenomena,
and human and social behavior are subsets of physical phenomena, is governed by a set of laws which is immutable. Comte's
only hedge in this regard is to see sociology as a relative, rather
than an absolute, science; that is, it is dependent upon evolution,
and the less than certain transformation evolution might bring
about.

With the fundamental tenet of his philosophy—the existence
of natural laws—Comte asserts that the sciences are hierarchical,
moving from the inorganic to the organic, the simple and abstract
to the complex and concrete. His hierarchy begins with "five
fundamental sciences in successive dependence—astronomy,
physics, chemistry, physiology, and finally social physics"
(Comte, 1975, 96). Moreover, "It is necessary not only to have
a general knowledge of all the sciences but to study them in their
order. What can come of a study of complicated phenomena if
the student has not learned, by the contemplation of the simpler,
what a law is, what it is to observe, what a positive conception is,
and even what a chain of reasoning is?" (Comte, 1975, 99) After
establishing the hierarchy of the five sciences Comte places
mathematics in the fore, since in his positive philosophy all of the
sciences are dependent on mathematics. This order has a

particular significance; it is seen by Comte as absolutely essential to the prime purpose of science, prediction. Edmund Ziegelmeyer assesses the aim of science and the purpose of the hierarchy: "Ferret out, the Positivist commands us, the unchangeable laws that govern phenomena in their relations of succession and similarity, and set aside all useless questions. Then man can foresee future events by the discovery of the unchangeable laws that govern the occurrence of natural phenomena" (Ziegelmeyer, 1942, 8-9).

Another trait of deterministic scientism remains to be discussed—reduction. To Hayek, reductionism is at the heart of Comte's sociology. "This new science of *social physics* [emphasis in original], that is to say, the study of the collective development of the human race, is really a branch of physiology, or the study of man conceived in its entire extension. In other words, the history of civilization is nothing but the indispensable result and complement of the natural history of man" (Hayek, 1979, 254). Hayek's position is an extreme one that suggests a literal equation of the social with the physical. Pickering denies that Comte's philosophy embodies reductionism at all. Rather, Comte separates physiology from sociology because the former is a study of humans as individual physical entities and the latter is a study of humans as part of society (Mary Pickering, 1993, 151). Both Hayek and Pickering overstate their cases, but Pickering's is by far the weaker. To begin with, the hierarchy itself is reductionist; it implies not only that sciences of the organic are dependent on and derivative of the inorganic, but also that the science of society likewise depends on and derives from the sciences of the physical. Perhaps even more to the point, while Comte does assert that the nature of sociology and biology are distinct, there is only one method of studying them: "As to the method, the logical analogy of the two sciences is so clear as to leave no doubt that social philosophers must prepare their understandings for their work by due discipline in biological methods" (Comte, 1975, 256).

What we have in Comte is a complicated, and far from consistent and clear, discourse on what constitutes science, how the study of the social fits into the construction, and what

methods should be employed. Apart from establishing a hierarchy, Comte's discussion of method is almost that of an excursus,
something appended because there had to be something there to
fill out his system. While Pickering maintains that the method is
well developed, it is sketchy at best. He invoked mathematics,
but there was no uniform application of mathematics throughout
the sciences. He wrote of induction and deduction, stating that
neither, alone, is adequate, but did not define precisely what he
meant by them. It is widely acknowledged that Comte's doctrine
was a very influential force in philosophy (which is why a
substantial amount of space is devoted to him here), but what did
he contribute? Laudan suggests, and rightly so, that some less
frequently admitted aspects of Comte's philosophy have had an
enduring influence. These include an admission that Comte:

(1) Recognized the structural similarity of explanations and
predictions;
(2) Used the notion of verifiability and predictability to resolve
the dual problems of meaning and demarcation;
(3) Recognized the *prediction* [emphasis in original] were not
essentially inferences from past to future but from the known
to unknown;
(4) Stressed the theory-laden character of observation; and
(5) Acknowledged the value of hypotheses, including those
dealing with theoretical (viz., nonobservable) entities. (Laudan,
1971, 36)

However, in addition to these contributions, Comte added
strength to claims of reductionism, the nomological nature of
science, determinism, and scientism. So, it remains to be seen to
what extent Comte influenced thinking in the nineteenth century
and beyond.

Mill

The matter of influence is a complicated one. The complexity
is manifest most clearly in John Stuart Mill's reception of Comte.
In the first edition of his *System of Logic*, published in 1843, Mill

made numerous references to Comte; many of these were laudatory and most were indicative of a strong effect of Comte on Mill's thinking. Perhaps because Mill was still rather young when the book first appeared, and perhaps because of a possible personal rift between the two (Hawkins, 1938, 8), Mill eventually drifted away from Comte to some extent. In any event, subsequent editions of the *System of Logic* contained revisions by Mill that lessened the apparent connection between him and Comte. What may be more probable as an explanation for Mill's alteration in assessment of Comte was the latter's espousal of his positivism, not just as a philosophy of science or method of thought, but as a form of civil order or organization and, eventually, as a religion (reminiscent of Saint-Simon in his later years). Over time the acknowledged influence of Comte on Mill was limited to method, and even in that area Mill questioned the efficacy of Comte's system. Granted, positive philosophy was not new with Comte, but Mill ultimately attempted to diminish his contributions further. Later editions of the *System of Logic* still included praise for Comte: "Within a few years three writers . . . have made attempts . . . towards the creation of a Philosophy of Induction: . . . greatest of all, M. Auguste Comte, in his *Cours de Philosophie Positive*, a work which only requires to be better known, to place its author in the very highest class of European thinkers" (Mill, 1852, 172). At a later time Mill's altered opinion was evident:

> Nor is it unknown to any one who has followed the history of the various physical sciences, that the positive explanation of facts has substituted itself, step by step, for the theological and metaphysical as the progress of inquiry brought to light an increasing number of the invariable laws of phaenomena. In these respects M. Comte has not originated anything, but has taken his place in a fight long since engaged, and on the side already in the main victorious. (Mill, 1961, 12)

Mill is, in many ways, a more direct descendent of a line of thought that has foundations in Baconianism and Newtonianism. This is particularly evident in his insistence on induction as the logical basis of science. He wrote, "We have found that all

Inference, consequently all Proof, and all discovery of truths not
self-evident, consists of inductions, and the interpretation of
inductions: that all our knowledge, not intuitive, comes to us
exclusively from that source" (Mill, 1852, 171). Moreover,
induction is based on an assumption that strikes at the foundation of nature. Mill asserts that the assumption is both a basis
and a result of inductive reasoning, central to and an outgrowth
of the process of inferring the universal from the individual. He
says that "the proposition that the course of nature is uniform, is
the fundamental principle, or general axiom, of Induction" (Mill,
1852, 184). Mill admits that if this proposition is not true, then
all other inductions prove false, since they are based on the
uniformity of nature. The implication of such a belief is that the
uniformity of nature is the first and most important of natural
laws. Twentieth-century physics has provided ample evidence for
something other than uniformity, so Mill's system must be called
into question.

Struan Jacobs notes that, in the course of revising his *System
of Logic*, Mill changed his assessment of the utility of hypotheses,
formulating more of a companion relationship between induction
and hypothesis (Jacobs, 1991). While this move is indicated in
Mill's writings, hypothesis is still distinctly subordinate to
induction.

> [H]ypotheses are invented to enable the Deductive Method to
> be earlier applied to phenomena. . . . [T]he Hypothetical
> Method suppresses the first of the three steps [in the process of
> explanation], the induction to ascertain the law; and contents
> itself with the other two operations, ratiocination and verifica-
> tion; the law, which is reasoned from, being assumed, instead
> of proved.
> This process may evidently be legitimate upon one supposi-
> tion, namely, if the nature of the case be such that the final
> step, the verification, shall amount to, and fulfill the conditions
> of, a complete induction. (Mill, 1852, 291-92)

Here Mill is substantially at odds with Comte and much more
sympathetic to his seventeenth- and eighteenth-century predecessors. He did claim that many intellectual ancestors, going back to

Bacon, were in error in their inductive reasoning, but the errors rested primarily with the rigor (or lack thereof) with which they applied induction. To the extent that Mill did mitigate his criticism of hypotheses he came closer to Comte's thinking and solidified the influence of Comte on his work.

Walter Simon claims that the principal effect Comte had on his contemporaries and followers was that of the method of positivism (Simon, 1963, 23-24). This is evidently true in the case of Mill (although the influence of Comte on Mill might have been greater if Mill had been guilty of fewer misreadings of Comte's work (Scharff, 1989). What is definite is that the determinism inherent in Comte's system endured in Mill's. The latter's principles of evidence display a mathematical reductionism:

> there is no science but that of number, in which the practical validity of a reasoning can be apparent to any person who has looked only at the form of the process. . . . A conclusion, therefore, however correctly deduced, in point of form, from admitted laws of nature, will have no other than a hypothetical certainty. At every step we must assure ourselves that no other law of nature has superseded, or intermingled its operation with, those which are the premises of the reasoning; and how can this be done by merely looking at the words? (Mill, 1852, 431)

The reductionism of Mill extends to the heart of his thinking. At once he equates epistemology with the philosophy of science (since he reduces knowing to the science of human mental faculties) and says that science itself can be pared down to the logic of its processes (Mill, 1961, 53). This reductionism surpasses Comte, who saw positive philosophy as a historical culmination with regard to the quest for answers to questions that were earlier subjected to theological and then metaphysical inquiry. Mill's stance is, by comparison, ahistorical; he negates the entire questioning process that predates the application of the logic of science. His position, then, is also more strongly deterministic than Comte's.

From Mill onward the genealogy of thought takes a variety of turns as many writers and theorists direct their attention to human society. While it is true that Saint-Simon and Comte purported to be setting forth a new science of society, their thoughts were still abstract, especially in comparison with many who wrote from the mid-nineteenth century on. This is certainly not to imply that elements of Baconianism and other aspects of deterministic scientism become submerged in the effort to articulate a *social science*. Beginning at that time, though, the various theorists took issue with one another regarding specific features of the vision for a science of society. Just as Mill disavowed particular tenets of Comtean positivism while retaining the essential goal of a scientific founding for society, so too did many of his contemporaries disagree with one another and with their predecessors even though they propounded ideas that focused on a scientifically determined theory of human society. The seeming disagreement among fundamentally like-minded writers has characterized the stream of thought for the last century and a half. The points of disagreement are certainly not uninteresting, but I would be hard-pressed to claim the existence of a genealogy of thought if there were no ties that bind. As we will see, the genuine disputations and departures from this line of thinking are more a product of our century than of any other.

Marx

Now that the foregoing paragraph has prepared the way for the tricky path ahead, we have to give at least some passing attention to a thinker who has presented more grounds for disagreement (sometimes violent) on more fronts than, possibly, anyone before or since—Karl Marx. There is neither time nor space here for a lengthy disquisition on Marx's far-reaching theories, but his writings on science deserve some attention here. One reason for a bit of an examination of Marx is the realization that there are almost as many interpretations of his stance regarding science as there are interpreters. Marx himself is a prime source for these multiple readings of his works. Two brief passages can serve to illustrate the problems he presents to interpretation. In writing of the foundation of science Marx stated, "Sense experience must be the basis of all science. Science is only genuine science when it proceeds from sense experience, in the two forms of sense perception and sensuous need, that is, only when it proceeds from Nature" (Marx, 1956, 77). This statement is quite reminiscent of much that has appeared thus far in these pages. He seems disinclined to make the reader's task an easy one, however. In his *Economic and Philosophical Manuscripts*, written in 1844 (and also the source for the previous statement), he wrote,

> Even when I carry out scientific work, etc., an activity which I can seldom conduct in direct association with other men—I perform a social, because human, act. It is not only the material of my activity—like the language itself which the thinker uses—which is given to me as a social product. My own existence is a social activity. For this reason, what I myself produce, I produce for society and with the consciousness of acting as a social being. (Marx, 1956, 77)

It is no wonder that there are still competing interpretations of Marx's stance on science. As Izabella Nowakowa and Leszek Nowak point out, there are, today, views of Marxism as an espousal of scientific philosophy, that is, as a reliable generalization of existence (Nowakowa and Nowak, 1978). They further recognize that some other interpretations deny that philosophy can be scientific, but many of those maintain a similar view of the essence of science as a depiction of truth. When Marx's inconsistencies are weighed, it is rather easy to see how opposing interpretations of his work continue to thrive. Yet despite some of Marx's assertions on science, he never developed a scientific approach to the examination of society's future. As Daniel Little reminds us, "much of Marx's science is rather dissimilar from the constructions of natural science: Marx's account is not a comprehensive, unified theory, it is not confirmed through test of its prediction, its explanations do not rely on laws of nature, and its hypotheses are generally couched in descriptive or observational terms" (Little, 1986, 200). Little's observation illustrates, in part, the problematic nature of Marx: the proliferation of ideological interpretations of Marx, that is, appropriations of the theories and conclusions of Marx regarding capital, production, power, etc. on some scientific grounds to lend credence to later conceptions of these phenomena. Little further writes that "Laws of nature are thought to arise from the determinate properties of natural processes and mechanisms, whereas social laws derive (directly or indirectly) from facts about individuals making decisions within conditions of constrained choice" (Little, 1986, 28). The interpretive problems arise when the latter is mistakenly translated into the terminology and thinking of the former.

The interpretive problem—what some might go so far as to call the interpretive fallacy—is not a completely newly discovered dilemma. Decades ago Antonio Gramsci wrote "Critical Notes on an Attempt at a Manual of Popular Sociologists" (Gramsci, 1971). In that piece Gramsci expressed opposition to those who appropriated Marx's works for sociology in the sense that laws, causality, and prediction could be applied to society in the same way they might be applied to the sciences. Gramsci's epistemology had a humanistic founding that strengthened his opposition to determinism. His epistemology led "him to belittle the efforts of positivist science to engage in objective analysis and value-free observation of society" (Kahn, 1989, 163). The debate over Marx is bound to continue with little hope of resolution. Such debate demonstrates, by its existence, the question of scientific determinism—and also it vitality.

Something Missing?

Some readers may wonder why one particular philosopher has not been mentioned up to this point. Of course Hegel is certainly one of the most influential thinkers who has ever lived. However, even with the generous definition of genealogy used here, Hegel does not really fit well. His thought did influence Marx, but much of Marx's work took a turn that was quite independent of Hegel. Hegel did not share the view of science that was held by many from Bacon well into the nineteenth century. He does not fall prey to the elimination of hum... that Toulmin says many seventeenth-century philosophers did. The empiricists have had difficulties with Hegel's metaphysics, especially since, at its most extreme, empiricism rejects metaphysics altogether. The very idea of a phenomenology of spirit (Hegel, 1967) may even seem rather foreign to a positivist thinker. Hegel's idealism was attractive to some of the earlier advocates of hermeneutics (see chapter 6 for a discussion of hermeneutics), but his writings are a bit afield of this heritage.

Spencer

I mentioned earlier that the genealogy takes some turns in the nineteenth century (and, to reiterate, it is the variability, as Foucault says, that is interesting). One of these variations is represented by Marx. Another, and a rather lengthy path continuing into this century, begins with Herbert Spencer. What is it about Spencer that marks a change in the legacy of deterministic scientism? From Bacon in the early seventeenth century through the early French positivists the vision of science and its place in inquiry has resided more in the philosophical realm than anywhere else. Many of the writers dealt with so far have searched for a scientific application to the problems facing humans, but the problem has largely been an intellectual one and the primary question has been how the certainty of science could extend to the rest of existence. This question hasn't changed by the nineteenth century, but application of the principles underlying the question are more directly applied in the social sphere. There is a strong hint of this dynamic in Comte, but he focused more on framing the question, on the search for a philosophical basis for the study of society's problems. It is Spencer, more than any other, who offered a means of applying sociology (that is, the study of society) in the light of science. With Spencer sociology begins to mature as a discipline.

Spencer follows a tradition in the nineteenth century (including Mill) that is an extension of application of Newtonian principles to "sciences" other than physics and astronomy. The application of the principles is partly conceptual (social science *conceived* as a science) and partly methodological (in the sense of a quest for explanatory laws). Valerie Haines uses as an example of the latter Spencer's application of laws of organic evolution to social evolution with the aim of discovering ultimate causation, with "ultimate" meaning incapable of further analysis (Haines, 1992). Spencer's incorporation and extrapolation of evolution to society establishes him as the author of social Darwinism in his concept of society as utilitarian. Two characteristics of deterministic scientism seem especially to pervade Spencer's sociology—reductionism and phenomenalism. He repeatedly refers to society as a thing and wrote, "Ignoring for the moment the peculiar traits of races and individuals, observe the traits common to members of the species at large; and consider how these must affect their relations when associated" (Spencer, 1971, 37). It is clear that he was reducing society to the physical. Phenomenalism (the claim that sensory observation is the best grounding for any truth claim) is evident in his 1893 statement that "Admitting, or rather asserting, that knowledge is limited to the phenomenal, we have, by implication, asserted that the sphere of knowledge is co-extensive with the phenomenal" (Spencer, 1971, 53).

Stanislav Andreski sums up Spencer's reliance on the encompassing power of science as the means by which society should be studied:

> Herbert Spencer firmly believed in the unity of science: not only in the sense that the basic logical methods are the same in all fields of scientific inquiry, which was the chief message of his somewhat resented illustrious forerunner Auguste Comte, but also in the sense that the basic processes in all realms of being are essentially identical, which he proceeded to prove in the successive parts of his System of Synthetic Philosophy. (Andreski, 1971, 7)

Spencer benefitted (if "benefitted" is the correct word) from the scientific upheaval caused by Darwin and the questions that his *Origin of Species* thrust upon not just science but philosophy, ethics, and, of course, sociology. In the most simplistic sense

Darwin's theory gave credence to a belief in the governance of natural laws and the extent to which such laws govern every aspect of existence, including the social. The belief in laws almost inevitably leads to a deterministic view of humans and human society and Spencer embraced this determinism, in the form of an inevitable path of history:

> the course of civilization could not possibly have been other than it has been. . . . [G]iven an unsubdued earth; given the being—man, appointed to overspread and occupy it; given the laws of life what they are; and no other series of changes than that which has taken place, could have taken place. For be it remembered, that the ultimate purpose of creation—the production of the greatest amount of happiness—can be fulfilled only under certain fixed conditions. (Spencer, 1971, 215)

Spencer was particularly influential in the U.S., where his fundamental conservatism seemed amenable to an "evolutionary" view of free markets and individualism. As Richard Hofstadter points out, "If Spencer's abiding impact on American thought seems impalpable to later generations, it is perhaps only because it has been so thoroughly absorbed" (Hofstadter, 1994, 50). In fact, there is at least some connection between Spencer and Charles Ammi Cutter, who admitted to having been influenced by an evolutionary model. Francis Miksa argues, convincingly, that the connection must not be overstated, though. Cutter, and other nineteenth-century librarians who turned their hands to organizing materials, did little to suggest formal, logical classifications of knowledge (Miksa, 1998, 36-37). On the other hand, the pragmatics of library classification in the nineteenth century is, itself, a paean to a phenomenalist approach to knowledge.

Durkheim

It seems that Spencer must be one of the most influential of the scientistic thinkers, but his impact on sociology—beyond as a pioneer who built respectability for the discipline—was rather short lived. Of more lasting influence was someone whose career began while Spencer was still active. Emile Durkheim not only proved a forceful and articulate advocate of a kind of positivist sociology, but he spoke more to the point of sociological method than had anyone up to that time. Durkheim was most assuredly a descendent of Saint Simon, Comte, and the rest, but he extended the reach of sociology beyond a philosophical stance. Whereas many of his predecessors contemplated the nature of a study of society and how it fit in with other disciplines (notably the natural sciences), Durkheim aimed to create a practice of sociology. There is no doubt that he was a believer in a science of society and that his belief was founded on reason and reliance on experience.

> Indeed our main objective is to extend the scope of scientific rationalism to cover human behaviour by demonstrating that, in the light of the past, it is capable of being reduced to relationships of cause and effect, which, by an operation no less rational, can then be transformed into rules of action for the future. What has been termed our positivism is merely a consequence of this rationalism. (Durkheim, 1982, 33)

While he attempted to distance himself a bit from the positivism of the past, his method is firm in its positivist roots.

Durkheim departed in some important ways, though, from the earlier sociologists. He agreed with Comte that social phenomena are akin to physical phenomena, that they are *things*; that is, that they are realities that are independent from ideas or conceptions of them. Durkheim, however, claimed that Comte, and Spencer for that matter, did not fully apprehend society and social fact as thing and that they reverted to a sociology based on ideas of society and social phenomena. Their sociology, then, was incomplete; they did not fully reject metaphysics in practice. Durkheim could be seen as having a Cartesian bent; he adhered to a belief in an absolute conception of knowledge. That absolute was, for him, rooted in the language and method of science. He wrote that the sociologist "must feel himself in the presence of facts governed by laws as unsuspected as those of life before the science of biology was evolved" (Durkheim, 1982, 55). This language is reminiscent of Comte, but Durkheim strove to apply the tenets of science in a search for fundamental laws of society. His nomological approach necessitated a forbearance of individual phenomena only insofar as, collectively, they constitute social phenomena. Moreover, social phenomena were to be viewed objectively.

Herein is perhaps the most important and enduring legacy of Durkheim. The sociologist, as a scientist, was required by him to be a neutral observer of social facts; in that neutrality was the sociologist's objectivity. But the concept of objectivity did not end there. The social fact, as a thing, was viewed as an objective phenomenon. The social fact, in such a conception, is no different from a physical fact—atomic weight, molarity, solubility, etc. Social phenomena are reduced in Durkheim's method to data, and Durkheim says as much.

> A thing is in effect all that is given, all that is offered, or rather forces itself upon our observation. To treat phenomena as things is to treat them as *data* [emphasis in original], and this constitutes the starting point for science. Social phenomena unquestionably display this characteristic. What is given is not the idea that men conceive of value, because that is unattainable; rather it is the values actually exchanged in economic transactions. . . . Social phenomena must therefore be considered in themselves, detached from the conscious beings who form their own mental representations of them. (Durkheim, 1982, 69-70)

This objectification of social phenomena was a foundation of Durkheim's method for sociology as a nascent science, and indeed of his positivist science generally.

The impact of Durkheim's method has not gone unnoticed. Jennifer Lehmann addresses his adherence to the language and method of science: "Through his insistence that social reality is part of nature, Durkheim sets the stage for the more radical claim that social reality is *like* natural reality, that *social* forces are *like* *natural* forces. Durkheim's terminology is the terminology of the natural sciences: determinism, causality, necessity [emphasis in original]" (Lehmann, 1993, 59). Note the observation that

Durkheim's program is deterministic. Durkheim believed that the answer to questions of society lay in ascribing causes to observable effects. His belief did not end there; it extended to verifying that the same causes are invariably ascribable to the same effects. Anthony Giddens claims that Durkheim has been the progenitor of most of the positivist sociology of the twentieth century (Giddens, 1977, 36-40). If I might be permitted to speculate, I would say that a fundamental reason for Durkheim's attractiveness is the strong claim of objectivity (in both of the senses noted above) that he makes. The attractiveness is not sufficient to counter the error of the strong claim of objectivity. Christopher Bryant offers a cogent counter to the claim:

> Now it is true that a thermometer recording eliminates the individual's subjective estimations of heat and that legal rules, etc., have an existence independent of any particular individual, but it is nonsense to suggest that physicists derive their *concept* [emphasis in original] of heat from thermometer readings any more than they do from sense impressions, or that legal rules present themselves to sociologists as sense data. Durkheim confused natural phenomena which exist independently of human conceptions of them, and social phenomena, which exist independently of individual manifestations, and called them both "objective"; and he supposed that in each case this objectivity is such to make possible the formation of concepts directly from sense perception when his own examples show that it is not. (Bryant, 1985, 37)

Bryant's argument accurately points out the flaw of believing that social phenomena are sense data. He succinctly uncovers the mistake of equating an object and one's concept of what the object is, of the idea of the object. The problem that is at the heart of this book goes deeper than that, however. Up to this point we have seen how many thinkers have conceived of science and the extent of science as embracing all knowledge. We have seen how many of these thinkers have founded their ideas and theories in the natural sciences and translated them into the realm of the human and the social. What we have yet to see is precisely why this is mistaken and how easy it is to fall into the trap of deterministic scientism. Theodor Adorno puts his finger on the problem:

> Disciplines and modes of thought are not justified by their mere existence but rather their limit is prescribed for them by the object. Paradoxically, the empirical methods, whose power of attraction lies in their claim to objectivity, favour the subjective—and this is explained by their origins in market research. . . . In general, the objectivity of empirical social research is an objectivity of the methods, not of what is investigated. (Adorno, 1976, 71)

We will return to this essential matter when the discussion focuses on the operational philosophy of library and information science. It is easy to mistake what is being studied for the method applied to the study, especially if certain specific methods are employed.

As we enter the twentieth century the genealogy accelerates the branching that began in the late nineteenth century. The occurrence of the branching is not surprising; from the late 1800s on we have seen a rapid growth in the enterprise of research that has been concomitant with the fragmentation of disciplines and the rise of the professions. What do I mean by the fragmentation of the disciplines? In the nineteenth century a number of thinkers, including many mentioned here, turned their attention to society—its compositions, its structure, its behavior, etc. At the same time many others focused on the natural sciences. Into this century inquiry has become much more targeted, with scholars and researchers defining realms of inquiry more and more narrowly. In the sciences, the narrowing process has been associated with, if not resultant from, the ability to examine physical phenomena in greater detail. For instance, physics has branched into a number of subdisciplines, such as chromothermodynamics, nuclear physics, condensed matter physics, electrodynamics, quantum mechanics, and others. In the social sciences, the narrowing has been associated with more specific questions regarding human behavior and society. With the branching has come a more complicated family tree, in the sense that the line of thought that has been traced thus far has had some influence in many of the emerging disciplines and sub-disciplines.

Language and the Genealogy

Before returning to the effects of the genealogy and determin-istic scientism on the social sciences generally, some attention must be paid to a movement that exerted a profound influence on philosophy, the philosophy of science, and the social sciences for a number of years. In the early part of this century the focus of some thinkers began to incorporate work in an emerging discipline—linguistics. The adherents of this movement took a cue from a few sources that took a different look at language. The first such look at language to be dealt with here was, essentially, a reformulation of linguistics—Ferdinand de Saussure's *Course in General Linguistics* (Saussure, 1966), published posthumously in 1916. Saussure's *Course* was not completely or overtly determinis-tic or positivistic, but it did share characteristics with Durkheim's sociology. Most notable, as Jonathan Culler points out, is a conception of language as social fact (Culler, 1986, 62-63). Culler asserts that one connection between Durkheim and Saussure is that social facts are objective. Saussure's linguistics, to a lesser extent than does Durkheim's sociology, depends on a method that is founded on the possibility of objective analysis. Saussure's linguistics aimed at the discovery of the fundamental structure of language; in the aftermath of the appearance of his *Course* his linguistics has been dubbed structuralist. This approach to linguistics has influenced other disciplines, such as literary theory and anthropology. The disciplinary stances that have derived from structural linguistics have tended to stress a search for underlying laws more strongly than did Saussure.

As is the case with almost all of the individuals discussed, Saussure certainly contributed many valuable ideas. Saussure, along with Charles Sanders Peirce, helped to establish a framework for semiotics, the study of signs. Such a study need not be deterministic. Umberto Eco clarifies Peirce's conception of semiotics, which emphasizes action, the combination of a sign, its object (what the sign signifies), and its interpretant (Eco, 1976, 15-16). This idea of semiotics embraces the role of the knowing and interpreting subject.

The philosophy of language was the focus of the earliest work of Ludwig Wittgenstein. In his *Tractatus Logico-Philosophicus*, first published in 1921, he proposed a foundation for an analytical approach to language. While a direct link with Saussure is elusive, the concerns of Wittgenstein in the *Tractatus* coincide with many of Saussure's in his *Course*. Of most relevance to the genealogy are his remarks regarding the logic of propositions. In particular, his analysis was focused on the ability of language to embody or convey, through such perceptible signs as the written word, meaningful communication. Communication, to be meaningful, must be based on what Wittgenstein called "facts"; that is, that words (signs) refer to objects. In short, Wittgenstein attempted to remove the metaphysical from the analysis of language and from the construction of propositions. If a proposition strayed from object, then it made no sense. "Most propositions and questions, that have been written about philosophical matters, are not false, but senseless. We cannot, therefore, answer questions of this kind at all, but only state their senselessness. Most questions and propositions of the philosophers result from the fact that we do not understand the logic of our language" (Wittgenstein, 1990, 63). In his later works, all of which were published posthumously, Wittgenstein recanted these early ideas. Nonetheless (perhaps due to propitious timing as much as anything else), the concepts in the *Tractatus* were influential (along with Saussure's linguistics to a somewhat lesser extent, and *Principia Mathematica* by Bertrand Russell and Alfred North Whitehead to an equal extent) in the formulation of logical positivism.

Logical Positivism

pre-determined
process,
procedure,
cause

Logical positivism (or logical empiricism) is the most famous, or infamous, manifestation of deterministic scientism. The disciplinary branching just noted is, in a sense, illustrated in this philosophical movement. Rather than depicting the splits experienced in the epistemological paths of several disciplines, though, logical positivism demonstrates the branching by allowing a convergence of members of several disciplines into the movement. Representatives from philosophy, physics, mathematics, and sociology contributed to the theoretical foundation of the school of thought. A great deal has been written about logical positivism from the time of its first articulation to the present. It is not the intention here to present a lengthy exegesis of its philosophical tenets, but some description is essential to the genealogy. It is essential because logical positivism was not without antecedents; it is, in fact, clearly descended from the totality of precursors we have dealt with to this point. It is also essential because logical positivism was a considerable force in philosophy for a few decades and because its influence lives on—either directly through the writing of it adherents, or indirectly as a link in the long line of deterministic scientism—particularly in the social sciences.

The Vienna Circle

The movement began in the 1920s as a group of individuals who found commonality in both the kinds of questions they sought answers to and the means of answering the questions. These individuals, of whom Moritz Schlick was most prominent in the early days, became known as the Vienna Circle. The group included A. J. Ayer, Rudolf Carnap, Otto Neurath, Kurt Gödel, and Hans Hahn, among others. Their acknowledged intellectual ancestors explicitly included Hume, Comte, Mill, and Spencer, as well as Russell, Whitehead, and Wittgenstein. The Vienna Circle itself lasted for only a decade or so (the encroachment of Nazism was largely responsible for dispersing its members), but, as a philosophical school, it lasted into the 1950s. Part of the influence of the movement was due to the intellectual breadth of, and respect commanded by, its members. Another contributory factor was the importance of the questions they addressed. Most especially, the logical positivists sought to respond to philosophical questions through the analysis of the language, the syntax, of the questions themselves and, then, their potential answers. One consistent means of defining the question and its answers is a reliance on experience, on what can be empirically verified, what can be true to all who experience a certain phenomenon. The importance of empiricism to logical positivism is almost encompassing; it is at the root of much of the thinking that is central to logical positivism.

One way that experience affects the construction of logical positivism is in its rejection of the metaphysical. This rejection is not new in the genealogy; this is one element of logical positivism's strong link to the tradition of deterministic scientism. The rejection of the metaphysical is made explicit by Carnap in his essay "The Elimination of Metaphysics through Logical Analysis of Language" (Carnap, 1959a). In that essay Carnap maintained that any metaphysical statements are "pseudo-sentences"; that is, they either include words which have no concrete meaning or take meaningful words and put them together in such a way as to violate rules of syntax so that the sentence containing the words has no meaning. The question addressed by logical positivism is: How can it be shown that a sentence is meaningful? The simplified answer is that the meaning can be verified. One means of verification is experience; there can be specific empirical criteria that can be applied to the sentence. The agreement of experience (the vast majority of people experiencing the same thing) may be one possible criterion. Another means is verification through logic, through the method of formal logic which might be employed to indicate the internal agreement of a sentence (that the rules of grammar and syntax are not violated) and agreement with that which has previously been verified. Those sentences which cannot pass these tests lie in the realm of the metaphysical and, according to logical positivism, are meaningless. Verification is a hallmark of the movement's theoretical foundation.

Unified Science

Another aspect of the logical positivist stance is the quest for unified science. In Carnap's conception, one basis for the unity of science was experience. Experience, as Carnap has attempted to demonstrate, is an element of the formal analysis that is part of every discipline. Logical analysis was, for him, the thread that constituted a commonality, regardless of the field of endeavor or question. He wrote,

> There are not different sciences with fundamentally different methods or different sources of knowledge, but only *one* [emphasis in original] science. All knowledge finds its place in this science and, indeed, is knowledge of basically the same kind; the appearance of fundamental differences between the sciences are the deceptive result of our using different sub-languages to express them. (Carnap, 1959b, 144)

Neurath took the idea of a unified language being part of unified science a bit further. This language, according to Neurath, was physicalist; it was placed in space and time and both subject to and expressive of physical laws (Neurath, 1959, 186-87). The logical positivism movement, and particularly Neurath, envisioned the creation of the *International Encyclopedia of Unified Science*. While the *Encyclopedia* was never fully realized, the philosophical foundation of the project embodied an openly reductionist claim. All disciplines are reducible to the physical. This notion has been challenged by many since its articulation. Oswald Hanfling provides a succinct and direct objection to its inclusiveness: "It does not follow that [connections between the language used in various branches of knowledge] must all be of one kind or that there must be a homogeneous class of terms to which others are reducible" (Hanfling, 1981, 113).

The claims of logical positivism held a definite attraction, especially to the then-burgeoning social sciences. (The attraction is not a new one; philosophers down the years found the lure of deterministic scientism strong enough to seek its application in fields of study beyond the natural sciences.) The notion that propositions can be verified suggests that there can be an

affirmation of truth claims. The belief in laws governing phenomena hints at causation and an underlying foundation for social, as
well as physical, phenomena.

> [The logical positivists] proposed a theory of meaning that
> showed how scientific discourse was grounded in sensory
> experience and thus certain to be meaningful. They provided an
> account of explanation that used deduction to show how
> particular events could be explained by laws and an account of
> confirmation that showed how particular events provided
> evidence for the laws that were developed. Finally, they showed
> how the laws of each science could be unified into axiomatic
> structures and ultimately grounded in a unified account of
> nature. (Bechtel, 1988, 29)

The attractiveness, however, could not overcome the numerous
objections to the logical positivist program. The collapse of the
system was evident when even its adherents began hedging their
positions. Ayer wrote, "A proposition is said to be verifiable, in
the strong sense of the term, if, and only if, its truth could be
conclusively established in experience. But it is verifiable, in the
weak sense, if it is possible for experience to render it probable"
(Ayer, 1952, 37).

Challenges to Logical Positivism

The attack on verification got its start with Karl Popper, a
contemporary of those in the Vienna Circle and one who
conversed with many of their number. Popper refused to accept
the verification principle; he claimed that inductive inference is
impossible, so there could be no logical basis for verification by
experience. Inductive inference begins with a general truth claim
and asserts statements about particular instances. For instance,
for the claim, "All swans are white" to be verifiable, we would
have to have observed the color of all swans that ever existed *and*
observe the color of all swans to come. Popper sought to replace
confirmation (which would be necessary for verification) with
corroboration. In the most important sense, Popper's use of
corroboration means "not falsified"; in other words, a hypothesis

or truth claim has not yet been shown to be false. This idea implies that there is a perpetually ongoing search and that we learn, we know more, by coming to an understanding of both the exploratory process and the system of finding that result from inquiry. As Popper said,

> Science is not a system of certain, or well-established, statements; nor is it a system which steadily advances towards a state of finality. . . . The advance of science is not due to the fact that more and more perceptual experiences accumulate in the course of time. Nor is it due to the fact that we are making ever better use of our senses. Out of uninterpreted sense-experiences science cannot be distilled, no matter how industriously we gather and sort them. Bold ideas, unjustified anticipations, and speculative thought, are our only means for interpreting nature: our only organon, our only instrument, for grasping her. (Popper, 1965, 278-80)

The attack on logical positivism itself intensified under W. V. Quine. Quine examined the logic of the central beliefs of the movement and found it wanting. In particular, he pointed out errors in the notion of logical analysis that Carnap and others propounded. He writes,

lack of good sense; publishers

> [I]t becomes folly to seek a boundary between synthetic statements, which hold contingently on experience, and analytic statements, which hold come what may. Any statement can be held true come what may, if we make drastic enough adjustments elsewhere in the system. Even a statement very close to the periphery can be held true in the face of recalcitrant experience by pleading hallucination or by amending certain statements of the kind called logical laws. (Quine, 1980, 43)

uncooperative attitude.

He also dispatches the principles of reductionism on similar grounds; for truth to be ascertained a phenomenon would have to be subject, not only to the sense experiences of the questioner, but also to the sense experiences of all humankind. The attacks prompted Ayer to admit that the Vienna Circle "thought that they had succeeded, where Kant had failed, in finding a way 'to set philosophy upon the sure path of a science.' This end has not been attained: it may, indeed, be unattainable" (Ayer, 1959, 9-10). Later in his life Ayer admitted, "I suppose the most important of the defects [in logical positivism] was that nearly all of it was false" (quoted in Hanfling, 1986, 261).

Philosophers mark the death of logical positivism with Quine's objections to the logical and analytical stance of the movement. Those aspects of logical positivism that made it unique—language as a manifestation of formal logic, the principle of verification—were indeed discredited by the mid-1950s. The demise of this particular philosophical school of thought should in no way be interpreted as an end to deterministic scientism. The elements that logical positivism shared with the rest of the genealogy continued and continue to live on. Part of the logical positivist program lived on in the writings of some of its earliest proponents. Carl Hempel collected a number of his essays for a volume published in 1965. In one essay, "The Function of General Laws in History," originally published in 1942, he wrote that "general laws have quite analogous functions in history and in the natural sciences, that they form an indispensable instrument of historical research, and that they even constitute the common basis of various procedures which are often considered as characteristic of the social in contradistinction to the natural sciences" (Hempel, 1965, 231). Hempel remained steadfast in his notions regarding explanation and retained the nomological approach (the reliance on the uncovering of general laws from empirical observation) and the assumption that the natural sciences and the human sciences are fundamentally consanguineous.

Latter-Day Positivists

The debate concerning positivism still occupies the pages of journals. Sometimes the literature keeps the issue alive by including anti-positivist papers, intended to illustrate precise errors in positivist thinking. The presence of so many items denouncing positivism suggests that it yet has some vitality as a mode of thought or operation. This literature is far too voluminous to deal with here (and it is not necessary to subject the

reader to the bulk of this literature), but a couple of works can be
used as indications of the nature of debate and analysis. Bernd
Baldus, for example, examines the promises offered by positivism
and finds that little has been accomplished by that program.
Nonetheless, positivism has a hold on much of the work in
sociology. Baldus writes,

> Two decades ago, positivists on one side confronted Marxist
> and hermeneutic critics on the other. Accusations of dogmatism
> and unscientific research met charges of conservatism and
> misguided empiricism. The outcome, if one can assess it so
> briefly, was a politically deeply divided discipline. Positivist
> sociology has taken firm charge of sociology departments and
> major journals in the United States. (Baldus, 1990, 150)

In reply to Baldus, Gerhard Lenski counters that

> The heart of [positivism]—and the one element that has
> persisted unaltered from the Comtean period—is the belief that
> scientific knowledge must be based on, tested by, and grounded
> in sensory experience, directly or indirectly (as with the use of
> the electron microscope or images transmitted by telescopes in
> space), and that neither intuition, logical reasoning, moral
> imperatives, or divine revelation can substitute for this. This
> has been the primary article of faith on which the whole of
> modern science rests. (Lenski, 1991, 188)

Lenski's statement is not so much a rejoinder to Baldus's
criticisms as it is a methodological assertion of some of the
natural sciences. I say some because many theoretical scientists
might well take issue with Lenski's blanket definition. Even in the
natural sciences there is the problem (which is not trivial) of the
equation of the measurement by instrumentation and direct
sensory experience.

The debate, as characterized by Baldus and Lenski, centers on
two principal points: definition—even where there is agreement
on the definitions of concepts, the agreement can be violent; and
the notion of the social sciences as a branch of the natural
sciences. The former point results in less-reasoned disagreements;
there is usually less dispute about the definitions of terms than

about the appropriateness of the terms in specific contexts. The latter point is the more contentious and is probably the single most pivotal issue in the debate today. In much of the rhetoric the matter is reduced to claims regarding the determination of causality and predictions of the future from the present. Adherents to a deterministic stance argue for both of these possibilities and opponents frequently argue against them. Omitted from much of the discourse is the observation by Baldus that "The complexity of social processes, acknowledged by most authors, raises the prospect of a potentially infinite causal regress. Causal explanation of the kind advocated by positivist sociology necessarily requires choice and simplification, and the omission of a large part of the variables that caused an event under study" (Baldus, 1990, 157). Complexity can confound efforts to predict, and sometimes to explain, human and social phenomena.

This, in effect, concludes the exploration of the genealogy of thought. Admittedly, the present discussion does not include *every* thinker or writer, nor does it include *every* articulation of deterministic scientism. It does, I hope, illustrate that there has been a line of thinking that has been transmitted, albeit with some evolutionary changes, over nearly five hundred years. The roots of some present-day thought extend back at least as far back as Bacon and Baconianism. In the next chapter an extension of the genealogy will be tackled. It is impossible to examine the philosophical (and even the methodological) stance of library and information science, and all of the social sciences, without understanding the contemporary conception of science. The genealogy presented here suggests that science is a unified entity and that philosophy of science is characterized by agreement as to purpose, approach, and method. As we will see, such is not the case. There is considerable discussion regarding what science is, what it does, how it is communicated, and what extrascientific elements (such as political) it may possess. This is all fodder for the discussion in chapter 3.

Chapter Three

What Is Real?:
Science and Ideas of Reality

The preceding two chapters are an attempt to trace an intellectual heritage. In the minds of some, the genealogy came to a culmination, for good or ill, with logical positivism. Those who maintain a strong belief in the promise of science rarely invoke the word positivism, but their behavior and some of their writings betray an abiding fondness for those perceived characteristics of a stance that seems to point to the perfectibility of knowledge. For them, the lure of deterministic scientism suggests some ultimate answers to enduring questions. Those who reject the notion of a transcendent science that is equipped to provide the method that will lead to an answer, if not the answer itself, to large questions see tenacious vestiges of positivist principles. I began this book by suggesting, and reiterate now, that a more encompassing epistemology has been a considerable force for centuries. At the risk of being repetitious I will state again that this epistemology is scientism. It is important at this juncture to emphasize that scientism is no mere operational means or methodological convenience. It is much more than that; it is a theory of knowledge, its creation, and its growth. What I tried to accomplish in

the first two chapters is to illustrate how, through time, scientism
has developed and endured as, for many, an epistemological
foundation, a fundamental intellectual stance on which inquiry
and praxis might be based.

facts which shape & change the world

Positivism Revisited

The most recent manifestation of deterministic scientism is
what is customarily called positivism. A number of commentators
adopt the term positivism to reflect a multifarious set of beliefs
and activities. As I mentioned at the outset of chapter 1, Michael
Harris, for instance, accuses positivism of shutting library and
information science off from the important questions and the
possibility of addressing those questions. As I also mentioned in
the first chapter, the strict constructions of positivism—those of
Saint-Simon, Comte, and the Vienna Circle—are specific
expressions of the more sweepingly dominant scientism. I do not
mean to imply that Harris, and many other writers, are wrong;
quite the contrary. As I hope to demonstrate, as those individuals
relate their observations on the specific characteristics and tenets
they ascribe to positivism, they are really describing the elements
of deterministic scientism. What we have, then, is the not
unfamiliar problem of linguistic inconsistency and categorical
uncertainty. Many have observed and critiqued the basic
structure of the epistemological stance of scientism; they just
happen to have referred to it as positivism. Because of the
vagaries of the term positivism, some writers have attacked the
critics of the epistemology on the grounds that they are not really
addressing the essential elements of either Comtean or logical
positivism. D. C. Phillips, for instance, illustrates that what is
called "positivism" is not a single school of thought or philosophical stance; there are differing intentions when the term is used in
different contexts (Phillips, 1983). As we will soon see, replacing
scientism for positivism enables us to examine, without the taint
of that imprecise label, the epistemological claims that must be
questioned.

Before turning to that concern it should be noted that, while
some philosophers have rung the death knell for positivism, it

[handwritten margin note: to defame, slander, make look bad]

certainly has not disappeared from the literature or from thought. Moreover, positivism is not universally vilified. Some go farther than a yearning for a simplified time when epistemological faith could anchor itself in the promise of certainty proffered by a deterministic scientism, a faith in the method and causal imperative of science. Arthur Staats, for example, calls for a unified positivism as the appropriate philosophical stance for psychology. The goal of this stance is unified science, characterized by a progressive mode of thought and action.

> As progress occurred in finding common underlying principles, the science endeavor took on an organized, consensual nature. Competition become that of being first to solve problems, rather than disagreement on fundamentals. The language of discourse became consensual, as did the slate of problems to be solved. Knowledge became more connected, simple, and parsimonious, easier for the scholar and scientist. The science became more directed, with more continuing, progressively profound investigation in place of the former study of anything that could be superficially justified. These are the characteristics of modern unified science. (Staats, 1991, 900)

[handwritten margin note: rejecting all religious & moral principles; belief that life is...]

There is much to take issue with in Staats's statements. The first thing that many readers would dispute is the claim that there has been progress (or even that progress is possible). Such a view, however, would lean toward the nihilistic, and only some extreme skeptics would deny the possibility of progress. Others, on the other hand, might question any sweeping claim that science has been responsible for progress in any but a rather narrowly applied sense. The second thing that springs from the page is Staats's claim, made without a hint of irony, that science is based on consensus. Many, myself included, would make the counter claim that science is, by its nature, based on contention, on dispute. Even Popper, the ultimate advocate of coming to knowledge by means of conjecture and refutation, would be loath to go so far out on a limb. There has been, and still is, disagreement over fundamentals. One would need look no farther than the arguments between strong evolutionary adaptationists, such as George Williams and Richard Dawkins, and those who disagree with the

[handwritten margin notes in right margin: meaning, lean, traditions, beliefs, etc., have, no, meaning, acting, established, laws]

encompassing nature of adaptationism, such as Stephen Jay Gould and Richard Lewontin. Since there is no universal epistemic consensus, there is not, and there could not be, any linguistic consensus. Staats appears to extend the rule of Occam's Razor (that, given two equally plausible solutions to a problem, the simpler solution is preferable) to mean that there will always be a simple solution, and that "science" will provide it.

In order to reach his conclusion, Staats must work through a willful misreading of Merton and, especially, of Kuhn. Staats extrapolates Kuhn's observation and conclusions regarding scientific discipline to psychology without a critical concern for the object of study. He then urges psychology to move itself, as a discipline, towards the respect and prestige accorded to science by emulating science's aspiration for a grand unified theory.

> Psychology must achieve compact, parsimonious, interrelated, and consensual knowledge to be considered to be a real science. . . . Unificationism says that psychology must begin to make a systematic investment in unification and that it could be strengthened greatly by a well-developed field devoted to weaving together, in many individual works, the endless diversity the science produces. (Staats, 1991, 910)

(Such urgings are not uncommon to LIS.)

Shortly after the appearance of Staats's article there was a reaction to his recommendations for psychology. Less than a year after his paper was published, *American Psychologist* included letters by five individuals who responded to his call for a unified positivism. None of the letter writers takes issue with the most fundamental premise of the article—psychology is a nascent science that needs to find a strategy for maturation so that it can be accepted as coequal with the natural sciences. Four of the respondents see unification (but not necessarily unified positivism) as an ideal, but disagree with particulars of Staats's program. One, Susan Schneider, makes it clear that she shares the scientistic goal set forth by Staats. She writes that "unification of psychology as a science surely must begin with the tacit understanding that a naturalistic approach will be taken to the subject matter: For example, scientific methods will be used, existence of the paranormal will not be assumed a priori, and the mind-body problem will not be an issue in the ontological sense" (Schneider, 1992, 1056). Cartesian dualism (which addresses the mind-body problem) is frequently negated, but it may be premature to relegate it to the philosophical scrap heap without more compelling arguments against it. From both Staats's paper and the responses it seems that scientism is viewed as a viable ambition for at least some psychologists.

A bit of evidence that bolsters the observation that "positivist" thinking persists in many disciplines can be provided by the fact that a number of writers continue to feel the need to counter the arguments of such thinking. Donald McCloskey characterizes the willingness of economists to embrace, uncritically, a "crude" version of positivism:

> An economist who uses 'philosophical' as a cuss word . . . and does not regard philosophical argument as relevant to his business will of course not reexamine the philosophy he lives by, regardless of what is going on in the philosophy department. Even grown-up economists, therefore, do not have an occasion to rethink their youthful positivism. Economists young and old still use the positivist way of thinking. (McCloskey, 1989, 226)

McCloskey's observation is a very important one, and it is applicable to LIS as well. (And I hope that librarians and information professionals will not use "philosophical" as a cuss word.) What McCloskey is calling for is reflexivity, self-examination. The need for reflexivity in fields such as economics and LIS is rooted in practice. Effective practice is, consciously or not, founded in particular ways of thinking and ways of conceiving knowledge. This book, I hope, is an exercise in reflexivity.

David Smith critiques a specific articulation of the efficacy of a positivist approach to the field of social work which advocates a scientific formulation for study and research (Smith, 1987). Not even history has been free from the lure of positivism (as many readers already know). Joyce Appleby, Lynn Hunt, and Margaret Jacob state that the desire to uncover laws, along the lines of those propounded by science, has substantial roots in the study of history. Further, contemporary work in history has not severed itself from those roots. "Explanatory history—the search for the laws of historical development—was born in the nineteenth century: it bequeathed a powerful analytical tool useful to all peoples trying to make sense of where they had been and what they were becoming. Every history book available today—including those about the 'end of history'—reflects the enduring power of that nineteenth-century vision of scientific history" (Appleby, Hunt, and Jacob, 1994, 52). I offer these examples to illustrate that the debates and concerns regarding what has been called positivism have by no means disappeared in the time since philosophers disavowed logical positivism. As I promised earlier, it is time to show why we must move beyond the constricted terminology of positivism.

What Characterizes Deterministic Scientism

A number of commentators have offered compilations of elements or claims that, they maintain, characterize positivism. Most of the elements, though, are consistent with the genealogy of thought chronicled in the first two chapters. The most consistently applied, and most accurate, characteristics are those that link the most fundamental tenets of the scientific tradition to knowledge claims of all disciplines. The tenets are not entirely consistent with any single conception of positivism but do characterize the basis of scientism. It is necessary here to relate some of the many litanies of fundamental elements of positivism. An exploration of some of the lists will help us to consolidate these essential characteristics of deterministic scientism.

One simple set of features is offered by Georg Henryk von Wright. He limits the core elements of "positivism" to three.

* One of the tenets of positivism is methodological monism, or the idea of the unity of scientific method amidst the diversity of subject matter of scientific investigation. A second tenet is

the view that the exact natural sciences, in particular mathematical physics, set a methodological ideal or standard which
measures the degree of development and perfection of all the
other sciences, including the [social sciences]. A third tenet,
finally, is a characteristic view of scientific explanation. Such
explanation is, in a broad sense, "causal". It consists, more
specifically, in the subsumption of individual cases under
hypothetically assumed general laws of nature, including
"human nature." (von Wright, 1971, 4)

The second tenet observed by von Wright has an obvious
connection to Comte and his classification of the sciences. As we
have already seen, however, the concept of classifying disciplines
(sciences) is even older than Comte. Hobbes's effort at discerning
a hierarchy of sciences predates Comte's by almost two hundred
years. This element has deep roots in the genealogy of scientific
thought. The third tenet has obvious deterministic implications.
If individual cases can be subsumed under covering laws, then the
identification of cases that can be similarly defined determines
that the same law applies to them. As Richard Miller notes, for
some the adherence to a covering law model constitutes "a
worship of natural science that serves a social interest in manipu-
lating people as if they were things" (Miller, 1987, 15). The
implications of Miller's observation are profound; the idea and
actions of social Darwinism illustrate the negative impact of such
a belief. The deterministic link, if the critics are correct, is
unmistakable.

A similarly simple list of "epistemological assumptions,"
specifically of logical positivism, is offered by Martha Brunswick
Heineman. She points out that the particular incarnation of
positivism was a manifestation of a frequently expressed philosophical goal of the twentieth century—the quest for certainty. As
indicated in chapter 2, this school of thought depends on a
premise of empiricism, not quite as strong as that of the
Baconians, but strong nonetheless. Heineman's list of characteristics centers on those things that are essential to scientific inquiry.
They are as follows:

> Correspondence rules (operational definitions)—. . . . the belief
> that, in order to preserve truth inherent in physical observa-
> tions, concepts, and definitions (theory) must be tied to these
> observations by logical operations. . . . The symmetry thesis—
> . . . explanation and prediction [are] formally the same thing.
> . . . The business of science is the justification, not the discov-
> ery, of theories— . . . scientific logic [is] deductive logic because
> deductive logic [preserves] truth. . . . [T]he discovery of
> hypotheses [is] not considered a process of logic but of psycho-
> logical creativity. . . . Reductionism—If the logic of science
> is deductive and if theories are merely abbreviations for
> observations, it follows that complex theories should reduce
> into simpler ones that are closer to basic observations.
> (Heineman, 1981, 375-77)

With respect to the last item, there is a long history of unease
between theory and observation. The purest of empiricists, such
as Bacon, eschew theory entirely; those who are less extreme
claim that theory is just an expression of the consistency of
observations. In both cases there is a strong reluctance to accept
that some disciplines, and the language they use, may be theory-
laden. The logical positivists, as depicted by Heineman, are
presenting nothing new, in this regard, to the history of scientific
thought.

Claims of Positivism

Paul Tibbetts recognizes that the claims of logical positivism
are connected to Comtean positivism and Mill's logic. He further
maintains that the claims of positivism are not merely an artifact
of the Vienna Circle; some aspects continue in sociology and
show no sign of disappearing despite the attention they receive in
the literature. The claims Tibbetts associates with positivism are:

> (P.1) Explicit adoption of the deductive-nomological model of
> explanation. . . . (P.2) The systematic and rigorous exclusion of
> all metaphysical claims form the domain of genuine cognitive
> assertions. . . . (P.3) Reductionism and the "unified language"
> thesis. . . . (P.4) The verification doctrine concerning cognitive

> significance. . . . (P.5) An operational definition of the empirical
> concepts of science. . . . (P.6) The doctrine of phenomenalism
> or that all empirical claims which purport to be genuine must
> ultimately be grounded and verified by sensory observation.
> . . . (P.7) The sharp dichotomy for [positivism] between factual
> and normative questions. . . . (P.8) A sharp distinction is to be
> drawn between the "context of discovery" and the "context of
> verification and justification." (Tibbetts, 1982, 185-87)

Some of these claims have been accepted as peculiar to the logical
positivism of this century. The verification principle, the hallmark
of logical positivism, is the element that might most clearly be
seen as unique to this incarnation of scientism. The belief in the
efficacy of science's ability to realize truth is not a new one, but
the arrival of verification through semantics is indeed a twentieth-
century activity. Logical positivism's hostility to metaphysics is
sometimes taken as original to that school of thought, but if we
recall Hume's admonition against metaphysics, quoted in chapter
1, we see that this aspect has a lengthy heritage.

Christopher G. A. Bryant delves a bit deeper in time, back to
earlier expressions of positivism. He does not confine his construction of a list of characteristics to a single source, since he sees
a complex of influential factors that evolved over a period of time.
Bryant focuses his attention on French positivism, as conceived
or adopted by Saint-Simon, Comte, and Durkheim, and how it
has had an enduring influence on sociology and social theory. He
identifies twelve tenets of French positivism:

> 1. There is but one world, and it has an objective existence.
> . . . 2. The constituents of the world, and the laws which govern
> their movements, are discoverable through science alone,
> science being the only form of knowledge. Therefore that which
> cannot be known scientifically, cannot be known. . . . 3. Science
> depends upon reason and observation duly combined. . . .
> 4. Science cannot discover all the constituents of the world, and
> all the laws which govern them, because human powers of
> reason and observation are limited. Scientific knowledge will
> remain for ever relative to the level of intellectual development
> attained and to progress in the social organisation of science.

... 5. What man seeks to discover about the world is normally suggested by his practical interests and his situation. ... 6. There are laws of historical development whose discovery will enable the past to be explained, the present understood and the future predicted. ... 7. There are social laws which govern the interconnections between different institutional and cultural forms. ... 8. Society is a reality *sui generis*. ... 9. Social order is the natural condition of society. ... 10. Moral and political choice should be established exclusively on a scientific basis. ... 11. The subjection of man before the natural laws of history and society precludes evaluation of institutional and cultural forms in any terms other than those of conformity with these laws. ... 12. The positive, the constructive, supersedes the negative, the critical. The positive, the relative, also supersedes the theological and the metaphysical, the absolute. (Bryant, 1985, 12-22)

Collection?

Bryant recognizes that his list is an amalgamation, that no one individual has ever embraced all twelve tenets, nor do these aspects characterize all French sociological thought of the period. He also emphasizes that the expression of positivism constitutes a tradition, a flow through time from Saint-Simon to Durkheim, and then beyond, although there are some differences between the French positivism of the nineteenth century and the positivism of the Vienna Circle.

Positivism in LIS

In our own discipline Harris takes a hard look at the genesis of research. The formal beginnings of research in, especially, library science, came together as a reaction against the "conception of librarianship as a mechanical art." At about the time of the founding of the Graduate Library School (GLS) of the University of Chicago in the 1920s there were strengthened calls for a more scientific approach to the field (although the calls were certainly not universal). Not accidentally, the lure of science as a cure for the ills of an anemic research program was strongest at the University of Chicago, where the influence of the Vienna Circle was quite powerful throughout the institution. The intellectual underpinnings of research in LIS can be traced, according to Harris, to the fact that graduates of the GLS dispersed to most library education programs and constituted a substantial portion of the faculties of those schools. The epistemology they tended to hold dear was, and is, characterized by a particular set of beliefs:

1. Library science is a genuine, albeit young, natural science. It follows then that the methodological procedures of natural science are applicable to library science; that quantitative measurement and numeration are intrinsic to the scientific method; that epistemological issues are best treated with respect to specific research questions; and that complex phenomena can best be understood by reducing them to their essential elements and examining the ways in which they interact.

2. The library (broadly defined) must be viewed as a complex of facts governed by general laws. The discovery of these laws and theories is the principal objective of research.

3. The relation of these laws and theories to practice is essentially instrumental. That is, once the laws and theories are in place, we will be able to explain, predict, and control—i. e., produce a desired state of affairs by simply applying theoretical knowledge.

4. The library scientist can and should maintain a strict "value-neutrality" in his or her work. (Harris, 1986, 518)

The spread of GLS graduates to other schools as faculty served to perpetuate the epistemology and create, in Harris's view, an intellectual hegemony.

I do not intend to dispute the observations of these critics of positivism. The primary reason for the fruitlessness of dispute is that each of these writers is concentrating on specific articulations of positivism. Some of the features they specify have long histories; others are more properly seen as developments of a particular time and place. For instance, there are aspects of French positivism that are outgrowths of the Revolution and are steeped in post-Revolutionary politics. The stance of the Vienna Circle members is, to some degree, a product of the state of Western Europe between the world wars. It is likely that each of the individuals cited above has a particular literature or segment of a literature in mind as they construct a list. The specific characteristics manifested in social work are a bit different from those apparent in sociology or library and information science. There is one idea that does unify the conceptions of positivism, and that links positivism explicitly with scientism. Jurgen Habermas assesses philosophical positivism and finds it wanting: "by making a dogma of the sciences' belief in themselves, positivism assumes the prohibitive function of protecting scientific inquiry from epistemological self-reflection. Positivism is philosophical only insofar as is necessary for the immunization of the sciences against philosophy" (Habermas, 1971, 67). In this sense positivism (scientism) is exclusionary; it admits to no rivals and no doubts in the power of its claims (be that power of an epistemic sort or a purely discursive sort). Those speaking from a positivist, as well as from a scientistic, point of view do so with an assumed authority that makes the reflexiveness Habermas mentions unnecessary. We will return to this thought when we look closely at specific works that embody a scientistic stance. For now, we can look to the above lists for evidence of consistency and agreement, and attempt to construct a single set of features of deterministic scientism.

Scientism

Drawing from the aforementioned lists, keeping in mind the genealogy of thought, and focusing on the most fundamental aspect of scientism—the belief that the premises and methods of the natural sciences offer the soundest road to truth—we can arrive at a cohesive set of claims that lie at the heart of deterministic scientism. What follows is, to me at least, the most essential and most consistent of such claims. This is not to say that someone cannot identify other claims that have more limited application or less central relevance, but these seem to be key. The first of the claims is that a deductive-nomological approach governs inquiry in any discipline that would aspire to be a science. The claim embodies two concepts. The first is that the logic of deduction is the most powerful tool in a discipline's methodological arsenal. This particular element is in opposition to Baconianism and its reliance on induction, but is in keeping with one line of thought in the genealogy—that knowledge flows from the theoretical, the general, to the practical, the particular. Explicit in this element is the confidence that theory is monistic (that is, that there is only one), and that it can provide the totality of a context for inquiry. Further, this view holds that the growth of knowledge lies in the confirmation of theories. As Miller observes, "a theory is portrayed as a set of premises for deductions of more directly observable phenomena; whether a theory is acceptable depends on its playing this deductive role in successful explanation" (Miller, 1987, 136). According to Miller successful theory embodies its own confirmation through empirical means. The second element of the claim is that the purpose of deduction from theories is the discovery of explanatory laws. These laws are empirical, based on observation and, ideally, cover all circumstances. A corollary purpose underlying general laws is that they be predictive. In scientism, the deductive-nomological approach necessitates treating humans as if they were physical entities with purely physical properties. Thus, theories can be constructed and tested empirically so as to explain and predict, say, human behavior.

A second claim of scientism is reductionism; that is, all can be reduced to a physical state. Mental activity, for instance, is nothing more than brain, or neural, activity. Such an attitude is extended to social phenomena as well; behavior is governed by physical factors. There can be no denying that human behavior is certainly influenced by human physiology, including both normal physiology and physiological pathology. The reductionist stance, however, asserts that the physical is the *determining* factor. An extreme reductionist stance (which is rare) holds that the physical is the *only* determining factor. Robert Trigg explicitly links reductionism and determinism, specifically in the realm of human behavior. He says, "Assuming that determinism is the thesis that every event has a cause, a belief in determinism embraces the claim that all human behavior is causally explicable." Trigg further recognizes that a belief in determinism is such an unmitigating position that the belief itself is subsumed in the determinant. "Even the adoption of the belief in determinism is the product of some causal chain, and those who advocate determinism have to accept that their own commitment to it is itself causally explicable" (Trigg, 1985, 172). He uses as an example of the ineluctable link of reductionism with determinism a particular work, *Genes, Mind and Culture*, by Charles J. Lumsden and Edward O. Wilson. Lumsden and Wilson are sufficiently confident in their strongly reductionist program that they can assert that "all domains of human life, including ethics, have a physical basis in the brain and are part of human biology," and "When the roots of ethics and motivation are fully exposed, political science, economics and sociobiology can be more easily uncoupled from the genetic and cultural biases of the specialists who originate them" (Lumsden and Wilson, 1981, 181, 174). Of course, if true, then the roots of knowledge would also have to have a physical foundation. If their claims are extended, then the conclusions of Lumsden and Wilson are, themselves, physically determined. Reductionism, which necessarily implies that natural and social explanations and predictions are the same, results in the reification of social action, the translation of the mental into the concrete and objective. Trigg further offers that "The extreme materialist who says that ideas are unimportant is, in fact, in the grip of an idea. Those who believe that society functions at a level untouched by human understanding have to come to terms with the irrelevance of their own understanding of this fact" (Trigg, 1985, 42).

Not unrelated to reductionism is the third scientistic claim, phenomenalism. In the phenomenalist conception sensory observation is the truest grounding for a claim or statement. Ernst Mach, one of the most influential physicists of the late nineteenth and early twentieth centuries, refused, for much of his life, to believe in existing atomic theories of matter since such particles were impossible to observe at the time. This objectivity of observation is tied to the notion of value-neutrality, mentioned by Harris (and others), and usually rhetorically attributed to Max Weber.

There is no doubt that Weber, particularly in *The Methodology of the Social Sciences*, expressed his awareness that value judgment and empiricism are necessarily separate. The phenomenalist claim implies that it is possible for a researcher or teacher to adopt a neutral stance with regard to the object of study and the researcher's (or teacher's) own value judgments and value interpretations. Weber's own position has problematic aspects, as he attempted to reconcile objectivity with human value judgment. "In the empirical social sciences, as we have seen, the possibility of meaningful knowledge of what is essential for us in the infinite richness of events is bound up with the unremitting application of viewpoints of a specifically particularized character, which, in the last analysis, are oriented on the basis of evaluative ideas" (Weber, 1949, 111). An interpretation of Weber has been that it is possible to separate empirical investigation from human evaluative means. Weber, however, presents a complex argument against an objectivism that would demand the independence of the observer and the observed.

The last two key claims of scientism are very closely related. One is the unity of science, or methodological monism. This means that the same goals and methods apply equally to all sciences, including the social sciences. This concept is itself reductionist; all disciplines, all means of inquiry can be reduced to what amounts to an almost metaphysical appreciation of science. Such an appreciation is paradoxical because the logical positivists worked vigorously to realize a unified science, yet they dismissed metaphysics as having no sense or being the antithesis of physicalism. Physicalism extended to the social sciences; human behavior was seen to be rooted in human biology (another connection with reductionism). Unity of science, though, is a conception that transcends any one articulation of scientism; it permeates every notion of scientistic thought. For instance, Habermas defines scientism as "science's belief in itself: that is, the conviction that we can no longer understand science as *one* [emphasis in original] form of possible knowledge, but rather must identify knowledge with science" (Habermas, 1971, 4). (This last suggestion by Habermas is a striking one; it is so powerful that we will have to explore it further in the context of contending ideas of science.) When Harris writes of positivism as the epistemological foundation of library and information science, he is acknowledging, consciously or not, that a more pervasive scientism is defining knowledge and that there is admission in the discipline of LIS that it is incapable of advancing knowledge except insofar as it is part of the unity of science. Again, the idea of unity of science fits the ideal classifications of knowledge set forth by Hobbes and Comte.

The last of the central claims of scientism is methodological idealism, or the view that the natural sciences, most especially physics, embody the degree of development and maturity to be sought after by all disciplines. This is an aspect of scientism that is frequently acknowledged. For instance, Andrew Sayer states that a widely held assumption is that "The 'soft' sciences are weak at prediction not because they deal with intrinsically unpredictable objects but because they have not yet developed theory and scientific methods" (Sayer, 1992, 130). The idealism of the "scientific method" is also part of the belief that science defines epistemology. Trigg observes that "methods developed by the physical sciences for predicting and controlling the physical environment are assumed to be the only ones available for gaining knowledge in other areas" (Trigg, 1985, 114). Methodological idealism is based on a vital, but questionable, assumption: there is a single unified scientific method.

To counter this assumption one can turn to a couple of sources. One, chemist Henry Bauer, illustrates convincingly that there are multiple methods at work in the sciences, each applied to the questions that it is best fitted to answer. The other source, and one that adherents to some claims of scientism may find convincing, is Karl Popper, who also asserts that there is no such thing as a single scientific method (Popper, 1983). The methods employed in a primarily descriptive science differ considerably in kind from those used in a primarily experimental science. Further, Bauer realizes that the common concept of *the* scientific method is an unattainable ideal, while still admitting that the ideal is a worthwhile intellectual and ethical construct (Bauer, 1992). It should be noted that the concept of methodological idealism is a useful heuristic; it can help with many critiques of existing methods in many disciplines.

If method is defined with sufficient vagueness, then the claim of methodological idealism becomes at once more palatable and more meaningless. It can also become more tenuous. Popper, himself an anti-positivist, but one who is not altogether unsympathetic to some aspects of scientism, states, "Labouring the difference between science and the humanities has long been a fashion, and has become a bore. The method of problem solving, the method of conjecture and refutation, is practised by both. It is practised in reconstructing a damaged text as well as in constructing a theory of radioactivity" (quoted in Bryant, 1985, 178). It is not difficult to turn the tables on Popper in this regard and say that the similarity between the sciences and the social sciences (and humanities) is that their methods depend necessarily on interpretive understanding, or hermeneutics. I cannot claim originality for this thought but, as we will see, it becomes integral to a reconception of epistemological grounding for LIS and the social sciences generally.

We can summarize the fundamental scientistic tenets in tabular form.

Table 3.1
Characteristics of Scientism

Claim	Meaning
Deductive-Nomological Aspect	The logic of deduction is the only means of analysis and the purpose is the discovery of covering laws.
Reductionism	Everything, even the mental and the social, can be reduced to the physical.
Phenomenalism	Sensory observation is the truest way to verify a claim or statement.

| Methodological Monism | There is only one method and that is the method of the sciences. |
| Methodological Idealism | The method of the mature sciences, such as physics, provide the ideal for all disciplines. |

Materialism

One particular expression of a scientistic stance which embodies the aforementioned properties is materialism. I should say that a particular form of materialism embraces the kinds of scientistic elements just outlined; it is what Paul Moser and J. D. Trout call "reductive materialism." It may also be known by the term "naturalism," but, again, there are varieties of naturalism. Reductive materialism holds "that every psychological property is equivalent or identical to a conjunction of physical properties" (Moser and Trout, 1995, 5). Moreover, they observe that this form of materialism can be identified with the specific kind of scientism I speak of here: "Historically, many materialists have held that causes in question must be deterministic. A system is deterministic, roughly speaking, if its state at any time is a necessary consequence of its states at an earlier time conjoined with the laws of nature" (Moser and Trout, 1995, 11). A proponent of this position is David Armstrong, who suggests the following argument, based on the notion that everything is phenomenal:

1 The cause of all human (and animal) movements lies solely in physical processes working solely according to the laws of physics.
2 Purposes and beliefs, in their character of purposes and beliefs, cause human (and animal) movements.
3 Purposes and beliefs are nothing but physical processes working solely according to the laws of physics. (Armstrong, 1995, 42)

Not everyone, of course, is sympathetic to Armstrong's argument. Donald Davidson says that "Mental events such as perceivings, rememberings, decisions, and actions resist capture in the nomological net of physical theory. . . . [T]here are no strict deterministic laws on the basis of which mental events can be predicted and explained" (Davidson, 1995, 107-8). The foregoing does serve to illustrate that deterministic scientism is far from being a distant dream; it has vitality among philosophers, and probably more strength among others, such as social scientists.

At this point I want to insure that there are no misunderstandings about my stance regarding the claims of scientism. First, deterministic scientism is an extreme position, one that depends on the adoption of absolutist claims. The five claims just mentioned do constitute an absolutist position. The quarrel I have with scientism is the unyielding absolute assertion that it is *the* means of defining knowledge and its growth. There are aspects of the claims that not only have appeal, but are compelling in a less absolute, more open, epistemological stance. For instance, Harold Kincaid says that "there is little reason to think physics shows there is a logic of confirmation, a single scientific method, as sharp distinction between laws and accidental generalizations, or that all adequate sciences are ultimately reducible to physics" (Kincaid, 1994, 111). Even given this statement, he defends the possibility of social scientific laws. His defense rests on an absence, however; law is not adequately or completely defined, so we do not know fully what constitutes a law. In actuality, and Kincaid does explain this dilemma, the concept of law, even in a discipline like physics, is problematic. For one thing, laws are usually conditional, expressed under the condition of ceteris paribus (all other things being equal or constant, which assumes that only specific independent and dependent variables might change and other factors do not). This condition considerably changes the conception of laws and forces a reconsideration of the possibility, and utility, of such laws in the social sciences.

Each of the other claims can be softened so that the effect is not that of an absolute requirement for knowledge. As I said earlier, it is undeniable that an individual's physiological state can have an effect on his or her mental state. The absolute claim asserts that the physiological state invariably *determines* the mental state. The examples illustrate that it is neither possible nor desirable to adopt an opposingly absolute position; rather, we should realize and understand that the problem of knowledge, in LIS or any other discipline, is a complex one.   It is also essential to realize, as Habermas tells us, that scientism reduces epistemology to methodology and, in so doing, shrouds the actual makeup of the world and of experience. Knowledge itself becomes irrational in that it is assumed that knowledge accurately describes reality (Habermas, 1971, 68-69). Method is not a substitute for knowledge, although scientism asserts that it is. This said, it is also undeniable that science has a measure of power and influence over non- and quasi-scientific disciplines. It is imperative that we explore in some depth the competing conceptions of science and scientific practice.

Science and Ideas of Reality

This section heading may well strike some as odd, since it seems to call into question whether there is anything we can call reality. It is certainly not the intention here to assert that there is no such thing as reality. However, this is one of the most heated areas of discussion among philosophers and sociologists of science. The contention is focused on whether there is anything that can exist apart from our mental conception of it. The position held regarding this issue carries important implications for the way one conceives knowledge and the concomitant ways of structuring inquiry and practice. In other words, the stance taken on the matter of science as defining or discovering reality tends to be indicative of the manner of conceiving the nature of the object of study and the methods used to study those objects. The weight of such a stance can strike at the heart of study in all of the social sciences. The import of the implications is evident when we consider the advice given by Abraham Kaplan in a work that has been very influential in many social science disciplines for a number of years: "The unity of science is more than an abstract philosophical thesis; it marks the ever-present potentiality of fruitful unions. It is in this sense that all the sciences, whatever their subject-matter, are methodologically of one species: they can interbreed" (Kaplan, 1964, 31). For there to be interbreeding, for there to be one method, there must be unity of conception; there has to be agreement on what, exactly, is the nature of what is examined.

Perhaps a more pertinent rationale for the examination that will follow is the presence of some arguments within the LIS literature in favor of viewing LIS as essentially the same as all of the physical sciences. A few examples illustrate this point. Some years ago, in a book intended to be a primer for research in LIS, Herbert Goldhor stated that science provides, not only the best, but the sole means to gaining knowledge. He further said that one hallmark of scientific research, testing hypotheses by quantitative means, is the way to get to the truth of any relationship between or among variables (Goldhor, 1972). This is a very strong claim, but it is shared by some others. Terrence Brooks agreed with Goldhor and urged the adoption of the methods and even the epistemology of the physical sciences. He said that "Information researchers are just now struggling to codify concepts and agree on units of measurement. There is hope that information science will coalesce into a science at some future point" (Brooks, 1989, 248). Implicit in his statement is the notion that a discipline can evolve from whatever state it is in at a given point in time into a "science." Lloyd Houser and Alvin Schrader issued a call for the transformation of the profession through the transformation of education. The proper grounding for librarianship and education for the profession is science (Houser and Schrader, 1978).

All of the writers just mentioned seem to confuse a very important distinction that Ian Hacking offers. What is studied in all disciplines may be categorized as to "kind." The LIS writers above assume that "objects" of study, usually human beings and their actions, are of what Hacking calls the "indifferent" kind. An indifferent kind is not aware or self-conscious; it is not necessarily passive (e.g., plutonium is not passive; it can kill), but it does not choose what it can be. Contrast this with "interactive" kinds, which *are* self-conscious and are affected by descriptions and classifications (e.g., someone may be affected by the ways that having a disability may be conceived or described) (Hacking, 1999, 103-5).

There is, by no means, universal agreement with the positions just summarized, but the arguments are persuasive to many. It is evident that the aforementioned writers, and many within LIS, have been influenced, explicitly or tacitly, by ideas circulating among philosophers and sociologists of science, as well as among scientists. These ideas have to do with the fundamental conception of the universe and everything in it. In the absence of universal agreement there is, and has been for a few decades, a debate over how to conceive of the world around us. If the debate is oversimplified, it could be seen as divided into two factions—realism and relativism. Such an oversimplification, however, does a serious disservice to the variations in thought regarding the world and our place in it. To reiterate, the positions held by some of the principals in the debate have exerted influence over social science and LIS. The influence is certainly not absolute; thought and practice in LIS can be an uneasy mixture of various beliefs. To a considerable extent, though, the prevailing influence is a manifestation of deterministic scientism. We need to have a very clear understanding of the complexities of the debate. And we need to realize that the debate, as an exercise in persuasion, may not be an objective examination of the foundations of science; there is a social element that pervades the debate itself. As Steve Fuller says, the debate "is a political battle over who has the right to speak for, or 'represent,' science, with all the benefits that are understood to accrue to its representative" (Fuller, 1993, 12).

Realism

The stance that appears to have held sway in much social science thought is that of realism. Menas Kafatos and Robert Nadeau offer what they see as the prevailing view of scientists: "Science in our view, and in the view of virtually all physical scientists, is, first of all, a rational enterprise committed to obtaining knowledge about the actual character of physical reality" (Kafatos and Nadeau, 1990, 3). The actual reality to which they refer can be defined in at least a couple of different ways, and the differences are vital to a conception of reality and a stance that would call itself realism. One version of realism we can call metaphysical realism, which holds that there are things that exist independently of our mental representations of them. Any metaphysical claim to realism is, as John Searle points out, an ontological theory (a theory of being), not a theory of knowledge. This may seem a fine point, but in a later chapter, in the discussion of epistemology, the discussion will prove to be important. For instance, consistent with metaphysical realism would be the belief that if there were no human beings on earth the mountain ranges, lakes, and oceans would still exist. Of course such a stance makes sense, and, in the example just given, we can agree that there are such entities because we can eventually observe them. A person who has never seen an ocean firsthand can still believe that oceans exist, and can travel to one to substantiate that belief. Perhaps more to the point, strong realism seeks to find a place for everything and to put everything in its place. According to Ronald Giere, realism is thus akin to set theory in mathematics: "Reality is conceived of as consisting of discrete objects, sets of discrete objects, sets of sets of objects, sets of ordered pairs of objects, and so on. True statements are those that describe objects as belonging to the sets to which they in fact belong" (Giere, 1999, 78). A strong version of realism, and the version most often dubbed *scientific* realism, holds that unobservable physical things exist independently of the mental.

The belief in the physicality of the unobservable is the metaphysical aspect of this stance. It is decidedly at odds with logical positivism, which tried (unsuccessfully) to remove the metaphysical from all consideration. It is also incompatible with earlier positivist, and broader scientistic, propositions. Recall that one of the tenets of deterministic scientism is phenomenalism, which holds that knowledge claims must be grounded in sensory experience. The example used earlier was that of Ernst Mach who denied atomistic theories of matter because atoms, at that time, were not observable. Most practicing scientists, even if they haven't given formal thought to metaphysical realism, behave *as though* unobservable entities are real. If they didn't, there would be far fewer interesting and potentially fruitful scientific theories.

A mitigated position is that of epistemological realism, which suggests that *observable* things exist independently of our representations of them. In these versions of realism there inheres the central idea that physical reality is extra-human; it exists regardless of our knowledge of it (in the case of epistemological realism) or our ability to know it (in the case of metaphysical realism). The first of the two, the existence of objects regardless of our knowledge of them, implies that we *can* know something of these objects. These objects are referred to by Roy Bhaskar as "the intransitive objects of knowledge" (Bhaskar, 1975, 21). This is opposed to transitive objects of knowledge, which include the theories, hypotheses, models, methods, and technologies (in short, the human interventions) used by humans to inquire into the intransitive objects. On the face of it, Bhaskar's division not only makes sense, but seems an essential distinction. In fact, I heartily endorse the distinction and urge that both practice and research in LIS be aware of the distinction. However, there are still problematic elements of the notion of intransitive objects of knowledge. Philosophers of science tend to limit that category to physical objects, but some open its inclusiveness. John Ziman says that "there is nothing in our basic model of science to say that the behaviours of human beings cannot in principle be studied by the same methods as the behaviour of neutrinos, nucleic acids, or nematodes" (Ziman, 1978, 158). A bit later, when our focus of attention is on the social sciences, we will see that Ziman's view is shared by a number of people.

Christopher Norris cites Bhaskar's categorizations and states, "To conflate [the intransitive and the transitive] . . . is the cardinal error of relativist philosophies and one that leads to disabling consequences in both spheres of inquiry. Thus it relativises 'truth' (in the natural and human sciences alike) to whatever form of discourse—or *de facto* regime of instituted power/knowledge—happens to prevail in some given discipline at some given time" (Norris, 1996, 159-60). The conflation Norris writes of is the assumption that the intransitive can be treated as though it were transitive, that the one can be studied in the same way as the other. A different kind of conflation, one consistent with scientism, is also possible. The transitive could be treated as though it were intransitive. This idea is (perhaps less than consciously) integral to the blueprint for an overhaul of LIS education posited by Houser and Schrader: "we assert that there are fundamental problems relating to the production, collection, organization, dissemination and utilization of knowledge in all its various media forms which demand to be treated and solved scientifically" (Houser and Schrader, 1978, 4).

It becomes evident that calls for realism are not entirely consistent in detailing what comprises a realist position. Jarrett Leplin lists a set of these that recur in various conceptions of realism (while making it clear that no group, possibly no individual, espouses all of the theses):

1. The best current scientific theories are at least approximately true.
2. The central terms of the best current theories are genuinely referential.
3. The approximate truth of a scientific theory is sufficient explanation of its predictive success.
4. The (approximate) truth of a scientific theory is the only possible explanation of its predictive success.
5. A scientific theory may be approximately true even if referentially unsuccessful.
6. The history of at least the mature sciences shows progressive approximation to a true account of the physical world.
7. The theoretical claims of scientific theories are to be read literally, and so read are definitively true or false.
8. Scientific theories make genuine, existential claims.
9. The predictive success of a theory is evidence for the referential success of its central terms.
10. Science aims at a literally true account of the physical world, and its success is to be reckoned by its progress toward achieving this aim. (Leplin, 1984, 1-2)

Some of the tenets are strong; that is, some of them are assertions of an almost absolute condition. For example, the assertion that terms in theories are referential means that the theory is an accurate picture of reality and that there is a clear linguistic link between what is said and what is. The linguistic and semantic elements have probably been the source of more dispute than any other aspects of realism. The language used to express a theory (in particular the individual statements that comprise the theory) is taken to represent what actually exists (at least to some realists).

These ten items present the ideas that most frequently create difficulties for anyone who thinks about realism. As was stated at the beginning of this section, metaphysical realism is the straight-forward claim that there are things that exist independently of our apprehension of them. Such a notion is consonant with Kant's idea of reality *an sich*, the reality of the thing in itself, independent of its reality for a perceiver. Laurence BonJour contrasts Kant's idea with a very different version of realism—what he calls semantical realism. Semantical realism is reflected in the list above. As BonJour says, "semantical realism is the thesis that our statements (and presumably also our beliefs) purport, in virtue of their meaning or content, to describe this *an sich* reality" (BonJour, 1985, 162).

Some philosophers, Donald Davidson perhaps more aptly than anyone else, point out a fundamental problem with the kind of language-based claims of realism depicted above. Drawing from Quine, he stresses the "inscrutability of reference." Even in cases of clarity of reference, there are referents that are either arbitrarily created or variable according to different constructions of reference. The example he uses is the sentence, "Rome is a city in Italy." This statement is true in relation S, where the word "Rome" is mapped to the place Rome, and the predicate "is a city in Italy" is mapped to cities in Italy. The statement is also true in relation S', where the word "Rome" is mapped to an area one hundred miles south of Rome, and the predicate "is a city in Italy" is mapped to areas one hundred miles south of cities in Italy. The truth conditions are equivalent, but unless all elements of reference are made clear there is no way of telling what a sentence like "Rome is a city in Italy" means. For most of our daily life there is agreement regarding reference. For disputable claims, including claims in LIS having to do with, say, information retrieval, there may be less than complete agreement, or even understanding, of the elements of reference.

Some realists believe that the goal of science is to discover truth, which in its strongest iteration necessitates a belief that absolute truth exists and is knowable. This is the stance of Popper (1983, 24-27). Theories provide a means to truth in this strong position: "Theories are not only instruments. What we aim at is truth: we test our theories in the hope of eliminating those which are not true" (Popper, 1982, 42). It seems that such a strong position would have to include the belief that language is capable of expressing truth, and expressing it unambiguously. A possible explanation for the accurate claim that no theory yet propounded has been able to express absolute truth is that we simply haven't gotten there yet, but we're on the right path. Both Karl Popper and Hilary Putnam attempt to handle the problem of truth not realized by saying that our theories, over time, have come progressively closer to approximating, or being similar to, truth. The notion of progress is one we'll return to shortly.

Two important criticisms have been leveled at the idea that theories (and the language of which they are construed) can correspond to truth. One, recognized by Philip Kitcher, is that scientific theories tend to be idealized. Generalizations and artificial conditions are inevitably used in both theorization and the testing of theories. These generalizations and artifices are at odds with truth and a correspondence to truth. Kitcher dismisses this criticism by saying that, "In general, I propose that we view idealizing theories as true in virtue of conventions. . . . Idealization is an appropriate substitute when we appreciate that the search for exact truth would bury our insights about explanatory dependence in a mass of unmanageable complications" (Kitcher, 1993, 126). This explanation creates a dilemma. On one hand, by the terms of a strong realist position it is an unsatisfactory rationalization. On the other hand, the idealization that exists in the sciences and the social sciences is necessary. There is no way to account for every aspect of a situation, especially since many of the aspects are unknown, and perhaps in the social sciences, unknowable. Kitcher's claim of progress to truth can be seen, variously, as the philosopher's rationalization of the scientist's pragmatism (the quest for theories that work better than existing theories), and as a statement of a weak claim of realism. The two ways of seeing Kitcher's explanation are not entirely incompatible; the weak version of realism includes some elements of pragmatism.

Truth

Another point, made by Putnam, is that truth is itself an idealization. The ideal nature of truth, and a potential explanation of the unproblematic aspect of that nature, rests, according to Putnam, in two essential ideas: "(1) that truth is independent of justification here and now, but not independent of all justification. To claim a state is true is to claim it could be justified. (2) truth is expected to be stable or 'convergent'; if both a statement and its negation could be 'justified', even if conditions were as ideal as one could hope to make them, there is no sense in thinking of the statement as having a truth-value" (Putnam, 1981, 56). The idealization of truth is clear in the two statements. However, the explanations why they are not problematic are less than convincing. The first presents a particular challenge, since a claim of truth founded on possible justification depends on an assumption that the possible justification is not itself an idealization and, further, that the claim to justification is actually an approximation of truth. The second statement is less problematic in the abstract, but still presents some challenges for the discovery of truth, especially given the complexity and seemingly possible justification of contradictory ideas in practice. The efficacy of the two statements depends heavily on a belief that language is able to describe truth or its approximation in unambiguous and noncontradictory terms. In any event, both Kitcher and Putnam appear to be softening realism to the point where one could question whether their positions still deserve the name. Putnam has since mitigated his stance, recognizing that, even if the concept of reality can be stable, the approximation of reality (and truth) is quite elusive. He writes,

?

Is truth a concept? or a construct?

It is not at all clear that [the idea that fact can be established beyond controversy] is correct even for the "hard sciences". Science has changed its mind in a startling way about the age of the universe, and it may do so again. If establishing something beyond controversy is establishing it for all time, as opposed to merely establishing it so that it is the accepted wisdom of one time, then it is far from clear how much fundamental science is, or ever will be, "established beyond controversy." (Putnam, 1987, 64)

One of the central notions of Putnam's skepticism, though not directly addressed by him, is the very idea of controversy and its bases—is a "fact" controversial because of differing evidentiary groundings, or because of vested interests (including financial support, influence, ego) in the adherence to one position or another? This is not a trivial question, but Putnam's later stance does hold more promise as a philosophical position.

Realism and LIS

So where do we stand with regard to realism? It seems obvious that there are some problems with strong realism, in particular that realism could be a claim of how the world must be or that it prescribes and regulates strategy for scientists. In fairness to many who call themselves realists, the strong version of realism is frequently a straw man held up by some opposing realism. For instance, in negating realism Bas van Fraassen must first define it; this he does by saying, "Science aims to give us, in its theories, a literally true story of what the world is like; and acceptance of a scientific theory involves the belief that it is true. This is the correct statement of scientific realism" (van Fraassen, 1980, 8). Softened positions of realism appear to be more common. Ernan McMullin takes issue with the claim that theory is a true account of the world. If it were, it would be irrefutable, and that (though McMulllin doesn't say this) would mean that the theorizers would be able to achieve infallibility. McMullin says, "Science aims at fruitful metaphor and at ever more detailed structure. To suppose that a theory is literally true would imply, among other things, that no further anomaly could, in principle, arise from any quarter in regard to it" (McMullin, 1984, 35). Similarly, Richard Boyd writes, "the realist conception of theory-mediated experimental evidence does not have the consequence that any traditional laws are immune from refutation. Instead, it provides the explanation of how rigorous testing of these and other laws is possible" (Boyd, 1984, 61). It seems evident, then, that we cannot judge realism on the basis of its strongest claims, since many of its adherents either don't accept those claims or weaken them.

This is not to say that there aren't those, even within LIS, who hold to strong versions of realism. Donald Davidson, in finding some serious problems with strong realism, recognizes that for such realism to apply to the human sciences, of which LIS is one (along with psychology, sociology, history, and many others), one would have to suppose that states are entities; that is, attitudes, beliefs, and the like are real in the same sense that physical objects are real (Davidson, 1997, 121). He says states are not entities in this sense, and I agree. The mental is of a different type; it is intentional and self-aware. I am not denying the possibility of truth with regard to the mental, but justification of the truth of the mental is not the same as justification of the truth of the physical. Again, these concerns are epistemological and will be discussed in a later chapter.

As we study information retrieval in LIS we inevitably have to recognize that the database and its content have an indisputably ontological existence. The information seeker, while also an ontological being, has an epistemic goal in employing strategies to search the database and to evaluate the retrieved material. The seeking and evaluating processes have to be examined on epistemic grounds.

A couple of softened positions represent efforts to retain what appears to many to make sense in realism, while avoiding pitfalls that might render the position obviously false. One of these softened stances is held by Alan Chalmers, who urges that we adopt an unrepresentative realism, which, he says, is realist in a couple of ways. "Firstly, it involves the assumption that the physical world is the way it is independently of our knowledge of it. . . . Secondly, it . . . involves the assumption that, to the extent that theories are applicable to the world, they are always applicable, inside and outside of experimental situations" (Chalmers, 1982, 163). The second sense of realism is weaker than some stances in that it recognizes that theories may not be absolute representations of reality. At the same time, though, Chalmers is stating that a theory that has not been refuted clings to life because of some, at least apparent, connection to the world as it is. He goes further with a softening of realism: "Unrepresentative realism is unrepresentative insofar as it does not incorporate a correspondence theory of truth" (Chalmers, 1982, 163). Abandoning the necessity of corresponding to truth is a major concession, and one that is probably amenable to many who would call themselves anti-realists. Another position is even weaker than Chalmers's. Giere suggests the stance of constructive realism, but only as it might be applied to scientific models and hypotheses. This position holds that theoretical models can be *similar* to the real world, but that the model is a human creation (Giere, 1988, 93-94). Giere straddles realism and relativism, but he emphasizes that there are substantive problems with a social constructivist position.

Relativism

Since we have to begin discussing alternatives to realism somewhere, let's start with the stance that is as far from realism as possible—relativism. In one very important way, the relativist position makes an interesting point: the practice of science is a social exercise. No matter what our conceptions of the various disciplines that comprise the natural, or for that matter the social, sciences, they are practiced by human beings. For that reason it is difficult to assert with the confidence Popper has that "To the scientist only truth matters, not power" (Popper, 1994, 194-95). To say that scientists, or anyone, act solely out of one specific motivation, such as the quest for truth, is to ignore the multifaceted social, cognitive, and affective influences on actions. Moreover, such a view is deterministic; the nature of the object of study determines the motivation of the practitioner. Doubtless there are some scientists who do what they do to attain power (or money, or fame, etc.). However, they couldn't gain power (except in extremely rare instances) without accomplishing something meaningful in the world of science. Conversely, no scientist seeks only power, or there would be little motivation to gain power through science in particular. Of course there is a social element to human behavior; only a fool would deny such an obvious truism. So relativism must be more complicated than such a self-evident assertion. Let's investigate relativism further.

The relativist position can be fairly simply stated. Steven Shapin says that he takes "for granted that science is a historically situated and social activity and that it is to be understood in relation to the contexts in which it occurs," and that "the task for the sociologically minded historian is to display the structure of knowledge making and knowledge holding as social processes" (Shapin, 1996, 9). Barry Barnes and David Bloor elaborate a bit on relativist doctrines; they include "(i) the observation that beliefs on a certain topic vary, and (ii) the conviction that which of these beliefs is found in a given context depends on, or is relative to, the circumstances of the users" (Barnes and Bloor, 1982, 22). They add a third element, which they call an equivalence postulate. This postulate maintains "that all beliefs are on a par with one another with respect to the causes of their credibility. It is not that all beliefs are equally true or equally false, but regardless of truth and falsity the fact of their credibility is to be seen as equally problematic" (Barnes and Bloor, 1982, 23).

There is another way of expressing the relativist position. Rom Harré and Michael Krausz observe that (again, simplistically stated) relativists may be divided into two camps—skepticism and permissiveness. They distinguish the two thusly: "1 Skepticism: no point of view is privileged, no description is true, and no assessment of value is valid. 2 Permissiveness: all points of view are equally privileged, all descriptions are true and all assessments of value are equally valid" (Harré and Krausz, 1996, 3). It seems as though there is no difference between the two, but, as Harré and Krausz point out, the first can be seen as malign and the second as benign. Skepticism is malign because it denies legitimacy to any point of view; perhaps another way of seeing this stance is as nihilism. Permissiveness is benign because it allows legitimacy for all points of view, although legitimacy is frequently situated (that is, it places a perspective within a particular temporal, spatial, cognitive, cultural, or other locus). One aim of relativism is to deny absolutism, the establishment of an ultimate truth, perhaps on the grounds that such privileging denies potentially meaningful points of view (meaningful at least to those who hold the belief in question) or constructs a hegemonic dominance that may be based on political, rather than epistemic, grounds.

In the cases of both skepticism and permissiveness the claims include their own demise. If no position is privileged, or if all are equally privileged, then there is no reason at all to accept either claim above any other stance. When we turn to the social sciences more explicitly later, we'll see that privileging is a problematic matter. A position may be epistemically privileged in that it is a justifiable knowledge claim, or it may be politically privileged in that it receives support from powerful adherents. One difficulty with most articulations of relativism is that the distinctions among kinds of privileging are not acknowledged. This itself may be a form of political privileging.

As is the case with realism, there are some compelling reasons to lean towards relativism. And as is the case with realism, it is the weaker version of relativism that is more attractive. One of the elements of a weak version of relativism includes a skeptical view of the claim of neutrality in science (which has been extended to the social sciences). The skeptical belief is that it is impossible for humans, who are acting agents in the practice of science, to eschew all bias, preference, or assignment of value. At a fairly basic level, for instance, there are preferences expressed for certain questions in a scientific subdiscipline, and pursuing those questions is privileged over the pursuit of others. As Andrew Pickering depicts this element,

> Relativists thus deny that science has the kind of objectivity that the philosophical tradition has sought to ascribe to it. Scientists are here revealed as genuine agents, by no means operating with their hands tied behind their backs. And scientific knowledge is consequently chained to particular communities: it is knowledge relative to them, with this relativity typically spelled out in terms of interests; it does not "float free" of its conditions of production and use as the objectivist hopes. (Andrew Pickering, 1994, 110)

The weak version does not overstate the influence exerted by interests, but admits that they do exist.

Problems of Relativism

Relativism is not without substantial difficulties, though. The idea of the social construction of knowledge is, at least in some form, an inescapable one, but it can be taken too far. Probably the most extreme expression of the constructivist position comes from Steven Shapin and Simon Schaffer, who write, "As we come to recognize the conventional and artifactual status of our forms of knowing, we put ourselves in a position to realize that *it is ourselves and not reality that is responsible for what we know* [emphasis added]" (Shapin and Schaffer, 1985, 344). It would be easy to heap ridicule on this notion; suffice it to say that such an extreme denial of ontology is without foundation. Modifications of such an idea are not at all uncommon in the sociology of knowledge. Karin Knorr-Cetina, who observed work done in a particular laboratory, suggests that "Scientific method is seen to be much more similar to social method—and the products of natural science more similar to those of social science—than we have consistently tended to assume" (Knorr-Cetina, 1981, 34). Her work builds on that of Bruno Latour and Steve Woolgar, who also observed laboratory work and conclude that the essential element of that work is the construction of facts, which is a step in the construction of reality (Latour and Woolgar, 1986). As

Hacking points out, even if some aspects of human action are socially defined, they are nonetheless real (Hacking, 1999).

The problematic aspect of the constructivist view is the unavoidably social element of knowledge, whether scientific or other. For instance, while many of us would dearly love to believe that there are "brute facts" that exert causal influence on phenomena, we can't evade the reality that, at least to some extent, as Alan Gross says, "the phrase 'brute facts' is an oxymoron. Facts are by nature linguistic—no language, no facts. By definition, a mind-independent reality has no semantic component" (Gross, 1990, 202-3). Even if there are nonsemantic forces at work in the world, we cannot conceive of them without language. Once language is employed, the goal of *absolute* objectivity disappears, and some alteration, intended or not, occurs. Some who adopt the relativist position aver that the alteration is intentional. Woolgar, in advocating a strong version of relativism, speaks of

> the ideology of representation, the set of beliefs and practices stemming from the notion that objects (meanings, motives, things) underlie or pre-exist the surface signs (documents, appearances which give rise to them). . . . The problem . . . is that any attempt to dismantle this ideology, rather than a particular set of claims which emerge from a specific disciplinary (natural scientific) application of this ideology, appears tantamount to dismantling one's own discipline. (Woolgar, 1988, 99)

This is an inherently confused position; Woolgar seems to believe that there is no possibility for agreement on the construction of the natural world because of the social element that is the foundation of our conceptions. At the same time, he appears to believe that a single ideology is possible. The latter belief should be refuted by the former.

Perhaps the most eloquent refutation of the relativist position regarding facts that is espoused by Latour, Woolgar, and others is offered by Alvin Goldman. In speaking of social epistemology, Goldman stresses that the epistemic program, the quest for knowledge, is necessarily a normative one that is comprised of rational as well as social elements. While the relativist argument centers on the essentialness of the negotiation of facts, Goldman points out that confusion also centers on this point.

> First, the sociologist who studies life in a scientific laboratory does not observe the negotiation of scientific facts. What is observed is only the negotiation of scientific assertions or beliefs, i.e., what the scientists agree to *say* or *believe* about the facts. That there are "negotiation" processes in social belief-fixation hardly demonstrates that there are no facts of the matter independent of this negotiation [emphasis in original]. (Goldman, 1987, 136-37)

Goldman's concepts pertaining to social epistemology will be very useful in the later discussion of knowledge.

The confusion reaches its peak with David Bloor and his "strong programme" (SP) for the sociology of knowledge. Bloor's goal is to set forth a scientific means for the study of knowledge. That science, though, is grounded completely in the social element of knowledge growth or, more appropriately, of belief. He articulates four tenets for SP:

> 1. It would be causal, that is, concerned with the conditions which bring about belief or states of knowledge. . . .
> 2. It would be impartial with respect to truth and falsity, rationality or irrationality, success or failure. . . .
> 3. It would be symmetrical in its style of explanation. The same types of causes would explain, say, true or false beliefs.
> 4. It would be reflexive. In principle its patterns of explanation would have to be applicable to sociology itself. (Bloor, 1991, 7)

He admits that there may be some nonsocial causes of beliefs, but these factors are neither necessary nor sufficient to those beliefs. Without dragging this discussion out, I have to point out that the most useful aspect of Bloor's SP, the realization that social factors influence social outcomes, is nothing more than a tautology (see Slezak, 1994).

Bloor's "strong programme" is fatally flawed; even though he denies it, his program is rife with internal contradictions, especially regarding causation. On the one hand, we cannot accept physical causation for beliefs about the physical world because of intervening social forces. On the other hand, we *can* identify social causes for those beliefs. Larry Laudan provides a thorough critique of Bloor's work, and concludes that much of what Bloor would have us believe is groundbreaking is really nothing more than the myth. His tenets are little more than obfuscation; science does not actually operate in the ways Bloor seems to believe (see Laudan, 1996, 183-209). In fact, Bloor's program, as is true of the constructivist theories of Woolgar, Shapin, Schaffer, and others, are exemplars of deterministic scientism, even though they would not only deny this, but would probably assert that they are trying to oppose scientism. All belief has social determination (there is no real epistemological difference between this and the stance that there is a purely physical determination). Further, these positions are highly reductionist; all is reduced to the social, and the ontological and epistemological (that is, anything normative) are dismissed. The positions also attempt to propound methodological monism; there is only *one way* to examine any question. For these reasons, we have to reject any *strong* relativist or constructivist stance.

How Did We Get in This State?

Interpretations of Kuhn

Relativism, and particularly social constructivism, has flourished in recent years. While it would be presumptuous to ascribe cause to one particular event, the ascendance of relativist thought received a boost in 1962 with the publication of the first edition of Thomas Kuhn's *The Structure of Scientific Revolutions*. Kuhn himself denied for the entirety of his life that he was a relativist, but his work *did* suggest that there are social underpinnings of scientific work. Kuhn's thesis is much more complicated than are those of Bloor, Shapin, and others, though. Moreover, his position is not entirely consistent, and that inconsistency has contributed to much of the debate surrounding his work. Few books have been cited more frequently than *The Structure of*

Scientific Revolutions (SSR), and few have been more frequently misread. It is important that we turn to the source and examine just what Kuhn has to say about science, progress, and the growth of knowledge. One of the most fundamental, and most challenging, points in SSR is the division of scientific work into periods of normal science and revolutionary science. Normal science is marked by stability, consensus on the problems that should be addressed, and agreement on the means by which those problems should be studied. The period is especially marked by acceptance of a paradigm. Here is where the problems begin with comprehending just what Kuhn meant. As Margaret Masterman shows, Kuhn employs over twenty distinct usages of "paradigm," and there is a lack of clarity in his employment of the word and a lack of consistency of meaning (Masterman, 1970, 61-65).

Much interpretation of Kuhn, especially in the social sciences, has fixated on "paradigm," with the frequent outcome that Kuhn is assumed to be prescriptive, that he is saying legitimacy as a science comes only with the development of a paradigm. There are numerous flaws in this interpretation. First, it is not a prescription for success so much as it is a strategy for continuing work. That is, the impetus is not simply to find a paradigm; rather, the paradigm emerges if it can provide "a new and more rigid definition of the field," and "The decision to reject one paradigm is always simultaneously the decision to accept another, and the judgment leading to that decision involves the comparison of both paradigms with nature and with each other" (Kuhn, 1970, 19, 77). The latter point has some grounding in realism; the new paradigm has a more effective link to the way things really are. Also, his point that one paradigm is not abandoned until another can replace it is an essential one. As he says, "Probably the single most prevalent claim advanced by the proponents of a new paradigm is that they can solve the problems that have led the old one to a crisis" (Kuhn, 1970, 153). In short, the paradigm (or "disciplinary matrix," the term Kuhn later used to illustrate that practitioners use a *set* of methods, theories, hypothesis, and other elements) emerges from scientific work; it is not artificially imposed upon that work. The complexity of scientific, or disciplinary, work is ignored by those who would

134

reduce the work to a single idea. The reducing is re‹
Feyerabend, who says, "More than one social
pointed out to me that now at last he had learned h‹   . .us
field into a 'science'—by which of course he meant that he had
learned how to improve it. The recipe, according to these people,
is to restrict criticism, to reduce the number of comprehensive
theories to one, and to create a normal science that has this one
theory as its paradigm" (Feyerabend, 1970, 198).

Another problem in the interpretation of Kuhn resides in the
locus of a paradigm. As is evident from Feyerabend's anecdote,
many assume that the discipline itself contains the appropriate
paradigm; it is the job of the practitioners to discover it. Kuhn's
explanation of the disciplinary matrix should be sufficient to
explode such a misguided notion, but that notion is persistent.
Kuhn is, at times, more explicit in what he means by paradigm
although even in his explanation there are the seeds of confusion.
He writes, "A paradigm governs, in the first instance, not a
subject matter but rather a group of practitioners. Any study of
paradigm-directed or of paradigm-shattering research must begin
by locating the responsible group or groups" (Kuhn, 1970, 180).
Yes, paradigm can refer to agreement, but we would ask if Kuhn's
expression of "paradigm" is the only possible way of conceiving
states of agreement on the parts of scientists.

> Even in Kuhn's own framework, "pre-paradigm" science is
> better described as *multi-paradigm* science. By his own character-
> izations of what constitutes *having a paradigm*, each of the
> competing schools has a paradigm. What is lacking at this stage
> are not paradigms, but a *dominant* paradigm that can guide the
> energies of the vast majority of practitioners concerned with the
> same general subject matter [emphasis in original]. (Giere,
> 1999, 35)

This clarifies that it is in the practice of science, not in science
itself, that the consistent elements of a disciplinary matrix apply.
His statement, however, seems to open the door to constructivism. A reader so inclined could take the passage to mean that the
only significance rests in the practice, rather than in the discipline, but this would be a gross misreading of Kuhn. He denied

relativism and expressed an abiding faith in scientific progress (Kuhn, 1970, 206).

All of this is not intended to dismiss some of the genuine problems with Kuhn's ideas. For instance, as Stephen Toulmin aptly points out, the distinctions between normal and revolutionary science are overstated. In fact, Toulmin maintains that Kuhn's essential relaxing of the demarcation between the two aspects of science amounts to a dissolution of the distinction altogether (Toulmin, 1970, 41). Toulmin himself may be overstating the case; there is an apparent disruption of both the epistemological grounding of a discipline and the work of its practitioners when a revolution occurs. Feyerabend also takes Kuhn to task for this seemingly absolute distinction; Feyerabend believes, with good reason, that the proliferation of theories alternative to the governing one exists all the time, not just in the event of a revolution (Feyerabend, 1970, 212). In other words, normal science is not as stable as Kuhn might have us believe. Criticism of Kuhn's notion of gestalt shift is offered by W. H. Newton-Smith. He says, "By and large this analogy is absurdly far-fetched. For few of us had anything like this dramatic shift of attitude when, having learned Newtonian mechanics in school, we came slowly and perhaps painfully to appreciate the greater virtues of Einsteinian mechanics" (Newton-Smith, 1981, 118).

Kuhn and Incommensurability

The idea of Kuhn's that has created the most stir among serious discussants is that of incommensurability. The adherents of competing paradigms are so grounded in their particular matrices that they are unable to communicate sensibly with one another. Kuhn goes so far as to say that "the proponents of competing paradigms practice their trades in different worlds. . . . Practicing in different worlds, the two groups of scientists see different things when they look from the same point in the same direction. Again, that is not to say that they can see anything they please. Both are looking at the world, and what they look at has not changed. But in some areas they see different things, and they see them in different relations one to the other" (Kuhn,

1970, 150). His thesis of incommensurability is consistent with his idea of revolutions; the change from normal science to revolutionary science entails a gestalt shift. A practitioner looks at the discipline in one way, and then shifts to a different view; the one vision precludes the other. Paul Hoyningen-Huhne, in his explication of the incommensurability thesis as articulated throughout Kuhn's career, points out that there are substantive inconsistencies in the thesis (Hoyningen-Huhne, 1993, 206-22). As is the case with other of Kuhn's ideas, there is overstatement in Kuhn's notion of incommensurability. The utility of his thesis lies in the possibility that communication is difficult between adherents of different theories because the terms used in description can have meanings that are not consistent across theories.

In fairness to those who would claim that there is such a thing as incommensurability in the sense that adherents of one paradigm are unable to communicate with those of another, Kuhn, in many places in his book, practically enables such a reading. However, Kuhn has repeatedly tried to correct the misreading. Michael Malone says that most misreaders of the incommensurability thesis presume that the invention or mastery of a particular paradigm necessarily means undergoing a transformation of perception, a gestalt shift. This shift, according to those who hold to a narrow view of incommensurability, equates insight into a possible way of conceiving something with conviction that this is the only way of conceiving something. There definitely can be difficulties with communication, though, and Malone says these difficulties are observed by Kuhn in the actions and expressions of scientists: "Kuhn's incommensurability thesis requires . . . two features: (a) *concepts and correlated ontologies sufficiently different that the world depicted in one theory cannot be fully represented by the rival theory*, and (b) *an inherently vague theory-fact distinction*" [emphasis in original] (Malone, 1993, 77). Kuhn, then, is not presenting as relativistic a stance as some believe, but he is pointing out the problem with the assumption that semantical realism holds for every scientific claim.

Some of the misreadings of Kuhn are indicative, first, of the wishes or desires of the commentators and, second, the leap from Kuhn to social constructivism. A couple of examples of the former can be found in LIS. Paul Metz, in his examination of citation analysis as a method to study library use, says that this means of analysis "has settled into what Kuhn has called 'normal science,' but as most bibliometricians well know, this very settling into comfort and habit may be the first sign that radically new perspectives and questions will soon emerge" (Metz, 1990, 160). Not so latent in his statement is the hope that a revolution is imminent and that bibliometrics can emulate the patterns of progress in the natural sciences. Jeffrey Gatten looks at interdisciplinary research in LIS and consistently assumes that "paradigm" is a normative criterion that describes a science (Gatten, 1991). His hope is very similar to Metz's. The latter product of the misreading of Kuhn can be seen in Stephen Cole's assertion that "For Kuhn, a new paradigm is simply a different, rather than a better, way of looking at reality" (Cole, 1992, 9). Likewise, E. Doyle McCarthy says that "There are no such things as bare facts, Kuhn argued, even scientific ones, since facts emerge and are known by virtue of a form of thinking within which they can be received and accepted" (McCarthy, 1996, 18). Cole and McCarthy are representative of some in the social sciences who are apparently looking for substantiation of constructivist claims. They ignore Kuhn's repeated acknowledgment of progress and of at least a weak realist view of the content of science.

This brief discussion of Kuhn is not meant to be an affirmation of all aspects of his thesis. There is quite a bit in his writings that presents conceptual and practical problems. Some of the more bothersome elements of Kuhn's thought are challenged by Imre Lakatos. For one thing, as Lakatos points out, normal science is not typified by monopolistic control of one paradigm. "The history of science has been and should be a history of competing research programmes (or, if you wish, 'paradigms'), but it has not been and must not become a succession of periods of normal science: the sooner competition starts, the better for progress" (Lakatos, 1978, 69). (In his championing competition Lakatos shares a modicum of common ground with Feyerabend [see Feyerabend, 1975].) In sympathy with Kuhn, though, Lakatos recognizes that there are some extrascientific, and not necessarily rational, factors that may influence the acceptance of a paradigm. To counter those factors, Lakatos suggests that "we must not discard a budding research programme simply because it has so far failed to overtake a powerful rival. We should not abandon it if, supposing its rival were not there, it would constitute a progressive problemshift" (Lakatos, 1978, 70). And throughout this discussion it must be remembered that Kuhn and Lakatos focused on the natural sciences and offered their descriptive and strategic analyses in that context only.

What Kuhn's work has meant for the conception of reality has been a heightening of the debate, even conflict. The controversy centers on the mixture of some realist premises and the realization that some social factors influence disciplinary practice. It is the mixture that is Kuhn's strength. Why? The mixture is not irrational; in fact, it is the most rational explanation for both content of disciplines and practice within those disciplines.

The Answer?

This section heading may seem pretentious, but I want to emphasize the question mark. What follows is an alternative to the two positions just discussed. The strong versions of realism and relativism are absolutist positions. Some people have no problem with the absolutist nature of the positions, but there are, at least in my view, unresolvable problems with the strong versions. The principal difficulty is that both stances are exclusionary; each maintains that one, and only one, force governs all aspects of the sciences. In the case of realism, that force is nature; the task of science is to discover what actually exists, and there are no substantive barriers to that discovery. In the case of relativism, that force is society; all knowledge, even putative knowledge of nature, is socially and culturally constructed. The inescapable conclusion is that both strong positions are, to some extent, irrational. Each position ignores aspects of the other that definitely impinge upon the growth of knowledge. In this section I hope to draw from balanced critical assessments to present a position that is sufficiently rational and inclusive that it can serve inquiry and practice in all disciplines. The position, as we will see, is a flexible one, taking into account objects of study that are more or less natural and more or less social, along with the challenging nature of the means of study.

Science and Feminism

To some, the strong version of realism includes a denial, intentional or not, of human agency in the practice of science or of any disciplinary inquiry. In particular, some who approach the matter from a feminist perspective point out that there are some clearly social elements of practice that work against full participation in disciplinary activities by all who might contribute to progress. Mary Hawkesworth suggests that claims of objectivity have been used for less than objective purposes. "Under the guise of objectivity, philosophy and science objectify women, deny their agency, silence their alterity, and condemn them to 'objectively' certified inferiority. . . . Under this construal, objectification approximates reification, a process that distorts as it concretizes. To reify a human being is to view a person as a thing, that is, as an entity devoid of consciousness and agency" (Hawkesworth, 1994, 154-55). Objectivity, then, might be used as an excuse to ensure that: (1) certain methods are used in inquiry, (2) certain results are more probable, and/or (3) certain individuals or groups are precluded from participation.

The feminist critique of science studies demonstrates that the *practice* of science is not absolutely objective. I cannot emphasize strongly enough that the most useful critiques are aimed at the practice, rather than the content, of science. It is a truism that science is distinct from the practice of science, that the content of study is an entity separate from the act of studying the content. The distinction implies that what scientists do may be influenced by the social relationships and cultural settings in which they work, as well as by the objects of study. This claim may be an oversimplification; it may be that the conception of science and the conception of the objects of study are also influenced by social and cultural factors. This latter notion is bolstered by the way science is practiced in the U.S. and elsewhere today. Scientific work in the U.S. depends to a considerable extent on support from sources other than the scientists' own institutions. Competition for external support is a strong force in practice; the sources of funding establish priorities and tend to support those projects that match their priorities. Even more subtly, the infrastructure of scientific practice, including the literature and the academic reward system, is less than objective in that there are decisions made that are not based solely on nature. Sandra Harding realizes these forces and says, "Science is politics by other means, and it also generates reliable information about the empirical world. Science is more than politics, of course, but it is that. It is a contested terrain and has been so from its origins. Groups with conflicting social agendas have struggled to gain control of the social resources that the sciences—their 'information,' their technologies, and their prestige—can provide" (Harding, 1991, 10).

To say that the practice of science is political is to address only the surface of the matter. It doesn't answer the question of how the politics may manifest itself. As Evelyn Fox Keller says, "Beliefs per se cannot exert force on the world. But the people who carry such beliefs can. Furthermore, the language in which their beliefs are encoded has the force to shape what others—as men, as women, and as scientists—think, believe, and, in turn, actually do" (Keller, 1992, 25). Even though there is the stated goal of objectivity, the language that is used to state theories, to assert claims, etc. is a human device, and, so, is not of the same "type" as the physical phenomena studied. At the least, we can surmise that our descriptions of what science is, of what knowledge is, are not entirely objective. An important difference between the kind of feminist critique that is the focus here and constructivism, as Joseph Rouse informs us, is that "feminist critics have tried to participate in the practices through which knowledge of the world is constructed as authoritative" (Rouse, 1996, 33).

Rationality

All this sounds as though there is no objectivity in scientific, or any disciplinary, work. It isn't that there is no rationality, just that there is no *absolute* rationality. This statement indicates, quite concisely, the quarrel I have with Enlightenment thinking. While elements of the genealogy suggest that emphasizing rationality goes along with eliminating the subject, I'd prefer to see humans as rational subjects. The difference between this and the Enlightenment view is that the inclusion of ourselves as subjects allows us to examine *both* the general and the particular, *both* the global and the local. Disciplinary practice is communal; there are positive and negative aspects of the determination of practice by community and, as Keller says, science is "not simply defined by the exigencies of logical proof and experimental verification" (Keller, 1995, 4). The structure of a community is not simple. That structure, as was previously mentioned, includes the politics of funding, the competition for rewards, and also some level of agreement (albeit reached through dialectical means). As Helen Longino relates, the complexity of community structure includes convention based on collective practice and also work that is substantially individual (such as hypothesis testing and experimentation) (Longino, 1992, 208). The duality (or perhaps multiplicity) that Longino speaks of is an inevitable part of disciplinary practice, and it leads to the healthy competition Lakatos speaks of and to both the rationality of practice and its occasional vagaries.

I make the claim that disciplinary practice, and here I lump the sciences and the social sciences together, is, by and large, rational. The claim to rationality is not a strong claim. First, I readily admit that rationality is not absolute, that it does not hold in all occasions. Second, I want to make clear that the rationality I speak of is applicable to the content of disciplinary matters. In this regard, rationality is specific and is targeted to the content of the questions and methodology of the disciplines. It could be argued that the politics and power relations of disciplinary practice have their own rationality, but it is separate from the rationality of disciplinary content. Third, rationality does not preclude debate, or even dispute. That one method of study is rational does not mean that it is the *only* rational means of study. It is frequently the case in the social sciences that multiple methods are necessary to address complex questions. Fourth, rationality does not eliminate errors. As Longino says, "If rationality is, at least in part, the acceptance or rejection of beliefs on the basis of evidence, then theory and hypothesis choice is, when based on evidence, rational. Rationality, however, is not the infallible road to truth or away from error that it is often claimed to be" (Longino, 1990, 59). Rationality is a very different criterion from objectivity. Chalmers stresses the distinction: "although individual judgements and wishes are in a sense subjective and cannot be determined by logically compelling arguments, this does not mean that they are immune to rational argument" (Chalmers, 1982, 138). In the social sciences it is frequently rational to recognize that phenomena such as human behavior are arbitrary or have arbitrary and subjective components. Seeking a completely objective answer to a question is not always rational.

A potential objection to the claim of rationality comes from the recognition, just noted, that, despite what Popper says, some actions are motivated by power. Perhaps Popper was taking the naive view of power as forcible domination, but it is not that simple a force. Rouse warns us that "the understanding of power as essentially repressive or censorious is inappropriate here. The power characteristic of scientific knowledge (at least in the natural sciences) does not operate directly upon or against persons and their beliefs. It is a constructive power that reshapes the world and the way it is manifested" (Rouse, 1987, 20). Further, he says that "power can influence our motivation to achieve knowledge and can deflect us from such achievement, but it can play no constructive role in determining what knowledge is" (Rouse, 1987, 14). What the force of power does imply is that rationality is, much more often than not, social rather than individual. It is the product of institutional dynamics, which means that, while it is not static, rationality is a collective criterion. Mature disciplines should be seen as having more fully developed collective conceptions of what is rational, instead of having an agreed-upon "paradigm."

Rationality is also inherent in a variation of Kuhn's incommensurability thesis. Instead of seeing competing visions as existing in different worlds it is more fruitful to recognize the challenges that surround understanding. If Kuhn were correct it would be unlikely that some revolutions would ever have been successful, since they are not understandable to the adherents of an opposing view. Let us focus on the dialectical nature of competing views. Richard Bernstein sees the efficacy of the incommensurability thesis in terms of dialectic: "What is sound in the incommensurability thesis is the clarification of just what we are doing when we do compare paradigms, theories, language games. We can compare them in multiple ways. We can recognize losses and gains. We can even see how some of our standards for comparing them conflict with each other" (Bernstein, 1983, 92). The recognition of a dialectic is useful in two ways: (1) it is the arena in which competing ideas are presented in their entirety, so that rational theory evaluations can take place, and (2) it provides a way to study the metadisciplinary aspects of the grounds of competition, compromise, agreement, and choice (the genuine grounding of cultural studies of a discipline). The dialectic is complicated by the idea that theories are underdetermined by data. That is, there is no amount of data that can fully verify a theory, so theory choice is made even more difficult. We need not see underdetermination as an insurmountable hindrance. As Laudan shows convincingly, the argument from underdetermination is usually overstated and it does not interfere substantively with theory choice (Laudan, 1996, 29-54). The concept of underdetermination is part of the dialectical challenge to disciplines.

All of the foregoing is intended to illustrate shortcomings of some widely held conceptions of reality, or its absence. What I suggest here is that the strong versions of realism and relativism are so exclusionary as to render themselves irrelevant. It is not productive to cling to either extreme stance. There are, however, weaker versions of both that have important and useful implications for disciplinary practice, including practice in LIS. From realism we can retain the belief that there are things that exist independently of ourselves, whether they be observable or unobservable. Even those, such as Michael Luntley, who thoroughly and convincingly reject the strong realist version, accept that "The characterisation of content requires the subject's possession of a conception of a world beyond that which is experienced" (Luntley, 1988, 4). What this means is that epistemology is grounded in an ontology; that is, knowledge is, fundamentally, knowledge *of* something, and that something is rooted to some extent in reality. Along with that, realism implies some correspondence to truth. Again, I am not referring to an absolute here, but to a nonarbitrary connection between knowledge and truth. This truth is corrigible (it can be corrected as we obtain more evidence or employ sounder means of analysis), but it is an approximation of what really is.

While we must reject strong relativism we have to come to grips with the social elements of knowledge. We reject the strong version because it falls victim to its own claims. If no theory or idea can be justified, then the very idea of social constructivism has no justification. The denial of strong relativism doesn't mean that there are no reasons or justifications for accepting some theories or rejecting others. What we have to admit is that the social makes both the acceptance and rejection of theories *and* the understanding of *why* theories are accepted or rejected more challenging. This realization includes the awareness that, as Longino says, "It is, of course, nonsense to assert the value-freedom of natural science. Scientific practice is governed by norms and values generated from an understanding of the goals of scientific inquiry" (Longino, 1990, 4). We can go even further with this idea. Taking our cue from Rouse, we can see that discussion of the value neutrality of disciplinary practice reifies value; it reduces value to an object (Rouse, 1996, 256). An example of this kind of reification of value in our own field can be found in Bruce Kingma's examination of the economics of information. He writes, "economists use mathematics to quantify the benefits and costs of decisions and make unbiased, scientific assessments of value" (Kingma, 1996, 9).

Other Ways of Thinking about Realism

The mitigated stance I advocate has, it seems to me, the greatest potential for richness in understanding the questions that face all disciplines and in comprehending the ways to inquire. The understanding I speak of depends on the acceptance of the suggestion that, while we are not absolutely rational, we are fundamentally rational. Roger Trigg describes a circumstance that does not fall prey to strong realism or strong relativism: "What goes on in the brain, what forces are at work in society, even what epistemological standards are acceptable, themselves need to be recognized by a human reason that is not totally constrained by its context" (Trigg, 1993, 219). He also states that, because we are fundamentally rational, we seek knowledge, and science is one way of seeking knowledge; we are not rational simply because we are scientists (Trigg, 1993, 62).

Another way of expressing the mitigated stance is, to borrow from Giere, perspectival realism.

> Imagine the universe as having a definite structure, but exceedingly complex, so complex that no models humans can devise could ever capture more than limited aspects of the total complexity. Nevertheless, some ways of constructing models of the world do provide resources for capturing some aspects of the world more or less well. Other ways may provide resources for capturing other aspects of reality more or less well. Both ways, however, may capture some aspects of reality and thus be candidates for a realistic understanding of the world. (Giere, 1999, 79)

What Giere proposes includes an inherent recognition of a fundamental point, one that is essential for us to admit. John Searle, who is himself a realist in a meaningful sense, states the point, which "presupposes a distinction between facts dependent on us and those that exist independently of us, a distinction I originally characterized as one between social and institutional facts on the one hand and brute facts on the other" (Searle, 1995, 149). Searle uses that distinction to address challenges to realism (which admits to the existence of brute facts). The challenges, he says, in the main conflate the two kinds of facts and try to use the existence of social facts to negate the existence of brute facts, and are wholly unsuccessful. In LIS we should be conscious of the distinction, since, while some of our practices deal with brute facts, more are concerned with social facts.

This perspectival realism spoken of by Giere is not absent in LIS. To give just one example, Donald Kraft and Bert Boyce stress perspective at the outset of their book on operations research. In defining models they state that models "are analogies of some real thing or some real system. They are not the thing they model, though. . . . There can be many models of the same thing that emphasize different characteristics and that are used for different purposes" (Kraft and Boyce, 1991, 12). They further advise us, "Never take a model too literally, substituting the model for reality," and "Never use a model for ends for which it was not designed" (Kraft and Boyce, 1991, 18).

The understanding we seek necessitates that we attempt interpretation of the world around us and of how we respond to it. And this interpretation is, or can be, a rational project. We can follow the lead of Rouse, who says, "the world is always interpreted, through language and practice. An uninterpreted world would be unintelligible. But the interpretation does not make the world the way it is; it allows it to show itself the way it is" (Rouse, 1987, 159). Interpretation is not, perhaps to the dismay of those who see virtue in deterministic scientism, entirely subjective. As we will explore later, interpretation is at the heart of both inquiry and practice in LIS. As such it is a methodology (a global approach to exploration) rather than a method (a specific means of study applied to a specific question). We must recognize, as Bernstein does, that there is a "claim for the ontological significance of hermeneutics, and [a] claim for its universality" because "We are 'thrown' into the world as beings who understand and interpret—so if we are to understand what it is to be human beings, we must seek to understand understanding itself, in its rich, full, and complex dimensions" (Bernstein, 1983, 113). Susan Haack also expresses this kind of constraint on interpretation: "My picture also acknowledges a partnership of perception with background belief, in the sense that our beliefs about what we see, hear, etc., are affected not only by what we see and hear, but also by already-embedded beliefs about how things are" (Haack, 1993, 110). We take her statement just a bit farther; our beliefs are also affected by what is, in the metaphysical sense.

Interpretation is not, of course, without challenges. A very practical challenge is the realization that interpretation is dynamic. In large part the dynamic aspect is a factor of what is interpreted. "One can start from the idea that the world is filled not, in the first instance, with facts and observations, but with *agency*. The world, I want to say, is continually *doing things*, things that bear upon us not as observation statements upon disembodied intellects but as forces upon material beings [emphasis in original]" (Andrew Pickering, 1995, 6). One genealogical line of hermeneutics has strong realist leanings. This line assumes that meaning—of the world and of our interpretation of it—is fixed. Our task, then, is to discover that meaning. This view of hermeneutics is too exclusionary to be productive. Another challenge is to identify ideology as it affects our interpretation *and* our means of investigation (along with determining the question that will be asked). Alan Chalmers provides a specific example:

> We have illegitimate extensions of biology and evolutionary theory in the form of social Darwinism and sociobiology posing as explanations of social phenomena, thereby disguising the political realities and serving to justify various kinds of oppression such as that of the poor or women or racial minorities, and in recent times we witness an increasing tendency to reduce social issues to economic ones to be dealt with by a (pseudo)science of economics. (Chalmers, 1990, 125)

There is one task left in this descriptive part of the examination of LIS thought and practice. Now that we have a glimpse of differing ways of defining reality in the context of science, we have to look at the social sciences and explore the currents of thought in disciplines that are closer in content to LIS. As we'll see, the positions regarding the social sciences owe a huge debt to the genealogy we've already delved into. In part the social sciences embrace the prevailing stances in the sciences; in part they react to these stances. The next chapter presents this exploration.

Chapter Four

False Starts and Dead Ends for Social Science and LIS

Most of the previous three chapters are concerned with what we might call the historical problematic, that is, the history, or genealogy, of the social sciences and LIS (informed by Foucault's idea of history). While largely descriptive, this background serves to enable us to understand the various, sometimes competing, influences on contemporary social science. The variety, even the competition, continues today, and this presents something of a dilemma for us as we try to analyze the current state and move towards a richer and more fruitful future. To simplify, the dilemma can be expressed as a dichotomy. On one hand, social science and LIS have embraced some form of scientistic determinism and that path has led to little conceptually sound theory or practice. On the other hand, some theory and practice in social science and LIS have been informed by other conceptual bases. In this chapter we'll examine the first path. We will do so with the full understanding that the dichotomy is, to some extent, an oversimplification (nothing in life is ever so easy that we can create a clear either-or division). The unproductive and unsound work that has been done is not always completely off the mark, but it can be found wanting. We should remember that the historical problematic (the various examples of thought and practice that have managed to find a foothold and exert some influence in the past) is present to a greater or lesser degree in the disciplines today.

Unity of Science

One idea that consistently recurs over time is the possibility and desirability of the unity of the sciences. This notion dates back as far as Bacon and finds champions over the centuries in Hobbes, Condorcet, Saint-Simon, Comte, the logical empiricists, and some (as we will soon see) today. A usual feature of this belief is trust in the eventual discerning of a set of covering laws that govern all disciplines. Appleby, Hunt, and Jacob refer to this as the "heroic model of science," and observe that a simple dictum guides thought: "Imitate mechanical science, follow its methods, seek laws for everything from human biology to the art of governing—that was the advice bequeathed to the Western world by the Enlightenment" (Appleby, Hunt, and Jacob, 1994, 15). The most fundamental underlying assumption of this belief is that there is nothing in our being or experience that is extra-natural, so natural laws hold sway over everything. Many have tried to support this idea, and point to regularities in the natural world and advances in natural science (perhaps most especially biomedical science, including biogenetics and neuroscience) as evidence of the correctness of this thought. Anomalies and even failures are accounted for by a claim to progress; while we haven't uncovered all the secrets of the natural world, we are on pace to do so at some future time.

The connection between unity of science and covering laws is a very important one. A persistent and widely held concept is that the social sciences are a part of the natural sciences and some fundamentals apply to both. The unifying link extends both to theoretical constructs and to methods. If everything is reducible to the physical world, then one set of laws should be discoverable that would explain everything. Philosophers through the ages have grappled with the debate between dualism and monism. The concept of dualism, usually associated with Descartes, holds that there are two mutually irreducible things, such as the mind and the body. For Kant the dualist distinction was based on a separation of the object of sensory experience (which he called phenomena) and the object of rationality (which he called noumena). The monist position, in brief, is that there is only one reality. That reality is most often assumed to be the physical, and the mind is taken to be rooted in the physical being of the brain. It would be rather difficult today to find many dualists; most philosophers agree that some form of monism more aptly captures human existence. Even with such apparent agreement, however, there are several conceptions of monism (including methodological monism) and they vary considerably according to the suggested strength of the determinism of the physical. Some stances, as we've seen, maintain that human behavior is governed by predictable physical processes. Others hold that, while the mind is not separable from the body, mental phenomena are too complex to allow any sort of facile prediction.

One version of the monist position may be labeled "materialism" or "physicalism." This stance was mentioned briefly in chapter 2, but a bit more explication would be helpful here. Materialism can be described as a position that

> affirms that philosophy is continuous with the natural sciences. . . . Historically, many materialists have held that causes in question must be deterministic. A system is deterministic, roughly speaking, if its state at any time is a necessary consequence of its states at an earlier time conjoined with the laws of nature. (Moser and Trout, 1995, 9, 11)

Materialism is an attractive stance in part because it incorporates an attempt at finding causal relationships. Materialists tend to agree that the source of causation lies in physical laws. For instance, David Armstrong suggests a syllogism that captures the causal strength of materialism based on natural law:

1. The cause of all human (and animal) movements lies solely in physical processes working solely according to the laws of physics.
2. Purposes and beliefs, in their character of purposes and beliefs, cause human (and animal) movements.
∴3. Purposes and beliefs are nothing but physical processes working solely according to the laws of physics. (Armstrong, 1995, 42)

There is no problem with the logic of the syllogism, but the premises are certainly disputable. If either 1 or 2 is erroneous, then this fundamental idea of materialism collapses. One of the points of materialism that is disputed is its ontological authority; that is, the authority of physical science to tell us what is real, what exists. We'll soon return to the strong physicalist stance when we look more closely at behaviorism and the computational theory of mind.

The assumption that covering laws can be found relies on a more basic assumption: a discreet set of facts describes any given phenomenon and the description of those facts enables complete understanding and prediction. This assumption is apparent in Fritz Machlup's assessment of the natural and social sciences:

> The main difference lies probably in the number of factors that must be taken into account in explanations and predictions of natural and social events. Only a small number of reproducible facts will normally be involved in a physical explanation or prediction. A much larger number of facts, some of them probably unique historical events, will be found relevant in an explanation or prediction of economic or other social events. This is true, and methodological devices will not do away with the difference. But it is, of course, only a difference in degree. (Machlup, 1994, 6)

What sort of thinking would lead someone to utter such a claim? For one thing, the social scientist, librarian, or information scientist would have to believe (or act as though he or she believes) that human behavior is no different from other phenomena in the natural world. This means that our behavior is governed by discernible, although possibly complex, physical processes. This idea denies that human will is anything other than a manifestation of those physical processes and that anything other than definite physical causation is responsible for what we do. I will take issue with this later; for now let's focus on the conceptual basis of this particular path.

What Is History?

The scientistic strain in social science and LIS has to resolve some formidable questions. One of the most important is how should we investigate our past, especially if the past functionally determines the present and future. In other words, an important question is, what is history? The path we're investigating now relies, explicitly or tacitly, on the definition offered by Carl Hempel (mentioned earlier, but reiterated here):

> [G]eneral laws have quite analogous functions in history and in the natural sciences, that they form an indispensable instrument of historical research, and that they even constitute the common basis of various procedures which are often considered as characteristic of the social in contradistinction to the natural sciences.
>
> By a general law, we shall here understand a statement of universal conditional form which is capable of being confirmed or disconfirmed by suitable empirical findings. (Hempel, 1965, 231)

Hempel's is an extreme claim; it is the equation of the physical and social sciences in terms of both the foundation of thought and of method. Of course this notion has not been adopted by everyone. Even those who believe firmly in objectivity and objective knowledge couldn't swallow such a view of history. Karl Popper, for instance, refuted such a notion in his *The Poverty of Historicism*. He defines historicism as an approach to social science that has prediction as its ultimate aim and seeks to accomplish this goal by means of the discovery of explanatory laws (Popper,

1957, 3). (There are several quite different definitions of historicism; Popper's is only one.)

The quest for historical laws did not originate with Hempel. As Applegate, Hunt, and Jacob point out, claims of explanatory history based on laws date back to the nineteenth century and were influenced by the success of Newtonian mechanics in predicting phenomena in the natural world. A science of society would have to account for the past (Appleby, Hunt, and Jacob, 1994, 52-56). It should be noted that, while such bold claims as Hempel's raise eyebrows and receive attention, they haven't been widely accepted by historians in this century (Novick, 1988, 393-95). It is other social sciences, such as economics, sociology, and LIS, that may be more accepting of the quest of general laws of history. Before we applaud the discipline of history for avoiding some of the dead ends of other social sciences, let's keep in mind that, as a discipline, it has found the goal of objectivity quite amenable. This goal has affected the practice of history for some in the profession:

> The assumptions on which it rests include a commitment to the reality of the past, and to truth as correspondence to that reality; a sharp separation between knower and known, between fact and value, and, above all, between history and fiction. Historical facts are seen as prior to and independent of interpretation: the value of an interpretation is judged by how well it accounts for the facts; if contradicted by the facts, it must be abandoned. Truth is one, not perspectival. Whatever patterns exist in history are "found," not "made." Though successive generations of historians might, as their perspectives shifted, attribute different significance to events in the past, the meaning of those events was unchanging. (Novick, 1988, 1-2)

Novick is obviously describing a strong realist stance; mitigated stances can readily admit to the need for interpretation.

Hempel's idea of history contains a couple of elements that invoke aspects of the genealogy, previously discussed. For one thing, Hempel's confidence in the eventual discovery of historical laws hearkens back to the Enlightenment. Alisdair MacIntyre observes that Enlightenment thinkers were "infant Hempelians"; they grounded explanation in generalization that would lead to uncovering regularity in the form of laws. Perfectability of the human condition would depend on the explanation and prediction that would result from the effort at uncovering laws (MacIntyre, 1984, 88). A second point in Hempel's conception (and also in the goal of historical objectivity) is that the inquirer approaches a question from a position of neutrality. Neutrality manifests itself in at least two ways: (1) the researcher does not commit to a particular theory, since such a commitment would blind that individual to the reality that waits to be discovered; (2) the researcher adopts no values and no valuation of the observed facts or of the researcher's position.

The first element is unabashedly Baconian and echoes Newton's claim, *"Hypotheses non fingo* [I feign no hypotheses]." The second is wracked with problems, not the least of which are logical. The very act of observing is a value judgment; some evidence is sought and examined on purpose. Something is leading the inquirer to observe certain things and not others; the alternative is hopeless confusion. For this reason numerous writers have discussed the theory-dependency of observation. Further, some quasi-theoretical position is leading the researcher to ask certain questions, and then gather the data; otherwise the researcher would be paralyzed by the possible questions with no way to begin the inquiry. Appleby, Hunt, and Jacob state,

> The notion of objectivity inherited from the scientific revolution made it sound as if the researcher went into a trance, cleared his mind, polished the mind's mirror, and trained it on the object of investigation. Of course, there were methods to be followed, but the beliefs, values, and interests that defined the researcher as a person were simply brushed aside in this deception to allow the mirror to capture the reflection to capture nature's storehouse of wonders. (Appleby, Hunt, and Jacob, 1994, 260-61)

The ideal of neutrality may also be expressed, as Brian Fay does, as objectivism. At the simplest level objectivism entails a view of reality that is based on its complete independence of the mental. At a deeper level objectivism derives from the importance of eliminating those subjective elements which becloud our mental perception. Since objective truth is achieved by ridding ourselves of deceptive mental elements, objectivity can also be defined as the cognitive state of lacking a priori categories and conceptions, desires, emotions, value-judgments, and the like which necessarily mislead and thereby prevent attaining objective truth. (Fay, 1996, 202)

As we saw in the last chapter, there is ample warrant to agree with the claim that there is a reality independent of our minds. A problem arises, though, when this belief is extended to the claim that we are able to shed all preconceptions, prejudice—in short, all theory. The dead ends we will examine momentarily tend to assume that ability. This error amounts to denying our humanity.

Progress and Advancement

Hempel aside, there are some persistent assumptions that tend to be included in most, if not all, of the unproductive peregrinations in the social sciences. Some of these assumptions subsume Hempel's version of historicism (in Popper's sense) and some transcend it. Alexander Rosenberg enumerates three fundamental assumptions that seem to capture a central dilemma. He writes that comparisons between natural and social sciences "presuppose (1) that we know what progress in natural science is and how to measure it; (2) that based on our measurements, the natural sciences have made more progress; and (3) that the social sciences aim for the same kind of progress as the natural sciences" (Rosenberg, 1995, 6). The line of thought that is our focus in this chapter embraces these assumptions uncritically. It boils down to a very particular definition of success that contains some key parts. For instance, when it comes to method it is supposed that the methods of the natural sciences are the product of those disciplines' maturity, so they will lead to the most successful results. This ignores the reality that there is no single scientific method, because the sciences are themselves different from one another. The assumptions affect theory and practice in the social sciences and LIS. One aspect of method that some of the natural sciences do share is the possibility to construct a closed system; that is, the opportunity exists to isolate certain variables and eliminate others so that effects of changing conditions or introduction of a particular variable can be observed. Not all sciences are able to construct closed systems, but *no* social science can. As Andrew Sayer explains, "Human actions characteristically modify the configuration of systems, thereby violating the extrinsic conditions for closure, while our capacity for learning and self-change violates the intrinsic condition" (Sayer, 1992, 123).

At this point it may seem as though I am constructing a straw man, that no social scientists embody the characteristics discussed so far. To be sure, not all in the social sciences and LIS operate according to the aforementioned assumptions. Many may agree with Michael Scriven, who draws an important distinction between two visions for the future of the social sciences: "First, there is the thesis that it will be possible to improve predictions and explanations indefinitely. Second, there is the thesis that it will be possible to improve predictions and explanation in *every case, and to an indefinitely high degree* [emphasis in original] of approximation" (Scriven, 1966, 76). Scriven agrees with the first thesis, but not the second, because of the elusiveness of data and the improbability of solving specific social problems. However, even someone as committed to the variability of human behavior and social action as Robert Merton can envision that sociologists may

> begin to ask: is a science of society really possible unless we institute a total system of sociology? But this perspective ignores the fact that between twentieth-century physics and twentieth-century sociology stands billions of man-hours of sustained, disciplined, and cumulative research. Perhaps sociology is not yet ready for its Einstein because it has not yet found its Kepler—to say nothing of its Newton, Laplace, Gibbs, Maxwell, or Planck. (Merton, 1967, 47)

At a fundamental level, Merton expresses a belief that unity of science is possible and desirable.

The points made so far in this chapter cry for evidence. We will now turn our attention to particular examples of the embodiment of the assumptions and practices mentioned above. The first examples are taken from the social sciences; they are not obscure instances but substantive and influential works. Next we will examine some examples from LIS. As we will see, LIS thought and work are consistent with other social sciences. The purpose of these examinations is not to rail against opposing views of theory and method; in fact, in each case there are many positive elements, just as there were positive elements of logical empiricism. Also, the purpose is not to denigrate the efforts of others. This book is intended to instruct, and instruction depends to a considerable extent on learning from the mistakes of the past. That said, there are some serious flaws inherent in the examples addressed. The falseness of the starts and the deadness of the ends will become apparent.

Skinner's Behaviorism

Just as it would be foolish to reject determinism in every sense, so too would it be foolish to say that we've learned nothing over the years from behaviorist psychology. We also must remember that, just as positivism does not mean one thing only, behaviorism is not a single, unified theory and research program. Behavior theorists such as John B. Watson, Edward C. Tolman, and Clark Hull were not entirely in agreement as to the causes of human behavior and where behaviorism should go in the future. As is the case with positivism, though, there are some theses or tenets that, while not held in their entirety by everyone who would claim to be a behaviorist, are common to the thinking of many. For the purpose of analysis, the focus here will be on the behaviorist claims of B. F. Skinner, particularly as stated in his *Science and Human Behavior* (all of the quotes from Skinner will be to this text (Skinner, 1965 [1953]); page numbers will be noted). Our attention will be on Skinner because his behaviorism was more radical than most and because he has had such a broad and deep influence.

There is another reason for focusing on Skinner that is appropriate to this book. Not only did he mount an extensive research program based on his behaviorist thought, but he also sought to develop a cogent epistemology. Suresh Kanekar sums up Skinner's position: "Knowledge is behavior and valid knowledge is effective behavior" (Kanekar, 1992, 132). Skinner did indeed contemplate what constitutes knowledge, but what passes for epistemology is actually a pragmatic philosophical stance that negates the possibility of epistemology. Why does his stance negate epistemology? Epistemology is defined by normative characteristics, including justification for knowledge and some approximation of truth. His stance is strictly empiricist; only the observation of demonstrable behavior has any validity. Skinner's empiricism begs comparison with the scientistic strain that is conventionally labeled positivism. His link with this school of thought is not based in logical positivism (or logical empiricism), though. For one thing, he was loath to seek or impose rules of logic on human behavior; behavior simply manifests itself with only biological rules to guide it. Another point of departure was Skinner's dismissal of the importance of language as either a synthetic or an analytic tool.

Skinner's affinity for positivism had its foundation in an earlier version, as propounded by Ernst Mach. In a previous chapter we got a taste of Mach's thinking, which is characterized by reductionism and phenomenalism. Skinner wrote his doctoral dissertation on the extension of the phenomenon of physical reflex to human behavior, using Mach's idea of history as a means of revealing the physicalist foundation of reality shorn of metaphysical obfuscation. Mach had taken his intellectual and methodological cues from Bacon. His empiricism was inductivist; he put little stock in theory or hypothesis. And even that empiricism, for Skinner, was instrumental; hypotheses and theories were avoided because they led the psychologist to "ineffective" behavior. We've already seen some of the serious flaws of inductivism; it is no more productive for Skinner and behaviorism. His operationalism and instrumentalism are further evidence that his position did not conform to most epistemologists' ideas of knowledge. Not only did he not see a correspondence between knowledge and truth, but he also did not see any correspondence between knowledge and meaning. As Laurence Smith says, "For Skinner, what is traditionally spoken of as the 'meaning' or 'reference' of a term was to be found only in its actual use. In this radically naturalized account of meaning, there could be no relation of correspondence between a term and its referent, much less between a mentalistic 'idea' and some object that it stands for" (Smith, 1986, 285). Smith's interpretation of Skinner's instrumentalism illustrates a problem with such instrumentalism generally. Skinner is not alone in avoiding, even denying, any meaning of a word or term that exists a priori to a person's use of it. If that were so, humans would be speechless. Imagine trying to find a way to express a thought, emotion, or action if you were unaware of previously established or agreed upon meanings of words. Imagine the existence of a dictionary if such meanings didn't exist.

Skinner's own words provide the most conclusive evidence of scientism and determinism. His scientism was also instrumental in its reductionism. All human behavior could be reduced to simple biological causes, causes that are no different from those that lead to certain behavior in animals. "Human behavior is distinguished by its complexity, its variety, and its greater accomplishments, but the basic processes are not therefore necessarily different. . . . We study the behavior of animals because it is simpler" (38). The latter statement is indicative of an operational leap that Skinner makes from the former. One problem is that he does not provide sufficient empirical grounding to make either statement. The examples that are rife throughout the book are of birds that are "conditioned" to peck at a button in order to effect a particular outcome. The leap occurs when the behavior of the bird is not distinguished from human behavior which, as many researchers have shown, is nowhere near so regular. Moreover, Skinner himself is engaged in something that no animal is remotely capable of—the explanation of behavior. Is this not different in kind from animal behavior? Skinner's determinism is absolute and works in two ways. First, all human behavior is determined by physical causes. Second, behavior, once its cause is understood, can be controlled. "We must expect to discover that what a man does is the result of specifiable conditions and that once these conditions have been discovered, we can anticipate and to some extent determine his actions" (6). Even intellectual activity is purportedly included by Skinner's behaviorism: "We cannot rigorously account for the origin of important ideas in the history of science because many relevant facts have long since become unavailable" (255). The assumption is that there are identifiable facts that determine thought and that they can be available, thus allowing explanation and prediction. The inability of behaviorists to explain contemporary thought didn't seem to affect Skinner's claim.

These shortcomings are closely related to limitations that have been detailed in earlier chapters. There is another failing that has also been discussed and that depends on a willful denial of the actual language of Skinner's. Throughout *Science and Human Behavior* are assertions of value neutrality; the researcher neither imposes value through theory or method nor assumes value in the behavior being examined. This assertion is a fiction; value judgments pervade the book. Skinner spoke of improving the efficiency of behavior; a criterion such as efficiency is ineluctably based on some assessment of value. Equating human behavior with animal behavior is also a value judgment. Perhaps most importantly, Skinner's program of controlling behavior can only be seen as an expression of value. Skinner tried to muddy this issue, but his denials of value judgment ring hollow. He wrote that reinforcement such as an edict to love one's neighbor "may also be used, of course, to coerce an individual into behaving in a fashion which resembles loving his neighbor, and indeed is probably most often used for this reason, but again this is not what is meant by a value judgment" (429). Barry Schwartz and Hugh Lacey, using the behaviorist's analysis of factory work, sum up a major source of behaviorism's dead end:

> Behavior theory may tell us why behavior in the factory looks the way it does. But it does not tell us how there came to be factories, or what work was like before them, or how factory organization might have changed the nature of work. By treating the factory as a general model of behavior, behavior

theory ignores social and historical influences that help make factory work intelligible. By ignoring those other influences, behavior theory mistakenly claims to have discovered princi- ples that are comprehensive. (Schwartz and Lacey, 1982, 257)

Whether Skinner accepted it or not, behaviorism was founded on a fairly elaborate theoretical construct. His book demonstrated quite clearly that his empiricism was not entirely inductivist, but was based on a set of hypotheses that are indicated by the assumptions mentioned above. The assumptions, over time, were shown by the behaviorist program to be inade- quate. As was the case with logical positivism, behaviorism wrote its own obituary: its findings could not support its premises. It was, as Larry Briskman observes,

a degenerating research programme. That is, specific theories developed within the programme were continuously refuted and constantly replaced with weaker, more trivial, and more *ad hoc* ones; fundamental notions such as 'stimulus' and 'reinforce- ment' became vaguer and vaguer, until virtually anything could qualify; and awkward, refuting results came to be explained in terms of assumptions which broke the internal constraints of the research programme itself. In other words, I want to suggest that the poverty of Behaviourism's achievements in helping us to understand behaviour was the result of its false theoretical assumptions. (Briskman, 1984, 110)

Behaviorism, however, is not dead and gone. A search of contemporary social science literature (including, but not limited to, psychology) yields numerous citations to contributions that address behaviorism in some way. Many of the publications indicate sympathy with, even acceptance of, the behaviorist program. One example will suffice to show that some of the fundamental ideas expressed by Skinner are embraced by some today. Kanekar, who takes issue with some of Skinner's positions, is nonetheless an apologist for strong behaviorism, going so far as to claim that an individual's beliefs are absolutely determined by the individual's past (Kanekar, 1992). Kanekar's stance is problematic for several reasons, not the least of which is his insistence on the efficacy of a scientific study of behavior while simultaneously adopting a strong anti-realist position (that is, there is no correspondence, for instance, between knowledge claims and external reality or truth) and claiming that empirical examination of behavior in the purely physical sense is the only path to knowledge. In short, Kanekar exhibits many of the practical and epistemological contradictions that Skinner did. The social sciences and LIS must examine their positions to see if similar contradictions are present.

Herrnstein and Murray on Intelligence and Race

It's not often that an ostensibly scholarly book results in massive sales, talk-show appearances, and raging controversy, but such has been the case with *The Bell Curve*. It may be one of those books that everyone talks about but few actually read. On the face of it, this is a massive study, based on large sets of available data, of the heritability of intelligence and the social implications of that possibility. The authors present every semblance of objectivity, completeness, and lack of a priori bias as part of what purports to be a serious examination of a serious subject. In fact, however, the authors are highly selective in their background information, slipshod in their presentation of statistical data, and contentious in their conclusions. A number of commentators have accused Herrnstein and Murray of abuse and misuse of data. Also, there are explicit political links between this book and work that has been funded by the Pioneer Fund, which has a history of supporting eugenics and, according to its charter, is connected to promoting "race betterment" (Lane, 1995, 127-28). If we accept, as I believe we must, that all inquiry is theory laden, then the theory (defined broadly as the conceptual foundation of study or thought) is certainly not only fair game for investigation, but essential to any understanding of inquiry.

As was just mentioned, *The Bell Curve* is massive; it is impossible (and unnecessary) to examine every detail. It is more fruitful to look at the premises, methods, and central conclusions

of the work as they betray a decidedly scientistic determinism. At
the very outset of the book the authors present perhaps the most
fundamental assumption: "that intelligence is a reasonably well-
understood construct, measured with accuracy and fairness by
any number of standardized mental tests" (Herrnstein and
Murray, 1994, 1; future page references will be to this edition].
Intelligence is by no means an agreed upon concept; scholars
disagree as to the definition of intelligence and how to assess it.
It is not uncommon, nor is it a cause of concern, for research to
be based on a controversial assumption; it is, however, disingenu-
ous for researchers to deny the controversy or to make claims for
consensus that are not warranted. Herrnstein and Murray
consistently assert that a particular measure of intelligence is
necessarily accurate and comprehensive. They sum up their
claims in six points:

> 1. There is such a thing as a general factor of cognitive ability
> on which human beings differ.
> 2. All standardized tests of academic aptitude or achievement
> measure this general factor to some degree, but IQ tests
> expressly designed for that purpose measure it most accurately.
> 3. IQ scores match, to a first degree, whatever it is that people
> mean when they use the word *intelligent* or *smart* [emphasis in
> original] in ordinary language.
> 4. IQ scores are stable, although not perfectly so, over much of
> a person's life.
> 5. Properly administered IQ tests are not demonstrably biased
> against social, economic, ethnic, or racial groups.
> 6. Cognitive ability is substantially heritable, apparently no less
> than 40 percent and no more than 80 percent. (22-23)

The last point is crucial; their entire program rests on the
assumption that intelligence is substantially heritable. They
further operate on the premise that a midpoint, 60 percent, is a
conservative estimate of the proportion of heritability. The claim
is made without substantive support, though. Other scholars have
conducted a careful and large-scale examination of studies of
heritability, and take issue with the authors' claim. The scholars
found that narrow-sense heritability, which they say is the
measure used by Herrnstein and Murray, is approximately 34

percent (Daniels, Devlin, and Roeder, 1997, 58). This figure is very different from the mark used in *The Bell Curve*; if the scholars' estimate is a reasonable one, then heritability is not nearly so strong a predictive element of intelligence as Herrnstein and Murray claim. But the authors persist in conveying "the impression that one's intelligence simply exists as an innate fact of life—unanalyzed and unanalyzable—as if it were hidden in a black box. Inside the box there is a single number, IQ, which determines vast social consequences" (Gardner, 1995, 66). Such a conclusion is warranted by statements made by Herrnstein and Murray themselves, such as, "In reality, what most interventions accomplish is to move children from awful environments to ones that are merely below average, and such changes are limited in their potential consequences when heritability so constrains the limits of environmental effects" (109). Two aspects of this statement cry for examination (and these are my points, not theirs):

A. Heritability is *the* determining factor when it comes to intelligence.

B. Environmental aspects are linear in effect; that is, movement from poor to better environments results in a clear linear improvement.

There is no evidence that leads us to concede either of these points.

Operating on these faulty premises, Herrnstein and Murray employ statistical methods to examine data and to affirm their assumptions. One point cannot be emphasized enough here—there is nothing inherently wrong with using quantitative methods to study social phenomena. To the contrary, statistical analysis is a powerful and extremely useful research tool. However, neither is quantitative analysis inherently correct. This is a point that will be reiterated later. It is not that Herrnstein and Murray falsify data, but they tend to report findings in such a way as to fortify their conclusions. For instance, on page 73 they present a table on the validity of the General Aptitude Test Battery. They claim the correlations presented are strong, but the figures range from .23 to .58 in rating proficiency. It is likely that few statisticians would make an unequivocal statement that the numbers represent strong correlations. In their appendix the authors note briefly that squaring the correlation coefficient yields an important number (564). This measure is usually referred to as the coefficient of determination and is taken to mean that the independent variable explains a certain percentage of variation in the dependent variable. (Of course the explanatory power is limited; there is no way for the statistical analysis to lead us to a clear understanding of *why* covariance occurs, for instance.) As a coarse example, if a researcher finds a correlation of .6 between library instruction and changes in students' grade point averages, then a conclusion might be that library instruction explains 36 percent ($r^2=.36$) of the change in grade point average. (There is, of course, much more to such research, but the example illustrates computation of the coefficient of determination, r^2.) Herrnstein and Murray do *not* report the r^2 figure in the table on page 73 or, by and large, in subsequent tables.

In another appendix the authors present all of the correlation data, a total of sixty-one measures. Here they do report the coefficient of determination, which contradicts their strong claims that border on statements of causation. At one point they state, "For most of the worst social problems of our time, the people who have the problem are heavily concentrated in the lower portion of the cognitive ability distribution. Any practical solution must therefore be capable of succeeding with such people" (369). This implies that low cognitive ability causes social problems. At another point they present more data that seem to show that IQ is *the* reason for lower earnings. We should take a closer look at the data they present in the appendix. (And we should ask why they do not report the coefficient of determination in the text, especially given the importance they attach to their findings.) For ease of reading, the coefficients of determination (translated as percentages) are shown in table 4.1. The table indicates how many of the sixty-one measures fall into each range of values.

Table 4.1
r^2 **Values (as Percentages)**

Range:	0<10%	10-20%	20-30%	30-40%	>40%
Number:	43	8	3	5	2

Range of r^2 values: .12% to 45.17%

Briefly stated, the data in the table show that in forty-three out of sixty-one cases, the independent variable explained less than 10 percent of variation in the dependent variable. These are indeed interesting findings, but the body of the book does not tell us *why* they're interesting. The obfuscation represents a major failing of *The Bell Curve*. In the last chapter I quoted Alvin Goldman, who provides the most effective response to the constructivist claim that facts are negotiated. He says that it is understanding, not facts, that is negotiated; to say otherwise is false. Herrnstein and Murray make the opposite of the constructivist claim, asserting that facts are simply there waiting to be discovered and then they conflate the stated understanding with the fact. Goldman's admonition still stands; Herrnstein and Murray do present an argument for understanding (an argument that is fatally flawed) and they take their argument to be a statement of fact.

In addition to Herrnstein and Murray's claim of heritability being much stronger than the data support, so is their unequivocal statement that there is a single, agreed upon measure of intelligence, the g factor. This is at the heart of the first of their six points which, they say, is "by now beyond significant technical dispute" (22). In a work such as *The Bell Curve* this sort of claim can only be taken as being unforgivably incompetent or willfully misleading. There certainly are psychologists who would agree with the authors, but, just as certainly, there are those who disagree. As David Layzer points out, Cyril Burt, an avowed hereditarian (and fraud) was convinced that intelligence cannot be directly measured (Layzer, 1995, 666). (Burt's work has been discredited as fabricated, but Herrnstein and Murray offer a defense of Burt's work.)

The case of Cyril Burt refuses to go away. It is still debated in psychology journals and in popular magazines. While Burt has a number of defenders, there is no doubt that he manipulated data. Further, he manufactured two collaborators who, if they existed at all, had no role in his research. The support of Burt's work flies in the face of the supposed objectivity of data analysis.

The authors barely acknowledge dissenters from their view, referring to some, such as Robert Sternberg, as revisionist, and some, such as Howard Gardner, as radicals. Such intellectual gerrymandering is irresponsible at the least.

While Herrnstein and Murray dismiss scholars who disagree with them, they do rely on a couple of individuals whose motives might be questioned. One is Richard Lynn, who stated in an article, "Who can doubt that Caucasoids and the Mongoloids are the only two races that have made any significant contribution to civilization?" (quoted in Giroux and Searls, 1996, 80). Leon Kamin has examined some of Lynn's work and has found that Lynn at times selectively reports the results of other research. Lynn has noted the results of a test of Zambian copper miners and derives an average IQ of 75 (based on an average of thirty-four correct responses on the Progressive Matrices test). He does *not* include, from the same study, the results of some Soweto students, who averaged forty-five correct responses on the same test (the average number of correct responses by white students at that time was forty-four) (Kamin, 1995, 85). More problematic is the reliance of Herrnstein and Murray on the work of J. Philippe Rushton. Rushton's reputation and scholarship has been defended by the likes of Irving Louis Horowitz, a widely respected sociologist. Rushton's work does, however, have strong physicalist elements that lead to conclusions that have been questioned. Some of his work has involved the measurement of cranial capacity, brain size, and penis size and has led him to the conclusion that there is an inverse relationship between some physical characteristics (penis size and sex drive) and intelligence.

The Bell Curve illustrates well that, regardless of the subject of inquiry, human understanding works out through language. Human behavior is, by and large, rational, but behavior also may involve rationalization. Herrnstein and Murray appear to have a specific political agenda; this is evident in the sections of the book dealing with public policy (for instance, they say their results support the policy of school choice, including vouchers). The language used by Herrnstein and Murray, especially in light of the serious methodological shortcomings of the book, may be seen as ideological; that is, the language used is an expression of domination and legitimation. Regarding the assertion in *The Bell Curve* that poverty is due to bad luck and genetics (130), Joyce King counters, "Suggesting that bad luck and bad blood explain societal inequity in this way represents just one instance of the 'oppressive language' in *The Bell Curve* that serves to legitimate the status quo by obscuring the relations of power that are largely responsible for it" (King, 1996, 183). Herrnstein and Murray essentially reify IQ; they take one measure of intelligence and use that measure to *mean* cognitive ability. Further, they take cognitive ability and use that to *mean* the cause of social ills. Stephen J. Gould sums up the only possible assessment of *The Bell Curve*: it is "biological determinism as a social philosophy. . . . The book is a rhetorical masterpiece of scientism, and it benefits from the particular kind of fear that numbers impose on nonprofessional commentators" (Gould, 1995, 5, 7).

Even in light of these criticisms, *The Bell Curve* still has its supporters. In a recent issue of the magazine *Commentary*, Christopher Chabris comes to the defense of the book. Some of his points are cogent and should be acknowledged here. It is possible to arrive at some measure of achievement; further, heredity does have something to do with the ability of each individual. No one would dispute these claims, but they are banal in their simplicity. The most sophisticated research warns us not to succumb to temptations of determinism when it comes to heredity and intelligence. Chabris faults political liberals for twisting the conclusions of Herrnstein and Murray. I gladly confess to being a political liberal, but my liberalism is not what informs my assessment of the methods employed by Herrnstein and Murray and the bias that is evident in their presentation. Chabris concludes by saying, "The most basic claim put forth by Herrnstein and Murray was that smart people do better than dumb people. What is so troubling about that?" (Chabris, 1998, 40). What is troubling is that their real claims focus on public policy and do so by ignoring the possible influences on intelligence and the social context in which we measure, report on, and act on the concept of intelligence. Scientistic determinism is, in large part, a denial of the social and the mental in favor of the exigency of facile reductionism.

Wilson and the Unity of Knowledge

This section is a bit of a departure in that it is not about practice in a social science. It is about a vision for the social sciences. Edward O. Wilson, renowned entomologist, has been working on his idea of the unity of knowledge for a number of years. For some time he has maintained that sociobiology is at the heart of the sciences and of life itself. In his most recent book, *Consilience*, he tries to articulate a complete argument for the unifying essence of knowledge. Of course other people have attempted this kind of ambitious program before, but Wilson's work has been very influential in the past and *Consilience* is receiving considerable attention in the popular and the scholarly press.

Wilson includes a brief and highly idiosyncratic history of the Enlightenment by relating a naively optimistic version of the period. He intends to focus on the Enlightenment aim of unifying all knowledge, but he neglects to tell us of the goal to be achieved by subsuming everything into some idea of what science should be. Wilson willingly acknowledges that the Enlightenment provided us with the deep roots of modernism, but he does not admit that eighteenth-century science was also a product of the culture and political economy of the day. He concludes his history of the Enlightenment with a jab at postmodernism, failing to understand two essential aspects of the postmodern: (1) it is *not* one simple, clear, definable, agreed-upon thing; (2) it is, in many important ways, an extension of modernism. He then acknowledges that Michel Foucault grasped that there is a power struggle between extremes—skeptics who see no grand narrative and no ultimate truth, no teleology at work, and materialists who admit to nothing at all but the physical. Wilson then dismisses Foucault completely, as though Foucault has said nothing worth listening to. One may disagree with Foucault (and others), but a serious attempt to understand the world and humans in it should address the kinds of concerns Foucault raised. Wilson's facade of tolerance appears to be shallow.

Wilson's materialism is most evident in his chapter on the mind. He begins it by asserting, "Belief in the intrinsic unity of knowledge—the reality of the labyrinth—rides ultimately on the hypothesis that every mental process has a physical grounding and is consistent with the natural sciences. . . . All that has been learned empirically about evolution in general and mental process in particular suggests that the brain is a machine assembled not to understand itself, but to service" (Wilson, 1998, 96; further references will be to this text). The latter statement is at the heart of a theoretical premise that defines Wilson's idea of sociobiology, as well as the strong adaptationist notions of Richard Dawkins and others. This adaptationist stance is anchored by the staunch Darwinian belief that, if something (some species of plant, insect, animal, or human) has survived, then its survival is due to its having adapted itself more effectively than have other species. Of course there's something to that idea. Many species have apparently adapted to take advantage of changes in the environment and have thrived. Many others have perished. The materialist thought of Wilson has it that the same biological determinism that may be witnessed with regard to, say, insect species, also applies to humans. This kind of biological determinism leads Wilson to proclaim, "The brain and its satellite glands have now been probed to the point where no particular site remains that can reasonably be supposed to harbor a nonphysical mind" (99). It may be that there is no nonphysical mind, but Wilson's statement is no proof of that assertion. If the premise is that there is no nonphysical mind, then a search for it in physical matter would be pointless; its existence could be neither proved nor disproved. While it is completely understandable to say, "I am skeptical of the existence of a nonphysical mind because I can find no evidence of it," it borders on the scientifically irresponsible (according to Wilson's own rules) to say, "I have found no evidence of a nonphysical mind, therefore it doesn't exist." The latter claim is not science; it is ideology. Also, it's the kind of faulty logic that advances neither science nor the social sciences.

Since Wilson is aiming at a kind of Theory of Everything, he eventually sets his sights squarely on the social sciences. He says, "People expect from the social sciences . . . the knowledge to understand their lives and control their futures. They want the power to predict, not the preordained unfolding of events, which does not exist, but what will happen if society selects one course of action over another" (181). At various points in his life Wilson has urged us not to confuse "ought" with "is." His notion of vox populi regarding the social sciences can be seen as the "is." Many social scientists for generations have tried counter with "ought"; the social sciences are not tools for control, but aids to understanding. With the social sciences Wilson is not exactly forgetting his rule of thumb, but he is rewriting "ought" to be the goal of prediction and control. Moreover, prediction and control are rendered possible if all is biologically determined. To Wilson, the social science with the greatest potentiality for achieving the deterministic end is economics, especially because it resembles the sciences "in style and self-confidence" and is "fortified with mathematical models" (195). Wilson doesn't bother to recount the failures of economics over the years, which may be due in large part to the creation of a model based on a closed system (which may be effective in some scientific fields, as we've seen, because the closed system adequately approximates some aspects of the natural world). A closed system, however, is a poor model of human behavior, and the rule of parsimony (Occam's Razor) that Wilson is so fond of is not very effective in the extreme in the social sciences. Further, as Theodore Porter aptly points out,

"Mapping mathematics onto the world is always difficult and problematical. Critics of quantification in the natural sciences as well as in social and humanistic fields have often felt that reliance on numbers simply evades the deep and important issues" (Porter, 1995, 5).

Very early in *Consilience* Wilson says, "The unification agenda does not sit well with a few professional philosophers. The subject I address they consider their own, to be expressed in their language, their framework of formal thought. They will draw this indictment: *conflation, simplism, ontological reductionism, scientism* [emphasis in original], and other sins made official by the hissing suffix. To which I plead guilty, guilty, guilty. Now let us move on, thus" (11). His dismissal is not sufficient; reductionism and scientism, as we have seen, are intensely problematic. The problems are rife throughout sociobiology generally and through this book in particular. Lewontin, Rose, and Kamin turn a critical eye to biological determinism and provide a cogent analysis that points out flaws. For one thing, this determinism is not apolitical, and Wilson must know this (the list of people he includes in his book as having influenced his thought includes Newt Gingrich). More to the point, Lewontin, Rose, and Kamin emphasize that "the relation between gene, environment, organism, and society is complex in a way not encompassed by simple reductionist argument" (Lewontin, Rose, and Kamin, 1984, 266). Tzvetan Todorov, in a review of *Consilience*, expressed agreement with their assessment:

> Surely the nature of knowledge differs with the object of knowledge. The laws of living organisms and the 'laws' of human history are differently known, with different standards of evidence and certainty. The qualities that are demanded of scientists and scholars in one realm are not the qualities that are demanded of scientists in another realm, beyond the common requirement of rigor. (Todorov, 1998, 33)

These notions maintain that more than one way of thinking is needed to understand human phenomena. Wilson, for his part, seems to interpret this pluralism as antagonistic to science. He says, the Standard Social Science Model "sees culture as an independent phenomenon irreducible to elements of biology and psychology, thus the product of environment and historical antecedents" (188). Here Wilson makes a serious error in his leap of reasoning: the claim that the social is not reducible to the physical is *not* a denial that the social is strongly influenced by the physical.

The major difficulties with Wilson's program center on what his science *can't* explain. If, for instance, postmodernism (or his version of it) is bankrupt, then how would people have conceived of it and why do people cling to it? If humans are rational creatures pointed toward survival of the species, then why have there been such devastating wars, the buildup of weapons of mass destruction, the destruction of rain forests, etc.? If Darwinism is an appropriate model for the study of humans and other species, how did social Darwinism and eugenics come to be? At one point Wilson claims, "Behavioral scientists from another planet would notice immediately the semiotic resemblance between animal submissive behavior on the one hand and human obeisance to religious and civil authority on the other. They would point out that the most elaborate rites of obeisance are directed at the gods, the hyperdominant if invisible members of the human group" (259). This thought experiment is absurd; the fundamentals of "obeisance" are different. Plus, how would Wilson explain atheism, civil disobedience, and even crime? If these are pathologies, why are they so widespread? He further claims that Western philosophy's "involuted exercises and professional timidity have left modern culture bankrupt of meaning" (269), but how did this come to be if humans are rational and striving for survival? To denounce all of philosophy with a wave of the hand is intellectually irresponsible.

Wilson's program is basically a severely strained tautology. Biological determinism is responsible for the present state of the human species; if certain behaviors are common to humans, then the deterministic state explains that behavior. He denies genetic determinism at one point in *Consilience*, but if he is true to that denial, then his program falls apart. The program depends on reductionism. As I've said before, some reductionism is essential to the study of a question; if we didn't reduce aspects of problems we would have no way of studying them. Wilson's reductionism is extreme, and therein is the dilemma. Lewontin, Rose, and Kamin examine Wilson's reductionism in sociobiology:

> Sociobiology is a reductionist, biological deterministic explanation of human existence. Its adherents claim, first, that the details of present and past social arrangements are the inevitable manifestations of the specific action of genes. Second, they argue that the particular genes that lie at the basis of human society have been selected in evolution because the traits they determine result in higher reproductive fitness of the individuals that carry them. (Lewontin, Rose, and Kamin, 1984, 236)

Where reductionism goes wrong is when it breaks things down, selects certain attributes, then conflates those attributes with the thing itself. The result is reification. For example, researchers inquiring into use patterns in public libraries may reduce the many potential variables to gender, personal income, and place of residence. Looking at the variables, they may find that library users tend to be upper-middle-class women who live less than a mile from a library branch. Based on that they may influence libraries to define the population of users *as* the community, develop collections, access, and services aimed at that population, thus turning the library into a mechanism geared to serve only a small portion of the community.

The principal message of *Consilience* is that science is the answer ("The only way either to establish or to refute consilience is by methods developed in the natural sciences" [9]). There is only one way to think about human and social phenomena. The determinism that guides and constrains the individual applies to society as well. A generous appraisal of Wilson's program would be that it is naive optimism. A more critical assessment would have to focus on the matter of control legitimated by determinism.

A Few More Examples in Brief

The three cases just discussed illustrate flaws in method, but, more importantly, illustrate conceptual flaws. The mistakes are misconceptions of human behavior, confusion regarding the nature of intention and will, and a physicalist or materialist bias that confounds most aspects of inquiry. One consistency in these cases is the narrowing of vision that results in a focus on only a few aspects of behavior or society or on a few variables. When, for instance, a small set of variables seems to be able to explain a phenomenon, albeit in rather shallow terms, then there may be a tendency to look no further for understanding. Other examples also illustrate this point. Let's take a quick look at a few more.

Gary Becker's Economics

Economics is an interesting, challenging discipline. Among the social sciences economics is probably the most quantitative. Its use of sophisticated mathematical models has drawn admiration from, among others, Edward O. Wilson. The work of one economist in particular demonstrates the false start of a specific way of thinking—rational choice theory. Gary Becker was awarded the Nobel Prize in economics in 1992, in large part for his economic analysis of human behavior. He has analyzed education, marriage, and the family in economic terms. Using rational choice theory, his analysis has focused on behavior as utility maximization. As we will see, rational choice theory is highly reductive; it reduces the reasons people have for the decisions they make to a formulation (conscious or not) of advantage and utility. When one alternative demonstrates greater promise of utility, then that alternative is overwhelmingly preferred. Becker says, "All human behavior can be viewed as involving participants who maximize their utility for a stable set of preferences and accumulate an optimal amount of information and other inputs in a variety of markets" (Becker, 1976, 14).

Becker turns his attention to education. Employing rational choice theory, he maintains that educational choice is based on the prospect for material gain. As evidence for his claim he states, "high school and college education in the United States greatly raise a person's income, even after netting out direct and indirect costs of schooling, and after adjusting for the better family backgrounds and greater abilities of more educated people" (Becker, 1993, 17). As is the case with some of the other claims examined here, Becker's assessment of the benefits of education is banal; it certainly comes as no surprise and is certainly not a revelation. He suggests further evidence for the material gain based on education: "women progressed most rapidly under the Reagan administration, which was opposed to affirmative action and did not have an active Civil Rights Commission" (Becker, 1993, 19). He attributes the gains to increasing divorce rates, declining birthrates, and growth in the service sector. He does not acknowledge underlying factors that might be influencing birthrates and divorce rates. For instance, he does not mention the recession that occurred during those years which may have led to tensions in homes and the need for a second income. In other words, it is possible that the dynamics of women entering the workforce have been complex; Becker reduces that complexity to a simple answer, but that answer doesn't enhance an understanding of the phenomenon. Further, he doesn't explain what he means by "progress."

His reductionism is perhaps most evident when he addresses matters related to marriage and the family. His program depends on an assumption of equality; everyone goes through the same stages of life in the same way. Or, more importantly, everyone has the same opportunity to live in the same way. "We also assume that everyone is identical and lives for two periods, childhood and adulthood, works T hours as an adult, and spends all his or her childhood time investing in human capital" (Becker, 1993, 331). The two stages affect not only the life of the individual, but also the life of the family. With regard to marriage Becker says, "A person decides to marry when the expected utility from marriage exceeds that expected from remaining single or from the additional search for a more compatible mate" (Becker, 1976, 10). As James Bohman points out, this analysis is vacuous; it amounts to an a posteriori imposition of reasons on what is also a complex phenomenon (Bohman, 1991, 74). No doubt some marriage decisions are made on the basis of expected material gain, but conversely, many marriages result in material hardship. Becker's facile answer is empirically simplistic and theoretically impoverished.

Rational Choice Theory

destitution, poverty, failure, hardship, ruin

The impoverishment can be placed on the shoulders of rational choice theory. The assumptions that characterize the theory are: utility maximization governs choice; consistency requirements are part of the definition of rationality; every individual maximizes the expected value of a choice, measured on some sort of utility scale; individuals, not society, are the units under investigation; and the models used apply equally well to all individuals and the models are stable over time (Green and Shapiro, 1994, 14-17). The fundamental reliance on rationality is probably the most questionable assumption. Alexander Rosenberg contends that people do sometimes behave irrationally; since they do behave that way, then the ordinal theory of preference (if I prefer *a* to *b*, and *b* to *c*, then I prefer *a* to *c*) is disconfirmed. Further, some defenders of rational choice counter that what seems to be irrationality is actually change in taste. But if taste can change daily, how is that different from irrationality (Rosenberg, 1995, 79)? There is a record of rational choice theorists, including Becker, to glibly explain away anomalies by redefining rationality or otherwise fudging data:

> The frequency with which rational choice theorists have explained away anomalies by manipulating the meaning of rationality, restricted arbitrarily the domain in which the theory applies so as to avoid discordant facts, constructed tests that adduce only confirming facts, or ignored competing explanations belies the suggestion that when employed as empirical science rational choice explanations are free from mercurial invention. (Green and Shapiro, 1994, 187)

Becker, as Bohman states, demonstrates "that the generalization of rational choice models of explanation can be done only by abandoning the idea that the theory was supposed to give an account of how reasons cause actions. Instead, the theory searches for unconscious maximizing motives and market mechanisms, making the rationality of actors themselves less and less important as an explanatory condition" (Bohman, 1991, 75).

According to the theory, rationality leads to the expression of preferences. The notion of preference, however, is problematic. There are a couple of recognized ways to conceive of preference—one is to see it as a choice between or among options; the other is to see it as a process of matching, in which the decision maker adjusts one option to match another. Tversky, Slovin, and Sattuth demonstrate empirically that these two conceptions are inconsistent and are frequently divergent. That is, different elicitation means can lead to different expressions of preferences. They write, "In the absence of well-defined preferences, the foundations of choice theory and decision analysis are called into question" (Tversky, Slovin, and Sattuth, 1988, 384). Becker does address some important questions and there is no doubt that the behavior of an individual does have material consequences, but he is unable to explain the complexity of human behavior solely in economic terms, and the empirical research conducted on the matter calls into question whether such a program is even possible.

Deterministic History

Another example combines the disciplines of economics and history. The application of quantitative methods to history, which has gained popularity in the last few decades, is frequently referred to as cliometrics. Employing multiple methods, including quantitative methods, has been a boon to historical research, increasing the breadth and depth of analysis. The particular work examined here, however, exhibits some of the same scientistic tendencies we've seen before. Also, the method used (along with the way it is used) seems to determine the results. In the 1970s, Robert Fogel (also a Nobel laureate in economics) and Stanley Engerman used quantitative economic analysis to study material aspects of slavery as a mode of production in the American South. (Their full study was published in two volumes, one narrative and one presenting data; the one-volume version of *Time on the Cross* will be cited here.) At the outset, Fogel and Engerman state that their research will correct some misconceptions of the slave economy; among their corrections are that "Slavery was not a system irrationally kept in existence by plantation owners who failed to perceive or were indifferent to their best economic interests" and "The slave system was not economically moribund on the event of the Civil War" (Fogel and Engerman, 1974, 4-5). In fact, the import of their conclusions, they say, rests on the corrections they claim to make. Although they say the misconceptions are pervasive, it is difficult to find many who hold the positions they wish to correct. As Oscar Handlin says, "Fogel and Engerman erected a straw man the more easily to demolish him: that tactic of controversy attracted attention; it did not win converts" (Handlin, 1979, 209).

Other corrections Fogel and Engerman try to assert are: "Slave agriculture was not inefficient compared with free agriculture," and "The material (not psychological) conditions of the lives of slaves compared favorably with those of free industrial workers" (Fogel and Engerman, 1974, 5). These corrections are dependent on some further assumptions (or perhaps obfuscations may be a better word). Slave economy was not inefficient if we remember that labor costs were extremely low, so there was little need or incentive for large-scale investment in mechanization. The cost of one acre's yield looks favorable, but only if the human cost is ignored. The claim that the conditions under which slaves worked compared favorably with those of industrial workers hides the reality of nineteenth-century industrial labor which, at its worst, was not particularly discernible from slavery. The claims, then, are couched in terms that render objection futile, unless the totality of the claims is critiqued. One doesn't have to object to the method to object to the claims. Handlin perhaps overstates his case, but he makes a cogent point when he cautions, "The new computer-driven techniques extend the ability to mobilize and use large amounts of information. But in themselves they solve no problems; and precisely because their power is greater than those of the weapons earlier historians commanded, their use requires more care. Those who disregard any but their own experience will be condemned to mistakes others have learned to avoid" (Handlin, 1979, 213).

Particulars of the data analysis of Fogel and Engerman should be scrutinized closely. To their credit they sought all available sources of data, including census records, sales and probate data, and records from plantations. However, these sources of data are incomplete—census records of the nineteenth century were less accurate even than today's; not all sales transactions were formally recorded; not all slave trade constituted sale in the strict sense; plantation records were seldom accurate. Just about all quantitative studies of complex human and social phenomena must tolerate limitations on the data available; this in itself does not render quantitative studies invalid. It does, however, necessitate the moderation of claims. It is impossible to make absolute statements on the basis of incomplete data. The authors tend to be extreme in their statements, as though they were able to have access to every possible data point. For instance, Novick relates that, when asked by other historians about their assessment of the exploitation of slaves, Fogel and Engerman's reply would be a mathematical formula (Novick, 1988, 588). The equation is only as good as the data that can be entered. Fogel and Engerman were also guilty of a sin against quantitative analysis—they did not always analyze comparable data. At times they use data on slavery from 1850 and data on the general population from 1870. The difference in the twenty-year period is not one that can be ignored.

Part of their correction depends on their demonstrating that the South was not behind in industrialization. The index they created built on previous work done by Fogel and relies heavily on railroad mileage per capita. They found, "In railroad mileage per capita she was virtually tied with the North, and both were far ahead of their nearest competitor" (Fogel and Engerman, 1974, 255). The railroad mileage is a very problematic index of industrialization. The index for the South is calculated as the standard, equal to 100; the index for Great Britain is reported to be 43. Fogel and Engerman do not, however, normalize these data for population density, geographic area, and other physical and demographic variables. The index is a primitive and misleading (at best) indicator of industrialization. Fogel and Engerman also tended to use counterfactuals to "prove" points. That is, they might say that if modes of transportation other than rail had been developed in the late nineteenth century, then there would have been specific economic results. Many of their conclusions (and the conclusions of Fogel's studies of the impact of railroads) depend on these kinds of counterfactuals. As Clayton Roberts warns, "Whether a counterfactual is given a negative or a positive expression, its truth depends upon the truth of the covering law," which may demonstrate scientistic leanings, and "Since it is undeniably true that the longer a chain of counterfactuals, the greater the chance of a mistaken conclusion at the end, Fogel has taken a dangerous path" (Roberts, 1996, 81, 255-56).

As was just stated, quantitative analysis has the potential to enrich research in all disciplines, but not if it is assumed to be the *only* viable means of examination. Fogel and Engerman, besides making some serious methodological errors, also erred in their claim for the method. Handlin's response, then, is not out of line: "The authors further fanned the flames of acrimony by stating their thesis in exaggerated and provocative terms. They trumpeted the book as a triumphant vindication of the pretensions of quantitative techniques and as a total revision of all previous interpretations of American slavery. On both counts Fogel and Engerman were wrong and misleading" (Handlin, 1979, 208).

Determinism and Organizational Theory

The next example from the social sciences is an unabashed adoption of scientistic and deterministic principles. Lex Donaldson asserts confidently that positivism is the soundest theoretical grounding for the study of organizations. By that he means, "That theory holds that organizations are to be explained by scientific laws in which the shape taken by organizations is determined by material factors such as their size. These laws hold generally across organizations of all types and national cultures" (Donaldson, 1996, 1). His definition of positivism is similar to those we've already seen: it is nomothetic (it seeks covering laws); it is empirical in method; it is materialist; it is determinist; and it emulates the natural sciences (Donaldson, 1996, 3). The tenets of scientism have already been examined and their problems detailed; there's little reason to reiterate those points here. Donaldson does differ from some of the other individuals already dealt with, such as Becker, in that he denies that players have any choice, rational or not. In this he comes closer to anyone we've seen to being absolutely deterministic. (One reason for the inclusion of Donaldson's thinking here is that readers may be tempted to assume that such a position doesn't exist in the world.) He does briefly acknowledge some of the counters to positivism, including the existence of political concerns, uncertainty, conflict, and sensitivity to context. He then ignores these factors and reduces anti-positivist thought regarding organizations to a limited set of ideal types, none of which embodies the kind of alternative propositions he previously acknowledged.

Since Donaldson's version of anti-positivism constitutes reduction to a set of straw men, it is easy to dismiss his program. He doesn't address the serious and formidable objections to positivism. The alternative he discusses is not far removed from his own ideal type. A large body of research in organizational theory has stressed the variable matters of context, including both external and internal cultures. His positivism may make Wilson smile, because there is an element of biological determinism in it. The positivist organization thrives through the process of adaptation, in the same way every successful species thrives. "There is extrapolation from successes in the past. The learning is within the organization rather than depending on comparison with radically different organizations somewhere else" (Donaldson, 1996, 170). How, then, would he explain organizations that perpetuate mistakes and still survive? If Donaldson intends his idea to be a strictly normative one (that is, a theory of how organizations *should* operate, not just a study of how they *do* operate), then he falls into the trap of defining factors solely in terms that fit his theory. The culture in which the organization works is irrelevant, but the positivist organization adapts itself according to a determinist imperative based on materialist elements. This amounts to facile side-stepping of important contextual issues. It also amounts to his theory constituting the error he sees other theories succumbing to—ideology: "The influence of ideologies shows the way that ideas have their effect. Ideas affect other ideas. A believer in an ideology consciously or unconsciously seeks out ideas that buttress that ideology" (Donaldson, 1996, 164). This statement demonstrates a simplistic notion of ideology. More than anything, Donaldson's idea is reductionist; he takes the complexity of the organization and the environment in which it works, and then tries to make it fit into a body of laws that are ultimately devoid of meaning.

NOT idealist *idealist*

Constructivism

It may seem to some that the examples offered here are criticized from a leftist perspective. Earlier I did admit to an affinity for the political left, and it's true that some of what has been discussed (*The Bell Curve* most prominently) takes on a right-leaning political agenda. However, the substance of the discussion here is grounded in the premise and methods put forth by their proponents—and they are found wanting. The last example is taken from a body of thought that is fundamentally different, on the face of it, from the examples discussed previously. Throughout this century an educational theory has gained currency, and its foremost champion, Jean Piaget, has gained fame. Constructivism is not universally accepted in education, but many agree with its central theme. I'll focus on one articulation, Ernst von Glasersfeld's *Radical Constructivism*. Right off the bat von Glasersfeld denies that the constructivist stance constitutes solipsism (the easily refutable view that the only thing that exists is own's one mind and thought), but his premises suggest a substantially solipsistic tendency. He says constructivism "starts from the assumption that knowledge, no matter how it is defined, is in the heads of persons, and that the thinking subject has no alternative but to construct what he or she knows on the basis of his or her own experience" (von Glasersfeld, 1995, 1). At the outset this position is on shaky ground, and von Glasersfeld does little to firm it up.

He offers what may be taken as a first principle: "Radical constructivism is uninhibitedly instrumentalist. It replaces the *Glasersfeld's* notion of 'truth' (as true representation of an independent reality) with the notion of 'viability' within the subjects' experiential world. Consequently it refuses all metaphysical commitments and claims to be no more than one possible model of thinking about the only world we can come to know, the world we construct as living subjects" (von Glasersfeld, 1995, 22). The problem here is the one we saw in the last chapter in the section on realism and relativism. As was shown, both positions, as extremes, are untenable. Von Glasersfeld's position is that of the extreme relativist. He uses, at one point, what he sees as the incommensurability of translation as support for constructivism. The absolute stance is flawed, though; if the only thing that exists is an individual's experience, then how is communication possible at all? If the answer is that there is something that subjects experience together, what is that something? He maintains that this position rejects metaphysics, but if there is a reality that can be shared and can be experienced by many, then the rejection of metaphysics doesn't work. He says, "Constructivism, as I explained earlier, has nothing to say about what may or may not *exist* [emphasis in original]. It is intended as a theory of knowing, not as a theory of being" and "knowledge does not constitute a 'picture' of the world. It does not represent the world at all—it comprises action schemes, concepts, and thoughts, and it distinguishes the ones that are considered advantageous from those that are not" (von Glasersfeld, 1995, 113-14). On the first point, this seems to be a neopragmatist rejection of epistemology (à la Richard Rorty, whom we'll talk about in the next chapter). That view is reinforced by the second point; this isn't a theory of knowing, but of doing. Also, according to the second point, it seems there is an affinity for rational choice theory, a notion supported by a later statement: "Empirical facts, from the constructivist perspective, are constructs based on regularities in a subject's experience. They are viable if they maintain their usefulness and serve their purposes in the pursuit of goals" (von Glasersfeld, 1995, 128).

The poverty of extreme constructivism is obvious; if it were to hold, then there would be no such thing as "misunderstanding." Every understanding, in the context of the individual cognizer, is valid. Further, *nothing* that is taught need be accepted, since what is taught is nothing more than the construct of the speaker. This stance is reductionist (in the sense we've seen previously) in that all can be reduced to the experience of the individual and nothing else matters. Again, the connection between extreme relativism and scientism is clear. As we've already discussed, some element of relativism, especially as it is manifest through discourse, exists. But some element of ontological reality also exists. The mediated stance is the only way to go. The extreme (in either direction) collapses under its own weight, as is the case with radical constructivism.

Examples from LIS

Acceptance of Scientism

The kinds of problems that can occur in the social sciences, such as those just mentioned, may also crop up in LIS. Commentators in our field have most often criticized method and application of method. Others, including Michael Harris, have found cause for concern with regard to the conceptual basis of inquiry and practice. Some have disagreed, at least in part, with Harris on the grounds that positivism prevails. For instance, Nancy Van House writes, "the positivist method remains the most widely accepted in the social sciences and LIS. The issue addressed here is not whether the positivist method is appropriate, but whether LIS researchers who have adopted it are using it capably and appropriately" (Van House, 1991, 87). This statement misses the point made by Harris and, I hope, by me. The broadly scientistic tradition that is imbedded in our past is not simply one of a number of legitimate approaches to inquiry. It is a failed, albeit mostly well-intentioned, program that has fatal conceptual flaws. The flaws obscure the kinds of questions that need to be addressed, the means for addressing questions effectively, and the practice that benefits from inquiry.

The kind of confusion that has seemed to plague LIS is also evident in Van House's thought. She says that two basic criteria can be used to assess the quality of research: "One has to do with the conduct of research: Its underlying logic and methodology, and the validity and robustness of its conclusions. The other has to do with the topic of the research: Does it address questions that are useful, interesting, or important?" She then adds, "Research cannot be of good quality in the second sense and not the first" (Van House, 1991, 90). Her reasoning is that if results are not valid, then the question asked is irrelevant. She conflates question and method in a manner that may tend to dismiss the importance of the question asked. The identification of questions or issues that should be addressed is essential and, to an extent, is a matter separate from method. That is, inquiry should begin with the conceptual issue before there is thought given to the method that might be applied. The discourse evident in the genealogy examined here is replete with essential questions. However, as we've seen, there are problems with subsequent conceptual contextualization of the questions (they are usually couched in terms that fit with scientism) and with approaches to answers to the questions (seeking answers on the basis of purely materialist and determinist assumptions).

Economics and Information

Most of the examples that follow do ask important questions. Difficulties arise with regard to the assumptions that are made and applications of method (though not necessarily the method itself). There has been something of an increase in recent years of applying economic methods to LIS problems and concerns. This effort should be applauded; despite the previous examples of Becker and Fogel and Engerman, economic analysis has the capability of enhancing our understanding. On the other hand, those instances dealt with above indicate that the method must be applied with caution (a warning that applies to all methods). In LIS, Bruce Kingma has written widely on the efficacy of economic analysis. Early in his book, *The Economics of Information*, he approvingly cites Becker. He writes, "The cornerstone of economic models of human behavior is the assumption that individuals behave rationally in ways they believe give them the most net benefit" (Kingma, 1996, 10). The illustrations used by Kingma in his book are based mainly on assumptions, especially assumptions of linearity. For instance, the quantity of books sold declines in a linear fashion relative to increases in price. Further, benefits exhibit the same linear pattern.

One of the most problematic elements of Kingma's book, which is intended to be something of a primer for information professionals, is the seeming equation of the economic aspects of libraries and information with consumer goods, such as used cars. The equation leads to some statements about benefit, such as, "Because the actual consumers of the good or service do not receive . . . external benefits, they are not expressed in the consumer's demand or willingness to pay for the good or service" (Kingma, 1996, 65-66). This statement is probably accurate for most consumer goods; does that mean it's accurate with regard to libraries and information? It may be descriptive of the attitudes of some, but others may see public good in individual action. Later Kingma states, "Books sold at a bookstore, newspapers sold on the street corner, computer software for individual use, individual journal subscriptions, and individual phone service are all examples of information goods or services as commodities" (Kingma, 1996, 114). These definitely are commodities and are part of a commodity market, but that doesn't mean they can't also function as public goods. Teachers purchase packages of information, but then use those items to disseminate information, to facilitate learning. I belong to some professional associations in large part for the personal benefits that accrue to me, but also because I receive journal subscriptions along with the membership. I can use the contents of those journals in courses I teach, and I can incorporate the contents into my own inquiry that may be communicated widely. Perhaps more importantly, books, journals, etc. may be inherently different from many commodities in that they may convey meaning to those who use them. That meaning might affect behavior in a public sense by having an impact on voting patterns, altruistic behavior, and other public manifestations of action. We must be careful not to reduce information to nothing more than a commodity; while the package may be bought and sold, information is more than just the package. We should heed the words of Georg Lukacs:

> The commodity can only be understood in its undistorted essence when it becomes the universal category of society as a whole. Only in this context does the reification produced by commodity relations assume decisive importance both for the objective evolution of society and for the stance adopted by men towards it. Only then does the commodity become crucial for the subjugation of men's consciousness to the forms in which this reification finds expression and for their attempts to comprehend the process or to rebel against its disastrous effects and liberate themselves from servitude to the "second nature" created. (Lukacs, 1971, 86)

Lukacs is warning against the reduction of things that may be complex in themselves and in their use to nothing more than the commodity.

At one point Kingma, in a discussion of fines for overdue library materials, mentions that prices can serve to finance the production of a thing. The implicit link is that fines can operate in the same way that prices do. In some organizations, such as corporate libraries, the link may be evident. In other libraries the analogy between fees/fines and movie tickets doesn't hold. In public organizations, for instance, the good is paid for by public funds, such as tax levies. Fines are particularly problematic because their primary purpose is to affect behavior, viz., the return of overdue materials. Kingma claims that fines prevent or lessen the incidence of overdue materials. Other evidence suggests that fines are not much of an incentive to return materials. Joy Greiner reports the experiences of several libraries, including one that eliminated fines, but blocked the borrowing of items until overdue items were returned. That library saw an increase in the return of items (Greiner, 1990). It seems that there may be a dynamic at work that is substantially different from typical retail transactions.

In another publication Kingma, with Gillian McCombs, turns attention to the opportunity costs of faculty status. The specific object of study is a group of catalogers in an academic library.

Some questions arise as they begin to define the study. For one thing, they state that there are also real costs of faculty status, such as travel expenses to attend conferences and resources to engage in some kinds of inquiry. The authors admit that some of these costs may be incurred by libraries without faculty status, but imply that the costs are greater for the libraries with faculty status. The question of whether one group of libraries incurs higher costs could itself be subjected to empirical inquiry, but the assumption is not substantiated. In the example the authors give, the work of four catalogers is detailed. One is on sabbatical and, of the remaining three librarians, a total of sixteen hours a week is spent in professional development. The authors calculate the cost in lost productivity and in replacement of the lost time: "If replacement catalogers are paid $15 per hour (or $525 per week), then faculty status results in a real cost to the library of $765 per week" (Kingma and McCombs, 1995, 259).

They also calculate an opportunity cost of $1,000 to the university community if replacements are not hired and some items do not get cataloged. They assume a productivity rate of four books cataloged per hour. The professional development of the three librarians, plus the one on sabbatical, results in 204 books not cataloged in a given week. Their implication is that the costs of faculty status may outweigh the benefits. A closer look at some underlying assumptions is called for. First, the example includes the anomaly of a librarian on sabbatical. If sabbaticals are not common, then this assumption inflates costs. Also, a constant and uniform rate of productivity is assumed (four books cataloged per hour). Many in libraries may question this level of output; it is not (apparently) based on empirical evidence, so the costs could be further inflated. And it assumed that professional development carries no benefit that might affect productivity. The unstated assumption is that a cataloger can work at nothing but cataloging for thirty-five hours a week and retain a constant level of productivity. Finally, the authors assume that each uncataloged book would be in demand immediately. All of the assumptions inflate costs, and some run counter to evidence (for instance, there is research that shows that some books acquired by libraries never circulate). The questions raised here are not intended to suggest that there are no costs to faculty status, but that the estimates provided by Kingma and McCombs are suspect, given the dubious nature of their assumptions.

Deterministic Management

Kingma is not alone in applying economic analysis to LIS questions. Malcolm Getz has examined some library management issues in economic terms. Regarding the potential impact of economic analysis he has stated, "The criterion for success is whether a change in library operation has increased the value of library services to the people who pay for them, net of the costs they incur. . . . The act of decision then requires that the decision maker assign a dollar value to the change in use or outcomes" (Getz, 1990, 192). A not inconsequential difficulty in such analysis is the assigning of a dollar value for certain actions. For instance, what is the cost to a person to search for an item in the library? There is no doubt that if a library can facilitate searching (such as implementing a system that offers more options in structuring a search), then the user may become more efficient at the task. However, what is required to make all users more efficient may be a number of actions, each aimed at a particular segment of the community. When a library chooses to facilitate use by one segment rather than another, the library is placing a higher value on one group. This may occur frequently in libraries, but the outcomes of decisions are social and political as well as financial; a purely economic analysis may fail to apprehend non-economic outcomes. Even in economic terms, value is an elusive variable. For one individual, the use of information sources or a library may have varying value. If a person goes to a public library to find a specific mystery novel, that person may place one value on the action. If the same person consults sources in advance of purchasing an automobile, the individual may place a different value on that search. As we saw with Kingma, library use may have benefits beyond the individual. How is that to be calculated?

Getz assumes that it is possible to estimate the probability of search success or failure, but he doesn't detail a means to reach such an estimate. These criticisms of economic analysis are not meant to denigrate the method, but to show the challenges in applying it well. Getz and Kingma tend to reduce their analysis to exchange value—what the action is worth in a commodity market. Exchange value in itself is very difficult to estimate in information transactions; use value is even more difficult to estimate, and it is all too frequently ignored. This view differs from others we've seen in that it is, in some important ways, a denial of materialism. Specifically, it eschews the material in favor of the symbolic. David Hawkes says, "In consumer societies of the late twentieth century, exchange-value (a purely symbolic form) has become more real, more objective, than use-value (a material phenomenon). Objects are conceived, designed and produced for the purpose of making money by selling them, rather than by practical utility" (Hawkes, 1996, 169). The view is reductionist, but the reduction is to the symbolic, rather than to the physical.

Conceptions of Customer

With the above examples it is not the quantitative aspect that is questioned; it is the conceptual aspect. This questioning seems to be consistently applicable. At times, perhaps, the attractiveness of quantification may affect the basic conception of a question and its possible solutions. In her book on customer service (itself a questionable concept in LIS; see Budd, 1997, 310-21), Darlene Weingand asks, "How can the library create and maintain *excellence* in a *changing environment* where responding to *customer needs* and focusing on *customer satisfaction* determines *survival* and *prosperity*?" [emphasis in original] (Weingand, 1997, 8). The question does have some validity, even in the face of some problematic elements. She goes further, though, and says that this challenge can be expressed as an equation (Weingand, 1997, 8):

Equation Denoting Factors Determining Survival (S) and Prosperity (P)

$$\frac{E \times X^{CE}}{CN + CS} = S + P$$

Nowhere are these variables defined in such a way that they can be conceptualized in ways that allow such a formulation. The equation, then, is meaningless. This view of libraries and customer service is fundamentally reductionist; the collections and services of a library mean only what can be expressed as instrumental satisfaction, which may mean nothing more than surface gratification. According to Weingand, the idea of information and libraries as public goods should be abandoned in favor of operation in a market economy. This reduces one organizational type to another without considering all implications of the change.

Deterministic Evaluation

The importance of a sound idea cannot be overstated. We've seen some criteria of assessment, but to sum up, the soundness of an idea should be judged according to logic (the proposition should be reasonable, internally consistent, and in concert with external constraints), completeness (the idea should encompass all necessary components and not simply defer to unsubstantiated assumptions), and clarity (all aspects of the idea should be clearly defined). These may not be the only applicable criteria, but they can provide benchmarks to assess any concept that is suggested in LIS (or the social sciences, or any discipline). Further, these criteria apply both to inquiry and to practice. In some instances in our literature, as we've seen, it is evident that there are some conceptual problems. In addition to those already discussed, other examples can be noted. In *Measuring Academic Library*

Performance, Nancy Van House, Beth Weil, and Charles McClure
intend to provide academic librarians with a model for evaluation
of services and operations. Such a purpose is necessary to the
advancement of LIS. This manual, however, falls short according
to some of the above criteria, especially completeness and clarity,
which are closely related. Early on, the authors try to tackle the
thorny matter of effectiveness since, after all, every library should
strive to be effective. The authors write, "Effectiveness has been
defined in many ways, including goal attainment, success in
acquiring needed resources, satisfaction of key constituent groups'
preferences, and internal health of the organization. This manual
defines an effective library as one that achieves its goals" (Van
House, Weil, and McClure, 1990, 12).

This provides no help in analyzing the internal and external
factors that influence effectiveness; rather, it glosses over this
essential element. In *The Public Library Effectiveness Study* Nancy
Van House and Thomas Childers also address the matter of
effectiveness (naturally), acknowledging its complexity and noting
four approaches to defining it. Unfortunately, these approaches
are no clearer; for instance, the goal model echoes *Measuring
Academic Library Performance*: "Effectiveness is measured by goal
achievement" (Van House and Childers, 1993, 1). Van House
and Childers, though, do attempt to arrive at a set of indicators
of effectiveness. One potential dilemma is that librarians, in
seeking to assess the effectiveness of their libraries, will treat the
indicators as a deterministic set of criteria, the absence of any of
which may signal lack of effectiveness.

Measuring Academic Library Performance contains other problematic passages. The authors state, "The outcome of the
reference transaction has three components: relevance of the
information provided, satisfaction with the amount of information provided, and the completeness of the answer received" (Van
House, Weil, and McClure, 1990, 96). At various points the
authors emphasize that some measures, for instance most user-
centered approaches to evaluation, are time intensive and so of
questionable worth. The concept of "relevance," however, is one
of the most charged, not only in LIS, but in communication and
philosophy as well. The authors rely here, and throughout the

manual, on a purely instrumental means of measurement. Such things as relevance and satisfaction are not defined; questions are to be asked of users whether they are satisfied and whether information and services are relevant. One of the difficulties of the instrumentalism of the manual is the inherent political position that is hidden behind the ostensible conceptual one. If "satisfaction" is defined by the responses by users to a simple question or set of questions, then, explicitly, the library's strategy should be to maximize expressed satisfaction. Such a goal should be scrutinized carefully according to the criteria noted above. The dicey goal of satisfaction may open libraries to the critique offered by Jean-Francois Lyotard, who said, "The question (overt or implied) now asked . . . is no longer 'Is it true?' but 'What use is it?' In the context of the mercantilization of knowledge, more often than not this question is equivalent to: 'Is it salable?' And in the context of power-growth: 'Is it efficient?'"(Lyotard, 1984, 51)

Others appear to be on the same page as the authors of the manual. Peter Hernon and Ellen Altman codify an instrumental approach to what they refer to as customer service in academic libraries. They advocate that librarians assess contributions to the institution's mission by creating a checklist that includes such items as:

> The percentage of courses using the reserve reading room; . . .
> The percentage of courses requiring term papers based on materials from the library;
> The number of students involved in those courses;
> The percentage of students who checked out library materials;
> The percentage of faculty who checked out library materials;
> The percentage of courses using reading packets based on materials photocopied from the library's collection. (Hernon and Altman, 1996, 1-2)

Of course these are data that any library might find useful, but they are not in themselves pertinent to an academic mission. The suggestions of Hernon and Altman share the focus on outputs that Van House, Weil, and McClure provide. In *Measuring Academic Library Performance* a repeated theme is the measurement of "use," but use is also defined only in instrumental terms—items circulated, items requested via interlibrary loan, items removed from shelves. There is no mention of outcomes—what differences do these resources make to the user? That is the kind of hard question the authors of the manual dismiss at the outset. These instrumental focal points illustrate an affinity for some elements of the genealogy. Specifically, they tend to be physicalist (actions that are taken by the library or by users), deterministic (the services and the structure of the library will lead to certain kinds of use by certain segments of the community), and are exemplary of the kind of discursive practice observed by Foucault (aimed at exclusion and power, and also descriptive of a fundamentally capitalist superstructure).

Another problem with the above examples is that they appear to be normative, but are not. Now this may sound like academic-speak, but it is a statement of a very important aspect of the thought and practice of any discipline. The examples purport to have established guidelines for action in libraries. I'm not quibbling with that goal; as I said earlier, it is an essential purpose. The guidelines, though, are reactive; they depend on first finding out what will serve an immediate and instrumental end, and then adjusting policy and action to foster that end. This is probably most evident, as has already been noted, with regard to user satisfaction. The dictum is to ask what leads to satisfaction and then to do more of that. The outcome that is achieved is a higher level of expressed satisfaction with some particular things by a set of people who are already positioned to respond to the question. Of course there are reasons, political among them, to enhance the good will of some segments of the library's community; if this becomes the driving force in policy and action, however, then there is no substantive foundation for the library.

Corporatizing the Library

Perhaps the extreme articulation of instrumentalism appeared recently in the pages of *American Libraries*. Steve Coffman suggests, without a hint of irony, that public libraries be run like bookstores (Coffman, 1998, 40-46). He says that superstores contain more titles and a more inviting ambience than most libraries. Also, bookstores have lower staff costs than libraries. This may be true, but it is true because the bookstore and the library are fundamentally different entities. The money to finance the construction and operation of a bookstore comes from the corporation, which finances itself through, primarily, sales and equity capitalization. The library doesn't have this opportunity to draw from a source of capital. The bookstore, Coffman says, features services that used to be the province of libraries, such as book talks and author signings. Most of these events are held with a particular end in mind—the sale of merchandise. It may be that an author appears at a bookstore through the support of the publisher, who foots the bill in anticipation of increased sales. Some things are not mentioned by Coffman: (1) bookstore chains tend not to build outlets in small towns; (2) the chains tend to build stores in certain parts of cities, and other areas are ignored by the corporation (but not necessarily by the library); (3) bookstores do not offer the range of services that libraries do; and (4) bookstores stock items with sales potential, and if the sales don't materialize, the stock disappears. The most basic difference between bookstores and libraries is the simplest—bookstores exist to sell; libraries exist to serve the community.

Again, what appears to be normative is actually what Lyotard calls "performative" (Lyotard, 1984). What is important is the performance of a system (like a bookstore or a library), and that performance is self-determined. This means that, for instance, the bookstore itself decides what is essential to effective or improved performance. If the bookstore establishes profit as the principal measure of performance, then the actions that are taken to optimize performance are, themselves, irrelevant except insofar as they affect performance. If a bookstore tries to reach out to, say, disadvantaged children, it does so as a means of improving performance, not necessarily because of altruism. On the other hand, a library reaching out to disadvantaged children tends to do so because that is essential to its purpose. While Coffman's suggestion is an extreme case, the previous examples are also expressions of performativity. I do believe that we should be seeking a normative basis for inquiry and practice, and in the next chapter I will explore what that might be.

Problematic Quantitative Analysis

Some other examples in the LIS literature show shortcomings with regard to the three criteria of judgment. Clarity is one of the criteria that may not be met. For instance, Robert V. Williams presents an analysis of data on libraries from 1850, 1860, and 1870 census records (Williams, 1986, 177-201). He presents some of this analysis in tables. The first table includes data from each census. While it is inadequately labeled, the table presents mean numbers of public, school, college, and Sunday school and church libraries. For example, there was an average of 402.23 school libraries per state in 1850. The standard deviation, though, was 1,969.48, indicating a very wide range (but the range is not reported). Further, no median data are reported. Similar patterns are indicated for other data on libraries (such as number of volumes), other types of libraries, and other years. These descriptive data are not particularly illuminating, since only selected measures of central tendency are reported. Williams then executes correlation and regression tests on the library data along with a set of social indicators, focusing on economics, education, and other factors. There appears to be nothing wrong with the statistical tests, but all of the variables are problematic to varying degrees. The data may vary in reliability and the relationships are probably very complex. The applied statistical tests are not sufficient to help us understand the complexity. In short, it is not clear what is being examined and what the results tell us.

Another example illustrates a technically competent, but conceptually unclear, application of quantitative analysis. Syed Saad Andaleeb and Patience Simmonds purport to explain user satisfaction with academic libraries (Andaleeb and Simmonds, 1998, 156-67). They formulate five hypotheses about satisfaction and, in expressing the hypotheses, muddy the picture a bit. The hypotheses are not so much relationships between variables as tautologies. The first is, "The higher the perceived quality of the library's resources, the greater the level of user satisfaction"

(Andaleeb and Simmonds, 1998, 158). The subsequent hypotheses deal with staff responsiveness, staff competence, staff demeanor, and the library's appearance. If these factors are accepted as determining satisfaction, then when they are highly regarded, satisfaction will be high. This doesn't allow for other potential factors influencing satisfaction. The results of the study are a bit unclear; there seems to be a disconnect between the descriptive results and the inferences. Assessment is difficult because the questions asked are not provided. Also, there are problems with sample size and questionnaire distribution. Ultimately, the authors find that the five independent variables explain 64 percent of the variation in the dependent variable of satisfaction. Given the tautology, the results are not surprising. One thing that is unclear is what might be responsible for 36 percent of the variation in satisfaction. The authors don't speculate on this matter. They then urge librarians to manage libraries to maximize the five variables and, so, maximize satisfaction. The problems with this notion—its instrumentalism and its performativity—have already been discussed.

Some conceptual problems plague information science as well as librarianship. For decades researchers have pondered what has been termed bibliometric "laws." The very notion that there are laws that govern communication is scientistic to the core. In physics, for example, it is recognized (although it is still a challenging and challenged idea) that some physical phenomena are the way they are *because* of a set of constraining or even determining forces. The statement of a bibliometric law such as Lotka's Law would require that a set of forces constrain or determine patterns of author productivity. There are two concerns with Lotka's Law (that apply in some form to other bibliometric laws as well): (1) there is no absolute, or nearly absolute, statistical regularity of author productivity, and (2) the law doesn't state *why* patterns of author productivity are the way they are. Moreover, the bibliometric laws may provide interesting evidence of tendencies in populations of information items, authors, etc., but they provide no help in predicting or explaining the behavior of any individual case in the population. Bradford's law may help us comprehend some gross patterns of scatter ex post facto, but it doesn't help us predict, for instance, the use patterns of a particular journal in a particular setting. In 1981 a *Library Trends* issue was devoted to bibliometrics. A recurrent theme in the articles was that more time and effort might yield a clearer link between empirical data and theory. In other words, some place faith in the inherent power of a law and think bibliometric laws might someday be as powerful as physical laws. The link between this belief and the thought of Comte (and others) is evident. In content and discourse, thinking about bibliometrics is connected to elements of the genealogy.

Some work in information has focused on particular ways to analyze and assess information retrieval. Again, this is a necessary task. One of the focal points, measurement of precision and recall, has proved problematic as has been recognized by Michael Buckland and Frederic Gey (Buckland and Gey, 1994, 12-19), among others. Still, some adhere to precision (defined as the number of relevant items retrieved divided by the number of items retrieved) and recall (defined as the number of relevant items retrieved divided by the total number of relevant items in the database). Both measures depend on the assessment of relevance, which is not fixed either temporally or spatially. Also, the measures mean little unless they are examined completely. For instance, if a search retrieves only one item, and that item is somehow determined to be relevant, then the precision measure is 1, or perfect precision. While the search may be precise, it may be largely useless to a user who is seeking to retrieve a body of relevant information. Louise Su (Su, 1994, 207-17) tried to study the efficacy of the measures of information retrieval. She claimed that precision is an easy measure to apply, but it is easy only insofar as the user designates a particular item as relevant, which is a complex and problematic process. Her claim for the ease of measuring precision is deterministic and dependent on the assignment of points on a scale. She examined mediated searches for forty users and then asked a set of questions about the retrieved information. One of her findings was that users rated precision lower than satisfaction with the precision of the search, on a seven-point Likert scale. It is not clear what the difference between these two categories might be and how they might be differently designated. The complexity of relevance is ignored, and Su concludes, "Precision is not a good indicator of success although it may be the most widely used or easily applied measure" (Su, 1994, 217). This conclusion is not warranted by this study, given the ambiguity of the assessment mechanism and the difficulty of making absolute statements about relevance.

Through the above examples I hope to have shown that the most basic challenges we face are conceptual ones. There is no favored method, necessarily, and no inappropriate method, necessarily. Not all in LIS seem to agree with that assessment. Charles Davis issued a plea for the use of quantitative methods, claiming superiority for them. He writes, "The best hypotheses are general and quantifiable" (Davis, 1990, 328). This is a kind of tautology, since hypotheses are usually testable in some way. Davis does urge researchers to become competent in multiple methods, but he also implies that there is a political cost to choosing qualitative over quantitative methods: "If qualitative research becomes the norm, a soft field will look even softer. Library schools will be thought inferior to other academic units, and they will seem increasingly expendable" (Davis, 1990, 328). Again, the Foucauldian genealogy helps us understand Davis's statements. They are assertions of power and exclusion, and seek to institutionalize that power in formal educational settings. What is missing from his plea is a conceptual foundation for the selection of an appropriate method.

This and the preceding three chapters have presented a detailed critical background and assessment of the current state of work in the social sciences and LIS. All this matter sets the stage for the next part of the challenge I set for myself in this book—search for a normative foundation for thought and practice that can apply not only to LIS, but to the social sciences generally. The search begins with the next chapter, which is an examination of ideas, primarily from philosophy, that can help us conceive of purpose and product of inquiry and action.

Chapter Five

Knowledge and Knowing in LIS

The social sciences, including LIS, claim to be about knowing something about human beings and human behavior. In LIS there has been frequent mention of refocusing on knowledge management, and even renaming professionals knowledge specialists. However, there has been precious little discussion about what knowledge management is, or even what constitutes knowledge. Can we afford, conceptually and practically, to ignore these issues? If we do ignore them, what is the cost?

This journey centers on that one particular philosophical idea (some might call it a dilemma)—knowledge. Several questions have been asked over the centuries regarding the theory of knowledge: Is knowledge possible? What constitutes knowledge? How do we know that we know? It would be impossible to address all questions regarding knowledge here, but we must delve into the fundamental issues relating to knowledge since this book is built on the premise that we can know something about the human elements of libraries and information. Moreover, this book is an argument in favor of our profession thinking seriously about what constitutes knowledge in LIS. Charles Davis, in suggesting what future research in LIS should focus on, says that, while some may ponder epistemological questions, the field will progress if we get down to the business of research (Anon., Editorial, 1997, 210). I maintain that attempting to conduct inquiry in LIS is meaningless if we haven't asked those epistemological questions. How else would we know what the business of research is, and how would we be able to evaluate the results of research. In this chapter we'll explore what epistemology is and why it's so important to us. In this respect LIS is no different from all other serious disciplines. We take the same generic approach as all other fields. Following Jacques Maritain, all disciplines, all "sciences," seek answers to two basic questions: "first, the question, AN EST—whether the things exists; and then the question QUID EST—what is its nature" (Maritain, 1995, 57). His simple statement provides us with a fundamental goal. In order to accomplish this goal, we'll have to answer those who claim that knowledge is not possible and that epistemology is an empty exercise.

This is not mainly a textbook on epistemology (which is an extremely large subject), so there's no need to seek answers to *all* of the questions relating to the theory of knowledge. There are, however, some very important points to cover before we explore knowledge in LIS. The first point is that we are talking about theories of knowledge. What that means is that we are examining sets of postulates that can be tested, either empirically or logically, to see if they hold. A major challenge for us rests on the recognition that knowledge is so complex, so imbedded in our assumptions, that it is extremely difficult to analyze fully a phenomenon that is such a part of ourselves. We have to ask if we can separate ourselves from the idea of knowledge to a sufficient extent that we can, ultimately, know something about knowledge. Why am I bringing up such a seemingly esoteric question? If we are to comprehend fully why someone bothers to formulate a query, why people seek "information," then we have to understand what it is we can know about the process of structuring a query aimed at finding a meaningful answer, and about the process of responding to the query. In other words, it is knowledge that defines the activities that take place in libraries and other, similar, environments. As Keith Lehrer says, "It is information that we recognize to be genuine that yields the characteristically human sort of knowledge that distinguishes us as adult cognizers from machines, other animals, and even our childhood selves" (Lehrer, 1990, 4).

All this may seem so specialized as to be useless to us in LIS. On the contrary (and to reinforce the statement above), we in LIS *must* be concerned with knowledge, both in the critical examination of our profession and in the daily workings of those who ask questions, seek information, and read. The pervasiveness of the place of knowledge in our work leads me to agree with Alvin Goldman, who, while stressing that epistemology deals with intellectual activities, says, "I mean the whole range of efforts to know and understand the world, including the unrefined, workaday practices of the layman as well as the refined, specialized methods of the scientist or scholar" (Goldman, 1986, 13). If we heed his words we quickly apprehend how the processes of organization of information, designing retrieval systems, and mediation between the user and the record are grounded in knowledge. I should also hasten to add that my view of epistemology, in keeping with the views of a number of prominent philosophers, is that the most effective idea of human knowledge is that it is fallible. That is, our beliefs are based in the best justification, or the closest approach to truth, that we can muster, given our own imperfect cognitive apparatus. Some might say that this stance is not related to knowledge. For example, Jonathan Kvanvig, after defining knowledge as a perfectible ideal, claims that epistemology is not necessary to study cognition (Kvanvig, 1998). I would hold that such a position is based on a straw man, an unrealistic ideal that few thinkers would seriously adhere to. Joseph Owens pleads the case that epistemology, as a study of knowledge, depends on the knowing subject's awareness, through cognition, of the world (and, further, understanding the world in the process of cognitive activity) (Owens, 1992). His case seems compelling. So now the stage is set to examine some core issues of epistemology.

What Constitutes Knowledge?

The traditional approach to epistemology is individualistic; the focus is on the individual knower and how knowledge is possible for the individual. In fact, we could say that we really can't even conceive of knowledge unless we can come to grips with the ability of an individual to make claims of knowledge. As we will see eventually, though, we need not stop there. Regarding the individual, I will draw from some of the foremost epistemologists to describe some fundamentals of knowledge. Perhaps the best place to begin would be to consider what conditions must be realized for us to claim to know something. Jonathan Dancy suggests two essential conditions for knowledge, which can be stated as the following: *S* believes that *p* and if *p* were not true, *S* would not believe *p* (Dancy, 1985, 37). (*S*, in this case is a symbol for any knowing subject, and *p* symbolizes some proposition that we can assess as a knowledge claim.) This gives us a partial beginning and stresses the individualistic element of epistemology. The conditions, in short, are *belief* and *truth*. Before we examine these aspects more closely, let's take a look at Keith Lehrer's expansion of these conditions. Instead of only two, Lehrer proposes four conditions: truth, acceptance, justification, and justification without falsity. The four conditions enable an analysis of knowledge, which he states as: "*S* knows that *p* if and only if (i) it is true that *p*, (ii) *S* accepts that *p* (iii) *S* is completely justified in accepting that *p*, and (iv) *S* is completely justified in accepting *p* in some way that does not depend on any false statement" (Lehrer, 1990, 18). The question might arise why include the fourth item; isn't it subsumed in the third? Suppose we can construct a justificatory argument that points to the acceptance of *p*, but our argument, while accurate and cohesive as far as it goes, omits some contradictory points. The contradictory points would render the argument false. We can think about language used in, for example, political campaigns. A candidate may list points that support a position, but the list is incomplete. We can agree that, because of the omissions, the candidate is not making a justified knowledge claim. The fourth item, then, is an essential one.

We might equate Lehrer's acceptance condition with Dancy's belief condition. Both concepts accomplish a very important goal: the knowing subject must have some awareness, some cognition, of the thing in question, and must acknowledge it to be true. If there is no acceptance (or no belief), there can be nothing we could call knowledge. The correspondence to truth condition, shared by Dancy and Lehrer, is a fundamentally realist position. For something to be true it first has to *be*, and for it to be true, its truth has to be something separate and apart from our apprehension of it. In other words, anyone who believes that knowledge is possible must accept metaphysical realism. For there to be knowledge, there must be knowledge *of* something; there is an ontological being to the world. As was discussed earlier, there can be variations on realism (and problems with realism). The strongest version holds that we can describe reality referentially, that the language we use to speak about something genuinely refers to that thing as it is (independent of our minds). We've already seen the problems of the strong version, but rejection of that version need not involve rejection of realism entirely. Frederick Schmitt indicates how realism can work on a metaphysical level while not being absolutely referential. An automobile, we can agree, exists independently of our minds; the shape and substance of the automobile does not depend on, nor are they created by, our representation of them. However, the design and function of the automobile are human representations; what makes the object an automobile (that is, something that humans can use for transportation) is extraontological—it is more than just its physical structure; it has a function imposed upon it by us. Here is an important difference between the physical (such as an automobile) and what I'll call the textual. Schmitt uses the example of Hamlet. The character Hamlet exists by virtue of being represented in the play *Hamlet*. There is no physical thing Hamlet (it is a character, an object of imagination), although there is a physical thing *Hamlet* (the text) (Schmitt, 1995, 13).

This distinction is not a fine one; it is a difference between physical being and mental being. A thought, an idea, does not have physical substance (if we reject the reductionist neurophilosophical claim that thought is completely reducible to physical events in the brain). I do not mean to suggest that the physical and the mental are absolutely separate and independent; such a claim would be ridiculous. What I do mean is that, while the two are related, there are some fundamental differences in the natures of the physical and the mental. The differences are sufficiently essential that we need to examine different ways to gain knowledge of them. A bit later in this chapter we'll explore the possibility of knowledge of the mental. In fact, that discussion will be most important for us in LIS, because what we deal with most is the mental—texts (in the broad sense), expressions, and queries. If knowledge of the mental is possible, it has to be conceived of somewhat differently from knowledge of the physical. The different conception has implications for the means used to gain knowledge. As should be clear from the exploration of the genealogy, the received tradition in LIS and the social sciences has been to emulate the physical sciences to the point of assuming that the phenomena of the natural sciences and those of the human sciences are identical in nature. This is a mistake. Maritain explains the mistake by saying that "the central error of modern philosophy in the domain of the knowledge of nature has been to give the value of an ontological explanation to the type of mechanist attraction immanent in physico-mathematical knowledge, and to take the latter for a philosophy of nature. It is not a philosophy of nature" (Maritain, 1995, 196). In other words, we have mistakenly taken the methods of the natural sciences, which are necessarily physicalist, to be the sole grounding for knowledge of all phenomena. Knowledge is not reducible to a method, although there are methods that help us to gain knowledge.

Foundationalism

To return to Lehrer, there are challenges pertaining to the element of justification. In the past, justification was frequently based in some form of foundationalism: "some beliefs, basic beliefs, are completely justified in themselves and constitute the foundation for the justification of everything else" (Lehrer, 1990, 39). The major question that arises is: What constitutes a foundational claim? One of the basic tenets of deterministic scientism (especially in its strongest empiricist form) is phenomenalism, the belief that sensory experience is the soundest grounding for knowledge. The aspects of the genealogy that adhere to phenomenalism are, in effect, statements of foundationalism. The assumption underlying phenomenalism is that our sensory experiences are directly received from the world as it is and so provide us with accurate meaning of the external world. Philosophers have offered two convincing objections to phenomenalism: (1) sensory data are not always accurate, so the data we receive are not necessarily indicative of the external world, and (2) sensory data are expressed through language aimed at explaining the sensory data, but there is no way to reduce language to a foundational claim, a claim that does not depend on another claim for justification. Some others have stated that logical reasoning can provide a foundation for beliefs. Such a claim was espoused earlier this century by many logical empiricists (logical positivists), who sought verification through logical analysis. Popper, Quine, and others successfully pointed out the impossibility of this goal. The critiques of foundationalism expose fatal errors in such a line of thinking.

The logical empiricists had to employ a kind of foundationalism for their program of verification to have any chance of succeeding. Sensory observation was important to them, but linguistic analysis was even more important. Building on early writings by Wittgenstein, they took to heart his claim regarding representation (that language, especially naming, is a true representation of what is referred to, of what is named). Wittgenstein writes: "The proposition is a picture of reality, for I know the state of affairs presented by it, if I understand the proposition. And I understand the proposition without its sense having been explained to me. The proposition *shows* its sense. The proposition *shows* how things stand, *if* it is true. And it *says*, that they do so stand" [emphasis in original] (Wittgenstein, 1990, 67). Popper challenged the ends of verification by stating that verification can't be achieved; only falsification (showing a statement to be *un*true) is possible. Quine more directly attacked the means employed by logicial empiricists. Analytical language, or meaning that is independent of particular matters of fact, can't be separated from synthetic language, or meaning that is grounded in fact. The logical empiricists' separation of the two amounts to what Quine calls a "metaphysical article of faith" (Quine, 1980, 37), which demolishes the roots of logical empiricism.

In short, as Dancy argues, "the main objection to classical foundationalism is that there are no infallible beliefs. The fallibilist holds, correctly in my opinion, that we are nowhere entirely immune from the possibility of error" (Dancy, 1985, 58).

The foregoing concentrates on the strongest claims of foundationalism. As we see repeatedly, there are weaker versions that can hold some interest and can have some validity. It is almost certainly the case that dependence on foundational statements for the sole grounding of truth is misguided. But, following Robert Audi, when we formulate beliefs and make claims to knowledge, do we do so by examining sets of related propositions? Audi's "moderate foundationalism" is a recognition that thought, and knowledge that emerges from thought and experience, is in part inferential (that is, we build one proposition from another by inferring from the earlier proposition) and is part noninferential. The noninferential element

> does not imply that such foundational beliefs are, e.g., epistemically certain, or not themselves grounded in something else, such as perceptual experience. Thus, it is left open that, psychologically, the presence of these elements can be explained, and, epistemically, an answer can often be given to the question of what justifies them. What is ruled out is simply that they are justified, inferentially, by other beliefs. (Audi, 1993, 3)

Furthermore, Audi stresses that, in reaching some kind of justification for beliefs, we employ reason and arrive at justification through rational means. Audi's position is that this kind of foundationalism is fallibilist, is always subject to correction. As he writes, "One can insist that what is not precisely true is simply not known. But we could also say that what is approximately true may be an object of approximate knowledge, and that beliefs of such propositions are both fallible and typically held with an openness to their revision in the light of new discoveries. I prefer the latter way of speaking" (Audi, 1998, 255). This is an important point; our knowledge is both contingent (upon methods for seeking and assessing evidence and the evidence available to us) and corrigible (it may be corrected as we develop more effective methods or find more complete evidence).

[handwritten margin note: quote + reflect!]

Coherentism

Even if we are able to accept some moderate foundationalism (*pace* Audi), it seems this stance is not sufficient for justification. What else can serve to justify knowledge? One answer suggested by many is called coherentism. Lehrer is a key proponent of coherence as justification for knowledge. If one's belief is considered consistent—logically, rationally, and (perhaps) experientially—with a body of beliefs, then that first belief is considered coherent, given the existing system of beliefs. One objection to this stance is that the system of beliefs may be internally consistent, but consistently erroneous, so a belief that fits into that system is likewise erroneous, since it may be false. According to Lehrer, this kind of coherence tells only half the tale. Agreement or consistency may help us decide what to accept, but it may not help us determine what is true. What is required is the twofold concept of coherence, just described, so that justification cannot be defeated (Lehrer, 1990, 132-52).

Donald Davidson agrees with Lehrer in that coherence, for him, rests on the veridical nature (or truth-relatedness) of belief. In stressing the relationship to truth, Davidson realizes that truth is not epistemic; it is independent of our (or anyone's) knowledge of it. That said, he also recognizes that truth is not absolutely

[handwritten note at bottom: Coherentism = one's beliefs consistent c̄ a body of beliefs AND there is a relationship to truth (truth relatedness)]

disconnected from belief; it becomes seen *as* truth through someone holding a belief. The complexity of the relationship results in coherence signaling a convergence of meaning, truth, and belief (Davidson, 1990, 135-36). A coherentist stance is also shared by BonJour, who connects coherence to justification. Justification, he says, depends on four stages of argument:

(1) The inferability of that particular belief from other particular beliefs and further relations among particular empirical beliefs.
(2) The coherence of the overall system of empirical beliefs.
(3) The justification of the overall system of empirical beliefs.
(4) The justification of the particular belief in question, by virtue of its membership in the system. (BonJour, 1985, 92)

Coherence also succeeds, according to BonJour, because it embodies a system of belief that holds over the long run, not just for that one moment in time. One difference between Davidson and BonJour is that, for Davidson, coherence is largely externalist; that is, the system of beliefs must not only be internally consistent, but also must cohere with truth (which is not determined by an individual). BonJour's stance is primarily internalist; of principal importance is the relationships among beliefs. BonJour doesn't ignore the external element, but it seems to be less important to him than it is to Davidson.

Coherentism, like foundationalism, may not be sufficient for knowledge. Haack and Goldman point out some shortcomings of coherentism—consistency of belief can't account for a departure from truth, for instance, and the charitable idea that beliefs are generally true can have too many counterexamples. Haack's response is to combine what she sees as the most efficacious elements of foundationalism and coherentism, such as the insight introspection gives us into our own mental workings plus the information that sensory experience gives us about the world around us (Haack, 1993, 213). Haack's position appears to be at least somewhat similar to William Alston's. Alston speaks of the "grounding" for knowledge, which he defines as including experiences and reasons (Alston, 1989, 176). (Alston, however, claims that each grounding may not be necessary for knowledge;

instead he emphasizes reliability, which is of primary importance to Goldman.) According to Goldman, something is reliable "if and only if (1) it is a sort of thing that tends to produce beliefs, and (2) the proportion of true beliefs among the beliefs it produces meets some threshold, or criterion, value. Reliability, then, consists in a tendency to produce a high truth ratio of beliefs" (Goldman, 1986, 26). Reliability has more than one form; there can be causal reliability, which has as its focus the causes for the beliefs we hold, and reliable causes tend to yield consistent beliefs. Also of importance, though, are the processes by which we arrive at beliefs and their reliability with regard to the generation of consistent beliefs and beliefs that are connected to truth (Goldman, 1986, 43-45).

Schmitt more directly addresses these "processes [which] are *relevant* [emphasis in original] in evaluating justified beliefs" (Schmitt, 1992, 140). He takes issue with some of Goldman's ideas (although the difference between him and Goldman are not drastic) and says that reliable processes may be supported by intuition, without the requirement of each individual arriving at a theoretical account of the relevance of processes to justification. This relative freedom does not mean, however, that there is no structure to the evaluation of relevant processes. Assessment is based on some prior constraints that help guide us to the factors that are important to evaluation. Schmitt identifies five such constraints:

(1) The Salience Constraint: (a) Relevant processes are those in terms of which evaluators think and talk; and (b) Ceteris paribus, relevant processes are individuated so as to maximize the accuracy of beliefs about whether subjects exercise reliable relevant processes. . . .
(2) The Folk Process Constraint: Relevant processes are (with extraordinary exceptions . . .) folk processes. . . .
(3) The Intrinsic Similarity Constraint: Ceteris paribus, relevant processes are individuated so as to maximize the intrinsic dissimilarity of the exercises of distinct relevant processes. . . .
(4) The Frequency Similarity Constraint: Ceteris paribus, relevant processes are individuated so as to maximize the similarity of the frequencies of true beliefs assigned stretches of belief belonging to a single process and the dissimilarity of the

frequencies of true beliefs assigned stretches of belief belonging
to distinct processes. . . .
(5) The Utility Constraint: Ceteris paribus, relevant processes
are individuated so as to maximize the utility of evaluating
beliefs, measured in number and proportion of true beliefs.
(Schmitt, 1992, 143-58)

These constraints are generally performed by all of us as we seek
justification for beliefs. Schmitt is attracted to these in particular
(with good reason) because they don't require the imposition of
a "metaprocess," a process governing processes. Instead, the five
constraints are enough for us to satisfy the condition of reliability.

Criteria for Justification

Amidst all the apparent disagreement among these philosophers, we can infer some elements that can help us assess
knowledge. If we agree that justification is essential, we have to
focus our attention on what justification is. Haack says that "The
concept of justification is an evaluative concept, one of a whole
mesh of concepts for the appraisal of a person's epistemic state.
To say that a person is justified in some belief of his, is, in so far
forth, to make a favourable [*sic*] appraisal of his epistemic state.
So the task of explication here calls for a descriptive account of
an evaluative concept" (Haack, 1993, 12). What, then, can
provide us with adequate justification for knowledge? It appears
that the best answer to that question, an answer that satisfies
Haack's evaluative criterion, is a combination of the elements
already discussed. As Audi suggests, we really can't escape some
kind of *foundational assumptions* (not foundations based on logical
analysis, perhaps, but some melding of empirical and rational
foundations that provides us with a starting point both for
cognition and for knowledge). We also need some *coherence* within
our systems of belief to ensure that we are not ignoring unavoid-
able falsifications for our beliefs (remember Lehrer's fourth
condition for knowledge). And the causes for our beliefs, along

with the processes by which we come to believe, must be *reliable indicators of truth*. At this point I have to disagree with Alston. His concept of grounding based in the experiences and reasons that lead to beliefs *is* necessary, but alone it is not sufficient. A combination of all of the above seems to suggest necessary and sufficient conditions for justification and, so, for knowledge.

Justification is not provided accidentally by a single bit of information, although information (in the sense of intentional data that is not knowingly false) is necessary for justification. This idea also implies that not every belief is a justified true belief, even in the fallibilist sense. An example might serve to illustrate this point. Suppose you read in a respectable LIS journal a study that concludes that faculty on college and university campuses prefer to use electronic journals over print journals, and that libraries should cancel print journal subscriptions in favor of electronic access to journal literature. Do you know something about faculty use of journal literature on the basis of this conclusion? The quick answer is no; you would have to evaluate the justificatory power of the claim first. In this case there is not likely to be any foundational belief that will help you with the evaluation. Perhaps you can turn to coherence and reliability. Those elements are not hostile to empiricism, so one means of evaluation is to examine the claim in the context of what you already know (always keeping in mind the fallible nature of our knowledge). Suppose you have examined the question locally, trying to find out from faculty at your institution (a university that emphasizes science and technology) which medium they prefer. Your findings agree with those of the published article. Now do you know something about the matter? Again, it depends on what you're assessing. If the claim you're evaluating regards the preference of faculty at your institution, the study can provide a statement that coheres with the beliefs you hold about the local faculty. The investigation you've done indicates that 80 percent of the faculty express a marked preference for electronic literature. Taking a probabilistic (rather than an absolutist) view of knowledge of such human behavior, you may see your belief as knowledge. There appears to be ample justification. To suppose further, let's say faculty expressions of preference have been accurate in the past. The belief about electronic journals may well be reliable; the belief is not false. But suppose you're evaluating the global claim—faculty everywhere prefer electronic journals. The article reports studying the preferences of faculty at three universities, all with emphases on science and technology. The three universities, at the time the study was conducted, had already canceled a number of print subscriptions and replaced them with electronic access. Now suppose you are affiliated with an institution that focuses on the humanities and social sciences. The findings of the article may not cohere with your system of beliefs. Moreover, the findings may not be reliable: given what you already know, the conclusion, in the global sense, may be false.

The example illustrates that knowledge is not easy to come by; the criteria of justification are not easy to meet. While difficult, however, knowledge is not impossible. Some philosophers do maintain, though, that knowledge, as we've been discussing it, is indeed impossible.

Denial of Epistemology

Perhaps because knowledge is not easy to arrive at, some philosophers assert that there really is no such thing as knowledge. The rationales for the claim are not entirely consistent, although there is something of a unifying thread running through their arguments. To begin, Stephen Stich tells us that we are mistaken to put any stock at all in what he refers to as "folk psychology," the stance that behavior can be explained, at least in part, by beliefs and desires and that explanatory theory can be grounded in such things as beliefs and desires. Stich advocates a principle called psychological autonomy, which suggests that psychological states or properties are part of physical states or properties. This suggestion should sound familiar; a principle of scientism is reduction to the physical. Stich presents some cases that, he claims, demonstrates the weakness of the premise that beliefs can help explain psychological states. His cases involve what can only be seen as deception, though. For instance, he posits that at the present time he believes he lives in the twentieth century (he is writing in 1978) and that strawberry fields are nearby. Then he is frozen, transported to Iceland, and left there for more than a century. Upon his being awakened, he still believes it is the twentieth century and that strawberry fields are nearby. These beliefs are false, so they are not tokens of the same type of beliefs as those he held before he was frozen. His explanation ignores what he *could* have known and, so, could believe when he was unfrozen. The case exemplifies a kind of delusion—that the physical is the only explanation for psychological states, so when the physical changes, psychological states necessarily change, and are independent of the mental (of beliefs or desires) (Stich, 1990, 345-61). In other words, Stich first assumes that psychological states are supervenient upon physical states (that is, the properties of the psychological are determined by the physical). Again, the thinking that underlies Stich's position has been examined critically earlier in this book. The key assumption by Stich is that beliefs are, or must be, grounded only in the physical. If that assumption is not true, then his position is seriously undermined.

Eliminative Materialism

This position (as is frequently the case in philosophy) has a name: eliminative materialism. Paul Churchland provides us with a definition: "the prospect we face is that a detailed neurophysiological conception of ourselves might simply displace our mentalistic self-conception in much the same way that oxidation theory (and modern chemistry generally) simply displaced the older phlogiston theory of matter transformation" (Paul Churchland, 1979, 5). Eliminative materialism indicates that our mentalistic psychological framework is a misleading idea of the causes of behavior. Another stance, reductive materialism, is the reduction of the concepts we hold as part of our "common-sense," or folk, psychology to neuroscience, the explanation of neurological events in physical terms. Or, stated more simply, "Mental states are physical states of the brain. That is, each type of mental state or process is numerically identical with (is one and the very same thing as) some type of physical state or process within the brain or central nervous system (Paul Churchland, 1988, 26). Churchland opts for the eliminative materialist position, as does Patricia Churchland, who asserts that sentential attitudes are irrelevant to any examination of cognitive activity. What that means is that, to the Churchlands, any theory that is based in a language of thought, or internal cognitive states that are identified by sentences, must be found wanting (Patricia Churchland, 1986, 386-99). They see eliminative materialism as having an explanatory advantage. Paul Churchland says,

> there are vastly many more ways of being an explanatorily successful neuroscience while not mirroring the structure of folk psychology, than there are ways of being an explanatorily successful neuroscience while also mirroring the very specific structure of folk psychology. Accordingly, the a priori probability of eliminative materialism is not lower, but substantially higher than that of either of its competitors. One's initial intuitions here are simply mistaken. (Paul Churchland, 1988, 47)

As is the case with Stich, Churchland seems to be reducing not only the event of the mental, but also the content of the mental. People conceive not just the physical elements of existence, such as time (what time of day it is, what year it is, what age we live in) and place (the town we live in, the address of our house, the scene of the garden next door). People also conceive of some contingent elements of existence, such as the willingness to act in a particular way, the defendability of a political stance, the kinds of ideas that connect one thought with another. While eliminativism seems to describe, and maybe even to explain, some simple actions and their rationales, it doesn't (in fact it can't) describe or explain them all. As Jerry Fodor says, for eliminative materialism to hold generally, we would also have to eliminate intentionality (something we'll return to shortly). The neuroscience (or neurophilosophical) position leaves no room for knowledge; the conditions for knowledge that we've addressed here are not sufficiently reducible to neurological states to make sense in that theory. This is a position argued against by Fodor, who states, "Content is constituted externally, by causal relations between mental symbols and the world. Often enough, internalized theories mediate these causal relations" (Fodor, 1994, 98). Of course, in keeping with what the Churchlands claim, the neuroscience explanation is itself determined by physical events in the brain. If that is so, why have not many other brains experienced similar enough events to have arrived at the same sort of eliminative materialism? The answer to that may be the following: the neurophilosophical approach is an extension of the scientistic version of Enlightenment thought that has been subjected to critique in earlier chapters.

Rorty's Pragmatism – denies epistemology "Realism"

A more interesting, but not necessarily more plausible, denial of epistemology is offered by Richard Rorty. Part of the interest of Rorty's thought lies in the seeming tensions between his propositions and his conclusions. In fact, his conclusions do not necessarily follow his propositions and arguments. In keeping with some of his conclusions, he would see nothing wrong with this tension; it is simply the product of a language that is incapable of representation (in the sense Wittgenstein espoused in his early writings) and, perhaps, even expression. For example, in part he is sympathetic to realism; he recognizes that it is reasonable to accept that the world is not our creation, that things exist apart from our mental representations of them. However, he separates the physical reality of the world from truth: "Truth cannot be out there—cannot exist independently of the human mind—because sentences cannot so exist, or be out there. The world is out there, but descriptions of the world are not" (Rorty, 1989, 5). There is no doubt that language presents challenges, but in some areas, such as mathematics, our symbolic codes appear to be referential (the code seems to refer to the world, or at least to properties of the world). I'm not suggesting that mathematics can provide a universal code than can apply to all of human behavior and human thought; language is far too complicated for such a reductionist cop-out. More fundamentally, Rorty assumes that truth and our expressions of what we hold to be true are the same. He denies that our expressions might approximately refer to something that exists independent of our representation.

What Rorty is not sympathetic to is the idea of truth as I've been using it here. To Rorty, true means "what you can defend against all comers" (Rorty, 1979, 308). Further, he translates a person knowing something into a statement about the status of that person's claim among peers (Rorty, 1979, 175). In short, according to Rorty, epistemology has no purpose; the traditional notions of knowledge have no meaning. In particular, individualist epistemology should be forgotten: "we need to turn outward rather than inward, toward the social context of justification rather than to the relations between inner representations" (Rorty, 1979, 210). Without any possibility of even approximate reference there is, of course, no defense against all comers, since a detractor can attack any idea on any grounds. Such a notion borders on anarchism. Throughout his career Rorty has denied being a relativist, but it's difficult to read him in any other way. Peter Munz says that Rorty denies justification and replaces it with a relativism in which claims are accepted because they have the consensus of the community (Munz, 1987, 360). Rorty's relativism, in *Philosophy and the Mirror of Nature*, takes the form of epistemological behaviorism, which entails, "Explaining rationality and epistemic authority by reference to what society lets us say, rather than the latter by the former" (Rorty, 1979, 174). I mention Rorty's challenge to epistemology because, for one thing, it is heeded by a number of philosophers, but also (and this is more important to our purposes in LIS) because on the face of it the dismissal of truth and rationality seems attractive. It appears to offer us in LIS a way to ignore some difficult questions by allowing a substantive denial of anything apart from ourselves. Rorty, in fact, goes so far as to say that "there is nothing deep down inside us except what we have put there ourselves, no criterion that we have not created in the course of creating a practice, no standard of rationality that is not an appeal to such a criterion, no rigorous argumentation that is not obedience to our own conventions" (Rorty, 1982, xlii). I've tried to show how a belief such as the one Rorty expresses can be used as an excuse for some knowledge claims; I'll revisit this notion in the next chapter.

Much more could be said about Rorty's dismissal of epistemology, but let me conclude by pointing out two errors in his thought. C. G. Prado observes that Rorty's attack on a correspondence theory of truth presumes an unlimited imaginative capacity. If there is no objective world that might correspond to our linguistic representations of it, then each of us has to have the capacity to imagine the world, so that we can find the words to speak of it (Prado, 1988). Every person has to have the ability to conceive of the world and (here's the real trick) we somehow reach a general agreement on what to say about the world. Also, as Alvin Goldman notes, Rorty mistakenly (or intentionally) reduces epistemology to infallible foundationalism (Goldman, 1999, 27). We've already seen the problems of foundationalism. I've also suggested that we have to adopt a fallibilist, but corrigible, stance regarding knowledge. To revisit what I said in the introduction, Rorty's version of pragmatism ignores the pragmatic intention and uses of epistemology by distorting what constitutes knowledge and its importance. In summary, Rorty appears to be seeking confirmation of his relativist position, while ignoring much contemporary thought on epistemology. He has not successfully confounded the theory of knowledge.

Rorty is indeed correct, though, in stating that language does present some difficulties for us, that our linguistic representations of the world are not perfect. This does not mean that they are solely our own creation and have nothing to do with the world around us. Instead it presents a particular challenge to us in our search for knowledge—a challenge that is rooted in the epistemic *and* in the social. That's what we'll take up next.

Where Does Information Fit In

Some readers may notice that, so far, I've made little mention of information in connection with theories of knowledge, and the omission is intentional. While the following section does discuss a conception of epistemology that has its origins in LIS, on the

LIS

whole I see information as something that supports, but is separate from, knowledge. There is a bit of historical grounding for my view. More than half a century ago, when Claude Shannon postulated his information theory, information was, at least in some constructs, divorced from knowledge (Shannon went so far as distinguish information from meaning). I'll admit that I think Shannon's information theory, while appropriate in some technical applications, has little import for most of LIS. This is not to say that there is no one in LIS that does connect knowledge and information. Perhaps the most noteworthy writer on the subject is Michael Buckland. In observing that being informed involves a change in beliefs he says that, "In this use of the term, information is an increment in knowledge, and, as such, it shares the characteristics of knowledge" (Buckland, 1991, 41). Unfortunately, Buckland does not expand on this idea.

I don't want to leave anyone with the impression that I see information as inferior to knowledge. To reiterate (and this will become clearer with the discussion of social epistemology), information is integral to knowledge. Aspects of information, such as relevance, organization, and discourse, must be linked in some way to what counts as knowledge and knowing, with how we think about justification. In the last chapter I'll present some of the most effective thought in LIS and hope the relationship between knowledge and information becomes crystal clear.

Social Epistemology—Jesse Shera

At first glance the term "social epistemology" may seem to be a contradiction. As we will see, though, there are social connections to justification and truth. But first a little background. As near as I can tell, the first conception of social epistemology (SE) comes from LIS. Jesse Shera, as early as 1953, was touting SE as the genuine purpose of librarianship. With Margaret Egan he distinguished SE from sociology and defined SE as "the study of those processes by which society *as a whole* [emphasis in original] seeks to achieve a perceptive or understanding relation to the total environment—physical, psychological, and intellectual"

(Egan and Shera, 1952, 132). They then outlined four underlying assumptions of SE:

> 1. That it is possible for the individual to enter into a relationship of "knowing" with respect to his own immediate environment or that part of the entirety of his environment with which he has personal contact.
> 2. That the instruments of communication which mankind has developed enable the individual to come into approximately the same kind of relationship with that of his total environment that is beyond his immediate personal experience but which he is able to comprehend because the symbols of communication relate this vicarious experience to his own immediate experience. In short, one must assume that man can achieve an intellectual synthesis with his environment and that environment, through our present mediums of communication, includes remote and vicarious as well as immediate and direct experience.
> 3. That, by co-ordinating the differing knowledge of many individuals, the society as a whole may transcend the knowledge of the individual.
> 4. That social action, reflecting integrated intellectual action, transcends individual action. (Egan and Shera, 1952, 132-33)

His conception, while putatively distinguished from sociology, evidently seems to have some connection to the sociology of knowledge.

Later Shera attempted to clarify what he meant by SE. He said it should be "a study of the ways in which society as a whole achieves a perceptive relation to its total environment. It should lift the study of intellectual life from that of a scrutiny of the individual to an inquiry into the means by which a society, nation, or culture achieves understanding of the totality of stimuli which act upon it" (Shera, 1972, 112). The last sentence sounds almost behavioristic, although it is doubtful that Shera intended such an interpretation. He also took some care to distinguish knowledge from information, which is an essential epistemological distinction. Despite his care, some conflation is apparent. Knowledge, to Shera, can be recorded and preserved, and the librarian "must also concern himself with the knowledge he communicates and the importance of the knowledge to the individual and to society" (Shera, 1970, 84). At one point he departed dramatically from traditional epistemology and asserted that knowledge "has nothing to do with truth or falsehood. Knowledge may be false knowledge, or it may be true knowledge. It is still knowledge, it is knowable and known" (Shera, 1970, 97). He seems to be confusing belief and knowledge and further magnifies the confusion by borrowing Fritz Machlup's classification of knowledge (Machlup, 1962): practical knowledge, intellectual knowledge, spiritual knowledge, pastime knowledge, and unwanted knowledge. I dare say epistemologists would take issue with this classification, especially with spiritual and unwanted knowledge.

Perhaps the most serious difficulty with Shera's conception of SE is his view of the relationship between knowledge and society. "Social epistemology is almost the reverse [of sociology of knowledge]: it deals with the impact of knowledge upon society—not the influence of society upon knowledge, but the influence of knowledge upon society" (Shera, 1970, 107-8). Perhaps this brief examination is less than fair to Shera. For the most part he was breaking new ground; at the time he wrote about SE, traditional, individualist epistemology ruled the day (and it still is dominant, although, as we'll soon see, there is an important challenge to the dominance). Shera was undoubtedly correct to emphasize the impact of knowledge upon society, even if he did not recognize that society has an impact on knowledge. He was also correct to point out that SE is fundamentally an interdisciplinary project and that LIS can learn from the disciplines that contribute to SE. The strengths of his idea were eventually discovered by some philosophers who today are developing programs based on SE (although they have, for the most part, been unaware of Shera's work).

Shera's SE has gone almost unnoticed in LIS. And when the idea of SE has been mentioned, it has tended to be problematic. Patrick Wilson claimed that his *Second-Hand Knowledge* was a work of social epistemology (Wilson, 1983). What he actually seemed to be asserting, however, was that knowledge is socially constructed and is relative to whatever set of social determinants happen to be present at the time. In fact, he drew most heavily from Rorty's *Philosophy and the Mirror of Nature* for his book. In particular, he took social interaction and social structure to most clearly define what is taken to be knowledge. Wilson earlier stated his position in *Public Knowledge, Private Ignorance.* He wrote,"The historian must construct his story, on the basis of the sources; and this is an act of invention. The reviewer of the state of knowledge is in an analogous position" (Wilson, 1977, 12). Rather than an act of invention, history is an act of interpretation, which should be inclusive in order to be justified. Wilson also departs from Shera's position by openly using the terms "information" and "knowledge" interchangeably throughout the book. Wilson's stance, then, is unabashedly relativistic, which creates a problem for any study of knowledge. While it is undeniable that the flow of information is indeed relative to individual abilities, group attachments, political dynamics, and other social factors, knowledge is normative. This does not mean that knowledge is separate from the social; rather, social elements inevitably contribute to knowledge, in a normative way.

One other writer from LIS who addresses social epistemology, though not in great depth, has been S. D. Neill, in his *Dilemmas in the Study of Information.* Neill expressed some skepticism regarding a seemingly inherent element of Shera's SE—society can know. He adopted a more individualist view of epistemology, but he did see that, beyond individual experience, there is a communicative aspect to knowledge growth. In developing his thought regarding that communicative aspect he drew heavily from Karl Popper, especially Popper's idea of objective knowledge. Popper's World 3, the record of knowledge (including, for instance, books and libraries), presents several problems, as we've seen, insofar as there can be knowledge without a knowing subject. Epistemology, whether individualist or social, is founded on the opposite premise, that there must be a knower for there to be knowledge. As I mentioned above, some contemporary philosophers have found the notion of social epistemology attractive. What do they have to say on the matter?

Social Epistemology—Philosophers

It may surprise readers to hear that social epistemology has not, until quite recently, captured the attention of philosophers. That realization alone should excite us in LIS; it points to the potential of this discipline and the possibilities presented by the study of libraries and information. It should also provide us with a warning, though, that we need to share ideas with inquirers in other disciplines.

A recent posting to a listserv asserted that there is little or nothing worth researching with regard to libraries. Obviously I heartily disagree with such a narrow-minded pronouncement; the author of the message could only be seen as correct if we limit our vision of fruitful inquiry to the simplest tasks that are executed in libraries. If we broaden our vision to the effective organization of information, the information-seeking behavior of users, and the mediation between users and the graphic record, we can readily see the feasibility of inquiry.

Just because philosophers have recently turned to SE does not mean that they have altogether ignored the social, but connections between knowledge and the social are not exactly common. Steve Fuller has written a considerable amount on SE. Perhaps the most notable thing in his writings that should be emphasized here is that the project of epistemology is a normative one. That is, it doesn't merely describe what is, it seeks to discover what should be. (It should be noted that the stance of epistemology as normative is a realist stance. Norms imply something that can exist independent of our representation of it.) In his earlier work he tried to distinguish SE from the sociology of knowledge, pointing especially to the shortcomings in social constructivist thought. These shortcomings uncover the naiveté of constructivists' work, which is founded on the assumption that "an account of knowledge production, as might appear in a book or a journal article, represents how knowledge is *actually* [emphasis in original] produced" (Fuller, 1988, 13).

Fuller, however, is certainly sympathetic to the sociological approach, even if he finds fault with some specific applications (and his sympathy seems to have increased in more recent years). Knowledge, in its social manifestation, is not purely individualist; in fact, for Fuller, knowledge depends not just on individual acceptance, but also on some form of collective acceptance.

> A producer 'has knowledge' if enough of his fellow producers *either* devote their resources to following up his research (even for purposes of refutation) *or* cite his research as background material for their own. The producer continues to 'have knowledge' only as long as these investments by his fellows pay off *for them* [emphasis in original]. (Fuller, 1988, 30)

There are some serious problems with this conception. For one thing, it assumes that the producer's knowledge is inextricably associated with the acceptance of his claims by others. This means that the producer's idea is not dependent on truth or justification, except as determined by the acceptance of others. For another thing, it assumes that acceptance counts as knowledge, even if the idea of the producer is false. As we'll see shortly, there must be more than acceptance for an idea to count as knowledge. In his more recent writings Fuller has further stressed the social aspect of knowledge: "A necessary (though not sufficient) condition for the appropriateness of a norm is that the people to whom the norm would apply find it in their interest to abide by the norm" (Fuller, 1993, 32). There seems to be little to distinguish an epistemic norm from ideology. Some have taken issue with Fuller's version of SE, finding gaps in his program. For instance, J. Angelo Corlett observes that Fuller does not ask what social belief or social epistemic truth is; Fuller doesn't specify possible subjects of social knowledge (Corlett, 1996, 15). Not all philosophers fall prey to these kinds of shortcomings.

Other philosophers acknowledge that accounting for the social in any conception of epistemology is essential. Most maintain the break with social constructivism, though. If one aspect of constructivism is that no a priori order inheres in the world—that order is imposed by us—then, according to Hilary Kornblith, knowledge would not be possible; there would be no object of knowledge (Kornblith, 1994, 95-96). For a naturalized epistemology, there must also be the realization that "human psychology must be richly structured as well, and structured in a way which dovetails with the structure of the world" (Kornblith, 1994, 96). Such a notion might be seen as a conservative sort of SE (more radical types tend to employ a stronger rejection of traditional, individualist epistemology along with a stronger acceptance of the social construction of beliefs, taken to be knowledge). The rather conservative approach favors the normative goal of SE. That approach may take the primary epistemological project, as Philip Kitcher does, as consisting

> in the investigation of the reliability of various types of social processes. Once we have recognized that individuals form beliefs by relying on information supplied by others, there are serious issues about the conditions that should be met if the community is to form a consensus on a particular issue—questions about the division of opinion and of cognitive effort within the community, and issues about the proper attribution of authority. (Kitcher, 1994, 114)

The ideas mentioned here are somewhat useful for us in LIS, but they still need development if they are to contribute to a fruitful intellectual foundation for us.

Social Epistemology—Alvin Goldman

Fortunately, there is a much more well-developed social epistemological program. I will draw heavily here on the recent work of Alvin Goldman. As we'll see, Goldman (although he was not aware of Shera's work at the time he wrote his book) owes an intellectual debt to Shera. Perhaps it is telling that two thoughtful individuals could arrive at similar conceptions independently, conceptions that offer a framework for thinking about how we come to know. He asserts that we need to move beyond individualist epistemology:

> But concentration on the individual to the exclusion of the social is inappropriate. The bulk of an adult's world-view is deeply indebted to her social world. It can largely be traced to social interactions, to influences exerted by other knowers, primarily through the vehicle of language. It is imperative, then, for epistemology to have a social dimension. (Goldman, 1987, 109)

In several of his works Goldman has described what he takes to define knowledge and to describe how we may gain knowledge. Knowledge, Goldman says, is true belief, that is, knowledge as contrasted with error or ignorance. The means by which we produce knowledge that may be correct and which replaces ignorance is by reliable mechanisms. Reliable mechanisms are those that, much more often than not, produce results that are not prone to error. I mention Goldman's definition because, first, he refers to his program as veritistic social epistemology (collective true belief) and, second, his definition and description appear to differ from some offered earlier in this chapter. Actually they are not that different. For example, one way that we might reach true belief is by some kind of justification. My point is that the differences between Goldman and other philosophers are sufficiently subtle that, for the purposes of understanding LIS's relation to knowledge, we can assume they are effectively the same.

One very real difference between Goldman and the philosophers discussed at the outset of this chapter is that he acknowledges the social element of knowledge production. He has recently written a book that fleshes out his idea of SE. Early in his book he tells us what is social about SE:

> First, it focuses on social paths or routes to knowledge. That is, considering believers taken one at a time, it looks at the many routes to belief that feature interactions with other agents, as contrasted with private or asocial routes to belief acquisition. . . . Second, social epistemology does not restrict itself to believers taken singly. It often focuses on some sort of group

> entity. . . . Third, instead of restricting knowers to individuals, social epistemology may consider collective or corporate entities. (Goldman, 1999, 4)

There are connections between these three points and Shera's conception. Shera's four assumptions of SE (see p. 233) could be seen to follow from (or precede, in the case of his first assumption) Goldman's points. In both cases there is a reliance, more explicit with Shera, on the records of thought and communication both as expressions of what is known and as evidence that could be used in the formation of true belief.

In examining how we arrive at true belief, Goldman responds to the constructivist criterion that is grounded in relativism. He turns to John Searle, who provides a cogent rejoinder to the relativism of Nelson Goodman and others: "we do not make 'worlds'; we make *descriptions* [emphasis in original] that the actual world may fit or fail to fit. But all this implies that there is a reality that exists independently of our system of concepts. Without such a reality, there is nothing to apply the concept to" (Searle, 1995, 166). The importance of the distinction Searle draws cannot be overstated. There is a world that exists apart from our representations of it. As we struggle to represent the world we inevitably employ individual and collective experience, individual and collective cognition, and language (which is indubitably a social construct). The tale of the seven blind men attempting to identify an elephant by feeling different parts illustrates how our experiences and our cognition can seem correct given the particular, and be erroneous given the whole. The tale points out the limitations to individual knowledge. Collectively, people can correct inferences, or at least eliminate false inferences. This matter was also recognized by Shera, who urged us to look beyond individual experience to the totality of the experiences of the group.

The realism that courses through the thought of Searle and Goldman implies that something can be true; that is, it can be unchanging insofar as it exists in the dimensions that are accessible to us (including time). If something can be true, it can be known. This element of realism makes possible the extension of belief to true belief. "Since knowledge involves belief, and belief is in contents that are [human constructs], there is merit to claim that knowledge is (partly) a social construct. But since knowledge is *true* [emphasis in original] belief, knowledge also involves truth; and what is true, as we have seen, is not a human construct as opposed to being of the world" (Goldman, 1999, 21). I should emphasize here that knowledge is not a necessary consequence of collective experience or collective belief. Language, agreed-upon description, assumptions, can all be shared (can even be consensual), but can also be erroneous. If, in some culture, there is the shared belief that the earth is stationary in space and everything revolves around it, the sharing does not create truth. Suppose, on the other hand, there is an individual who looks at the sky and surmises that everything revolves around the earth, and then that individual studies physics and astronomy by reading published works and listening to teachers. That individual then abandons the prior belief in the light of the evidence that is offered. This example illustrates Goldman's first point—that people take many routes to knowledge, some of which can involve interaction with others.

Another criticism that constructivists, or postmodernists generally, submit is that claims of knowledge amount to the privileging of some beliefs in the less malignant sense, and are used as instruments of domination in the more malignant. Goldman successfully answers both versions of this criticism. True belief is indeed privileged, but not by means of politics or ideology. Certainly politics, ideology, and other factors affect belief and can be employed in the privileging of some positions and even the exercise of domination (and it is essential that we recognize these possibilities), but they do not affect truth. It is incumbent, then, upon those who seek knowledge to work through nonepistemic rationales for belief en route to true belief.

It is possible for us to employ epistemic (truth-seeking) means to study those beliefs that are based in, say, ideology. Ideology, at least in some usages of the word, distorts truth as a means of persuasion or domination. An inquirer, or group of inquirers, can, however, study ideological discourse, can set out to arrive at true beliefs—normative, epistemic beliefs—*about* the non-epistemic beliefs that people also hold.

With regard to the second version, two things can be said: (1) the uses to which knowledge is put is, in a very real sense, independent of the knowledge itself (Einstein's theories contributed to the manufacture of the first atomic weapon, but the use does not denigrate Einstein or his theories); (2) much of the stuff that is used for the purpose of domination is, in fact, false (in Goldman's sense in that it is erroneous, albeit purposefully so, or it is intended to perpetuate ignorance). It must be reiterated that the nonepistemic beliefs are legitimate subjects for examination and, further, we can add to our social epistemic knowledge by understanding them more clearly.

If we accept that SE offers us a fruitful framework for examining knowledge in LIS, there is an important question that remains. How do we arrive at knowledge through social interaction? Goldman offers three means by which we can reach true belief (Goldman, 1999, 103-88). I won't go into great detail here; instead, I recommend Goldman's book to readers. Some summary of the processes by which we can attain knowledge is necessary, though. One path to veritistic knowledge is through (1) *testimony*, or the communicative sharing of discoveries. At the most basic level testimony denotes a means by which we can become aware of things. Of course knowledge necessitates much more than awareness; testimony leading to knowledge depends at least on what Goldman refers to as "good veritistic intent" (Goldman, 1999, 107), or the speaker's own knowledge plus the desire to communicate it to an audience that cares about it. Goldman's idea of reliabilism (the reliability of a process leading to, or yielding, truth) also enters here. The hearer should be able to assess the reliability of the speaker; this is one way to justify belief in what the speaker says.

A second mechanism that can be employed in SE is (2) *argumentation.* By argumentation Goldman does not mean heated debate (necessarily) or forensic competition with winning as the goal. He is referring to factual argumentation which involves presenting a case for a particular point and then trying to respond successfully to challenges to that point. There are conditions that a discourse must satisfy for it to have the potential of leading to knowledge. On the speaker's side, that individual must believe in what he or she is arguing in favor of and must also believe in all the premises that lead to the conclusion. Further, the speaker is justified in believing the premises and the premises, taken together, support the conclusion. These conditions are normative and rational, two elements that are necessary for knowledge. The social aspect of argumentation lies in the dialogic nature of this kind of communication. There is not only a speaker; there is also a hearer. And the hearer can respond to or challenge the speaker's premises or conclusion. There are conditions that must be met on the hearer's side. Any rebuttal offered for a speaker's point should be accurate and it should directly address the speaker's point. If a speaker's claim survives the challenges, if it is not defeated, then it tends to be reliable. If a speaker's claim is defeated by a body of evidence that is contrary to the conclusion, then that conclusion should be rejected. Throughout the process all involved must be committed to finding truth.

Goldman's third mechanism is the one that is of most interest to us in LIS. There are modes of communication that are not testimonial and are not dialogic (at least not in the sense of dyadic communication); there are (3) *mass media* that are used for the purpose of increasing and sharing knowledge. The collections of libraries, the products of some information producers, the contents of some databases, are intended to assist people with knowledge growth. We should ask to what extent they meet the goals of veritistic social epistemology. These kinds of formal communication may not contribute to SE. There are, fundamentally, four categories of individual communications. They may contain errors or inaccuracies; they may be weakly argued and may not respond to reasonable objections; they may not be flawed, but they may add nothing new; or they may not only avoid flaws, but also present new findings or theories. If we are committed to knowledge growth we should seek to maximize the occurrences of the fourth category and minimize the occurrences of the first three. Our communication mechanisms attempt to achieve such an end by subjecting communications to peer review. Another is to replicate work to ensure that results are reliable. Such efforts are employed to produce academic or research communications that are as veritistically sound as possible. Success certainly isn't automatic, though. Mass communication tends to use fewer epistemic gatekeeping approaches and more economic ones. Goldman argues in favor of some regulatory mechanisms that do not rely solely on market forces to determine success. More broadly, Goldman speaks of the role of the gatekeeper:

> Given the importance of gatekeepers, especially in mass communication, social epistemology must inquire into the practices available to gatekeepers and the veritistic consequences that might flow from these practices. Casting our net more widely, we should examine not only the practices of individual gatekeepers, but the fundamental institutional arrangements or frameworks that influence the dissemination of thought and ideas. (Goldman, 1999, 189)

In a subsequent chapter I will review some work and some questions in LIS and will examine actual and potential applications of SE to inquiry and practice in LIS. This later examination will be conducted in the context of what Goldman calls the "mental infosphere"—the states of beliefs of everyone in the world at a given time.

> If we are lucky, a goodly proportion of the mental infosphere consists of true beliefs, or knowledge. This, then, is the totality of human knowledge at the time in question. However impressive this totality may be, it can undoubtedly be enlarged. First, many truths are initially known by only a single person, or only a select few. . . . Second, entirely new truths may be acquired by society, items of knowledge that no individual previously possessed. These new truths may be acquired by either independent or collaborative inquiry. Communication can play a

critical role in both old knowledge dissemination and new knowledge acquisition. . . . In general, the social advance of knowledge hinges on communication. (Goldman, 1999, 161)

Goldman could have been writing about LIS.

Related Ideas of Knowledge— Feminist Epistemology

The program of social epistemology, just outlined, can also serve as an effective response to some who criticize aspects of traditional epistemology. One critique in particular will be addressed here—feminist epistemology—because the elements that form part of the critique offer some very cogent points about knowledge. In short, the feminist critique argues that what has passed for knowledge at times has been grounded in a privileged androcentric framework that has eliminated or subverted other epistemological stances. The principal point of this argument, first of all, assumes that there is a social aspect to knowledge and knowledge growth. Secondly, the argument, with the social aspect in mind, asserts that some knowledge claims have ignored substantial and essential elements of society. Feminist epistemology frequently makes an explicit connection with the social. Naomi Scheman argues that "neither the descriptive nor the normative task [of epistemology] can be adequately accomplished by abstracting knowers and knowledge from their concrete, historically specific incarnations" (Scheman, 1995, 179).

At times the connection is made clear as part of articulations of the feminist epistemological position. Elizabeth Anderson says, "An adequate feminist epistemology must explain how research projects with such moral and political commitments can produce knowledge that meets such epistemic standards as empirical adequacy and fruitfulness" (Anderson, 1995, 54). Anderson's idea of the social aspect of epistemology adds to Goldman's by incorporating nonepistemic behaviors that may impinge upon knowledge. She also adds that the social elements do not preclude meeting epistemic criteria, including empirical adequacy. If we think about the means of communication that Goldman speaks of, the stance of Anderson makes a great deal of sense. The mechanisms, such as academic or mass media, undoubtedly include degrees of openness and exclusion; understanding the dynamics of the media is essential to understanding of the social aspects of knowledge.

Although it doesn't analyze knowledge in the same way that epistemologists do, the landmark study, *Women's Ways of Knowing*, provides us with some insight into the social dynamics of such factors as acceptance, justification, and authority (Belensky, Clinchy, Goldberger, and Tarule, 1997). The study demonstrates that there are different manners of deciding upon accepting received views, different ways of connecting between knowing *what* and knowing *that*, and different ways of assessing cognitive authority. The principal lesson the book offers us is that there are more ways of examining justification and truth than we may tend to be taught. This is indeed a valuable lesson, especially insofar as it can lead us to a clearer understanding of what should be included as part of a program of social epistemology. The authors do at times tend to try to legitimize a constructivist approach to knowledge. This attempt may lead to a confusion of social epistemology with social constructivism; the difference between the two is essential, though. At the risk of being repetitive, the epistemic approach is normative; the social epistemic approach helps us more accurately to conceive of the norms that should be applied to the evaluation of knowledge claims. The constructivist approach, in denying a normative aspect, effectively denies the possibility of knowledge. I don't think this latter effect is intended by the authors of *Women's Ways of Knowing*, but it is a fairly easy trap to be captured in. This criticism aside, the book can be read in a positive light; it can help to clarify the norms by which knowledge is to be assessed.

As we can see, while feminist epistemology can help us appreciate social epistemology, we have to take care to evaluate specific statements. For instance, Lynn Hankinson Nelson offers some reasoned support for feminist epistemology, but she tends to group alternative theories of knowledge together. There certainly are alternative theories (several have been discussed so far in this chapter). The alternatives tend to treat the question of *how* we justify, *how* we identify reliable processes, and *how* we arrive at truth. Far fewer theories differ on *what* justification and truth are (Nelson, 1995). In part, Nelson's stance almost advocates replacing one kind of privileging with another; she also seems to be speaking of belief and not necessarily of knowledge. In other words, we have to be careful to distinguish between sociology and epistemology, especially with regard to the difference between belief and true belief.

If readers wish to find out more about feminist epistemology, perhaps the single source I could recommend is Sandra Harding's *Whose Science? Whose Knowledge?* She provides a clear explication of standpoint epistemology, and the fundamental elements of her position are grounded in the mixture of the social with knowledge. She makes the very valuable point that epistemology should offer a theory about how we perceive and how we reach understanding of the world. She writes, "it is not the experiences or the speech that provides the grounds for feminist claims; it is rather the subsequently articulated observations of and theory about the rest of nature and social relations—observations and theory that start out from, that look at the world from the perspective of, women's lives" (Harding, 1991, 124). Goldman makes particular reference to Harding's thought and acknowledges the affinity with SE. He especially notes Harding's point that standpoint epistemology necessitates, not only acceptance of social situation, but also critical evaluation of those social situations that lead to objective knowledge claims (Goldman, 1999, 35).

It probably won't surprise readers to learn that some dispute the claims of feminist epistemology (and, by extension, those of social epistemology). I will treat only one objection, mainly because it has received a considerable amount of attention and because the argument actually supports feminist and social epistemology. Paul Gross and Norman Levitt see Harding as emblematic of an antiscience bias perpetrated by the political left. The very ascription of this bias to a competing political group demonstrates that social factors do indeed have an impact on the process of belief formation. Gross and Levitt reduce Harding's work to an argument whose sole claim is that multicultural participation in science will alter the results of scientific work (Gross and Levitt, 1994, 126-32). Their own bias is apparent in their polemic: "The propositions of science, by and large, escape humiliation, while those of the humanities, including venerable philosophic areas as ethics and aesthetics, emphatically do not" (Gross and Levitt, 1994, 87). In a more recent work Harding argues that scientific work tends to occur in localized communities, with limited social interaction (Harding, 1998). Again, this reinforces Goldman's point that knowledge grows along social, as well as rational, lines. A feminist examination of science and its epistemic claims does not necessarily negate the content of scientific knowledge; it does explore how that knowledge is arrived at and what veritistic means are used to do science. Gross and Levitt undoubtedly do not suspect it, but they provide some of the strongest evidence in favor of social epistemology.

Epistemology and the Philosophy of Social Science

We've seen the philosophers' conception of knowledge, including the less abstract idea of social epistemology. A question that may come to mind at this point is: Are the social sciences sensitive to the criteria and the import of epistemology? A principal feature of epistemology is that it is normative. One thing needs to be pointed out here. Just because theories of knowledge maintain that the criteria for what counts as knowledge are normative, that doesn't mean that all of our actions and beliefs are normative, that they are all rational. So when I say normative I do not mean that human behavior is completely, or even predominately, generated by norms. Human behavior is too individualistic, variable, and sometimes idiosyncratic to be said to be determined by universal norms. On the other hand, the study of human behavior, thought, and interaction can be guided by norms. The foregoing illustrates the difficulty of knowledge acquisition and knowledge growth—there are rational processes and we are *capable* of rationality, but we do not always behave rationally. This glitch affects both the object of study (human behavior and action) and the means of inquiry (our own knowledge-seeking actions).

Observers of the social sciences most frequently see evidence for, or suggest the efficacy of, norms in the methods applied to inquiry. This activity is certainly legitimate, but, alone, however, the focus or method is not sufficient; it must be accompanied by an examination of norms pertinent to the way we think about theory and practice and agreement on what constitutes knowledge in the social sciences and LIS. Conflict has a potential impact on knowledge; let's see what some have to say about epistemology in the social sciences. (We have already seen some positions that are less than sympathetic to epistemology; let's use this limited space to see if there are any who do believe that there is a connection between social science and knowledge.) The ideas presented here are those that have the most to say to us in LIS.

The most useful of social science philosophy demonstrate the flaws of deterministic scientism. It's not sufficient to deny determinism or to ignore that there are influences on thought and action, but it is necessary to examine determinism to see where it falls short. As I just mentioned, we certainly must recognize that there are factors, natural and social, that influence what we do and how we think. Does that mean those factors determine our responses? Brian Fay offers an explanation of influences that we can find helpful:

> But if by "make" you mean "determine" then our culture and society do not make us what we are: in the process of enculturation and socialization we are not passive entities upon which cultural imperatives and social rules are impressed as if we were a wax tablet (though we must be careful not to picture our appropriative activity as unconstrained or as possible absent the resources provided by our culture and society). (Fay, 1996, 69)

Our consciousness enables us to become aware of the impact of surroundings on us, including self-awareness. Consciousness also enables our affective and rational responses to that impact. James Bohman affirms the acknowledgment of self and consciousness: "the indeterminacy of social action requires that explanations in

the social sciences take into account the fact that knowledgeable
social agents are not mere bearers of social forces or norms, but
can change themselves and alter their circumstances" (Bohman,
1991, 233).

Realization of indeterminacy is not new with Fay and
Bohman. In 1958 Peter Winch noted that discovery of laws
depends on accurate representation of initial conditions but, even
with such a representation, "even given a specific set of initial
conditions, one will still not be able to predict any determinate
outcome to a historical trend because the continuation or
breaking off of that trend involves human decisions which are not
determined by their antecedent conditions in the context of
which the sense of calling them 'decisions' lies" (Winch, 1958,
92-93). Even before Winch, Max Weber, in 1904, addressed one
particular element of determinism—objectivity. If human
behavior or thought can be determined, then there must be a way
to identify those criteria or ideals that will allow us to derive
precisely what can direct action. Weber shows how such ideals do
not exist, so "An empirical science cannot tell anyone what he
should do—but rather what he *can* [emphasis in original] do—and
under certain circumstances—what he wishes to do" (Weber,
1949, 54).

Perhaps most importantly, these social science philosophers
recognize that human and social phenomena are based in
language. This recognition implies that our behavior and actions,
as well as our thought, are linguistic. Of course this has methodological consequences, since we frequently rely on what people
say, even if they are describing what they do. Language helps us
to construct what we believe, how we act, and what we know. It
permeates justification, conclusions regarding truth, and identification of reliable mechanisms. If much of our knowledge is
propositional knowledge (statements about how things are,
relationships among factors, etc.), the import of language is
obvious. Also, the challenges introduced by language become
obvious. As Andrew Sayer reminds us, the phenomena we deal
with are "*concept-dependent* [emphasis in original]. Unlike natural
(i.e. non-social) objects they are not impervious to the meanings
ascribed to them. What the practices, institutions, rules, roles or

relationships are depends on what they mean in society to its members" (Sayer, 1992, 30).

Awareness of indeterminacy, of the effects of consciousness on the processes of both the knower and the known, reinforce a fallibilistic conception of knowledge. Add language to the mix and we can see clearly how knowledge claims are fallible and corrigible. I would submit that there is no alternative for us but to accept a fallibilist stance regarding knowledge. It does not mean that knowledge isn't possible, but it is a realization that our knowledge is not complete and absolute. Neither, however, is what we call knowledge arbitrary. We examine evidence—call this action justification or reliabilism—in order to develop *reasons* for our beliefs. The justificatory process separates knowledge from doxa (opinion). Fallibilism also implies a particular usage of "objectivity." Fay says it "suggests an alternative account of objectivity, one which construes objectivity not as a property of the results of inquiry but as a property of *the process of inquiry itself*. To fallibilists the *method* [emphasis in original] of scientific analysis, not its conclusions, is what is or is not objective." Further, he asks,

> What makes a process of inquiry objective? In a word, that it be *fair* [emphasis in original] in the sense that its procedures and the judgments it underwrites be responsive to the evidence as best it can be determined, and responsive to other possible interpretations of this evidence. To be objective, an investigation must require its practitioners to seek out facts which appear relevant to the preconceptions or commitments, to put their explanations up against other explanations to show that theirs are superior, and to be willing to revise or abandon their conclusions if later work warrants it. (Fay, 1996, 212)

For us in LIS, and for all engaged in the work of the social sciences, we have to grasp a fundamental difference between knowledge of social phenomena and knowledge of natural phenomena. We have to resist scientism and comprehend the difference. In other words, we must adhere to Sayer's admonition; we must not "think of knowledge as a product or thing which exists outside of us, which we can 'possess' and which is stored in finished form in our heads or in libraries," and we must "think in terms of *knowing*, which is in the process of becoming, 'in solution', as consciousness" or "consider the *production* of knowledge as a *social activity* [emphasis in original]" (Sayer, 1992, 16). This admonition is consistent with social epistemology. Now that we have this framework we have to turn our attention to *how* we might come to true belief.

Chapter Six

Paths to Knowledge

If a principal purpose of LIS practice and inquiry is the growth of knowledge, then one task for us is to examine ways by which we might come to knowledge. I should emphasize that I'm not speaking of particular methodologies of research or practice (in fact this book is not about methodology). Instead, I'm exploring possible approaches, ways of thinking about both the questions that are central to LIS and the thinking that guides our quest for answers. In part, the importance of the approach is rooted in the way we tend to do things anyway. While I have disagreed with Karl Popper on some matters, he really does put his finger on the need for considering the intellectual approach we adopt. He says, "I contend *there is no such thing as instruction from without the structure* [emphasis in original], or the passive reception of a flow of information which impresses itself on our sense organs" (Popper, 1994, 8). In other words, everything we do is theory dependent. I don't mean that each of us has some elaborate theoretical construct in mind every time we handle an information organization or retrieval problem. What I do mean is that we frame our observations and our actions according to a set of assumptions and connections that are consciously formulated.

The notion that theory precedes action may encounter some resistance in LIS. The ostensible debate between theory and practice has been evident in the professional literature for several decades. The dichotomy is a false one, though. What we do as part of the fulfillment of professional responsibility is based on an idea of the best way to accomplish our goals. Where criticism has been most valid is the observation that there may have been insufficient thought given to effective action. With regard to one element of our discipline, Birger Hjorland writes, "We do not have many explicit theories in IS. Actually it is difficult to name just one good example. . . . Most work is of a pragmatic nature, which resists scientific analysis and generalisation [*sic*]" (Hjørland, 1998, 607). Hjorland's statement implies another challenge for us—defining theory. There are several ways to examine theory, including developing or identifying specific theories aimed at explanation and understanding of a particular phenomenon (such as patron use of online public catalogs) and proposing encompassing conceptual frameworks within which particular phenomena can be addressed. Both definitions are legitimate, but my focus will be on the latter idea. A successful approach could inform the development of theories in the first sense.

Recognition of the need for some far-reaching conceptual framework is not new. Ian Cornelius says, "Without a clear and conscious high-level theory, there is no basis for a clear understanding either of where the field presently stands or where it is going" (Cornelius, 1996, 6). He further observes that "Senior commentators in the field commonly skip over difficult questions about the nature of the profession, and the most sophisticated analyses rarely reach below the surface description of technical performance" (Cornelius, 1996, 7). (Cornelius's book is an excellent attempt to propose a high-level theory; while I don't agree completely with his proposition, I will revisit his work later in this chapter.) Rather than quibble over whether the conceptual framework should be empirical, nomological, or something else, we should attempt to construct an idea that will facilitate knowledge growth. In addressing literary theory, Paisley Livingston says the study of literature should be grounded in what might constitute knowledge of literature and knowledge in literature (Livingston, 1988). He suggests that "Only a theory, the word being taken here in a very broad sense, specifies a question that can be given anything like a precise result" (Livingston, 1988, 205-6). We could borrow from Livingston: a framework that could work for us should be an epistemological one, leading to knowledge of LIS and knowledge in LIS. This means developing a conceptual grounding that can help us know more about our own actions and thoughts and also know more about the outward focus of library and information work. Moreover, as we'll see, this framework should have individual, social, historical, and textual elements.

Prelude

The title of this chapter is "Paths to Knowledge." The plural is not accidental; it would be either folly or arrogance (or both) to suggest that there is a single means by which we gain knowledge. As we saw in the last chapter, the most reasonable approach to epistemology is to realize the social *and* the rational elements of knowledge. If the social is to be a part of how we come to know things, then there is no one method (empiricism, positivism, ethnography, etc.) that will provide the framework we need. Specifically, what I'm proposing here is an epistemological framework, a way to evaluate paths to knowledge and to select the path, or set of paths, that makes the most sense at a given time and for a given purpose.

In a recent article Archie Dick has argued for a kind of epistemological pluralism. The grounding for what he refers to as holistic perspectivism (the recognition that knowledge claims are based in particular contexts and that we should examine entire systems of thought instead of individual hypotheses) is that we do not apprehend reality per se; we structure our view of reality according to sets of assumptions and propositions (and this is somewhat related to Searle's distinction between social facts and brute facts). He writes that "standpoint epistemology, cognitivism, poststructuralism, phenomenology, positivism, and so forth, do not offer radically different accounts of LIS realities but instead account differently for the same LIS realities" (Dick, 1999, 319). (His argument may sound so reasonable as to be obvious, but recall the false starts and dead ends in LIS.) While there is considerable merit to his position, I have to differ with him on a couple of key points. First, we do indeed interpret reality from the point of view of differing theoretical perspectives, but we need to evaluate these perspectives in a way that relates to the reality they attempt to explain. Second, phenomenology is not simply another perspective in the same way that, say, positivism is.

Elsewhere I have suggested that the most efficacious framework for LIS is hermeneutical phenomenology (Budd, 1996). I'll detail what I mean by this momentarily, but I should explain at this time that hermeneutical phenomenology is fundamental to philosophy as a whole. The purpose of philosophy is ontological, that is, the examination of being in the most basic sense. Phenomenology is closely linked to ontology, as Martin Heidegger says. Ontology and phenomenology "are not two distinct philosophical disciplines among others. These terms characterize philosophy itself with regard to its object and its way of treating that object. Philosophy is the universal phenomenological ontology" (Heidegger, 1962, 62). Admittedly, phenomenology implies a method of examination, but it might be better seen as a metamethod—an informing means by which we can inquire into the nature of a vast variety of questions. As I've stated, "It is a stance, a position—one that opens the inquirer to possibilities instead of barricading avenues. It is also a vocabulary, a means of expression, a way of describing and explaining" (Budd, 1995, 304).

Phenomenology is, as we'll see shortly, necessarily interpretive. An inquiry into being has to be hermeneutical; it has to include the formal and structured interpretation of the expression of being (through behavior, text, speech, or other means). I emphasize "formal and structured" interpretation because the interpretative act is not merely the occurrence of a chance impression. It is the product of a process of examination into history, context, language, reference, etc. In a sense the term hermeneutical phenomenology is redundant, but it stresses both the process of interpretation and what is being interpreted.

I'll close this prelude by stating again that this framework is not a disconnected intellectual exercise. It is intended to help us understand the purpose of LIS and to practice in this profession. It is a theoretical framework, but not simply for theory's sake. The goal is to provide us all with a way to look at LIS and a way to *act* within LIS. In other words, the intent here is to help us not only to think, but to live. To accomplish this goal, we have to remain open to the possibilities that research and practice offer. In presenting his opinion, anthropologist Richard Wilk says, "It's perfectly healthy when a theory prompts research activity, and scholars then use the results to modify the theory. But when theory becomes a rarefied domain . . . , theory has lost touch with reality" (Wilk, 1999, A52). The framework that will be articulated in the coming pages is admittedly somewhat eliminativist; it does, through evaluation, turn us from paths (such as deterministic scientism) that lead nowhere. That said, the framework not only allows, but necessitates, examination of the essential elements of our work.

Phenomenology

There are a couple of questions that have to be answered right away. First, what is phenomenology? Second, how does it assist interpretation? The first question seems straightforward, but, as is the case with many ways of thinking, there is no single approach to phenomenology. There's no need here for an exhaustive account of all phenomenological thought, but some description of this way of thinking will, I believe, give direction to our research and practice. An early expression of phenomenology by Hegel focused on the absolute self-awareness of mind. That extreme ideal vision was not adopted by subsequent philosophers—at least not nearly to the extent that Hegel did.

That is not to say that others do not share *any* part of the idealist stance. For example, a hallmark of Edmund Husserl's phenomenology is the idea of the essence of Being that is manifested through consciousness of some phenomenon. This means that, through phenomenological investigation, it is possible to identify the true essence of a thing. There are problems with this idea, as we'll see. Others after Husserl attempted to move beyond idealism. Heidegger stressed the importance of existence, which can be complex. In order to reach understanding of existence we have to examine the ways that we might apprehend Being. Paul Ricoeur has emphasized that phenomena are evident to us largely through action, and our studies should recognize the actions that reach our consciousness and our own consciousness *as* action.

An examination of phenomenology has to begin by detailing what is meant by a phenomenon. The simple description is that a phenomenon is anything we experience, that we have consciousness of. In fact, Husserl defined consciousness in terms of being conscious *of* something; that is, consciousness entails both being aware of or perceiving *and* the thing that is perceived. What one is conscious of is not arbitrarily limited, as Michael Hammond and his colleagues point out:

> One important class of such experiences of things is perception—seeing, hearing, touching, and so on. But it is by no means the only one. There are also phenomena such as believing, remembering, wishing, deciding, and imagining things; feeling apprehensive, excited, or angry at things; judging and evaluating things; the experiences involved in one's bodily actions, such as lifting or pulling things; and many others. (Hammond, Howarth, and Keat, 1991, 2)

Phenomena are all those things we can be conscious of.

There remains the need to define phenomenology. Herbert Spiegelberg offers one particular definition:

> Phenomenology . . . is a cognitive approach to any field of studies which aims at being rigorously scientific, i.e., to achieve systematic and intersubjective knowledge; it does so by (a) describing first what is subjectively experienced ("intuited") insofar as it is experienced, whether real or not (the "pure

phenomenon") in its typical structure and relations ("essences" and "essential relations"), and by (b) paying special attention to its modes of appearance and the ways in which it constitutes itself in consciousness. (Spiegelberg, 1975, 112)

His definition focuses on the cognitive kind of experience, leaving out emotions or other noncognitive kinds. This doesn't present a problem here; I also focus on cognitive experiences in LIS. As a cognitive approach to phenomenology, our program here recognizes that there are cognitive elements of experience:

(1) the ability of someone to comprehend the language used in the source (the thing experienced);

(2) the ability to comprehend the structure of the source;

(3) the content-dependence of the source;

(4) the perceiver's present cognitive state; and

(5) the perceiver's store of knowledge.

The first element is self-explanatory. The second has to do with an individual's ability—whether innate or learned—to grasp the intricacies of, say, a database of information, including search protocols and the like. The third depends on the nature of the content itself—whether it provides sufficient explanation and background to be understood by a novice or is tacitly assuming prior knowledge. The fourth takes into account the temporal condition of the individual, including illness, emotional distress, etc. The fifth is based in what the individual knows when approaching a content source and how the knowledge facilitates or impedes understanding of the source's content.

There are some differences in the programs of the aforementioned (and other) thinkers; our attention here will be on those elements that are most useful to us in LIS. One basic aspect of phenomenology is that it tries to be presuppositionless. It may be impossible to eliminate all assumptions and presuppositions, but the goal is to perceive phenomena with as few barriers as possible between the thing and the perceiver. If someone is adhering to a particular theory, say, of relevance, then that person may try to explain something only in terms of that theory, thus missing other possibilities. For instance, an error of neurophilosophy is to reduce cognition to the theoretically convenient ideas it espouses.

Or, as J. N. Mohanty says, "A reduction of consciousness to states of the body . . . loses sight of the very essence of consciousness, i.e., its intentionality. A reduction of morality to social and psychological conditions would inevitably miss the very essence of morality, i.e., its 'ought'-character" (Mohanty, 1997, 3). Since phenomenology is itself a theoretical stance, the way we seek knowledge is accordingly influenced by that stance. Its strength, though, is the awareness of the implications of the presuppositions with which we may begin inquiry.

If we accept, as we must, that LIS is a complex discipline (including, as it does, the collection of materials, the organization of information, the design of organizational and technical structures, the understanding of information-seeking behavior, and the mediation between seekers and the graphic record), then we must also be prepared to embrace a conceptual framework that is complex. The framework that holds the most promise for us should correct some of the problems that other philosophical stances entail. Decades ago Husserl wrote that the philosophy of the time threatened "to succumb to skepticism, irrationalism, and mysticism" (Husserl, 1970, 3). Phenomenology requires close investigation to understand what really comprises being. As Husserl further says, "True being is everywhere an ideal goal, a task of *episteme* or 'reason,' as opposed to being which through *doxa* is merely thought to be, unquestioned and 'obvious'" (Husserl, 1970, 13). Going beyond doxa (opinion) is precisely what LIS needs today. For instance, as we've seen, some in LIS assert that science (which is a naive shorthand for the principles of the physical sciences) provides the only conceptual and methodological tools we need. This kind of assertion exemplifies the presupposition that phenomenology warns us against. Max Scheler tells us that "to presuppose the validity of science or of any of its propositions is not to explain its essence but to obscure it" (Scheler, 1973, 139).

There is another difference between phenomenology and later elements of the genealogy, such as the neurophilosophy posited by Stich and the Churchlands. The scientistic view of ourselves, and especially our consciousness, is that we are objects to be studied in the same way any other physical phenomena should be studied. This kind of thinking is represented in LIS in much of the writing dealing with what are frequently referred to as bibliometric laws (such as Bradford's, Lotka's, and Zipf's Laws). It is also represented in the practice of librarianship in the form of objectifying selection (treating books as nothing more than physical objects that are acquired) and information seeking (treating the queries of users as objects). One of the most common examples of objectification is the phenomenon referred to as information retrieval. This term implies an outcome, rather than the complex process that underlies search strategy, inference of relevance, etc. Of course LIS practice does not consist entirely of objectified reductions, but objectification is too common to ignore. Borrowing from David Stewart and Algis Mickunas, the difference can be stated succinctly as, "(1) consciousness itself is not an object among other objects in nature, and (2) there are conscious phenomena which cannot be dealt with adequately by means of the quantitative methods of experimental science" (Stewart and Mickunas, 1990, 4).

Avoiding falling prey to the temptation of objectification can help us to accomplish some of our goals relating to knowledge. Understanding that our beings, our consciousnesses, are not the same as physical phenomena can aid in the process of interpreting the phenomena that are most important to us. Once we can grasp more completely the nature of being we will be able to comprehend our own selves and how we interact with others. It might be said that phenomenology can help us to understand understanding. By that I mean that this framework can provide us with the grounding we need to see how we come to understand the complex events around us. Let's now look at some of the particulars of phenomenology.

Elements of Phenomenology

Even with the differences in individual conceptions of phenomenology there are some central aspects that are included, in some way, by all philosophers. Given the purpose of this book, I'll focus on those aspects that can contribute the most to LIS. It may help to present a rather crude graphic sense of the aspects of phenomenology.

===

Elements of Phenomenology

Being   Essence

Interpretation

Perception   Intentionality

Self and Other

===

The individual elements—being, essence, perception, intentionality, and self and other—are related to one another. Further, each element is necessary for, and contributes to, interpretation. Let's examine each element in turn.

Being

Many philosophers have tried to tackle the seemingly simple, but actually complicated, problem of existence. Perhaps "problem of existence" is not the correct way to refer to the challenge; "problem of understanding existence" may be more descriptive. In all accounts of phenomenology, being is closely related to consciousness (i.e., there is no being, in the phenomenological sense, without consciousness). Husserl expressed his view of being by the term *Lebenswelt*, or life-world. For Husserl, the life-world is something that exists a priori; it is there for us to experience. Without going into great detail (and thus risking obscuring the point), Husserl most fully described the life-world in *The Crisis of European Sciences*, where he located the life-world as it relates to physical science. The life-world "is always there, existing in

Husserl

advance for us, the 'ground' of all praxis whether theoretical or extratheoretical" (Husserl, 1970, 142). The world, however, is not a static thing. It exists for us in our experiencing of it. The way we see objects in the world—our sciences of the world—is founded on the experience we have of the world (we see *through* our experience). Joseph Kockelmans explains the connection between life-world and scientific theory:

> The operations and procedures whose outgrowths and constituted correlates are objective theory and, generally speaking, the objective world of science always imply those acts of consciousness in and through which the life-world appears as always present and pregiven, as existing in its own right prior to all scientific endeavor. Therefore, for a really fundamental understanding of the world of science, we must return to the life-world and elucidate the role it plays in several respects in the constitution and development of science. (Kockelmans, 1994, 336-37)

Within LIS, we should pay attention to being, consciousness, and experience before positing a theoretical position on the phenomena of our discipline and profession.

Mohanty makes an observation that has particular pertinence for us in LIS. As a profession centered on seeking and finding information, LIS is a way of experiencing certain parts of the world (and these parts help inform the way we experience the totality of the world). So, as Mohanty says, "The lifeworld is a world of *practice* (of action, making and doing) and *praxis* (of social action, of production of goods, exchange of goods, and distribution of goods) [emphasis in original]" (Mohanty, 1997, 60). There's more to the experiencing than just acting, though. We don't simply absorb the world around us; we think about it, ponder it. "It would also be a mistake to hold that the lifeworld is not a *cognitively* apprehended world [emphasis in original]. . . . There is a core of perceptual cognition at the heart of the experience of the lifeworld—a perceptual cognition that is inextricably linked with action and evaluation" (Mohanty, 1997, 60). Experience, as we may know it, involves a kind of theorizing (if we take theory to signify a means to understanding).

Praxis

A somewhat different conception of being comes from Martin Heidegger, who was Husserl's student. Heidegger's conception is referred to as *Dasein,* or being-in-the-world. Heidegger's idea incorporates existentialism. Being, to Heidegger, exists both in time and outside of time. Being is fundamentally always in the process of happening. It is not simply historical, since there is a sense of detachment that usually accompanies history. Being-in-the-world embodies a view that each human being is participating in the world. There is a tendency among some to interpret life-world as being more akin to history (somewhat detached observation). For Heidegger, being is always the being of someone, in the same way that consciousness is always consciousness of something. He is linking the idea of being to ourselves and our lives. Also, for Heidegger being-in-the-world is that which has meaning:

> Meaning is an *existentiale* of Dasein, not a property attaching to entities, lying "behind" them, or floating somewhere as an "intermediate domain". Dasein only "has" meaning, so far as the disclosedness of Being-in-the-world can be "filled in" by the entities discoverable in that disclosedness. *Hence only Dasein can be meaningful or meaningless.* That is to say, its own Being and the entities disclosed with its Being can be appropriated in understanding, or can remain relegated to non-understanding [emphasis in original]. (Heidegger, 1962, 193)

Now no one said Heidegger was easy to understand, but this statement of his deserves some contemplation. What he is urging *against* is the thinking that objects have meaning inhering in them. What has meaning is the experience of things and events—understanding the meaning necessitates inquiring into the thing oneself, and the temporal process of the event of experiencing the thing. The experience is, in many instances, both individual and collective. That is, we may, as a group or collective, examine common experience and reach common understanding regarding meaning. As an example of what Heidegger is talking about we can look at, say, an undergraduate student who comes to the library to find background material for a paper. The student does not simply absorb information from the books, periodicals, or databases provided by the library. That student's

Heidegger

experience is shaped by the teacher's assignment, the content of the course (including readings), other courses the student is taking/has taken, *and* the contents of the materials consulted. Another way of approaching Heidegger's point is to think about what underlies an information seeker's assessment of the relevance of a set of documents. The assessment of the first document is made in the context of what the individual knows and, perhaps, what that person *expects* from the document. The assessment of the second document includes the experience of reading the first document. The evaluation of the documents is not a series of independent judgments (it is not objectifiable), but of interrelated and transforming experiences that are ongoing.

The articulations of Husserl and Heidegger are not really all that different. Husserl did not completely disassociate the observer from the experience; the observer participates in the life-world. He did not, however, adopt a fully existentialist stance. While Heidegger makes the necessary point that the event of experiencing something is itself an integral part of the experience, Husserl's conception seems more amenable to us in LIS. The reason for the attractiveness of his idea is the process of reflection that accompanies observation. There is, of course, substantial rhetoric advocating that LIS and other professions be based in reflective practice. Husserl helps us to grasp what this might entail: "reflexion [*sic*] . . . is an expression for acts in which the stream of experience, with all its manifold events (phases of experience, intentionalities) can be grasped and analyzed in the light of its own evidence" (Husserl, 1962, 200). And as I've written elsewhere, "One result of reflection is the moving of what is past into the present in the sense that consciousness and analysis of the past is a phenomenon of the present. As a consciousness of the past, reflection is a means to knowing" (Budd, 1995, 310). That is, after all, our goal.

Essence

As I mentioned earlier, the elements of phenomenology are interrelated. As we proceed with each element in turn it may be useful to look for the connections among them all. For instance, the concept of essence is closely related to being. Both are rooted in ontological principles; they are expressions of what is real and what really exists. In fact, one way to see essence is as the fundamental components that constitute a thing. The concept of essence is most closely tied to Husserl, and is seen as problematic by a number of subsequent commentators. There is a tradition that accompanies past definitions of essence that has mystical and idealist overtones. At times this part of Husserl's phenomenology is interpreted as being consonant with that idealist tradition. His efforts to link essence with ontological being should militate against such an interpretation, though. So what did Husserl mean by essence?

There is no doubt that Husserl created some difficulties for us with his use of the word essence. For him, essence was not apprehended through empirical observation (although observation may be a first step toward understanding the essence of a thing). It is understood cognitively and intuitively. He argued with positivism primarily on the grounds that positivism unnecessarily and unjustifiedly restricted what can be seen as given (essential) to particular and limited data. Empiricism is not necessarily incorrect, but it is circumscribed along prejudicial conceptual and methodological lines. The idea of the essence of a thing extends beyond the mundane limits of sensory observation. Understanding essence requires going beyond our particular time and place, beyond our particular instance. Husserl tried to delineate the difference between individual and essence:

> The acts of cognition which underlie our experiencing posit the Real in *individual* form, posit it as having spatio-temporal existence, as something existing in *this* time-spot, having this particular duration of its own and a real content which in its essence could just as well have been present in any other time-spot; posits it, moreover, as something which is present at this place in this particular physical shape (or is there given united to a body of this shape), where yet the same real being might just as well, so far as its own essence is concerned, be present at any other place, and in any other form, and might likewise change whilst remaining in fact unchanged, or change otherwise

than the way in which it actually does. Individual Being of every kind is, to speak quite generally, "*accidental.*" It is so-and-so, but essentially it could be other than it is [emphasis in original]. (Husserl, 1962, 46-47)

Maurice Natanson helps us comprehend this difficult idea. First, he speaks of essences rather than of essence; each thing is comprised, at least potentially, of more than one essence. More importantly, essences, as he says, are not hidden, are not mysteries to be divined; they are the intentional character of the thing itself. Essences can reveal unities of meaning—one object can be apprehended by the same person at different times or by different people at different (or the same) times. Natanson offers the following example:

The White House is essentially the same intentional object whether viewed earlier or later in the day, remembered or directly perceived or even imagined, today or last year. The "real" White House was once burned by the British army and the re-built White House is subject to fire, but the White-House-as-intended cannot be destroyed, its essentiality cannot be scorched. (Natanson, 1973, 14)

Given Natanson's assistance, we can better comprehend essences related to LIS. Information, for example, can be seen as more than the individual cases of physical packaging, or even of content. Information has an essential character that includes not just words on a page or images in a screen. It includes the process of reading and seeing, of argreeing and arguing, of evaluating and dismissing, of contextualizing and compartmentalizing. Gary Radford illustrates the essence of informing with the help of Michel Foucault (Radford, 1992). Foucault likens informing to the fantastic, but with real outcomes:

the visionary experience arises from the black and white surface of printed signs, from the closed and dusty volume that opens with a flight of forgotten words; fantasies are carefully deployed in the hushed library, with its columns of books, with its titles aligned on shelves to form a tight enclosure, but within confines that also liberate impossible worlds. The imaginary now resides between the book and the lamp. (Foucault, 1977, 90)

Foucault presents an idea of informing that goes beyond any one specific experience.

LIS, and librarianship in particular, is, at the time of this writing, grappling with essences of the profession. In 1999 the American Library Association sponsored a Congress on Professional Education. Recommendations emanating from the Congress include efforts aimed at identifying core values of the profession and fundamental competencies for those entering the profession. The phenomenological framework could be valuable in guiding these processes. What we in LIS do *not* need at this time is focus on specific, temporally fixed, solely empirically defined, "facts" of the profession. Instead, we need to think about essences, about those things that form the idea of librarianship. For example, if one of the eventually identified core values is "service," then "service" cannot be defined in terms of particular structures that occur in particular places. It should be defined in terms of what everyone can recognize as responding to the kinds of requests people may make and the reasons and purposes they may have for making the requests. Further, the attention should be on the character of responses to the requests, rather than on the instrumental actions that are executed in retrieving specific items or records. The task for us, in short, is to transcend time and place in considering such things as values and competencies.

Perception

Just as the concept of essence is most frequently (though not exclusively) linked to Husserl, the concept of perception is likely (though not completely) linked to Maurice Merleau-Ponty. And as did other phenomenologists, Merleau-Ponty took issue with some contemporary views of how we perceive our selves and the world around us. He found fault with what could be termed the associationist approach (an empiricist stance) and its physicalist and scientistic limitations (perception, in that approach, was based on stimulus and impression). He also found the intellectualist approach wanting because it tended to see the world as a construction created by a perceiving subject. Merleau-Ponty's stance is more of a unified one, in which our selves, including our physical selves, are what connect us with the external world. He tended to speak in terms of the lived world as a way of expressing the unity of our selves and the world. He wrote,

> The world is not what I think, but what I live through. I am open to the world, I have no doubt that I am in communication with it, but I do not possess it; it is inexhaustible. "There is a world", or rather: "There is the world"; I can never completely account for this ever-reiterated assertion in my life. (Merleau-Ponty, 1962, xvi-xvii)

Merleau-Ponty argues against a determinate explanation of perception. The view he opposed holds that perception is a function of sensation, or what the physical human senses and what, in the physical world, can be sensed. Such a view is a product of the intellectual genealogy whose shortcomings we've already seen. Also, as we've seen, this product of the genealogy is somewhat attractive because it provides a certain answer to questions we may have relating to perception. Instead of the deterministic position, Merleau-Ponty suggests that perception is ineluctably indeterminate. I should hasten to add that his position does not hold that perception is nondeterminate, but that the dynamics of perception (integrating, as it does, self and world) include humans confronting the world. We have to realize that we are constantly reconstituting our understanding of the world in light of changing perceptions of our selves, and vice versa. He spoke of the dynamic in the context of an individual trying to understand his/her past:

> In the same way, although my present draws into itself time past and time to come, it possesses them only in intention, and even if, for example, the consciousness of my past which I

now have seems to me to cover exactly the past as it was. The past which I claim to recapture is not the real past, but my past as I now see it, perhaps after altering it. (Merleau-Ponty, 1962, 69-70)

A similar conclusion could, and probably should, be reached regarding history generally. A deterministic version of history is not fruitful; history is a product of interpretation (there's the interrelatedness among elements again) based on changing perception.

Perhaps the difference between the phenomenological view of perception and the objective view can't be overstated. I say this because of the persistence of the idea of objective thought and the even more pervasive treatment of many human actions, including perception, objectively. An assumption of the empiricist stance is, fundamentally, that the subject is actually an object (e.g., a human being is an object in the same way that, say, a book is). If that assumption is an accurate component of empiricism then, as Gary Brent Madison says, *no one* can perceive in such a construct; perception is, effectively, impossible (Madison, 1981). Merleau-Ponty himself made this point: "Objective thought is unaware of the subject of perception. This is because it presents itself with the world ready made, as the setting of every possible event, and treats perception as one of these events" (Merleau-Ponty, 1962, 207). Hammond, Howarth, and Keat emphasize Merleau-Ponty's point with regard to language. The ambiguity we may experience is not a function of a multiplicity of possible definitions of words or terms.

> Instead it is a feature of the lived world itself—that its objects often display mutually incompatible properties. In claiming this, what [Merleau-Ponty] has in mind is quite close to the way in which one commonly talks of certain human situations or relationships as "ambiguous". For example (ours, not his), a personal relationship between two people might be described as "sexually ambiguous", in that it could equally well be interpreted as sexual or as non-sexual. . . . It would be "open to both interpretations", not because one had failed to discover which was the correct one, but because of the co-existence of

(and indeed the tension between) both "meanings".
(Hammond, Howarth, and Keat, 1991, 135)

If the empiricist position were correct and perception were equal to sensation (and, so objective), then we would face the challenge of trying to explain multiple, even conflicting, accounts of the same thing. This challenge can be examined in the context of LIS. If there were objective sensations, how would we come to grips with the different views people hold of the library? How would we explicate the debate about the purpose of the public library (ongoing almost since the founding of the public library in this country)? These questions may extend beyond perception, but the way we perceive a thing is basic to answers to the questions. More particularly, if sensation were objective, would we not be able to design information systems that all users could successfully manipulate? It is obvious that there are disagreements about the matters central to these questions. Our understanding of the questions could be enhanced by accepting that perception is dynamic and not entirely determinate. If we try to determine the outcomes of library use and information seeking through system design (the imposition of particular subject headings to works or the creation of particular search protocols), the result is likely to be frustration for us and for the users. If we accept that perception is complex we may well be able to reconceive our goals and to address them more effectively. "Once the prejudice of sensation has been banished, a face, a signature, a form of behaviour cease to be mere 'visual data' whose psychological meaning is to be sought in our inner experience, and the mental life of others becomes an immediate object, a whole charged with immanent meaning" (Merleau-Ponty, 1962, 58).

Intentionality

Intentionality may be the most central and important element of phenomenology. It is a matter that just about every philosopher who focuses on phenomenology addresses. The statement, mentioned a few times here already, that consciousness is consciousness *of* something is integral to the idea of intentionality. Our consciousness is always directed *toward* some object. The idea has a history that predates Husserl (extending at least as far back in time as Descartes), but it is certainly fundamental to his program, and those of his successors. Intentionality has been criticized over the years as being rather trivial; critics maintain that of course there is an object of consciousness, but that awareness doesn't help us understand human action. On the face of it, statements such as the following by Husserl seems self-evident:

> It was in the explicit *cogito* that we first came across this wonderful property to which all metaphysical enigmas and riddles of the theoretical reason lead us eventually back: perceiving is the perceiving of something, maybe a thing; judging, the judging of a certain matter; valuation, the valuing of a value; wish, the wish for the content wished, and so on. Acting concerns action, doing concerns the deed, loving the beloved, joy, the object of joy. (Husserl, 1962, 223)

There is much more to intentionality, though, and it has particular relevance to us in LIS.

For one thing, as Heidegger has pointed out, "Essentially the person exists only in the performance of intentional acts, and is therefore essentially *not* [emphasis in original] an object. Any psychical Objectification of acts, and hence any way of taking them as something psychical, is tantamount to depersonalization" (Heidegger, 1962, 73). His words strengthen the need to avoid objectification in the consideration of human action. Where the tendency at times in the social sciences and LIS is to reify human action, phenomenology points clearly to the error of such thought. As we consider the behavior and actions of others, we must keep in mind that those "others" are behaving intentionally—they are directing their thoughts and actions *at* something. They are not merely *re*acting to some physical stimulus, internal or external. (This is, of course, opposed to Skinner's myopic position.) There may be physical stimuli, but they become potential intentional objects. We must also remember that our own actions are intentional, including such actions as the design of information systems, the organization of information, and the mediation between users and the record.

With the reader's forebearance, it is necessary to introduce a bit of Husserl's technical language so that we might understand intentionality better. In particular, this language, as it is used by Husserl, demonstrates that phenomenology is not a relativistic position. It certainly recognizes, even embraces, indeterminacy in interpretation, but phenomenology, as I'm describing it here, does not admit to complete indeterminacy. The dynamic that includes subject and object is complex; subject and object are not completely separate, but are both components of the life-world. Husserl described two concepts that are important to the process of consciousness. One of these concepts is *noesis*, which literally means perception or thought. The other concept is *noema*, which means that which is perceived. These two concepts, *together*, are necessary components of consciousness. What this means is that we cannot connect noesis with subject and noema with object; the two concepts form a unity that should not be separated. One way to look at this unity is to recognize that we are not simply perceiving beings seeking objects to perceive. Without the things there can be no perception; without perception there are no intentional objects. In other words, consciousness is comprised of both noetic and noematic *actions*. I am stressing these concepts because they apply to the basic actions of LIS. For example, the consciousness that is necessary for materials selection in libraries should be shaped by the content of those things that might be selected. Moreover, the content of the things is related to the conscious act of selecting. We can't effectively conceive of selection without the content or the content without selection.

Intentionality illustrates that phenomenology is a realist stance. While some detractors of phenomenology claim that it is relativistic, the claims are mistaken. The fundamental premise of the phenomenon, the noetic and the noematic as a unity, point to the realism of the framework. Granted, phenomenology is not realist in the strong sense of scientific realism, with its attendant criteria of referentiality and representation. The insistence on the connection between consciousness and the thing one is conscious of clearly places phenomenology in the realist camp. The strength of phenomenology, through intentionality, is that we are able to comprehend the complexity of intentional action and we are not trapped by the restrictive physicalist or narrowly empirical limitations. As Stewart and Mickunas cogently observe,

> The intentionality of consciousness also points up the absurdity of dividing up reality into such mutually exclusive categories as minds and bodies, subjects and objects, and so forth. . . . The noetic dimension of any mental process is, in fact, the meaning of that process understood intentionally; that is, consciousness is always directed toward something, it can be a material object in some cases, or a nonmaterial object in other instances. This *object* [emphasis in original], which is the correlate of any conscious activity, is the noematic dimension of consciousness. (Stewart and Mickunas, 1990, 9, 120)

I'll offer one comment on intentionality and LIS at this point. At the risk of being reductionist, we might say that action in LIS is grounded in communication. Structures of information collections and information systems are designed to communicate to information seekers how they might be most effective in their quest. The seekers query the system or ask people questions about actual or potential information content. Responses follow those queries, and so on. At each stage the participants are engaged in complex intentional action. The participants are directed at something throughout the process. And the initial query by an information seeker is itself informed by previous intentional actions (assignments in school, household challenges, political events, etc.) that are, at the time of the query, brought into the present and are reflected upon. When we realize the nature of this action it becomes much more readily apparent that there is no concrete object to be examined as a static thing. The realization can help us speak of the phenomenon of information seeking (which unites the seeker and the content record in a process), instead of, for example, a transaction that has a discrete beginning and end. We can learn from Alfred Schutz's description of communication and the action based on communicative phenomena:

> Every act of communication has, therefore, as its in-order-to motive the aim that the person being addressed take cognizance of it in one way or another. . . . [I]f I happen to know that the completed act is only a link in a chain of means leading to a further end, then what I must do is interpret the subjective experience the other person has of that further goal itself. (Schutz, 1967, 130)

Self and Other

The realization that the phenomenon of perception, an intentional phenomenon, blurs distinctions between the perceiver and the perceived raises questions about our conception of self. We come to know that each of us is shaped, in part, by the world. The knowledge is integral to the idea of being-in-the-world. Self-awareness necessitates awareness of those things that are not self. Just as the delineation of subject and object becomes impractical, the idea of self isolated from the world becomes impossible. Again, this conception is part of the fundamental phenomenological principle that consciousness is consciousness *of* something. The consciousness we have is of the world and ourselves in the world. There are some literal implications of such a seemingly abstract statement. Imagine yourself driving a car on an interstate highway. You are aware of the traffic flow, the movement of other cars, because they can affect what you do. If another driver cuts into your lane you apply the brakes because your vehicle and the other are both occupying this part of the world. Also, you pay attention to signs that guide you to your destination, not because they are abstract communication devices, but because they inform you when to turn off the highway, which direction to head, and so on. Those signs exist for you as intentional things.

When someone enters a library for the purpose of locating a book, the unity also applies. The catalog, from which the user gets a call number, the map of the physical layout of the library, the labels on ranges of shelves, the call number on the book itself all exist to help the user fulfill the original purpose. As I've said elsewhere,

> What is primary about intentionality is that it constitutes an unmistakable link between "I" and "other." The other may be a physical object that spurs memory or some kind of conscious cognitive activity. The other may be another person, another I, which means that a pair (or set, in the case of more than two) of intentional stances are at work. The other may be the physical product of another I, such as a text in the form of a poem or a novel or a library's catalog. We cannot forget that the entirety of the library signifies, directly or indirectly, the product of intentionality. The catalog, the physical and conceptual organization, even the physical structure itself are consciously created by an I (be the "I" individual or collective). The library user—another I—adopts an intentional stance when perceiving the aspects of a library. To the user, then, the library (or its catalog or classification system) is the other. (Budd, 1995, 312)

Communication, central to LIS, should be seen as a discursive process. The rules of language—syntax, grammar, etc.—apply, but there is a difference between language and discourse. We might see discourse as language in action. Discourse, then, is a phenomenon; it is intentional. Paul Ricoeur reminds us that "To say that discourse is an event is to say, first, that discourse is realized temporally and in the present. . . . Moreover, whereas language has no subject insofar as the question, who speaks? does not apply at this level, discourse refers back to its speaker by a means of a complex set of indicators, such as personal pronouns" (Ricoeur, 1991, 77). Discourse is defined by an exchange of messages and is at least potentially meaningful. Ricoeur adds, "So discourse not only has a world but has an other, another person, an interlocutor to whom it is addressed" (Ricoeur, 1991, 78). Discourse is always the conjoining, through language, of an I and an other. The conjoining can be complex. In a profession, such as LIS, there are multiple means of discursive practice. There is, of course, the traditional dialogue—two people engaged in conversation, each explicitly aware of the exchange between self and other. There is direct, though not exactly dialogic, communication, such as a presentation before a group (common at professional conferences). The most effective presentations (and the most effective classroom presentations) also entail an acute awareness of self and other. The above two means involve situations in which it is reasonably easy to conceive of the other as another self. Another means, publication, makes such an awareness a bit more problematic. Ricoeur says that textual communication is not really dialogic, but others, such as Mikhail Bakhtin, disagree (we'll return to Bakhtin in the next chapter). In any event, textual communication is also intentional. All of these forms of communication, as Goldman points out, can contribute to knowledge by conjoining the rational and the social.

In all of these means of communication there is a necessarily intentional exchange at work. Other ways of thinking about human action, especially the kinds of scientistic, objectivist ways of thinking, do not admit to the intentional imperative. To stick with some examples already mentioned, there may be a temptation to see a library user or information seeker as an object. The kind of objectification that may occur could tend to be reductionist; the user or seeker may be seen (though certainly not overtly) as an automaton following certain rules or patterns of behavior. In this context the chosen response may be seen to be the application of prescribed instructions aimed at eliciting "appropriate" behavior. No one would admit to doing this, but the temptation exists nevertheless to treat users or seekers as "types" and to initiate programmed responses to various types. This action amounts to a denial of the consciousness of the other and, in practice, can be seen as solipsism (the belief that only the self exists). Merleau-Ponty diagnosed the problem:

> There is thus no place for other people and a plurality of consciousness in objective thought. In so far as I constitute the world, I cannot conceive another consciousness, for it too would have to constitute the world and, at least as regards this other view of the world, I should not be the constituting agent. Even if I succeeded in thinking of it as constituting the world, it would be I who would be constituting the consciousness as

such, and once more I should be the sole constituting agent.
(Merleau-Ponty, 1962, 349-50)

Merleau-Ponty's observation also serves as a critique against the
strong relativism that maintains that each of us, individually or
in some groups, defines the world around us. This kind of
relativism is actually as objectivist as the strongest scientism. The
phenomenological framework in intended to address the problem
of solipsism.

Addressing the problem, or the occasional charges, of
solipsism is indeed an important aspect of phenomenology. It is
undeniably tempting to think that I am the sole subject and
everything else is an object that might warrant my attention.
There are, however, some very important things to remember that
can help us see the relationship between self and other more
clearly. And, fortunately, Paul Ricoeur elucidates these points:

> [A]lthough, speaking absolutely, only one is subject, I, the
> Other is not given simply as psycho-physical object situated in
> nature but is also a subject of experience by the same right as I
> and as such perceives me as belonging to the world of his
> experience. . . . [T]he world is not simply a private scene but a
> public property. This is not so easy to understand, for on the
> one hand there is the "world-phenomenon" opposite to all
> subjects of experience and to all their "world-phenomena." . . .
> [T]he constitution of objects of a new type attaches to the
> experience of the Other. Cultural objects—books, tools, works
> of all sort—which specifically refer back to an active
> constitution on the part of alien subjects, these cultural objects
> are "there for everybody," more precisely for every member of
> a particular cultural community. (Ricoeur, 1967, 117-18)

The points Ricoeur makes have readily apparent connections to
LIS. The first has clear relevance to all mediation (and, in fact,
argues against the recent suggestion that disintermediation
should be common in information services). The second is the
recognition of the global phenomenon of social interaction, and
corroborates the need for a social epistemological stance for us in

LIS. The third affirms that, for every work in a collection or in any body of works, there is a consciousness responsible for that work and there is conscious reception of the work by all readers/viewers/listeners.

Interpretation

As should be evident (I hope) from the graphic representation (p. 252) of the elements of phenomenology, interpretation is key to each element and is fundamental to phenomenology itself. Ricoeur refers to the relationship between phenomenology and hermeneutics as one of "mutual belonging." He describes this relationship more explicitly:

> On the one hand, hermeneutics is erected on the basis of phenomenology and thus preserves something of the philosophy from which it nevertheless differs: *phenomenology remains the unsurpassable presupposition of hermeneutics.* On the other hand, phenomenology cannot constitute itself without a *hermeneutical presupposition* [emphasis in original]. (Ricoeur, 1991, 26)

The full realization of the relationship, as I've said, is hermeneutical phenomenology. While there may be some philosophers who would take the term to be tautological, it is necessary to make the connection as explicit as possible. The goals of phenomenology are achieved primarily through hermeneutical analysis. This kind of analysis really constitutes what we might call a metamethod, a way of conceiving any analysis, whether quantitative or qualitative methods are employed.

The process that enables us to understand each of the elements of phenomenology is necessarily interpretive. This does not mean that there are no constraints, but it does mean that there is some indeterminacy at work. By that I mean that our experiences, our use of language, our access to cultural products (books, films, Web sites, letters, etc.), are all shaped by the time in which we live. To an extent, our consciousness is also influenced by history. As we attempt to understand anything that is temporally and/or spatially removed, we face limitations. We cannot directly experience the consciousness, the self, that lived in that other time and place. We then must construct understanding with less than optimal tools. Even when we can engage someone directly we have less than full access to that other consciousness. When we don't have the temporal limitations we can at least try to engage in mutual reflection to, we hope, reach understanding. In any event, we must adopt a kind of realist position; we must examine what exists, what is accessible, and try to understand it. Such a realization argues against infinite possibilities. As Umberto Eco says, "If there is something to be interpreted, the interpretation must speak of something which must be found somewhere, and in some way respected" (Eco, 1990, 7). Since interpretation is so vital for us, we need to look more closely at hermeneutics.

Some Background to Hermeneutics

Hermeneutics actually has quite a long history, but there's no need to go into great historical detail here. We can take a brief look at some key figures to help us comprehend the main points of discussion over the years. While hermeneutics was originally intended to aid with the explication of scriptural meaning (specifically, interpreting the Bible), it began to move beyond that application in the nineteenth century in particular. Friedrich Schleiermacher, a German theologian and philologist, helped bring hermeneutics into a wider frame of application. He certainly still employed hermeneutical techniques to reach a clearer understanding of scripture, especially of the New Testament, but he was also concerned with the possibilities and practices of understanding more broadly. In his efforts to devise principles of general hermeneutics he (rightly, I think) touched on a vital point: "Understanding has a dual direction, towards the language and towards the thought" (Schleiermacher, 1998, 229). His principle presaged some twentieth-century linguists' (such as Ferdinand de Saussure) distinction between language and speech. Language refers to the entire universe of a linguistic body—for example, the English language. Speech generally refers to the particular utterances individuals make, using components of the language. Schleiermacher further made the distinction that an utterance reflects the thought of the speaker.

In referring to the thought of the speaker Schleiermacher included the psychological state of the speaker. In fact, there is a psychologistic strain throughout Schleiermacher's hermeneutics. This strain is problematic inasmuch as it depends on our ability to gain access to the inner workings of a speaker's state of mind. It is also problematic in that it is based on the assumption that what is said (or written) is an accurate and honest reflection of what is thought. Husserl, who originally was sympathetic to such a psychologistic approach, eventually recanted and claimed that it is not possible (nor is it necessarily desirable) to gain a full understanding of the state of another person. More recent critics of Schleiermacher have targeted his psychologism.

There are, however, ideas expressed by Schleiermacher that clarify the aims of interpretation and also link it with phenomenology. For example, he indicated that context is extremely important to interpretation and that history must be taken into account: "The vocabulary and the history of the era of an author relate as the whole from which his writings must be understood as the part, and the whole must, in turn, be understood from the part" (Schleiermacher, 1998, 24). In part the historical awareness is "objective" in that interpretation depends on knowing language as it could have been used by the author/speaker. In our experiences of studying the plays of Shakespeare we most likely used annotated texts to help us know what certain words or terms would have meant in Elizabethan times. Now if we have the potential for understanding, we also have the potential for misunderstanding. For us in LIS it is important that we know why some things can go wrong. Schleiermacher wrote, "Misunderstanding is either a consequence of hastiness or of prejudice. . . . The latter is a mistake which lies deeper. It is the one-sided preference for what is close to the individual's circle of ideas and the rejection of what lies outside it" (Schleiermacher, 1998, 23). Prejudice is certainly not always malicious, but may be the result of preformed ideas. For instance, we may develop ideas of the "ideal search" or of what constitutes relevance and may misinterpret an information seeker's query or the results of a search.

Later in the nineteenth century and into the early twentieth century the idea of hermeneutics was picked up by Wilhelm Dilthey. One of Dilthey's main concerns was to describe how one might gain knowledge through the human sciences (what we today would call the humanities and social sciences). He made the distinction clear between the human sciences and the natural sciences not just in disciplinary terms, but with regard to purpose:

> The nature of knowledge in the human sciences must be explicated by observing the full course of human development. Such a method stands in contrast to that recently applied all too often by the so-called positivists, who derive the meaning of the concept science from a definition of knowledge which arises from a predominant concern with the natural sciences. (Dilthey, 1989, 57)

The goal of the human sciences, to Dilthey, is understanding, particularly understanding of the individual. This is in contrast to explaining, the goal of the natural sciences, which is aimed at general types or categories. The link with phenomenology is even stronger with Dilthey than with Schleiermacher. Richard Palmer explains Dilthey's quest for a method for the human sciences as, "(1) an epistemological problem, (2) a matter of deepening our conception of historical consciousness, and (3) a need to understand expressions from out of 'life itself'" (Palmer, 1969, 100).

One of the principal phenomenology-related elements of Dilthey's thought is his conception of experience. For him experience is the totality of an individual's life in the world. The idea of life-world in Husserl and being-in-the-world in Heidegger are concepts that either spring from Dilthey or have very similar origins as Dilthey's idea of experience. Dilthey also separated the reflection upon an event in one's life from the event itself. The conscious act of reflecting is an experience in its own right. This idea of experience also is related to the phenomenological imperative of blurring the lines between subject and object.

Understanding (Dilthey's goal) involves comprehension of what another human being may think, may experience. Another person is not an object of study, but a consciousness that might be understood. In focusing on the totality of experience Dilthey was aware that life is dynamic. There may occur an event which prompts a person to reconceive what has gone before; former meaning may be replaced by reshaped meaning. This does not signify that meaning is capricious or completely subjective (that is, completely *within* the subject who experiences the world). It is tied to the phenomenon of experiencing the world. That meaning may be variable or may change over time for someone is not a mark of complete relativism; it is an indication of the dynamic nature of experience.

Contemporary Debate

In the last half of the twentieth century there has been a rather adversarial debate regarding the purpose of hermeneutics and the means of hermeneutical investigation. We've already seen (with positivism and phenomenology, for example) that philosophical concepts are not indisputable, that there can be disagreements as to definition, goals, methods, etc. Such is the case with hermeneutics. Let me say at the outset that much of this debate is irrelevant. Yes, there are some different visions of and for hermeneutics, but there is also substantial common ground. It is the common ground that is most fruitful and holds the greatest potential for us in LIS. Let's first turn to the disagreement, so that we can better understand the areas of agreement.

The debate centers on two figures—Hans-Georg Gadamer and Emilio Betti. Schleiermacher also comes into play here. Betti adheres to Schleiermacher's claim that it is possible to recapture the meaning intended by the author of a work. Betti is sympathetic to Schleiermacher's psychological analysis that is aimed at analyzing an author's time and life as a means of reaching that authorial intent. Gadamer's focus is on the text rather than the author. He has criticized Schleiermacher's psychologism as, first of all, difficult if not impossible to apply. Further, Gadamer maintains that the text holds the key to interpretation and, from there, to understanding. This is a very brief and simplistic synopsis of the issue, but it illustrates a dilemma that anyone seeking to interpret something faces: Is it possible to discern a final and complete meaning of a text or a discourse? Palmer sums up the conflict:

> The problem arises in the fact that Gadamer's ontology is such that the possibility of objective historical knowledge is called into question. From Betti's standpoint, Heidegger and Gadamer are the destructive critics of objectivity who wish to plunge hermeneutics into a standardless morass of relativity. The integrity of historical knowledge itself is under attack and must be stoutly defended. (Palmer, 1969, 47-48)

Betti tends to look upon interpretation as having an objective target—the text that has become concrete. He says,

> Here, the mind of an Other, speaks to us not directly but across space and time through transformed matter that is charged with mental energy—which makes it possible for us to approach the meaning of this product, since it is part of the human spirit and is, to speak with Husserl, born of the same transcendental objectivity; but it nevertheless remains a steadfast, self-contained existence that can confront us owing to the fact that here the mind of an Other has objectivated itself in meaning-full forms. (Betti, 1990, 173)

The objectified text becomes part of what Betti refers to as the triad of interpretation: the interpreter (the mind that seeks meaning), the author (the mind that created the work), and the objectified form (the text). The text is, in a way, the mediator between the two minds. Meaning, for Betti, is knowable, since it exists as the author's intent. There is, of course, a connection with phenomenology; no one would deny that a text (or utterance, for that matter) is the intentional product of a conscious being. The question here is the extent to which the intentional act of an author or speaker can be retrieved and known. Gadamer claims that context, in the sense of the author's psychological state at the time of creation, is not absolutely knowable; it is at least to some degree indeterminate. The reader brings a context (both in terms of knowledge of the author's time and life and of an intentional state of his/her own) to, or imposes a context upon, a text in an effort to understand it. Ron Bonetkoe suggests that the difference between Betti and Gadamer lies in what counts as context.

Betti's staunchest defender is E. D. Hirsch (of *Cultural Literacy* fame). Hirsch is adamant about making a distinction between meaning and significance. "Meaning is that which is represented by a text; it is what the author meant by his use of a particular sign sequence; it is what the signs represent" (Hirsch, 1967, 8). Hirsch appears to be falling into the same trap the strong scientific realists did in taking language to be completely and univocally representational (what is said means one, and only one, thing). What others take to be meaning Hirsch calls significance, which "names a relationship between that meaning and a person, or a conception, or a situation, or indeed anything imaginable. . . . Significance always implies a relationship, and one constant, unchanging pole of that relationship is what the text means" (Hirsch, 1967, 8). In order for an individual to find significance in a text, that person must first determine the meaning which, Hirsch says, is determinate. One major problem with that conclusion is that meaning is a prior condition of significance. If interpretation of meaning is fallible and unending, significance would be impossible to find. In claiming that an author's intent is knowable Hirsch seems to assume that the author didn't equivocate, was uniformly determinate in intent, and was stable in communicating throughout the text. I say seems to assume because Hirsch admits that an author can alter opinion regarding the meaning of a work or may no longer understand his or her text. He then says that has no effect on finding meaning. His stance rests solely on the possibility of fixed philological analysis that results in fixed meaning. If, however, a word or phrase can have multiple meanings, in the philological sense, his stance collapses. As we know, multiple meanings are not uncommon, in literary or other kinds of discourse. Ricoeur has

what is perhaps the most effective rejoinder to Hirsch's insistence
on relying on the intended meaning of the author:

> In fact, however, the intention of the author is lost as a
> psychical event. Moreover, the intention of writing has no other
> expression than the verbal meaning of the text itself. Hence all
>
> information concerning the biography and the psychology of
> the author constitutes only a part of the total information
> which the logic of validation has to take into account. This
> information, as distinct from the text interpretation, is in no
> way normative as regards the task of interpretation. (Ricoeur,
> 1976, 100)

Gadamer presents his own set of problems. In particular, he
leaves himself open to accusations of relativism. He repeatedly
makes claims that the meaning of texts is not fixed; it is a product
of history. Also, at times he says that reaching a "true"
interpretation does not depend on the work's background.
Bonetkoe recognizes that some of Gadamer's statements create a
phenomenological problem: "[Gadamer's approach to
interpretation] involves, both a recognition of the author as an
Other, but a determination that, since there is no possibility of
recognizing *all* [emphasis in original] that is other in another, we
will ignore him entirely" (Bonetkoe, 1987, 8). Bonetkoe also
observes that, while Gadamer criticizes Schleiermacher's
psychologism, he glosses over Schleiermacher's repeated warnings
that the task of interpretation in unending, "that our
understanding of another can *always* [emphasis in original] be
improved by further research into the circumstances of his life
and the language of his texts" (Bonetkoe, 1987, 8). Gadamer
himself is not the relativst some claim him to be, though. In *Truth
and Method* he states unequivocally that the purpose of
hermeneutics is to seek truth. Palmer recognizes that Gadamer
sees the difficulty of interpretation since "Historical knowledge
is itself an historical event; subject and object of historical science
do not exist independently of each other" (Palmer, 1969, 52).
Palmer clearly sees the phenomenological aspect of hermeneutics.

He also sees that hermeneutics is connected to epistemology and has a practical purpose of linking language, thinking, and reality (Palmer, 1969, 54).

Agreements about Hermeneutics

As I mentioned, we can learn more from what philosophers have in common, since there are fundamental areas of agreement. Further, these areas of agreement emphasize the relationship between phenomenology and hermeneutics. One of the most fundamental components is that hermeneutics aims to attain understanding. The word understanding has significance that transcends the usual usage. Understanding extends to the universality of the human condition, incorporating all of the elements of phenomenology, and so helps us to approach the criteria for knowledge. Hermeneutics is a way to approach the life-world and being-in-the-world. Betti admits to this fundamental purpose: "Drawing on the familiar distinction between action and outcome, procedure and its result, we may tentatively characterize interpretation as the procedure that aims for, and results in, Understanding. . . . [S]peech produced by our fellow-men cannot be regarded as a ready-made physical object simply to be received by us" (Betti, 1990, 162). For Betti the way to achieve understanding is through the triadic process that includes the interpreter, the creator of the text, and the text itself. In light of the challenge to the importance of the creator (attributed to Gadamer, among others), we have to recognize that Betti's triad speaks to many of the actions that occur in information agencies, especially direct mediation. When a librarian or information specialist tries to mediate between the record and the information seeker, we can readily see the utility of Betti's vision. The librarian must consider both the question and the person asking it. The phenomenon of mediation includes the three aspects.

Both Betti and Gadamer include an ontological element in their ideas of hermeneutics. Actually, we can include the ontological element in the thought of the phenomenologists discussed above. For example, the very concept of being is frequently linked to truth. James DiCenso, in addressing the work of Heidegger in particular, observes that "What is required is an inquiry into Being that is capable of addressing issues concerning the *way* [emphasis in original] things are, that is, their manner or mode of existing" (DiCenso, 1990, 30). Richard Bernstein affirms the importance of being and emphasizes the ontological side of being, and its universality: "We are 'thrown' into the world as beings who understand; and understanding itself is not one type of activity of a subject, but may properly be said to underlie all activities" (Bernstein, 1985, 274). I'll repeat again, hermeneutical phenomenology is a kind of realist stance and, inherent in a realistic stance, is the aim of understanding the truth of being.

While this section focuses on agreement, there is an area where Betti and Gadamer seem unable to come to terms with one another—the historian's understanding of history. This point does have relevance for the formal study of history, but it has broader ramifications. All of what we can call the human sciences have a historical aspect. This is true of LIS as well. The issues we deal with have historical roots and necessitate interpretation of the past. Betti maintains that it is possible to come to objective historical knowledge, that it is possible for the interpreter to eschew all preconceptions and to "exclude any personal preference concerning the result" (Betti, 1990, 170). Even in this apparent steadfastness in favor of objectivity Betti hedges. He says, "objective truth can now be glimpsed from any standpoint and point of view within the limits of their perspective; the picture that is arrived at would only be misleading if that particular perspective was claimed to represent the only admissable and legitimate one" (Betti, 1990, 172). In admitting to multiple possible legitimate approaches Betti is necessarily admitting the melding of history and historical understanding, a principal element of Gadamer's thought. Although he is not responding directly to Betti, Ricoeur explains a problem with historical objectivism:

The error of the proponents of nomological models is not so much that they are mistaken about the nature of the laws that the historian may borrow from other and most advanced social sciences—demography, economics, linguistics, sociology, etc.—but about how these laws work. They fail to see that these laws take on a historical meaning to the extent that they are grafted onto a prior narrative organization that has already characterized events as contributing to the development of a plot. (Ricoeur, 1991, 5)

Another point of common ground is the connection of hermeneutics with knowledge. In seeking understanding we are seeking knowledge. There is a richness and a particular character that hermeneutics presents to us, though. I am indebted to Bernstein for demonstrating the practical aspect of knowledge, especially as Gadamer envisions it. The importance of knowledge to praxis is of paricular interest to us in LIS.

As I indicated in the introduction, I'm using the word *praxis* deliberately here, instead of practice. While praxis, which comes from the Greek, is frequently translated as practice, the word has a more specifc meaning, especially to Aristotle. As Bernstein points out, praxis refers to action in the social and ethical sense, whereas practice refers to the technical performance of a task (Bernstein, 1971, ix-xiii). In LIS practice is of vital importance; it is essential that we, as professionals, are proficient in the tasks of information work. Likewise, though, praxis is essential. We must continuously remind ourselves that LIS has a social meaning as well as a technical application. We might even say that our praxis is a combination of all our practices *plus* the ethical basis of our being.

Bernstein, in examining Gadamer's stance regarding knowledge, recognizes that there are several kinds of knowledge. As we saw in the last chapter, there is knowing how (we might use the Greek word techne for this) and knowing that (which we've referred to as episteme, and is taken to mean the universal knowledge of a field or discipline). Episteme was the focus of chapter 5 and, in fact, is at the heart of this book. There is another kind of knowledge to Gadamer (and to Aristotle)—phronesis, or the ethical knowledge that mediates between the universal and the particular. In other words, phronesis helps to unite being and knowing.

Gadamer says that a product of phronesis is understanding, not in a technical sense (such as understanding how an operating system works), but of the relationship of self and other. "The person with understanding does not know and judge as one who stands apart and unaffected; but rather, as one united by a specific bond with the other, he thinks with the other and understands the situation with him" (Gadamer, 1989, 288). As Bernstein explains, to Gadamer understanding helps us to realize our humanity, including our shared humanity, more fully. For this reason Gadamer sees the human sciences as moral-practical sciences. For us this brings home the importance of LIS as a praxis (including research within praxis) with ethical imperatives, with obligations beyond individuals and beyond the profession. As Gadamer put it, phronesis involves knowledge of both means and ends (Gadamer, 1989, 286). Gadamer's concept also helps us in LIS to comprehend that information seekers are, at their cores, seekers of understanding. He writes,

> The interpreter dealing with a traditional text seeks to apply it to himself. But this does not mean that the text is given for him as something universal, that he understands it as such and only afterwards uses it for particular applications. Rather, the interpreter seeks no more than to understand this universal thing, the text; i.e., to understand what this piece of tradition says, what constitutes the meaning and the importance of the text. In order to understand that, he must not seek to disregard himself and his particular hermeneutical situation. He must relate the text to this situation, if he wants to understand at all. (Gadamer, 1989, 289)

The information structures, including libraries, that we work with are universal. We can see this most plainly in our catalogs, classification systems, information products (such as databases), and their operation. These universals, for information seekers, are means, and we need to focus our praxis on that realization.

With knowledge as our goal, we cannot remind ourselves often enough that all of the kinds of knowledge must be part of our praxis. Techne without episteme and phronesis places us in the position of adopting practices that are not aimed at information seekers. The elements of phenomenology are lost in such narrow practices. Concern with means dominates and the ends may be forgotten. Jurgen Habermas warns against dismissing episteme and phronesis:

> The positivistic self-understanding of the nomological sciences does in fact promote the suppression of action through technology. If practical questions, which involve the adoption of standards, are withdrawn from rational discussion, and if only technologically exploitable knowledge is considered to be reliable, then only the instrumentalist values of efficiency participate in what is left of rationality. (Habermas, 1988, 20)

Paul Ricoeur

At this point I want to focus a bit of space on the work of Paul Ricoeur. I've already quoted him in a few contexts earlier in this chapter to point to the usefulness of phenomenology and the purposes of hermeneutics. As is true of most mature thinkers, Ricoeur's ideas regarding phenomenology and hermeneutics have changed somewhat over time. Many of his later writings reflect the thought he has given to the issues discussed in this chapter. I do not agree with everything he says, but much of his work can be appropriated by us in LIS. I've mentioned that he has taken issue with Hirsch and the tradition of Romanticist hermeneutics in critiquing the psychologistic program aimed at understanding an author's intention better even than the author. His critique is largely well founded, but it presents some problems for us, even as it suggests an alternative. In rejecting psychologism he rejects the influences that acted upon the author/speaker. His alternative is to examine a text semantically as a way of finding meaning. He says, "The surpassing of the intention by the meaning signifies precisely that understanding takes place in a nonpsychological and properly semantical space, which the text has carved out by severing itself from the mental intention of its author" (Ricoeur, 1976, 76). The principal difficulty with his alternative is the accompanying assumption that semantics is temporally and spatially static, that the analysis we may make here today holds for discourse originating at another time and another place. It seems that, while Hirsch is in error, some attention to the author's time and life can augment the semantic analysis.

Ricoeur's conception of semantic analysis does hold promise for us, though. A fundamental element of his idea is one that has been mentioned briefly above—the distinction between language and speech. He refines the distinction by separating language and discourse. Discourse, according to him, is a phenomenon that is temporal and is realized in the present. Language, as a universal, is not so time bound. Another difference is that "the signs of language refer only to other signs in the interior of the same system so that language no more has a world than it has a time and a subject, whereas discourse is always about something" (Ricoeur, 1991, 78). The phenomenological aspect of discourse is evident in the distinction. Discourse includes an other; it is addressed to someone. Also, it shares a feature with consciousness; it is about something. Further, discourse has its own structure; it is not merely an aggregation of words, or even an aggregation of sentences. Discourse, as he states, is a message intended for a reader or hearer; it is intended to be understood. It has meaning. As an intentional event, discourse contains both noesis (thought or perception) and noema (that which is perceived). What is written or what is said embodies the intention of the writer/speaker (noesis) *and* the meaning of the speech act, of the event (noema).

Discourse is dialectical; it is an event, which is temporally fixed, and it carries meaning, which transcends time. The meaning endures even though the event is fleeting. We experience both sides of the dialectic. Ricoeur focuses on writing in this dialectic, since the event of writing is recorded in what is written. Speaking is usually not recorded, but it can continue in the memory and consciousness of the hearer. The major differences between writing and speaking have to do with audience and with time. The writer is not in the presence of the audience (and there may be audiences that are not anticipated by the writer), and the writer's text has already been created by the time a reader has access to it. Ricoeur observes that "there is no longer a situation common to the writer and the reader, and the concrete conditions of the act of pointing no longer exist" (Ricoeur, 1991, 85). The dialectic is evident in information work. Direct mediation, such as a reference transaction, most obviously represents an event, but it also depends on discernment of meaning. A person searching a database is most obviously a quest for meaning, but it is also an event, albeit one in which the connection between the "writer" and the reader (searcher) is not concrete. In both cases there is intentional action that is undertaken in an effort to find meaning.

Ricoeur acknowledges the complexity of interpretation. For one thing, we have to deal with polysemy; many words have more than one meaning. Further, sentences may be ambiguous. The hazards we come up against are not insurmountable, however. In most instances we can determine which of the polysemic meanings of a word apply from the context of the sentence. And we can determine which reading of a sentence is appropriate when we look at it in the context of the whole work. Ricoeur at times advocates a structural analysis as a means of finding meaning (that is, examining the specific words and their possible meanings within the structure of the discourse itself). This method may be effective in many cases, but it can also be limiting. For instance, Bakhtin says that structuralism assumes "a listener who is immanent in the work as an all-understanding, ideal listener.

. . . It is an abstract ideological formulation. Counterposed to it is the same kind of abstract ideal author. In this understanding the ideal listener is essentially a mirror image of the author who replicates him" (Bakhtin, 1986, 165). In LIS discourse, for example, a structural analysis may be insufficient to draw connections among propositions and ideas as a way to gain knowledge. The structure alone may not hold the key to the phenomenological elements that open up discourse to interpretation and, so, to knowledge.

At his clearest, Ricoeur avoids the problems his thought is sometimes prone to (for instance, avoiding the primacy of language over discourse, which most structuralists concede). For the most part, as I've said, he reacts against Romanticist hermeneutics and closes himself off to the world of the author. At other times he recognizes that the two facets of authorial intent and the semantics of the text are also a necessary dialectic contributing to understanding. For example, at one point he writes,

> On the one hand, we would have what W. K. Wimsatt calls the intentional fallacy, which holds the author's intention as the criterion for any valid interpretation of the text, and, on the other hand, what I would call in a symmetrical fashion the fallacy of the absolute text: the fallacy of hypostasizing the text as an authorless entity. If the intentional fallacy overlooks the semantic autonomy of the text, the opposite fallacy forgets that a text remains a discourse told by somebody, said by someone to someone else about something. It is impossible to cancel out this main characteristic of discourse without reducing texts to natural objects, i.e., to things which are not man-made, but which, like pebbles, are found in the sand. (Ricoeur, 1976, 30)

When he accepts this dialectic he is on the surest footing with regard to the normative aim of interpretation—understanding through explanation. And the outcome of such understanding, the outcome we seek, is knowledge.

LIS and Hermeneutics

There are few writings in LIS that directly address hermeneutics (and fewer that address phenomenology). It is useful, however, to take a look at some of these publications in order to see how our field is receiving the ideas of philosophers and theorists. The first work I'll deal with briefly is *Librarians in Search of Science and Identity* by George Bennett. This book is a published version of his dissertation, in which he attempts to apply hermeneutics to praxis in LIS. The attempt should be applauded, but there are some conceptual problems with his view of hermeneutics and its application. First, he borrows from Ricoeur, but he does so uncritically. He accepts Ricoeur's critique of Romanticist hermeneutics but he doesn't see some of the shortcomings in Ricoeur's insistence on the primacy of the text. That said, there is a paradox in Bennett's book. While he claims to use Ricoeur's thought as a guide, he also turns to the sociology of science as support for the claim that there are multiple, socially constructed, realities. In drawing from some of the sociological stances (examined in a previous chapter here) Bennett neglects to investigate the determinism of some of those claims. In particular, he accepts that reality is a social construction; this is a fundamentally anti-realist stance that negates any ontological truth. Further, the determinist stance is necessarily skeptical about agreement among cultural groups; if there happens to be agreement, it is accidental. Bennett does observe that, in any setting, there may be some interpretive conventions that become ingrained in the day-to-day life of the group. Where he falls short is in his assumption that, because these conventions are interpretive, they are grounded in hermeneutics. Hermeneutics, as we've seen, is normative and not relative. In short, what he takes to be interpretive conventions are really more like dicta—pronouncements intended (in many cases explicitly) to influence action. Bennett does not make the neccesary distinction in his book, and his aim of constituting hermeneutics as the theory of practice falls short of its mark.

Daniel Benediktsson has also focused directly on hermeneutics. He has offered an erudite summary of some of the background to hermeneutics as well as to some of the major strains of thought in hermeneutics. Despite the service he provides LIS in raising the questions he does, he takes the more psychologistic path of Betti and finds the most problematic elements of Ricoeur's thought the most attractive. Benediktsson rightly recognizes the phenomenological underpinnings of hermeneutics, but he limits his critique of phenomenology to Husserl and neglects some of the glosses on Husserl provided by other philosophers—glosses that clarify some points and emphasize the positive aspects of phenomenology. For example, he takes Husserl to task for isolating consciousness in the emphasis on intuition as a means to knowing essences (Benediktsson, 1989, 206-9, 219). Intuition, for Husserl, is indeed a challenging idea, but others who have examined this idea have refined the concept and its application. Emmanuel Levinas has placed intuition into an ontological philosophy and has demonstrated that it can be useful to understanding of reality (Levinas, 1995). Benediktsson does accept that Gadamer's thought provides some useful grounding for us in LIS, but he chooses to adhere to Betti's idea of meaning-full forms and Ricoeur's structural analysis. Perhaps the major problem with Benediktsson's paper is his complete dismissal of empiricism. Strong empiricism (what we might call intolerant empiricism) is seriously problematic, but empiricism in general is not illegitimate; it is limited. It must be accompanied by hermeneutical phenomenology if we are to reach understanding of phenomena. Perhaps the greatest service Benediktsson provides is his concrete links between hermeneutics and LIS praxis: "At least two major subfields can be named: Information retrieval (IR), in terms of bibliographic organization retrieval and indexing, and personal interaction within reference theory" (Benediktsson, 1989, 227).

I made reference to the work of Ian Cornelius earlier. His book is an important one and I recommend it to all in LIS. At the outset he states what he hopes to communicate to readers, that "An interpretive approach gives practice an enhanced role in theory construction for the field by binding practice and theory into a closer and more complex relationship" (Cornelius, 1996, 2). I mention this because of the frequent criticism of writings in LIS that there is no connection to practice. Cornelius's work actually addresses praxis, the social importance of action as well as the techniques applied. As he points out, "Practice has received increased attention in the professional literature, but as an idea it has been poorly treated, concentrating more on the performance of tasks than on the problem of what practice in the profession means for the self-identity of each practitioner" (Cornelius, 1996, 35). Regarding praxis, he admonishes writers in LIS for ignoring difficult questions and especially for avoiding serious discussion of theory that could help us better understand the field. He also, quite rightly, adds that the discussion should not be couched in quantitative-qualitative terms but in terms of conceptual foundations that can guide the application of specific methodologies. He further, again quite rightly, emphasizes that an interpretive approach is based on experience and is intended to foster understanding of shared experience.

Rather than summarize Cornelius's many excellent points (he does this job much more completely than I could attempt here in a synopsis), I'll focus on one principal feature of his book. A fundamental purpose of any praxis is to find meaning in what is done. What is needed in LIS is much more attention given over to the meanings that, first of all, inhere in the things we do and the things we say and, next, are to be sought and found by us (in other words, what do we *really* mean). At the heart of a discussion about meaning is a genuine acceptance of reflexive practice, of a consciously interpretive and intentional approach to praxis. Reflection necessitates moving beyond the instrumental tasks that are undertaken in order to understand purpose. Cornelius illustrates this necessity by saying that "the practice of filing catalog cards in a drawer does not have as its meaning or ultimate purpose conformity to some set of rules about filing, rather observing those rules give effect to some other objective that requires the filing of records in some order" (Cornelius, 1996, 111). Reflection also means that theorizing is a part of life for serious practitioners. The professional, in constantly reflecting on action, is constantly theorizing, is constantly apprehending shared meaning (Cornelius, 1996, 125). Cornelius draws quite heavily from the thought of Charles Taylor, who succinctly connects theory and praxis:

> In any case, it is clear that theories do much more than explain social life; they also define the understandings that underpin

ms of social practice, and they help to orient us in
orld. And obviously the most satisfying theories are
do both at once: they offer the individual an
orientation which he shares with his compatriots, and which is
reflected in their common institutions. (Taylor, 1985, 108)

Cornelius, perhaps more thoughtfully than anyone in recent
years, offers LIS a way to think about what this praxis is really
about.

Summary

The foregoing has been based on the premise that inquiry in
LIS, and in all of the social sciences, needs to be founded on a
way of thinking that recognizes the characteristics and qualities
of humans. What we in LIS deal with are human beings and
human constructions. Our dealings can be seen as events in the
phenomenological sense. One of the implications of these events
is the blurring of subject and object. This means that the event is
shared and affects all involved in it. Further, the event is
intentional; the participants mean something by their actions and
are pointed to an outcome. The phenomenological way of
thinking, incorporating hermeneutics, provides us with a way to
see ourselves and our actions that will enable us to understand
these actions and ourselves. Or, stated another way, it gives us a
means to gain knowledge. And, hermeneutical phenomenology is
a way to investigate reality; it is grounded in ontology.

Richard Palmer encapsulates hermeneutics in a concise set of
theses, some of which are as follows:

The hermeneutical experience is intrinsically historical. . . .
The hermeneutical experience is intricically linguistic. . . .
The hermeneutical experience is dialectical. . . .
The hermeneutical experience is an event—a "language event."
. . .

The hermeneutical experience understands what is said
light of the present. . . .
The hermeneutical experience is a disclosure of truth. (Palmer,
1969, 242-45)

An important aspect of phenomenology, at least as conceived
by Husserl, is that it is presuppositionless. As an absolute goal,
this is unattainable. Everything that we do in a formal discipline
like LIS is purposeful, is in some respect theory laden; even the
avoidance of presuppositions is a theoretical construct. We can,
however, admit to an openness to the phenomena we're
examining. By that I mean that we need not constrain our study
of phenomena in LIS or our praxis by assertions that specific
constructs govern action. For example, if we begin by assuming
that mediation between information seekers and the graphic
record functions like a system, with a particular set of actions,
reactions, and flows of communication, then we may impose that
structure on the act of mediating (whether the structure
facilitates understanding or not). Instead of trapping ourselves in
abstract ideals, we would do better to follow the advice of
Mikhail Bakhtin, who argues against what he calls "theoreticism,"
which is a fundamentally a theory about itself, not a theory about
being. "A theory needs to be brought into communion *not*
[emphasis in original] with theoretical constructions and
conceived life, but with the actually occurring event of moral
being" (Bakhtin, 1993, 12). The phenomenological framework,
focusing as it does on being, is more responsive to essences,
perception, and other.

We must remember that this framework is normative; it does
not admit to a permissive relativism. Spiegelberg reminds us that
"phenomenology is more than phenomena and their direct
inspection. It is a systematic account of these phenomena. As
such it is expressed in descriptive statements which claim to be
true. . . . Their claim of truth has always to be checked against
the facts, if only the facts of the phenomena" (Spiegelberg, 1975,
117). As he has stated, phenomenology is means to achieve
knowledge, and knowledge that is intersubjective, knowledge that
is shared. His statement reinforces the social epistemic goal of
hermeneutic phenomenology.

Next, we'll look at some work in LIS and some possibilities
that have the potential to achieve the epistemological goal we've
set for ourselves.

truth- seeking

Chapter Seven

Products and Possibilities in LIS

In past chapters we've seen an intellectual heritage of the social sciences and LIS, some representations of the limitations of that heritage, an argument for the purpose of LIS, and a framework for achieving that purpose. The goal of knowledge, achieved through hermeneutical phenomenology, points to one thing quite clearly—the action we engage in LIS, including facilitating information seeking, are inseparable from being, especially as conceived by Husserl and Heidegger. In this chapter we'll see some works that have the purpose of LIS in mind and employ productive means to meet their ends. I'm not saying that these works are perfect, but they do not succumb to many of the temptations of scientism and, by and large, they do not resort to deterministic methods. The examples used are not exhaustive; they don't represent all of the well-conceived, well-executed contemporary inquiry in LIS. The examples are intended to be illustrative of the need to remember that the goal is knowledge (for its own sake *and for application in practice*). They further illustrate that physicalist methods are not sufficient for understanding. Instead, they are sensitive (although usually implicitly) to the framework proposed in chapter 6. In addition to the examples, taken from the pages of our literature, this chapter will suggest some conceptual strategies from other disciplines for inquiry and praxis (keeping in mind that praxis includes both the techniques used from day to day plus the social and ethical imperatives of LIS).

Relevance

A considerable amount of work identified as part of information science deals directly with, or depends on, ideas regarding relevance. I've mentioned some aspects of relevance earlier, but I believe it's now necessary to look at some fairly common, but misguided, ideas about relevance so that we can better appreciate the more conceptually sound work. Of course one of the first and most important challenges in any study that includes relevance is to define the word. In application, relevance is overwhelmingly associated with topicality. This means that a document could be judged relevant if the topic of the document matches the topic of the search (or, more appropriately, the terms used in a search). For instance, an information seeker may express a query as: voting patterns of naturalized U.S. citizens. Investigators may then ask the seeker to judge the relevance of items in a retrieved set. In some cases the seeker has access only to a title, in some cases the seeker has access to an abstract, and in other cases the seeker may be able to examine the entire document. The seeker then judges each document (or abstract or title) as relevant or not. In many studies the relevance judgment is a binary one—yes or no. Lesk and Salton, in a heavily cited article published more than three decades ago, offer an explicit operational definition of relevance. A document is to be considered relevant "if it is directly stated in the abstract as printed, or can be directly *deducted* [emphasis in original] from the printed abstract, that the document contains information on the topic asked for in the query" (Lesk and Salton, 1968, 347). Lesk and Salton treat retrieval in an objectivist way. A document "contains" relevant information in the same way that a glass can "contain" water. Further, there is an objectivist connection between the abstract (they do not refer to the entirety of a document) and the search strategy. Both abstract and search statement are objects that have some determinate relationship. Studies that follow the lead of Lesk and Salton may be geared toward answering questions about information seeking generally, or toward the design of technical systems.

In any event, the assumption, which is more often than not implicit, that relevance can be assessed in binary terms is a product of the outlined genealogy. A practical flaw of some work dealing with relevance is that assumptions regarding judgments are unstated, leaving the reader to infer them from the study. The inferred assumptions generally follow a few lines:

(1) information seekers are able to peruse documents, parts of documents, or abstracts and make immediate binary judgments;

(2) information seekers' queries are complete and explicit, allowing others to make judgments about the relevance of documents;

(3) the relevance judgment, once made, is permanent;

(4) the documents in a retrieved set can be effectively assessed independently of one another; and

(5) relevance inheres in the document, making reliable relevance judgments possible.

Not all work contains these assumptions, but they are not uncommon. All of the assumptions are based on a physicalist view of relevance—it exists as part of the stated query and/or it is part of each document (that is, every document is discernibly relevant or not to any stated query). In other words, relevance is a verifiable, empirically measured property of the query or of the document.

Some of the measures, closely related to relevance, that have been a part of information retrieval research for a few decades are precision and recall. These measures were employed some years ago in the Cranfield studies (Cleverdon, 1960; Cleverdon, 1962).

(It should be noted that Cleverdon himself recognized the limitations of recall and precision and urged caution in their use.) Recall is usually defined as the number of relevant documents retrieved divided by the number of relevant documents in the database. So if an information seeker constructs a query that yields 100 relevant documents and it is determined that there are 200 relevant documents in the database, the recall figure is 50 percent. Precision is defined as the number of relevant documents retrieved divided by the total number of documents retrieved. So if an information seeker constructs a query that yields 100 documents, and twenty-five of the retrieved documents are relevant, the precision figure is 25 percent. Of course the measures depend on the ability to make an absolute relevance judgment. In the case of recall it is further assumed that it is possible to make a relevance judgment about each document in the database. When librarian-mediated online searching was common in libraries some training tools were used to improve the effectiveness of librarians' searches. Natural language queries were presented to librarians and they would then structure queries according to system protocols and, perhaps, database thesauri. The system would then calculate recall and precision figures (which means that relevance was determined beforehand). The shortcomings of such training tools are readily evident. As Linda Schamber says, "Generally, recall, precision, and similar measures concern the ability of the system to identify relevant documents without error, or . . . the degree to which system relevance response predicts user relevance judgment" (Schamber, 1994, 14).

The difficulties with a naive view of relevance (the premise that, if the topic of a document matches the terms of a search, the document is relevant) are recognized in some work that is more sensitive to the human quest for knowledge. In a couple of studies Taemin Kim Park questions the objectivist definition of relevance:

> Topical relevance is context-free and is based on fixed assumptions about the relationship between a topic of a document and a search question, ignoring an individual's particular context and state of needs. It is an [*sic*] unidimensional view of users'

> information problems, disregarding the changing nature of the individual's information problem and its subsequent impact on the search. It fails to focus on the complexity of the individual's background and task situation. (Park, 1994, 136)

Recognizing the importance of context is a step toward recognizing the phenomenological nature of being and the connection between being and the world. A query does not simply appear from nowhere; it is an expression that is rooted in an intellectual situation that includes some knowledge and the desire to know more. Much of traditional thought on relevance tacitly assumes that a seeker's knowledge is definite and the desire to know more is clearly directed, with no confusion or ambiguity. Park disputes this assumption.

Another kind of questioning of the assumption regarding relevance is made by Nicholas Belkin. Belkin advocates what has come to be called the cognitive viewpoint. He admits that some proponents of the cognitive viewpoint incorporate some aspects of phenomenological thinking, especially thinking that adds social to individual being. Ostensibly, the cognitive viewpoint is intended to replace an approach to information seeking that is object-centered with one that is user-centered. I say ostensibly because, despite the seeming user-centered orientation, Belkin's vision of the cognitive viewpoint tends to be reductionist. He coins the term Anomalous States of Knowledge (ASK) to describe in some way the information seeker's reason for searching. The term itself creates a problem for us, though, since it implies that there are definable states that can be altered by some action on the parts of librarians or systems designers. (In one sense, all knowledge is anomalous if we take it to be fallible and corrigible.) He says that we can expect a seeker to describe "goals, problems, and knowledge, and that such a description can be represented and used in comparison with similar document representations for retrieval purposes" (Belkin, 1990, 14). According to such a position, knowledge can be translated into information needs in terms specific enough to generate representations and then matched with other representations determined from the documents themselves. Two objects (the representations) can be compared so that relevance can be assessed. While initially attractive, the cognitive viewpoint has shortcomings, many of which are noted by Bernd Frohmann. Frohmann details the diminshing of social elements of knowledge, the reduction of intellection to specific internal cognitive processes, and ultimately the commodification of information seeking (Frohmann, 1992). Belkin's work serves as a warning to us to look past claims of user-centeredness and to examine closely the nature of any theoretical and practical position for its relation to being.

Perhaps a more reasonable description of relevance is offered by Park. Relevance is, as Park says, temporal and fluid. A document (or any potentially informing text) can only be evaluated at a point in time and in the context of being at that time. Traditional thinking maintains a clear subject-object separation. The phenomenological framework, as we've seen, negates a clear separation. This means that relevance does not inhere in the document, nor does it reside in the information seeker (solely). The fluidity of relevance includes not only the seeker's knowledge, but also the seeker's perception, which is intentional. A claim that relevance is temporal and fluid implies that relevance judgments are not fixed; they may change with time. Park says that it may be possible to "trace an individual's view of relevance and its changing patterns during the whole process of one's information seeking and use" (Park, 1993, 346). In other words, a study could be conducted to collect relevance judgments from the seeker at various stages of research (treating the judgments as historical data) and then examining the judgments qualitatively. Park's work can help us see the short-comings of the traditional views of relevance. One limitation of his work is that there seems to be an assumption that judgments progress through discrete stages. Such an idea runs somewhat counter to the notion of fluidity.

Park's work (along with that of several others) is cited by Peiling Wang and Marilyn White. Early in their article they state, "The current paradigm related to relevance considers it a complex, multidimensional concept based on both cognitive and situational factors that is derived from dynamic human judg-ments" (Wang and White, 1999, 99). They then construct a study that has participants from a previous examination of relevance judgments reassess the relevance of retrieved documents. Wang and White recorded comments about the relevance of documents at the time they were retrieved in 1992. They then interviewed the participants in 1995 and asked them about subsequent assessments of the relevance of the documents. One respondent said in 1992 that a title looked promising and should be examined right away. In 1995 that respondent said that, upon reading the full document it was not appropriate for citation, even though the document fits generally with the respondent's research interest. Wang and White conclude in this instance that, "In the comments across the two studies, it is apparent that this participant applied different criteria in the citing decision than in the selecting decision" (Wang and White, 1999, 101). While it could have been stated more explicitly, this study includes a number of instrumental aims that might be linked to relevance. Such aims include inserting citations to pioneers in the field or to journals that are deemed important to the discipline. A next step in this kind of inquiry could be to explore how relevance assessments fit into the more complex dynamic of being.

One of the voices most critical to the physicalist view of relevance belongs to David Ellis. His remarks at times strike at the heart of the physicalist way of thinking and expose its limitations:

> But it is not objection to measurement which underlines criticism of the employment of relevance as a performance criterion; rather the lack of recognition that there is a difference in kind between the employment of a device to measure a physical process, and the employment of human judgements of relevance as the basis of the measures of retrieval effectiveness. (Ellis, 1990, 21)

Ellis correctly and necessarily articulates what is probably the central shortcoming of the genealogy of thought that contributes to a physicalist position. The genealogy, accepted widely in the social sciences and LIS, logically leads to the acceptance of simplistic empirical means of measurement. I will not argue that empirical, quantitative methods have no value in LIS; they can contribute to understanding. For instance, data about library acquisition and circulation trends can help us greatly in our understanding of the nature and use of materials. These methods, however, have severe limitations and Ellis points out how they fall short:

> The goal of attempting to retrieve all and only those documents which are relevant to the searcher becomes not so much a theoretical ideal, unattainable in practice, as an unsustainable construct. . . . [W]hile it is feasible to describe or analyze changes in knowledge in response to new information qualitatively, to attempt to do the same quantitatively seems to have no tenable theoretical or practical foundation and represents a similar unsustainable research goal. . . . The original vision of information retrieval research as a discipline founded on quantification proved equally restricting for its theoretical and methodological development. (Ellis, 1996, 33-34)

It is time for information retrieval, as a field of study and as it applies to praxis, to transcend those restrictions.

In at least one published piece Park makes reference to a book entitled *Relevance: Communication and Cognition*, by Dan Sperber and Deirdre Wilson. While nominally a work in the realm of cognitive science, *Relevance* focuses on the linguistic and philosophical side of that discipline. At one point Sperber and Wilson make an observation that seems eminently sensible, even though it is an idea that is missing from much traditional LIS thinking: "As a discourse proceeds, the hearer retrieves or constructs and then processes a number of assumptions. These form a gradually changing background against which new information is processed. Interpreting an utterance involves . . . seeing the contextual effects of this assumption in a context determined, at least in part, by earlier acts of comprehension" (Sperber and Wilson, 1988, 118). A judgment of relevance, such as one that research subjects may be asked to make, might well be based on intuition. As such it is, as Park says, temporal and fluid. The contextual elements within which relevance is assessed include both external and internal frames. In the external frame, something may be deemed relevant if it fits logically, substantively, spatially, and temporally into a situation. A student may find a text relevant if it fits into the content of a course, specifically if it fits into the content that is currently being studied or is the focus of an assignment. Further, that text may be relevant if it fits into the kind and depth of treatment of the course. With the internal frame, a text may be deemed relevant if it fits with what an individual is currently thinking about and if it fits into the way an individual is thinking about the topic.

These frames seem self-evident, but let me elaborate on them a bit to illustrate the complexity of relevance. Sperber and Wilson write, "We have suggested that the context used to process new assumptions is, essentially, a subset of the individual's old assumptions, with which the new assumptions combine to yield a variety of contextual effects" (Sperber and Wilson, 1988, 132). When a person seeks information, that person does not have a blank mind. She or he is constructing a query (in the broad sense) based on existing knowledge. For example, if I am unaware that some medical authorities question the direct link between HIV and AIDS I may construct a search on the treatment of HIV as part of the control of the spread of AIDS. If I retrieve a document that denies HIV's connection to AIDS I may not judge it relevant. However, as new propositions are uncovered I may begin to include these new propositions into my perception. If I retrieve several documents questioning HIV as a cause of AIDS I may reassess the relevance of those documents. The dynamic of questioning already held propositions in the face of new ones is a complicated and dialectical one. There is no simple algorithm that effectively predicts some kind of gestalt shift to a different way of thinking. Individual context may be based on a claim by John Searle: not all intentional beliefs are conscious. I may believe something about the cause of AIDS, but I may not be thinking about that at the time of a search. Nonetheless the unconscious belief is affecting assessment of relevance, in large part because, as Searle says, every unconscious intentional belief *could* be conscious (Searle, 1992, 132). Context, as we can see, is extremely difficult to discern fully. Searle offers a reason for the difficulty; most of computational cognitive science makes a serious mistake. "The mistake is to suppose that in the sense in which computers are used to process information, brains also process information. . . . In the case of a computer, an outside agent encodes some information in a form that can be processed by the circuitry of the computer. . . . In the case of the brain, none of the relevant neurobiological processes are observer relative" (Searle, 1992, 223-24). (Searle's approach is physicalist, but in a way that is substantially different from neuro-philosophers.)

Information and Communication

Recent work has attempted to combat any inclination to reify information (to treat it as an object) by emphasizing the communicative action engaged in by people when seeking information. It generally isn't stated, but stressing communication embodies an acceptance of the intentionality of human action. The communicative stance may be articulated most explicitly and most forcefully by Brenda Dervin, whose work is cited heavily in the LIS literature. In her view information is more of a means to an end (the end being the result of communication—making sense of some situation). She writes, "Information is essentially seen as a tool that is valuable and useful to people in their attempt to cope with their lives. . . . The core assumption is that information exists independent of human action and that its value lies in describing reality and therefore in reducing uncertainty about reality" (Dervin, 1977, 18, 20). The idea that information is a tool is not an altogether common one in LIS. The word "information" is frequently much more sweeping. The disagreement over what information is illustrates the problematic aspect of the word. Dervin seems to equate information with data; if "data" were to replace "information" in her statement there would probably be less disagreement (at least with regard to that statement). Or, looked at another way, Dervin advocates stressing communication, which is a fundamental human action that may depend on a process of informing, of giving shape to data.

Dervin reiterates the limitations of an objectivist approach to information and informing. The approach, which ignores the essential nature of being, is, according to Dervin, grounded in two assumptions: "one is that information can be treated like a brick; the other is that people can be treated like empty baskets into which bricks can be thrown" (Dervin, 1983, 160). The act of reification may be one of the most serious mistakes we can make (and is opposed to phenomenology). The tradition of scientistic determinism necessarily depends on objectifying, not only human products, but also human action. As might be expected, the scientistic stance requires the reification of language. This means that an objectivist treatment of language reduces the elements of language—syntax, grammar, semantics—as things. This is precisely what Dervin (rightly) criticizes. Reification of language transfers meaning entirely to the language itself and eliminates the intentions of the speaker/writer. The intentionality of communication is implicit in Dervin; it is inherent in her idea of information as a User Construct: "[I]t is assumed that the individual is a sensemaker by mandate of the human condition" (Dervin, 1983, 169). At times her work suggests a kind of anti-realism, bordering on constructivism, but her insistence on the importance of communication indicates that there must be some way for communication to share meaning. The intentionality of language use is much more explicit, for instance, in the work of Paul Grice. He demonstrates how a speaker/writer expresses intentions in ways that can be understood by a hearer/reader (Grice, 1989, 86-116).

If we combine Dervin's important body of work with some other thought on language and communication that has not become a part of the literature of LIS, the phenomenological nature of communication becomes clearer. Dervin repeatedly says that an individual's information seeking is situated, contextual. The only way to understand information seeking behavior is to understand the context in which it takes place. We can't assume that every information seeker will come to content in the same way for the same reason. What can go wrong, according to Dervin is that "The user's unique situation, then, is treated as a typical or normatively defined situation and is thus made amenable to a match in an information system designed normatively" (Dervin, 1977, 19). In other words, a query is reified, treated as an object; and that object has a single discernible meaning. The tendency to reification is powerful, though, and is exacerbated by both the nature of language (as something more or less fixed by rules and conventions) and possible assumptions regarding language (as determinate of meaning and as universally shared). These two factors lead to an observation by Schutz on reification:

> I leave out of my awareness the intentional operations of my consciousness within which their meanings have already been constituted. At such times I have before me a world of real and ideal objects, and I can assert that this world is meaningful not only for me but for you, for us, and for every one. This is precisely because I am attending not to those acts of consciousness which once gave them meaning but because I already presuppose, as given without question, a series of highly complex meaning-contents. The meaning structure thus abstracted from its genesis is something that I can regard as having an objective meaning, as being meaningful in itself. (Schutz, 1967, 36)

The kind of reification Schutz speaks of is apparent in some conceptions of relevance, which is seen as universal and determined by the content itself, rather than as part of the complex intentional perception of the seeker *and* the intentionality of the content.

The way we treat language when it comes to information retrieval further illustrates the tendency to reification. Everyone involved in the process—information seekers, systems designers, librarians, indexers—engages in an effort to normalize the range of queries through categorization. What I mean by this is that everyone translates a complex event (keeping in mind an information seeker's perceptions, the intentional act of querying, and the intentional act that results in creating the content that might be retrieved) into a highly structured, and usually simplified, one. This doesn't mean that categorization is bad or that it should be abandoned. It does mean, though, that the act of categorizing should not be oversimplified. Patrick de Gramont suggests that a metaphor for the act of categorizing is to see language as a filing system. "Filing systems have two distinguishing characteristics which enable one to compare them to the way language works. First, they operate on the basis of the fact that the information to be filed has meaning before it is filed. Second, the system under which the information is filed is geared, not to the information per se, but to an ulterior purpose" (de Gramont, 1990, 65). In common usage of language the process of categorization may be shared by all speakers of a language and is usually based in shared or common experience. The commonality of experience is generally the grounding for establishing a verbal category to describe the experience. We can see that there is a difference between categorization in everyday usage and categorization in much of information retrieval. The categories in a database include a structured vocabulary (such as subject headings in a library catalog or descriptors in a bibliographic database) are not customarily established by the information seekers (although there may be exceptions). In other words, the information seeker is not the one who created the filing system or filed the information. Understanding, in the sense of shared meaning, exists insofar as the information seeker can infer what the filer did in the process of categorization (including both the establishment of a thesaurus or vocabulary and the application of that vocabulary to specific content). Categories, which can be at least somewhat predictable, can facilitate finding content that closely fits the accepted definition of the category. Given that much language is characterized by polysemy and that content is frequently semantically rich, simplified, a priori, categorization is of some, but limited, value to an information seeker.

Carol Kuhlthau, in many ways, builds on Dervin's work. She, too, makes a distinction between an almost exclusively objectivist approach to information services and a more phenomenological approach. She writes, "The traditional approach is limited to the task of locating sources and information but does not take into account the tasks of interpreting, formulating, and learning in the process of information seeking" (Kuhlthau, 1993, 168). Locating sources implies that meaning is fixed and, further, inheres in the information objects. Meaning, as we've seen, is a result of action, specifically communicative action. Kuhlthau's model of information seeking includes a combination of the analysis of content with the seeker's *doing* something with the content. The model owes a debt to Habermas's insistence that understanding stems from the joint interpretation of language *and* experience (Habermas, 1971, 171). Such necessary interpretation is central to Habermas's idea of lifeworld (which is similar to, but differs somewhat from, Husserl's idea). Habermas's lifeworld also has being at its heart, but being, for him, is shaped by, and helps to shape, society and cultural production (which includes, among other things, both libraries and their contents). And the personal is, of course, a part of being (Habermas, 1998, 215-55).

Some aspects of Habermas's lifeworld are incorporated by Kuhlthau. She says, "Within the [Information Search Process], the user interprets information to construct new understandings and knowledge that add valuable information for addressing problems and making judgments" (Kuhlthau, 1999, 400). Action is a vital outcome of the information seeking process. Kuhlthau's program, however, is much more focused on the individual than on the individual's place in society. She does include experience, but internalizes that experience; she doesn't fully explore the richness of societal relations and influences and cultural production. In one study she concludes that librarians can become active in the information seeking process, but the phenomenological challenges of incorporating self and other are not addressed (Kuhlthau, 1999). The process of inferring meaning, or of making sense, is not purely internal in her program. It is by its nature communicative and linguistic. More attention to Habermas might strengthen Kuhlthau's information seeking model. In particular, an explicit recognition, left implicit in much of her work, that information seeking is a directed action with pragmatic purposes could lead to emphasis of the communicative action that contributes to understanding. The pragmatics of communication generally include cooperation aimed at shared (entirely or partially) interpretations based on claims of validity (or what Goldman would call veritism), if not truth, that can be mutually arrived at (Habermas, 1998, 299). Cooperation necessitates a transformation from an objectivist to a phenomenological attititude. As Habermas says,

> The ⟨telos⟩ of reaching understanding inherent in the structures of language compels the communicative actors to alter their perspective; this shift in perspective finds expression in the necessity of going from the objectivating attitude of the success-oriented actor, who seeks to *effect* something in the world, to the performative attitude of a speaker, who seeks to *reach understanding* with a second person about something [emphasis in original]. (Habermas, 1998, 300)

Comprehension of the interaction between self and other is integral to understanding.

In evaluating Kuhlthau's method and program, Hjørland points out that her work has sound grounding in principles that follow from phenomenology and is aimed at helping us to understand, to know more about, information seeking. He identifies her methodological principles as:

- User orientation instead of focusing on the information system itself
- Process orientation, that is, the perception of information seeking as a process
- Orientation toward both cognitive and affective processes
- Qualitative studies (interviews and case studies) and quantitative studies
- Longitudinal studies. . . .
- Studies of real users with real problems in real libraries.
  . . .
- Studies that build upon a theoretical framework of users as constructive information seekers. (Hjørland, 1997, 116)

He also points out that her work is limited by its "methodological individualism," and could benefit greatly by inclusion of social aspects of experience. Expansion of the conceptual base could help LIS more directly address its central questions. Hjørland is, I believe, correct both in his praise for the strengths of Kuhlthau's program and in his criticism of its limitations.

Other LIS Work

Those who are familiar with writings in LIS are probably aware of the work of Ross Atkinson. Atkinson has built a record of thoughtful scholarship; everyone studying or practicing librarianship should pay attention to what he has to say. Some years ago he suggested that the materials selection process in libraries is complicated by the multiple contexts that can affect decisions. Citations (references in published works) can be used to help make selection decisions. The existence of citations creates a relationship among texts, a relationship so intricate as to signal an indication of intertextuality, or the interweaving of the ideas in texts that blur lines among individual works. Atkinson quotes Roland Barthes, who recognizes the phenomeno-logical element of intertextuality, especially the linking of "I" and "other." As Atkinson observes, "The reader is very much the product of the texts he or she has come upon before; an individual's ability not only to understand but also to evaluate and make other decisions about newly encountered documents (or other utterances) depends upon his or her reference to such personal textual experience" (Atkinson, 1984, 110). The multiple contexts of selection include the social environment that constitutes demand and use (and that responds to the actions of selectors). Atkinson also recognizes that selection, as an epistemic act, is both an individual and a shared event.

> Written policies may, of course, be used to provide some regulation and coordination among selectors, but such policies no matter how detailed must still always be interpreted by each selector on the basis of his or her personal experience at the time of each selection decision. . . . Contexts overlap greatly between individuals, so that most instances of selection invite little dispute. (Atkinson, 1984, 118)

He demonstrates how interpretation need not be entirely relativist, but may lead to some normative social epistemic agreement.

More recently Atkinson has turned his attention to collection management in an online environment. Although he doesn't state it, there are some familial links between this later work and his earlier thinking on intertextuality. He recognizes that in an online environment the connections between and among texts are more apparent than when we handle physical artifacts. The connections that are made depend on both the information seeker and the content. It is possible to examine library service from either perspective: ensuring that local users have ready access to the content they need

> can be viewed from either a subjective or an objective perspective. From a subjective position, the goal of information services is—given a particular set of information objects—to provide local users with the tools and skills they need to make the most effective use of those objects. But the service can also be approached from the objective perspective: assuming a particular group of local users with clearly defined needs, the goal of the service is to add selected values to the specific information objects, such that those objects can be used more effectively to respond to those local needs. (Atkinson, 1998, 8)

As we examine the goals of information services we can see that there is another way to see the apparent dichotomy of the subjective and the objective. Atkinson says we can divide the values of our goals into functionality (ensuring a person's ability to work within an object such as a text) and maintenance (ensuring stability and accesibility to objects over time). The dichotomies he illustrates, and especially the subjective and objective designations, are, essentially, false. Just as phenomenology dissolves subject-object distinctions, Atkinson attempts to minimize the dichotomies by advocating what he calls the "digital mentality." The information seeker makes and breaks connections with content in an intentional manner given changing wants and needs. The digital mentality allows seekers and librarians to envision a fluid environment, characterized by, among other things, what Atkinson refers to as embedment. "Both transferability and analyticity entail embedment. Transferability is the potential to move objects within a wider universe, while analyticity is the capacity for the user to move within the object. Thus while every database is an object, we must also recognize that every object is a database" (Atkinson, 1998, 19). In his body of work Atkinson gives a way of thinking about familiar matter in unfamiliar, but fruitfully epistemic, terms.

Information services can certainly be as complex as collection management, and some thought in LIS displays not only awareness of the complexity, but effort at understanding the root of the problems we face. Melissa Gross investigates a particular kind of information seeking, the imposed query. Most information services assume that user-generated queries begin the service action, but at times people are urged, asked, or assigned to seek information. The dynamics of an imposed query are quite different from a user-generated one, and the central difference is epistemic. Gross tells us that

> The imposed query model describes a process in which the imposer or end user passes the question to another who will act as the agent in the transaction of the query and then return to the imposer with an answer or resolution. Since the person who formulated the question is not present in the reference negotiation process, the performance of reference service is to some degree dependent on how well the agent really understands what the end user wants and the degree to which the agent feels licensed to add to or change the question. (Melissa Gross, 1998, 291)

She recognizes that the same approach to service will not be effective with both the imposed query and the user-generated query. The will to knowledge is not the same in the two instances. With an imposed query, as Gross points out, the information seeker does not necessarily have knowledge of the origins of the question and, so, may not be able to consult with a librarian or assess the outcome of the service. Gross also acknowledges that examination of such instances as imposed queries can help us understand statements about relevance. What the information seeker may be able to know is how to assess content that may satisfy the originator of the query. Gross states that relevance judgments are usually assumed to be based on subject knowledge. Her work suggests that an epistemic event does take place; rather than evaluating on the grounds of subject knowledge, the information seeker evaluates content on the grounds of knowledge about the nature and situation of query imposition—the information seeker may know what will succeed in the eyes of the person who began the process. That success may be based to varying extent on perceptions of the content, but is more likely to be related to topicality.

All information services are related to the ways we have tried to organize information for retrieval, including our frequently used systems of classification. Investigations into the frameworks of classification systems aren't uncommon, but some investigations are more sensitive to the conceptual underpinnings of classification. Francis Miksa offers such a sensitive analysis. He admits that some library catalogs, particularly in the nineteenth century, were based on Francis Bacon's hierarchy of the sciences. Others owed a debt to later scientistic organizational premises. Miksa writes,

> Charles A. Cutter, for example, lauded by his contemporaries for the scientific accuracy of his classificatory work and well acquainted with John Fiske, the American populizer of Herbert Spencer's philosophy of evolution, was quite straightforward in asserting in 1897 that his Expansive Classification was based on the idea of evolution, a basic theme of Spencer's philosophy. (Miksa, 1998, 36)

Hierarchical classification continued into the twentieth century, but was accompanied by other (although related) approaches that illustrate a kind of Enlightenment optimism that knowledge is perfectable. Underlying the optimism is a belief that science (or, more appropriately, scientism) provides the instrumental means to address all issues and solve all problems. Miksa points out that Henry Bliss "established this argument by putting forth an elaborate philosophy of realism. He posited an objective world apart from humankind's observation of it and asserted that not only are 'objects' of this world discovered progressively, but also that individual minds together constitute a unity in perceiving such objects" (Miksa, 1998, 60). As has already been admitted in previous chapters, a softened realism is an appropriate conception of the world, but strong realism is insufficient to an understanding of being.

The assumption that nature exhibits a hierarchy of organization and influence and, by extension, our knowledge mirrors the hierarchy is, according to Miksa, questionable. Relationships among things in the world are much more complex than a simple deterministic hierarchy, and our perceptions of relationships are at least as complex. The complexity does not render classification impossible, but it does suggest some critical response to traditional hierarchical structures. Miksa suggests that one response is to allow a deeper level of specification that information seekers can use; another response is to create alternatives that can exist alongside existing structures, such as the Dewey Decimal Classification. One alternative might be to allow flexibility in facet sequences so that users could alter sequences (for example, the user might want place or time to be earlier in the sequence because of the nature of the query). Another alternative could be to employ collocation so that content on a topic could be linked. Miksa provides an example:

> if a classifier wished to collocate a wide variety of information resources (or electronic links to them) related to jewelry, the template should allow the user to move the topical areas and subclasses of, say, gem metallurgy (553.8), gem mining (622.38), synthetic gems (666.88), gem carving (736.2), jewelry and gems in religion (the categories of individual religions from the 270s to 290s), and so on into a structure at, say, 739.27 (Jewelry) with links from their standard positions to the new locations. (Miksa, 1998, 89)

Miksa's analysis incorporates the nature of being, perception, and intentionality into an examination of existing practice in LIS *and* into proposals for future practice. Such reflexiveness is imperative to the knowledge-based goals of our profession.

Miksa's example above represents both a challenge and an opportunity for the retrieval of pertinent information. I've addressed the opportunity elsewhere. In examining the difficulties of retrieving all materials on a specific topic I suggested that "There is no conceptual reason why a single work cannot be assigned multiple call numbers [in bibliographic records of a library's online catalog], with one primary call number serving as a shelf locator. The multiple call numbers could be used to assist retrieval in the same way multiple subject headings do" (Budd, 1996, 115).

I've already made reference to Birger Hjørland's work, but it deserves a bit more attention. As does Miksa, Hjørland examines access to information from the perspective of knowledge and communicative action. Perhaps in response to potential skepticism, Hjørland explains why we in LIS should concern ourselves with epistemological matters:

- Level 1: Information science should develop a theory of subject for analyzing [disciplinary literatures in the context of the knowledge bases of the disciplines].
- Level 2: Information science is itself a science influenced by the same paradigms or epistemological positions as those influencing psychology and other human and social sciences. (Hjørland, 1997, 92)

He further says that human knowledge can only be understood as a social process that depends on communication. While I agree that an investigation of how we know depends on social influence and social action, I believe we can't ignore, in fact we can't entirely separate the social context from, the ways individuals come to knowledge. By disagreeing in part with it, though, I definitely do not mean to suggest that he is incorrect, just that his position could be strengthened by recognition of the confluence of the individual and the social. Hjørland further states that his position is pragmatic, although not so radically pragmatic as to deny epistemology. In recognizing the shortcomings of radical pragmatism, he objects to "the problem with a pragmatic concept of the subject [which] lies in the most basic sense in the condition it shares with pragmatic philosophy: even though the goal is to develop human practice, a narrow practice-orientation is too short-sighted and superficial in its truth criteria" (Hjørland, 1997, 78). He realizes that knowledge and human action tends to be functional and directed (which is admitted by phenomenology).

The social element, according to Hjørland, can be explicit in what he calls a domain analytic approach to the subject analysis of content. The approach is characterized by: realism; the social functioning of disciplines; focus on the knowledge domain of a discipline (or comparisons of different disciplines and their knowledge domains); and a collectivist, rather than an individualist, methodology (Hjørland, 1997, 109). It is evident that he advocates a social epistemic foundation for our discipline. In practical terms, Hjørland maintains that the approach he urges can result in a more complete analysis of content leading to subject representation that is consonant with the retrieval purposes of information seekers. There may well be variation in subject headings among different settings (libraries) and that a merged database, or union catalog, can present the totality of possibilities that individual libraries can choose from for local access. "Information retrieval systems should be made user-friendly, and this can be done by having knowledge of the users' language and subjective perceptions and use this knowledge, for example, in cross-references to the preferred terms" (Hjørland, 1997, 66).

Birger Hjørland's thought demonstrates that there is interesting, well-conceived work emanating from places other than North America. His writings are not anomalous. In the last chapter I spent some time reviewing Ian Cornelius's ideas on theory. Others offer readers fresh points of view on matters that are central to LIS. Søren Brier, for instance, agrees with Hjørland in stating, "I want to show that LIS has to move from the cognitive science's information processing paradigm towards more pragmatically semiotic, cybernetic and social-linguistics theories of understanding, improving and designing document mediating systems" (Brier, 1996, 24). He emphasizes the importance of semiotics (sign systems) to the communication process of which

LIS is an important component. A sign is representational; it stands for something. Moreover, it represents something *to* someone. Interpretation is inescapable in the field of representation. The kind of linguistic understanding that Brier says systems such as libraries, databases, etc. exist to facilitate is dependent on the variety of meanings that exist in the range of producers (what Hjørland and Brier refer to as domains) plus the range of mediators (libraries, information systems, databases). There is not a single lingua franca that everyone recognizes and uses. The challenge, according to Brier, is "how we can map the semantic fields of concepts and their signifying context's into our systems beyond the logical and statistical approaches the technology up till now has made us focus on as the only realistic strategies" (Brier, 1996, 40). The work of these non-Americans brings home the fact that we cannot be parochial in our quest for understanding.

Possibilities

As is readily evident by now, there is a substantial record of conceptually and methodologically sound work in LIS. Maybe there is also some work that is grounded in the errors of scientism as well, but the same could be said of all social science disciplines. And, as is true of the social sciences generally, we in LIS can learn from some thought in other disciplines. Throughout this book I've mentioned work in philosophy, sociology, and other fields that is directly related to the kinds of questions and concerns we have. At this time I'd like to focus on a couple of strains of thought that can help us frame some of those questions and increase our understanding of the complex issues of our discipline and profession.

Mikhail Bakhtin

A considerable amount of the foregoing discussion of intellectual direction and of productive work has included a linguistic element. The communicative nature of study and practice in our discipline necessarily encompasses the nature and working of language. The role of language is manifest in more than one way: practice in libraries and other agencies depends on the effective communication of professionals; the content information seekers need; regardless of the medium, the content is in large part textual; and formal study in LIS is, of course, communicated textually. Language and communication are essential to knowledge and are related to phenomenology. Given the importance of language, we should incorporate study of it into our inquiry and practice. And if we are committed to hermeneutical phenomenology we must investigate how language functions in concert with the elements of phenomenology. One approach to language and thought is that of Mikhail Bakhtin. Bakhtin's work is usually linked to literary study; he does address literary and aesthetic texts. His writings are broader, though, and include the human sciences generally. I'm willing to admit that the texts and communication we most frequently deal with in LIS are not literary, but Bakhtin's ideas relating to both literary and other texts have something to offer us.

Bakhtin adopts the position that our conceptions of human action must be rooted in ethical considerations. As is the case with ethics generally, judgments based in language and communication can fall into one of two categories—judgments of value or quality, or judgments of obligation or action. It should come as no surprise at this point in the book that the ethical considerations apply to LIS. The very nature of epistemology implies that there are value judgments that must be made on the bases of justification, correspondence to truth, or veritism. The nature of professional practice implies judgments of obligation that lead to actions based on principles of equal access to information, balance in library collections, and mediation between information seekers and content. Ethical considerations, in some ways, can concretize the abstract, can make ideas real in the way we inquire and practice in LIS. Bakhtin addresses the ethical considerations in discussing the purpose of theory:

> A theory needs to be brought into communion *not* with theoretical constructions and conceived life, but with the actually

occurring event of moral being—with practical reason, and this
is answerably accomplished by everyone who cognizes, insofar
as he accepts answerability for every integral act of his cognition, that is, insofar as the act of cognition as *my* deed is
included, along with all its content, in the unity of my answerability, in which and by virtue of which I actually live–perform
deeds [emphasis in original]. (Bakhtin, 1993, 12)

The acceptance of answerability or responsibility is, as might be
expected, a major criterion for ethical application of theory.
Bakhtin criticizes what he calls theoreticism, which is no more
than theory about itself, not theory of being.

The space remaining in this book is not sufficient to approach
a complete examination of Bakhtin's thought, but some of his
most important (to LIS) observations should be mentioned here.
(A much deeper investigation of whether we can learn from
Bakhtin will have to be relegated to a subsequent piece of work.)
In one of his earliest writings, *Toward a Philosophy of the Act*, he
stresses that each of us participates in being. In other words,
being is concrete; *I* exist and *you* exist and we have actual
histories filled with particular events. The concreteness of being
emphasizes the ethical aspect of our lives; while we live *within*
ourselves, we do not exist solely for ourselves. Participation
defines the way we live our lives, so any examination of the
elements of being can only be fully realized if we accept and
comprehend the nature of participation in being.

There *is* no acknowledged self-equivalent and universally valid
value, for its acknowledged validity is conditioned *not* by its
content, taken in abstraction, but by being *correlated* with the
unique place of a participant. . . . Theoretical cognition of an
object that exists by itself, independently of its actual position
in the once-occurrent world from the standpoint of a participant's unique place, is perfectly justified. But it does not
constitute ultimate cognition; it constitutes only an auxiliary,
technical moment of such ultimate cognition [emphasis in
original]. (Bakhtin, 1993, 48)

We can relate his idea to some of the most pressing concerns of our discipline. Information seeking by several people are distinct moments in what Bakhtin calls being-as-event. The act of seeking is unique to each seeker and involves individual knowledge of, for instance, information content. Assuming that all information seekers and all acts of seeking are alike, and understanding based on such an assumption, can only come from the perspective of non-participation. As such, the study becomes something less than fully human; or it is divorced from a more complete understanding of being.

Elsewhere Bakhtin embellishes upon the participative idea. Participation is frequently manifest through expressions (speech, writing) that can be formulated as a text, in the broadest sense of the word. The text can be received. This communicative action is not limited to literary texts, but describes perception that can only occur through some literal act of expression. As Bakhtin tells us,

> The transcription of thinking in the human sciences is always the transcription of a special kind of dialogue: the complex interrelations between the *text* (the object of study and reflection) and the created, framing *context* (questioning, refuting, and so forth) in which the scholar's cognizing and evaluating thought takes place. This is the meeting of two texts—of the ready-made and the reactive text being created—and, consequently, the meeting of two subjects and two authors [emphasis in original]. (Bakhtin, 1986, 106-7)

His conception of dialogue is one of the most essential features of his writing, and one of the most discussed. The nature of dialogue is very closely related to the phenomenological linking of self and other, and the connection is made through language.

> As a living, socio-ideological concrete thing, as heteroglot opinion, language, for the individual consciousness, lies on the borderline between oneself and the other. The word in language is half someone else's. It becomes "one's own" only when the speaker populates it with his own intention, his own accent, when he appropriates the word, adapting it to his own semantic and expressive intention. (Bakhtin, 1994, 77)

With regard to the human sciences (and we can, of course, include LIS) Bakhtin recognizes that knowledge is not a matter of comprehending a physical thing. In many cases what we seek to know something about is another subject, an "other," who perceives, intends, and also lives in the world. The place of other as subject denotes a clear distinction between the human and the natural sciences.

> The exact sciences constitute a monologic form of knowledge: the intellect contemplates a *thing* and expounds upon it. There is only one subject here—cognizing (contemplating) and speaking (expounding). In opposition to the subject there is only a *voiceless thing*. Any object of knowledge (including man) can be perceived and cognized as a thing. But a subject as such cannot be perceived and studied as a thing, for as a subject it cannot, while remaining a subject, become voiceless, and, consequently, cognition of it can only be *dialogic* [emphasis in original]. (Bakhtin, 1986, 161)

I realize that Bakhtin's use of the word dialogue can create some confusion; we may be tempted to think in terms of conversation. He does, as might be expected, include such events as conversation within dialogue, but dialogue encompasses more than a simple linguistic exchange. Michael Bernard-Donals explains,

> Dialogue is not so much a discourse between two people (as in Saussure's notorious model of one interlocutor "pitching" and another "catching" meaning), as it is a metaphor for the welter of communication that exists in the social world generally. Rather than involving an exchange of meanings, there occurs an exchange of selves, since language is the medium with which subjects conceive their world and their placement in it. (Bernard-Donals, 1994, 34)

Dialogue, then, is both cognitive (it involves comprehension of the language used as well as the meaning of the language event) and ethical (it necessarily involves understanding of value and obligation). Dialogue, in Bakhtin's usage, doesn't guarantee understanding; there remains the reality that speaker and hearer are exterior to one another. Dialogue does, however, admit to the consciousness, and by extension the directedness of that consciousness, of the other.

Imagine the kind of mediating action that takes place regularly in libraries and other information agencies. The information seeker has a purpose in asking a question, even if the query is imposed by someone else. Does that seeker initiate a dialogue, in the Bakhtinian sense? There isn't a clear answer to that question; at times an information seeker is communicating at a deep level, but at other times the seeker is closing off some cognitive and ethical possibilities by adopting an objectivist approach. A person may say, "I need information on Hemingway." This may be an expression of, for example, an imposed query, an assignment to find biographical data on the author. Or it may hide a desire to read critical receptions of *The Sun Also Rises* because the questioner has been touched by the characters in the novel. If the query goes no further it amounts to the kind of monologic expression Bakhtin associates with the natural sciences. There is a sharing of self in such a query.

The mediator's response to a query can likewise be examined in dialogic or monologic terms. A librarian or information professional may be closed off to the possibilities a query can initiate and may objectify the question. Since two selves are involved in mediation, there must be an openness for dialogic communication to occur. The difference, in epistemological terms, between monologue and dialogue is a striking one. Tzvetan Todorov observes that the difference is "that in the natural sciences we seek to know an *object*, but in the human ones, a *subject* [emphasis in original]" (Todorov, 1984, 18). Pam Morris also tries to signal the difference:

> There is no existence, no meaning or thought that does not enter into dialogue or "dialogic" relations with the other, that does not exhibit intertextuallity in both time and space. "Monologue" and "monologic" refer to any discourse which seeks to deny the dialogic nature of existence, which refuses to recognize its responsibility as adressee [*sic*], and pretends to be the "last word." (in Bakhtin, 1994, 247)

The concept of intertextuality is a complex one, as we've seen in the brief discussion of Ross Atkinson's work. Todorov helps us understand it—intertextuality is not an aspect of language, but of discourse (the purposeful use of language), and every utterance exists within a context of other utterances (Todorov, 1984, 60-61). How we know, and what we know, then, is inherently constructed by both an individual understanding of language and its meaning *and* a collective employment of discourse. For knowledge to be possible at all in the human sciences, and certainly in LIS, discourse must be dialogic. By dialogic I mean Bakhtin's recognition that

> *word is a two-sided act.* It is determined equally by *whose* word it is and for whom it is meant. As word, it is precisely *the product of the reciprocal relationship between speaker and listener, addresser and addressee.* Each and every word expresses the "one" in relation to the "other". I give myself verbal shape from another's point of view, ultimately, from the point of view of the community to which I belong. A word is a bridge thrown between myself and another. If one end of the bridge depends on me, then the other depends on my addressee. A word is territory shared by both addresser and addressee, by the speaker and his interlocutor [emphasis in original]. (Bakhtin, 1994, 58)

Knowledge depends on the sharing, on the actual bridging that can occur. And dialogue is not an unconscious act; it is intentional.

Ideology

If we accept, as I think we must, that communication is essential to a discipline and profession like LIS, then we should also accept that communication has an ideological aspect. Let me emphasize at the outset that "ideology" is not always negative or pejorative, although the term "ideological" usually signals a negative connotation. (The original meaning of the word had to do with the study of ideas.) There are, in a simplified conception, two ways of looking at ideology. One way has nothing to do with truth or falsity; its focus is on the functioning of ideas as part of our social lives and social interaction. According to this conception each of us is guided by a socially influenced set of beliefs that lead to particular actions. For example, I was raised in a particular part of the U.S., in a particular religious tradition, with particular schooling, and in a particular familial setting. All of those strong forces have implications for the way I look at the world. The extent to which my thinking and acting are shaped by those forces is the extent to which my thinking and acting are ideological. This neutral idea of ideology is described by Terry Eagleton as

> the general material process of production of ideas, beliefs and values in social life. Such a definition is both politically and epistemologically neutral, and is close to the broader meaning of the term "culture". Ideology, or culture, would here denote the whole complex of signifying practices and symbolic processes in a particular society; it would allude to the way individuals "lived" their social practices, rather than to those practices themselves which would be the preserve of politics, economics, kinship theory and so on. (Eagelton, 1991, 28)

Much more frequently ideology refers to the contests between true and false thinking, between honest and deceptive expressing, between straightforwardness and distortion, between clarity and illusion. That conception is an oversimplification, though. Ideology is not merely a matter of deception or illusion. It is a way of describing reality, so, at least in some way, it must attempt to conceive reality. The effort at prescribing, legitimating, and spreading the thinking of one group can be based in establishing the identity of the group. This conception has something of a negative connotation, mainly because there is usually some distortion or deception employed in the effort at legitimation. In the most extreme conception of ideology, one group or class is seeking domination over others and is seeking to extend that domination as far as possible. One clear example of the effort at domination based on distortion is the state of science during Stalin's rule in the Soviet Union. Reasonable empirical evidence counted for little and political approval allowed Tromfin

Lysenko's absurd dictates regarding agriculture (among other things) to hold sway. I will submit here that a much more subtle ideological force is that of deterministic scientism. That way of thinking distorts both what knowledge is and how we come to knowledge.

That last point explains why I'm spending some time on ideology here. In the first, neutral, sense, each of us is a member of, probably, several ideological groups—religious, political, professional, social, etc. We maintain the memberships isofar as our identities are formed by the fundamental elements of those groups. In the second, negative, sense, each of us is subjected to purposeful forces that aim at co-opting or dominating us. As we in LIS seriously consider how we know and what we know, we must be aware of the possibility of ideological impact. If we follow the proposition that constitutes the heart of this book, we can identify ideology in operation through its intentionality, its mode of perception, and its manipulation of the relationship between self and other. To return to communication, the examination of ideology involves study of the uses of symbols and signs as they are used in purposive ways (sometimes for domination, sometimes for legitimation). The ideology of deterministic scientism focuses on a particular instrumental use of "fact" that holds it to be objective and immutable, separate from social and historical context. Our investigation should include the most basic assumptions and premises of the scientistic program.

The implications of such an investigation extend to inquiry and practice in LIS. I'll focus on just a couple of instances where ideological influences can affect the ways we think and act. And in doing so, I'll urge readers to keep in mind Eagleton's observation that "at least some of what we call ideological discourse is true at one level but not at another: true in its empirical content but deceptive in its force, or true in its surface meaning but false in its underlying assumptions" (Eagelton, 1991, 16-17). One, that has been addressed in many ways by a number of commentators, is technology. (By technology here I am referring to existing and emerging information technologies, including networks, telecommunications, etc.) No reasonable person would dismiss technological development as completely false; there are numerous things possible in the world of LIS *because* of technological development. However, claims are made on behalf of technology that extend beyond its material capability. Advertisements state, for example, that human differences disappear in cyberspace, or that only the latest developments contribute anything of value to society. There is, of course, some truth to the statements. Technology is not separate from society, but is embedded in it. But what force does it exert, and for what purposes? In some utopian visions technology has the power to transform education, work, and the ways we are informed. The power is, to a considerable extent, real, but the power may also be imparted by us. Andrew Feenberg says that technology acquires meaning by three main means: "(1) rhetorical procedures that invest [it] with symbolic meaning, such as myths or advertising; (2) design features that embed values in the artifact; (3) interconnections with other technologies in a network that imposes a specific way of life" (Feenberg, 1995, 227). As is the case with scientism, technology has a large body of applications that are reasonable and appropriate; the extent of that body of applications is not universal, though. The framework of phenomenology can help us examine critically which applications are best fitted to technology and which are not.

Related (at least somewhat) to technology is consumption, especially mass consumption. Robert Bocock reminds us that "Consumption, in late twentieth-century western forms of capitalism, may be seen . . . as a social and cultural process involving cultural signs and symbols, not simply as an economic, utilitarian process" (Bocock, 1993, 3). In LIS consumption is best typified by the discourse on customer service. Elsewhere I have examined the rhetoric of customer service and conclude that, as an economic and a social idea, it affects our perceptions of the nature of service and of the most fundamental conception of information (Budd, 1997). In fact, the customer service premise necessitates a reconception of LIS and of everything related to the profession, including the content which we provide access to. It is grounded in a claim that there is a diminishing of the use value of information in favor of information's exchange value. The content and the service related to it are objectified, and their meaning is defined by their value *as* objects. The danger is that the services offered by libraries and information agencies, including the access mechanisms we design, are not seen in terms of the knowledge enhancing potential they represent. Instead, as Slavoj Žižek points out, as a commodity it "is reduced to an abstract entity which—irrespective of its particular nature, of its 'use-value'—possesses 'the same value' as another commodity for which it is being exchanged" (Žižek, 1989, 17).

With knowledge as our goal, we can examine claims and statements critically. Since we are looking for truth-value, or veritistic-value, we will be able to assess the claims on their own terms. Any distortions or deceptions can be uncovered, and our inquiry and practice can contribute to the combatting of ideologies that obscure the genuine purposes and contributions of LIS.

Bourdieu

Other scholars from disciplines outside LIS can suggest ways we can inquire into matters that are important to us. Pierre Bourdieu has examined many aspects of human action, and some of his ideas in particular have relevance to action in LIS. Let's pay special attention to what he has to say about language and its use. (The scope of his work extends beyond language, but I believe this element of his program addresses some of the societal aspects of LIS.) Bourdieu's focus is not on the individual (he doesn't study conversation, for example), but on societal dynamics (how language supports or creates relationships within the structure of society). The societal dynamics of LIS operate in (at least) two ways—internally as we continuously constitute and define ourselves, and externally as we communicate with, and are influenced by, other societal elements.

Bourdieu also addresses one particular issue that is of vital concern to us, censorship. He deals with censorship, though, from an internal perspective, pointing out the ways that a field expresses itself and who controls that expression. He writes,

> The metaphor of censorship should not mislead: it is the structure of the field itself which governs expression by governing both access to expression and the form of expression, and not some legal proceeding which has been specially adapted to designate and repress the transgression of a kind of linguistic code. This structural censorship is exercised through the medium of the sanctions of the field . . . ; it is imposed on all producers of symbolic goods, including the authorized spokesperson, whose authoritative discourse is more subject to the norms of official propriety than any other, and it condemns the occupants of dominated positions either to silence or to shocking outspokenness. (Bourdieu, 1991, 138)

We have to remember that the kind of censorship he speaks of has to be exercised *by* someone. The library, especially the organizational (through ALA), stance regarding the larger issue of censorship in the external sense provides us with a venue for examining internal censorship. The organizational statements, such as the "Library Bill of Rights," express a particular point of view that not all librarians agree with, for instance when it comes to access to some sexually explicit materials via the Internet. According to the ethos of our profession, we should openly discuss the grounding for dispute, and we should also examine the extent to which an open discussion is possible. That is, we should investigate whether there is some structural silencing of dissenters. In some ways Bourdieu's conception of censorship also provides a connection between the internal and external uses of language.

One way the power of authority manifests itself is in our interactions with information seekers. The explicit goal we cling to is the provision of complete and individualized service aimed at meeting the seeker's needs. We might ask if the language we use in interactions helps realize that goal or if it inhibits service. Bourdieu examines the language that typifies academic communication, the interaction between teachers and students. The setting is different, but his observations strike a familiar chord. Teachers are systemically sensitized to the use of a particular code (something that transcends the occasional use of jargon) that embeds ideas in a dense rhetorical cloud. Librarians have been accused at times of using jargon, but the more serious charge may be that we have also adopted and institutionalized a code that hinders clarity in interactions with information seekers. The lack of understanding in such interactions, then, is not accidental; it is formalized by the systems under which we operate. For example, the code may permeate presentations and discussions at conferences, the language of our literature, and the daily communication with information seekers. A possible outcome, as Bourdieu says is that "language is the most effective and the most subtle of all the techniques of distancing" (Bourdieu and Passeron, 1994, 19). If we are to overcome the distancing and misunderstanding we must comprehend the nature and origin of the code, which tends to be deeply rooted. As is the case with the teacher, we can't leave our "linguistic and cultural 'ethnocentrism' to discover that the language [employed] is that of a particular social class" (Bourdieu and Passeron, 1994, 22).

The "social space" Bourdieu keeps returning to is powerful, but it is also substantially of our own making. Part of the construction relies on what counts as symbolic capital, which can be cultural or social, and which can be recognized and valued when perceived by those who are sensitive to it. There can, however, be a "shift from a diffuse symbolic capital, resting solely on collective recognition, to an *objectified symbolic capital* [emphasis in original]" (Bourdieu, 1998, 50). There may have been, over time, a shift in the symbolic capital of the library from an accepted recognition of selectivity of contents (collections) and purpose based on edification of the reader to a received symbol of public institution (i.e., publicly funded or publicly owned). The symbolic shift here is, in part, a transference of control from within the organization to what could be termed "the people." Once objectified, the definition of the symbolic capital is removed from its previous holder. In the past the library has generally maintained a "pure" purpose grounded in uplifting and educational reading. As a cultural good, the library has in many ways drifted from the realm of the pure to that of the commercial. The current symbolic capital of the library allows it to transform itself from an agency in denial of the economy to one embracing it. The danger in the transformation is a particular kind of reduction, one closely related to scientism. Bourdieu calls it "economism," which leads to "considering the laws of functioning of one social field among others, namely the economic field, as being valid for all fields" (Bourdieu, 1998, 83). The ideas of customers, customer service, and commodity applied to libraries are just such examples of economism. A potential outcome of the reduction is, as Michel de Certeau says, that "What is counted is *what* is used, not the *ways of using* [emphasis in original]" (de Certeau, 1984, 35). Purpose and being can become altered by a process that operates in some ways sub rosa; the transformation is not necessarily agreed to through discussion, but may be insinuated into institutional discourse.

De Certeau addresses some of the challenges that Bourdieu and others grapple with, including the place of ethics in praxis. He contrasts the ethical responsibility of practitioners with what he calls dogmatism. Dogmatism sets itself up as being nomological by defining the reality it purports to represent. Ethics, on the other hand, "is articulated through effective operations, and it defines a distance between what is and what ought to be. This distance designates a space where we have something to do" (de Certeau, 1986, 199). The ethical responsibility can help us examine, among other things, the role of technology in LIS. De Certeau provides provides some warnings regarding a departure from ethical responsibility. Media can have the effect of obscuring the act of consumption, can solidify the mistaken idea that consumption is passive. The "technocracy of the media" reinforces the assumption of passivity; "the 'informing' technicians have thus been changed, through the systematization of enterprises, into bureaucrats cooped up in their specialties and increasingly ignorant of users" (de Certeau, 1984, 167).

Bourdieu's thought is not without its problems. He tends to be less than willing to admit to normative criteria for knowledge, for example. Also, he is not entirely consistent in his use of the term "field." The definition I've selected here includes the complexity of societal and cultural influences, but at times "field" designates a much more autonomous construction, separate from exterior forces. Even with such limitations, Bourdieu can contribute to the framework I'm arguing for.

Knowledge and Ethics

In a profession such as ours no one would deny that we all should have what is called *techne*, or "knowing that." This is the kind of practical knowledge that is the foundation of every action we take. This book has been an argument that, as essential as *techne* is, practical knowledge is grounded in *episteme*, or "knowing that." It is now time to introduce a third kind of knowledge, which is referred to as *phronesis*, or "ethical knowledge." The organization of information, the design of systems, and the provision of services that LIS is based on undeniably has an ethical component. Ethics has been a concern of our professional associations for many years. *Phronesis* is the knowledge on which we base our ethical arguments and ethical praxis. It is necessary for us to ask of ourselves (individually and collectively), what should I/we do, and how should I/we act? A key element of the questions is "should," which implies two things that we must recognize: (1) there is an underlying responsibility that we accept as part of praxis, and (2) there is some normative aspect of analysis that can guide our answers to these questions (see, for example, Cullity and Gaut, 1997). In some ways, most notably the recent attention within the American Library Association to the profession's core values, LIS has been cognizant of the ethics of praxis. There is sound philosophical grounding for such attention to values (even if the ALA process and product may be flawed), and Hans Jonas expresses the grounding clearly:

> It is therefore necessary, where ethics and obligation are concerned, to venture into the theory of values [which is technically known as axiology], or rather the theory of value as such. Only from the objectivity of value could an objective "ought-to-be" in itself be derived, and hence for us a binding *obligation* [emphasis in original] to the guarding of being, that is, a responsibility toward it. (Jonas, 1984, 50)

To focus on just one element of LIS to illustrate the importance of ethical knowledge, we can turn to technology. Our praxis-based relationship with technology is not merely technical; that is, we are not simply concerned with what information technology is capable of doing. We are concerned with how the technology is used, how it may be transformative, how it may privilege some people over others, the economics of technology, the politics of technology, and other factors. All of these concerns are ethical. They affect the decisions we make in our organizations; they have an impact on the services we design for our communities. As Jonas says, "technology, apart from its objective works, assumes ethical significance by the central place it now occupies in human purpose"; this carries a serious implication: "If the realm of making has invaded the space of essential action, then morality must invade the realm of making, from which it has formerly stayed aloof, and must do so in the form of public policy" (Jonas, 1984, 9). The criteria for knowledge that have been presented here, and especially phenomenology as a path to knowledge, provide us with ways to inform praxis and to ensure that praxis is not only efficient in the technical sense, but also effective in the ethical sense.

Epilogue

The future of library and information science is bright. The contributions of our field have been monumental. While there may be some who question whether the contributions will continue, there is no foundation for the kinds of doubts based on technological, or other, myths. Reasons for optimism include the archival functions of libraries, the mechanisms for access that have been designed, and the commitment to knowledge demonstrated by the profession. If there is any grounding for doubting the future of LIS, and particularly of librarianship, it would be any betrayal of the commitment to knowledge. As we've seen, there are a number of intellectual forces pulling and tugging at us. Some of those forces are attractive and are shared by a number of other disciplines. They are, however, epistemologically weak siren calls, even if they are ideologically strong.

The genealogy of thought in the social sciences and LIS has wound with some fits and starts from the seventeenth century to the present, but the tie that has bound the ideas that have been inflluential has been the presumption that everything we can study is physical and can be examined objectively. The presumption of objectivism affects praxis as well as inquiry. The erroneous way of thinking that can be identified as scientism leads to a program of practice based on the false premise that the process of information seeking is objectively knowable and predictable. The shortcomings of the program should be sufficient for us to look elsewhere for epistemological foundations. What I've tried to offer here is a consistent idea of knowledge—what it is, how we come to knowledge, and what role communication plays in knowledge growth. I've tried to present a framework within which we can seek knowledge. The framework of hermeneutical phenomenology combines a kind of realism with understanding of the dynamics of human action and perception. It confounds scientistic thinking and praxis. It resists the repression that scientism can exert by emphasizing the intersubjectivity of human action. The intersubjectivity pervades thought (through, for instance, research by reminding us that researchers are *part* of the structure they study) and praxis (by stressing the phenomenological elements of communication, including the social implications of communicative action).

As does every author, I hope this book will be read critically and that it will contribute to the discourse on the purpose and future of LIS. And I hope this will open us up to the possibilities that have been, and are being, explored in other disciplines. An open mind can help us realize the bright future that's possible for us.

References

Adair, Douglas. 1976. That Politics May Be Reduced to a Science: David Hume, James Madison, and the Tenth Federalist. In *Hume: A Re-Evaluation*, edited by Donald W. Livingstone. New York: Fordham University Press.

Adorno, Theodor. 1976. Sociology and Empirical Research. In *The Positivist Dispute in German Sociology*, edited by Theodor Adorno, et al. London: Heinemann.

Alston, William P. 1989. *Epistemic Justification: Essays in the Theory of Knowledge*. Ithaca, N.Y.: Cornell University Press.

Andaleeb, Syed Saad, and Patience L. Simmonds. 1998. Explaining User Satisfaction with Academic Libraries: Strategic Implications. *College and Research Libraries* 59 (March): 156-67.

Anderson, Elizabeth. 1995. Feminist Epistemology: An Interpretation and a Defense. *Hypatia* 10 (Summer): 50-84.

Andreski, Stanislav. 1971. *Herbert Spencer: Structure, Function, and Evolution*. New York: Scribner.

Appleby, Joyce, Lynn Hunt, and Margaret Jacob. 1994. *Telling the Truth about History*. New York: Norton.

Armstrong, David M. 1995. Naturalism, Materialism, and First Philosophy. In *Contemporary Materialism: A Reader*, edited by Paul K. Moser and J. D. Trout. London: Routledge.

Atkinson, Ross. 1984. The Citation As Intertext: Toward a Theory of the Selection Process. *Library Resources and Technical Services* 28 (April/June): 109-19.

————. 1998 Managing Traditional Materials in an Online Environment: Some Definitions and Distinctions for a Future Collection Management. *Library Resources and Technical Services* 42 (January): 7-20.

Audi, Robert. 1993 *The Structure of Justification*. Cambridge: Cambridge University Press.

————. 1998. *Epistemology: A Contemporary Introduction to the Theory of Knowledge*. London: Routledge.

Ayer, A. J. 1959. *Language Truth and Logic*. New York: Dover.

Bacon, Francis. 1899. *Advancement of Learning and Novum Organum*. New York: Colonial Press.

Bakhtin, Mikhail. 1986. *Speech Genres and Other Late Essays*. Austin: University of Texas Press.

————. 1993. *Toward a Philosophy of the Act*. Austin: University of Texas Press.

————. 1994. *The Bakhtin Reader: Selected Writings of Bakhtin, Medvedev, Voloshinov*. London: Edward Arnold.

Baldus, Bernd. 1990. Positivism's Twilight? *Canadian Journal of Sociology* 15 (Spring): 149-63.

Barnes, Barry, and David Bloor. 1982, Relativism, Rationalism and the Sociology of Knowledge. In *Rationality and Relativism*, edited by Martin Hollis and Steven Lukes. Cambridge, Mass.: MIT Press.

Bauer, Henry H. 1992. *Scientific Literacy and the Myth of the Scientific Method*. Urbana, Ill.: University of Illinois Press.

Bechtel, William. 1988. *Philosophy of Science: An Overview for Cognitive Science*. Hillsdale, N.J.: Lawrence Erlbaum.

Becker, Carl L. 1932. *The Heavenly City of the Eighteenth-Century Philosophers*. New Haven: Yale University Press.

Becker, Gary S. 1976. *The Economic Approach to Human Behavior*. Chicago: University of Chicago Press.

————. 1993. *Human Capital: A Theoretical and Empirical Analysis with Special Reference to Education*. Chicago: University of Chicago Press.

Belensky, Mary Field, Blythe McVicker Clinchy, Nancy Rule Goldberger, and Jill Mattick Tarule. 1997. *Women's Ways of Knowing: The Development of Self, Voice, and Mind*. New York: Basic Books.

Belkin, Nicholas J. 1990. The Cognitive Viewpoint in Information Science. *Journal of Information Science* 16, no. 1: 11-15.

Benediktsson, Daniel. 1989. Hermeneutics: Dimensions Toward LIS Thinking. *Library and Information Science Research* 11 (July-September): 201-34.

Bennett, George E. 1988. *Librarians in Search of Science and Identity: The Elusive Profession*. Metuchen, N.J.: Scarecrow Press.

Berkeley, George. 1986. *A Treatise concerning the Principles of Human Knowledge and Three Dialogues between Hylas and Philonous*. La Salle, Ill.: Open Court.

Bernal, J. D. 1965. *Science in History*, Vol. 2: *The Scientific and Industrial Revolutions*. Cambridge, Mass.: MIT Press.

Bernard-Donals, Michael F. 1994. *Mikhail Bakhtin: Between Phenomenology and Marxism*. Cambridge: Cambridge University Press.

Bernstein, Richard J. 1971. *Praxis and Action*. Philadelphia: University of Pennsylvania Press.

―――. 1983. *Beyond Objectivism and Relativism: Science, Hermeneutics, and Praxis*. Philadelphia: University of Pennsylvania Press.

―――. 1985. From Hermeneutics to Praxis. In *Hermeneutics and Praxis*, edited by Robert Hollinger. Notre Dame, Ind.: University of Notre Dame Press.

Bertman, Martin A. 1991. *Body and Cause in Hobbes: Natural and Political*. Wakefield, N. H.: Longwood Academic.

Betti, Emilio. 1990. Hermeneutics As the General Methodology of the Geisteswissenschaften. In *The Hermeneutic Tradition: From Ast to Ricoeur*, edited by Gayle L. Ormiston and Alan D. Schrift. Albany: State University of New York Press.

Bhaskar, Roy. 1975. *A Realist Theory of Science*. London: Verso.

Bloor, David. 1991. *Knowledge and Social Imagery*. Chicago: University of Chicago Press.

Bocock, Robert. 1993. *Consumption*. London: Routledge.

Bohman, James. 1991. *New Philosophy of Social Science*. Cambridge, Mass.: MIT Press.

Bonetkoe, Ron. 1987. A Fusion of Horizons: Gadamer and Schleiermacher. *International Philosophical Quarterly* 27 (March): 3-16.

BonJour, Laurence. 1985. *The Structure of Empirical Knowledge*. Cambridge, Mass.: Harvard University Press.

Bourdieu, Pierre. 1991. *Language and Symbolic Power*. Cambridge, Mass.: Harvard University Press.

―――. 1998. *Practical Reason*. Stanford: Stanford University Press.

Bourdieu, Pierre, and Jean-Claude Passeron. 1994. Language and Relationship to Language in the Teaching Situation. In *Academic Discourse*, edited by Pierre Bourdieu, Jean-Claude Passeron, and Monique de Saint-Martin. Stanford: Stanford University Press.

Boyd, Richard N. 1984. The Current Status of Scientific Realism. In *Scientific Realism*, edited by Jarrett Leplin. Berkeley: University of California Press.

Brier, Søren. 1996. Cybersemiotics: A New Paradigm in Analyzing the Problems of Knowledge Organization and Document Retrieval in Information Science. In *Proceedings: Integration in Perspective, October 13-16, 1996: Second International Conference on Conceptions of Library and Information Science*, edited by Peter Ingwersen and Niels Ole Pors. Copenhagen: The Royal School of Librarianship.

Briskman, Larry. 1984. Behaviourism, Positivism, and Kuhn. *New Ideas in Psychology* 2, no. 2: 105-13.

Brooks, Terrence A. 1989. The Model of Science and Scientific Models in Librarianship. *Library Trends* 38 (Fall): 237-49.

Bryant, Christopher G. A. 1985. *Positivism in Social Theory and Research*. New York: St. Martin's Press.

Buckland, Michael. 1991. *Information and Information Systems*. Westport, Conn.: Praeger.

Buckland, Michael, and Frederic Gey. 1994. The Relationship between Recall and Precision. *Journal of the American Society for Information Science* 45 (January):12-19.

Budd, John M. 1995. An Epistemological Foundation for Library and Information Science. *Library Quarterly* 65 (July): 295-318.

———. 1996. The Complexity of Information Retrieval: A Hypothetical Example. *Journal of Academic Librarianship* 22 (March): 111-17.

———. 1997. A Critique of Customer and Commodity. *College and Research Libraries* 58 (July): 310-21.

Budd, John M., and Douglas Raber. 1998. The Cultural State of the Fin De Millenaire Library. *Library Quarterly* 68 (January): 55-79.

Burke, Edmund. 1898. *Select Works of E. Burke*. Oxford: Oxford University Press.

Butler, Pierce. 1961. *An Introduction to Library Science*. Chicago: University of Chicago Press.

Carnap, Rudolf. 1959. The Elimination of Metaphysics through Logical Analysis of Language. In *Logical Positivism*, edited by A. J. Ayer. New York: Free Press.

———. 1959. The Old and the New Logic. In *Logical Positivism*, edited by A. J. Ayer. New York: Free Press.

Cassirer, Ernst. 1951. *The Philosophy of the Enlightenment*. Princeton: Princeton University Press.

Chabris, Christopher F. 1998. IQ Since 'The Bell Curve.' *Commentary* 106 (August): 33-40.

Chalmers, Alan. 1982. *What Is This Thing Called Science?* Indianapolis: Hackett.

———. 1990. *Science and Its Fabrication*. Minneapolis: University of Minnesota Press.

Churchland, Patricia Smith. 1986. *Neurophilosophy: Toward a Unified Science of the Mind/Brain*. Cambridge, Mass.: MIT Press.

Churchland, Paul M. 1979. *Scientific Realism and the Plasticity of Mind*. Cambridge: Cambridge University Press.

————. 1988. *Matter and Consciousness*. Cambridge, Mass.: MIT Press.

Clarke, Desmond M. 1992. Descartes's Philosophy of Science and the Scientific Revolution. In *Cambridge Companion to Descartes*, edited by John Cottingham. Cambridge: Cambridge University Press.

Cleverdon, Cyril W. 1960. *Report on the First Stage on an Investigation into the Comparative Efficiency of Indexing Systems*. Cranfield: College of Aeronautics.

————. 1962. *Report on the Testing and Analysis of an Investigation into the Comparative Efficiency of Indexing Systems*. Cranfield: College of Aeronautics.

Coffman, Steve. 1998. What If You Ran Your Library Like a Bookstore? *American Libraries* 29 (March): 40-46.

Cohen, I. Bernard. 1985. *Revolution in Science*. Cambridge, Mass.: Belknap Press of Harvard University Press.

Cole, Stephen. 1992. *Making Science: Between Nature and Society*. Cambridge, Mass.: Harvard University Press.

Comte, Auguste. 1975. *Auguste Comte and Positivism: The Essential Writings*. New York: Harper & Row.

Condorcet, Marie-Jean-Antoine-Nicolas Caritat, Marquis de. 1976. *Condorcet: Selected Writings*. Indianapolis: Bobbs-Merrill.

Corlett, J. Angelo. 1996. *Analyzing Social Knowledge*. Lanham, Md.: Rowman and Littlefield.

Cornelius, Ian. 1996. *Meaning and Method in Information Studies*. Norwood, N.J.: Ablex.

Cranston, Maurice. 1985. *Philosophers and Pamphleteers*. Oxford: Oxford University Press.

Crosland, Maurice. 1987. The Image of Science As a Threat: Burke versus Priestley and the "Philosophic Revolution". *British Journal for the History of Science* 20 (July): 277-307.

Culler, Jonathan. 1986. *Ferdinand de Saussure*. Ithaca, N.Y.: Cornell University Press.

Cullity, Garrett, and Berys Gaut, eds. 1997. *Ethics and Practical Reason*. Oxford: Oxford University Press.

Dancy, Jonathan. 1985. *Introduction to Contemporary Epistemology*. Oxford: Blackwell.

Danford, John W. 1990. *David Hume and the Problem of Reason: Recovering the Human Sciences*. New Haven: Yale University Press.

Daniels, Michael, Bernie Devlin, and Kathryn Roeder. 1997. Of Genes and IQ. In *Intelligence, Genes, and Success: Scientists Respond to "The Bell Curve"*, edited by Bernie Devlin, Stephen E. Feinberg, Daniel P. Resnick, and Kathryn Roeder. New York: Copernicus.

Davidson, Donald. 1990. A Coherence Theory of Truth and Knowledge. In *Reading Rorty*, edited by Alan R. Malachowski. Oxford: Basil Blackwell.

———. 1995. Mental Events. In *Contemporary Materialism: A Reader*, edited by Paul K. Moser and J. D. Trout. London: Routledge.

———. 1997. Indeterminism and Antirealism. In *Realism/Antirealism and Epistemology*, edited by Christopher P. Kulp. Lanham, Md.: Rowman & Littlefield.

Davis, Charles H. 1990. On Qualitative Research. *Library and Information Science Research* 12, (October-December): 327-28.

De Certeau, Michel. 1986. *Heterologies: Discourses on the Other*. Minneapolis: University of Minnesota Press.

———. 1984. *The Practice of Everyday Life*. Berkeley: University of California Press.

de Gramont, Patrick. 1990. *Language and the Distortion of Meaning*. New York: New York University Press.

Dervin, Brenda. 1977. Useful Theory for Librarianship: Communication, Not Information. *Drexel Library Quarterly* 13, (July): 16-32.

———. 1983. Information As a User Construct: The Relevance of Perceived Information Needs to Synthesis and Interpretation. In *Knowledge Structure and Use: Implications for Synthesis and Interpretation*, edited by Spencer A. Ward and Linda J. Reed. Philadelphia: Temple University Press.

Descartes, Rene. 1989. *Discourse on Method and the Meditations*. Buffalo, N.Y.: Prometheus Books.

DiCenso, James J. 1990. *Hermeneutics and the Disclosure of Truth: A Study in the Work of Heidegger, Gadamer, and Ricoeur*. Charlottesville: University Press of Virginia.

Dick, A. L. 1999. Epistemological Positions and Library and Information Science. *Library Quarterly* 69, (July): 305-23.

———. 1991. Influence of Positivism on the Design of Scientific Techniques: Implications for Library and Information Science Research. *South African Journal of Library and Information Science* 59, (December): 231-39.

———. 1995. Library and Information Science as a Social Science: Neutral andNormative Conceptions. *Library Quarterly* 65 April): 216-35.

Dilthey, Wilhelm. 1989. *Selected Works:* Vol. I. Princeton: Princeton University Press.

Donaldson, Lex. 1996. *For Positivist Organization Theory: Proving the Hard Core.* London: Sage Publications.

Dreyfus, Hubert L., and Paul Rabinow. 1983. *Michel Foucault: Beyond Structuralism and Hermeneutics,* 2d ed. Chicago: University of Chicago Press.

Dunn, John. 1992. Locke. In *The British Empiricists.* Oxford: Oxford University Press.

Durbin, Paul T. 1988. *Dictionary of Concepts in the Philosophy of Science.* Westport, Conn.: Greenwood Press.

Durkheim, Emile. 1982. *The Rules of Sociological Method.* New York: Free Press.

Eagelton, Terry. 1991. *Ideology: An Introduction.* London: Verso.

Eco, Umberto. 1990. *The Limits of Interpretation.* Bloomington: Indiana University Press.

———. 1976. *A Theory of Semiotics.* Bloomington: Indiana University Press.

Editorial: A Research Agenda Beyond 2000. *Library and Information Science Research* 19, no. 3: 209-16.

Egan, Margaret E., and Jesse H. Shera. 1952. Foundations of a Theory of Bibliography. *Library Quarterly* 44, (July): 125-37.

Ellis, David. 1990. *New Horizons in Information Retrieval.* London: The Library Association.

———. 1996. The Dilemma of Measurement in Information Retrieval Research. *Journal of the American Society for Information Science* 47, (January): 23-36.

Fay, Brian. 1996. *Contemporary Philosophy of Social Science.* Oxford: Blackwell.

Feenberg, Andrew. 1995. *Alternative Modernity: The Technical Turn in Philosophy and Social Theory.* Berkeley: University of California Press.

Feyerabend, Paul. 1975. *Against Method.* London: Verso.

———. 1970. Consolations for the Specialist. In *Criticism and the Growth of Knowledge,* edited by Imre Lakatos and Alan Musgrave. Cambridge: Cambridge University Press.

Fodor, Jerry A. 1994. *The Elm and the Expert.* Cambridge, Mass.: MIT Press.

Fogel, Robert William, and Stanley L. Engerman. 1974. *Time on the Cross: The Economics of American Negro Slavery.* Boston: Little, Brown.

Force, James E. 1990. Hume's Interest in Newton and Science. In *Essays on the Context, Nature, and Influence of Isaac Newton's Theology,* edited by James E. Force. Dordrecht: Kluwer Academic Publishers.

Foucault, Michel. 1972. *The Archaeology of Knowledge and the Discourse on Language*. New York: Pantheon.

———. 1977. Nietzsche, Genealogy, History. In *Language, Counter-Memory, Practice: Selected Essays and Interviews*, 139-64. Ithaca, N.Y.: Cornell University Press.

———. 1980. *Power/Knowledge: Selected Interviews and Other Writings, 1972-1977*. New York: Pantheon.

Friedman, Michael. 1992. Causal Laws and the Foundations of Natural Science. In *The Cambridge Companion to Kant*, edited by Paul Guyer. Cambridge: Cambridge University Press.

Frohmann, Bernd. 1992. The Power of Images: A Discourse Analysis of the Cognitive Viewpoint. *Journal of Documentation* 48 (December): 365-86.

Fuller, Steve. 1988. *Social Epistemology*. Bloomington: Indiana University Press.

———. 1993. *Philosophy of Science and Its Discontents*. New York: Guilford Press.

———. 1993. *Philosophy, Rhetoric, and the End of Knowledge: The Coming of Science and Technology Studies*. Madison, Wis.: University of Wisconsin Press.

Gadamer, Hans-Georg. 1989. *Truth and Method*, 2d ed. New York: Crossroad.

Galgan, Gerald J. 1982. *The Logic of Modernity*. New York: New York University Press.

Gardner, Howard. 1995. Scholarly Brinkmanship. In *"The Bell Curve": History, Documents, Opinions*, edited by Russell Jacoby and Naomi Glauberman. New York: Times Books.

Gatten, Jeffrey N. 1991. Paradigm Restrictions On Interdisciplinary Research into Librarianship. *College and Research Libraries* 52 (November): 575-84.

Gay, Peter. 1969. *The Enlightenment: The Science of Freedom*. New York: Norton.

Getz, Malcolm. 1990. Analysis and Library Management. In *Academic Libraries: Research Perspectives*, edited by Mary Jo Lynch and Arthur Young. Chicago: ALA.

Giddens, Anthony. 1977. *Studies in Social and Political Theory*. London: Hutchinson.

Giere, Ronald N. 1988. *Explaining Science: A Cognitive Approach*. Chicago: University of Chicago Press.

———. 1999. *Science without Laws*. Chicago: University of Chicago Press.

Giroux, Henry A., and Susan Searls. 1996. "The Bell Curve" Debate and the Crisis of Public Intellectuals. In *Measured Lies: "The Bell Curve"*

Examined, edited by Joe L. Kinchloe, Shirley R. Steinberg, and Aaron D. Gresson III. New York: St. Martin's Press.

Goldhor, Herbert. 1972. *An Introduction to Scientific Research in Librarianship*. Urbana, Ill.: University of Illinois, Graduate School of Library Science.

Goldman, Alvin I. 1986. *Epistemology and Cognition*. Cambridge, Mass.: Harvard University Press.

———. 1987. Foundations of Social Epistemics. *Synthese* 73: 109-44.

———. 1999. *Knowledge in a Social World*. Oxford: Oxford University Press.

Gould, Stephen Jay. 1995. Mismeasure by Any Measure. In *"The Bell Curve": History, Documents, Opinions*, edited by Russell Jacoby and Naomi Glauberman. New York: Times Books.

———. 1998. In Gratuitous Battle. *Civilization* (October/November): 86-88.

Gramsci, Antonio. 1971. *Selections from the Prison Notebooks*. New York: International Publishers.

Green, Donald P., and Ian Shapiro. 1994. *Pathologies of Rational Choice Theory: A Critique of Applications in Political Science*. New Haven: Yale University Press.

Greiner, Joy. 1990. The Philosophy and Practice of Fines. *APLIS* 3 (December): 233-38.

Grice, Paul. 1989. *Studies in the Way of Words*. Cambridge, Mass.: Harvard University Press.

Gross, Alan G. 1990. *The Rhetoric of Science*. Cambridge, Mass: Harvard University Press.

Gross, Melissa. 1998. The Imposed Query: Implications for Library Service Evaluation. *Reference and User Services Quarterly* 37 (Spring): 290-99.

Gross, Paul R., and Norman Levitt. 1994. *Higher Superstition: The Academic Left and Its Quarrels with Science*. Baltimore: Johns Hopkins University Press.

Guerlac, Henry. 1958. Newton's Changing Reputation in the Eighteenth Century. In *Carl* Becker's *Heavenly City Revisited*, edited by Raymond O. Rockwood. Ithaca, N.Y. Cornell University Press.

Haack, Susan. 1993. *Evidence and Inquiry: Towards Reconstruction in Epistemology*. Oxford: Blackwell.

Habermas, Jurgen. 1971. *Knowledge and Human Interests*. Boston: Beacon Press.

———. 1988. *On the Logic of the Social Sciences*. Cambridge, Mass.: MIT Press.

———. 1998. *On the Pragmatics of Communication*. Cambridge, Mass.: MIT Press.

Hacking, Ian. 1999. *The Social Construction of What?* Cambridge, Mass.: Harvard University Press.

Haines, Valerie A. 1992. Spencer's Philosophy of Science. *British Journal of Sociology* 43 (June): 155-72.

Hamilton, Paul. 1996. *Historicism*. London: Routledge.

Hammond, Michael, Jane Howarth, and Russell Keat. 1991. *Understanding Phenomenology*. Oxford: Blackwell.

Handlin, Oscar. 1979. *Truth in History*. Cambridge, Mass.: Harvard University Press.

Hanfling, Oswald. 1981. *Logical Positivism*. New York: Columbia University Press.

———. 1986. Ayer, Language, Truth, and Logic. *Philosophy* 20: 261-83.

Harding, Sandra. 1991. *Whose Science? Whose Knowledge? Thinking from Women's Lives*. Ithaca, N.Y.: Cornell University Press.

———. 1998. *Is Science Multicultural? Postcolonialisms, Feminisms, and Epistemologies*. Bloomington, Ind.: Indiana University Press.

Harré, Rom, and Michael Krausz. 1996. *Varieties of Relativism*. Oxford: Blackwell.

Harris, Michael H. 1986a. The Dialectic of Defeat: Antimonies [*sic*] in Research in Library and Information Science. *Library Trends* 34 (Winter): 515-31.

———. 1986b. State, Class, and Cultural Reproduction: Toward a Theory of Library Service in the United States. *Advances in Librarianship* 14: 211-52.

Hawkes, David. 1996. *Ideology*. London: Routledge.

Hawkesworth, Mary E. 1994. From Objectivity to Objectification: Feminist Objections. In *Rethinking Objectivity*, edited by Allan Megill. Durham: Duke University Press.

Hawking, Stephen W. 1988. *A Brief History of Time*. New York: Bantam Books.

Hawkins, Richard Laurin. 1938. *Positivism in the United States (1853-1861)*. Cambridge, Mass.: Harvard University Press.

Hayek, F. A. 1979. *The Counter-Revolution of Science: Studies on the Abuse of Reason*. Indianapolis: LibertyPress.

Hegel, G. W. F. 1967. *The Phenomenology of Mind*, translated by J. B. Baillie. New York: Harper & Row.

Heidegger, Martin. 1962. *Being and Time*. New York: Harper Collins.

Heineman, Martha Brunswick. 1981. The Obsolete Scientific Imperative in Social Work Research. *Social Services Review* 55 (September): 371-99.

Hempel, Carl G. 1965. *Aspects of Scientific Explanation and Other Essays in the Philosophy of Science*. New York: Free Press.

Hernon, Peter, and Ellen Altman. 1996. *Service Quality in Academic Libraries*. Norwood, N. J.: Ablex.

Hernon, Peter, and Cheryl Metoyer-Duran. 1992. Literature Reviews and Inaccurate Referencing: An Exploratory Study of Academic Librarians. *College & Research Libraries* 53 (November): 499-512.

Herrnstein, Richard J., and Charles Murray. 1994. *The Bell Curve: Intelligence and Class Structure in American Life*. New York: Free Press.

Hirsch, E. D., Jr. 1967. *Validity in Interpretation*. New Haven: Yale University Press.

Hjorland, Birger. 1997. *Information Seeking and Subject Representation: An Activity-Theoretical Approach to Information Science*. Westport, Conn.: Greenwood Press.

———. 1998. Theory and Metatheory of Information Science: A New Interpretation. *Journal of Documentation* 54 (December): 606-21.

Hobbes, Thomas. 1968. *Leviathan*. Harmondsworth: Penguin.

Hofstadter, Richard. 1944. *Social Darwinism in American Thought*. Boston: Beacon Press.

Horkheimer, Max, and Theodor W. Adorno. 1994. *Dialectic of Enlightenment*. New York: Continuum.

Houser, L., and Alvin M. Schrader. 1978. *The Search for a Scientific Profession: Library Science Education in the U.S. and Canada*. Metuchen, N.J.: Scarecrow Press.

Hoyningen-Huhne, Paul. 1993. *Reconstructing Scientific Revolutions: Thomas S. Kuhn's Philosophy of Science*. Chicago: University of Chicago Press.

Hume, David. 1969. *A Treatise of Human Nature*. London: Penguin.

———. 1988. *An Enquiry concerning Human Understanding*. La Salle, Ill.: Open Court.

Husserl, Edmund. 1962. *Ideas: General Introduction to Pure Phenomenology*. New York: Collier Books.

———. 1970. *The Crisis of European Sciences and Transcendental Phenomenology*. Evanston: Northwestern University Press.

Iggers, Georg G. 1958. *The Doctrine of Saint-Simon: An Exposition; First Year, 1828-1829*. Boston: Beacon Press.

Im Hof, Ulrich. 1994. *The Enlightenment*. Oxford: Blackwell.

Jacobs, Struan. 1991. John Stuart Mill on Induction and Hypotheses. *Journal of the History of Philosophy* 29: 69-83.

Jardine, Lisa. 1990. Experientia Literata or Novum Organum? The Dilemma of Bacon's Scientific Method. In *Francis Bacon's Legacy of Texts: "The Art of Discovery Grows with Discovery"*, edited by William A. Sessions. New York: AMS Press.

———. 1996. *Worldly Goods: A New History of the Renaissance*. New York: Doubleday.

Jonas, Hans. 1984. *The Imperative of Responsibility: In Search of an Ethics for the Technological Age*. Chicago: University of Chicago Press.

Kafatos, Menas, and Robert Nadeau. 1990 *The Conscious Universe: Part and Whole in Modern Physical Theory*. New York: Springer-Verlag.

Kahn, Beverly L. 1989. Antonio Gramsci's Critique of Scientific Marxism. *Thought* 64 (June): 158-75.

Kamin, Leon J. 1995. Lies, Damned Lies, and Statistics. In *The Bell Curve: History, Documents, Opinions*, edited by Russell Jacoby and Naomi Glauberman. New York: Times Books.

Kanekar, Suresh. 1992. Reflections on the Epistemological and Ethical Implications of Skinner's Radical Behaviorism. *Genetic, Social and General Psychology Monographs* 118 (May): 133-55.

Kant, Immanuel. 1950. *Prolegomena to Any Future Metaphysics*. Indianapolis: Bobbs-Merrill Educational Publishing.

———. 1990. *Critique of Pure Reason*. Buffalo, N. Y.: Prometheus Books.

Kaplan, Abraham. 1964. *The Conduct of Inquiry: Methodology for Behavioral Science*. New York: Harper & Row.

Keller, Evelyn Fox. 1992. *Secrets of Life, Secrets of Death: Essays on Language, Gender and Science*. New York: Routledge.

———. 1995. *Reflections on Gender and Science*. New Haven: Yale University Press.

Kincaid, Harold. 1994. Defending Laws in the Social Sciences. In *Readings in the Philosophy of Social Science*, edited by Michael Martin. Cambridge, Mass.: MIT Press.

King, Joyce E. 1996. Bad Luck, Bad Blood, Bad Faith: Ideological Hegemony and the Oppressive Language of Hoodoo Social Science. In *Measured Lies: "The Bell Curve Examined"*, edited by Joe L. Kinchloe, Shirley Steinberg, and Aaron D. Gresson III. New York: St. Martin's Press.

Kingma, Bruce. 1996. *The Economics of Information*. Englewood, Colo.: Libraries Unlimited.

Kingma, Bruce R., and Gillian M. McCombs. 1995. The Opportunity Costs of Faculty Status for Academic Librarians. *College and Research Libraries* 56 (May): 258-64.

Kitcher, Philip. 1993. *The Advancement of Science: Science without Legend, Objectivity without Illusions*. New York: Oxford University Press.

———. 1994. Contrasting Conceptions of Social Epistemology. In *Socializing Epistemology: The Social Dimensions of Knowledge*, edited by Frederick F. Schmitt. Lanham, Md.: Rowman and Littlefield.

Knorr-Cetina, Karin D. 1981. *The Manufacture of Knowledge: An Essay on the Constructivist and Contextual Nature of Science.* Oxford: Pergamon Press.

Kockelmans, Joseph J. 1994. *Edmund* Husserl's *Phenomenology.* West Lafayette, Ind.: Purdue University Press.

Kornblith, Hilary. 1994. A Conservative Approach to Social Epistemology. In *Socializing Epistemology: The Social Dimensions of Knowledge,* edited by Frederick F. Schmitt. Lanham, Md.: Rowman and Littlefield.

Koyré, Alexander. 1968. *Metaphysics and Measurement.* London: Chapman and Hall.

Kraft, Donald H., and Bert R. Boyce. 1991. *Operations Research for Libraries and Information Agencies.* San Diego: Academic Press.

Kraynak, Robert P. 1990. *History and Modernity in the Thought of Thomas Hobbes.* Ithaca, N.Y.: Cornell University Press.

Kühlewind, Georg. 1986. *The Logos-Structure of the World: Language as a Model of Reality.* Hudson, N. Y.: Lindisfarne Press.

Kuhlthau, Carol Collier. 1993. *Seeking Meaning: A Process Approach to Library and Information Services.* Norwood, NJ: Ablex.

———. 1999. The Role of Experience in the Information Search Process of an Early Career Information Worker: Perceptions of Uncertainty, Complexity, Construction, and Sources. *Journal of the American Society for Information Science* 50 (April): 399-412.

Kuhn, Thomas S. 1970. *The Structure of Scientific Revolutions.* Chicago: University of Chicago Press.

Kvanvig, Jonathan L. 1998. Why Should Inquiring Minds Want to Know?: Meno Problems and Epistemological Axiology. *Monist* 81 (July): 426-50.

Lakatos, Imre. 1978. *The Methodology of Scientific Research Programmes.* Cambridge: Cambridge University Press.

Lane, Charles. 1995. Tainted Sources. In *"The Bell Curve" Debate: History, Documents, Opinions,* edited by Russell Jacoby, and Naomi Glauberman. New York:Times Books.

Laplace, Pierre Simon, Marquis de. 1814. *Essai philosophique sur les probabilités.* Paris: Courcier.

Latour, Bruno, and Steve Woolgar. 1986. *Laboratory Life: The Construction of Scientific Facts.* Princeton: Princeton University Press.

Laudan, Larry. 1971. Towards a Reassessment of Comte's "Methode Positive". *Philosophy* 35 (March): 35-53.

———. 1996. *Beyond Positivism and Relativism: Theory, Method and Evidence.* Boulder, Colo.: Westview Press.

Layzer, David. 1995. Science or Superstition? In *"The Bell Curve" Debate: History, Documents, Opinions*, edited by Russell Jacoby and Naomi Glauberman. New York: Times Books.

Lehmann, Jennifer M. 1993. *Deconstructing Durkheim: A Post-Post-Structuralist Critique*. London: Routledge.

Lehrer, Keith. 1990. *Theory of Knowledge*. Boulder, Colo.: Westview.

Lenski, Gerhard. 1991. Positivism's Future—And Sociology's. *Canadian Journal of Sociology* 16 (Spring): 187-95.

Leplin, Jarrett. 1984. Introduction. In *Scientific Realism*, edited by Jarrett Leplin. Berkeley: University of California Press.

Lesk, M. E., and G. Salton. 1968. Relevance Assessments and Retrieval System Evaluation. *Information Storage and Retrieval* 4: 343-59.

Levinas, Emmanuel. 1995. *The Theory of Intuition in Husserl's Phenomenology*. Evanston: Northwestern University Press.

Lewontin, R. C., Steven Rose, and Leon J. Kamin. 1984. *Not in Our Genes: Biology, Ideology, and Human Nature*. New York: Pantheon.

Little, Daniel. 1986. *The Scientific Marx*. Minneapolis: University of Minnesota Press.

Livingston, Paisley. 1988. *Literary Knowledge: Humanistic Inquiry and the Philosophy of Science*. Ithaca, N.Y.: Cornell University Press.

Llobera, Josep R. 1979. Newton, the Scientific Model, and Social Thought in the Enlightenment. *Dialectical Anthropology* 4 (July): 147-53.

Locke, John. 1974. An Essay Concerning Human Knowledge. In *The Empiricists*. New York: Anchor Books, Doubleday.

Longino, Helen E. 1990. *Science as Social Knowledge: Values and Objectivity in Scientific Inquiry*. Princeton: Princeton University Press.

———. 1992. Essential Tensions—Phase Two: Feminist, Philosophical and Social Studies of Science. In *The Social Dimensions of Science*, edited by McMullin, Ernan, 198-216. Notre Dame, In.: University of Notre Dame Press.

Lorenz, Edward N. 1963. Deterministic Nonperiodic Flow. *Journal of the Atmospheric Sciences* 20 (March): 130-41.

Lukacs, Georg. 1971. *History and Class Consciousness: Studies in Marxist Dialectics*. Cambridge, Mass.: MIT Press.

Lumsden, Charles J., and Edward O. Wilson. 1981. *Genes, Mind, and Culture: The Coevolutionary Process*. Cambridge, Mass.: Harvard University Press.

Luntley, Michael. 1988. *Language, Logic and Experience: The Case for Anti-Realism*. La Salle, Ill.: Open Court.

Lyon, Peyton V. 1961. Saint-Simon and the Origins of Scientism and Historicism. *Canadian Journal of Economics and Political Science* 27 (February): 55-63.

Lyotard, Jean-Francois. 1984. *The Postmodern Condition: A Report on Knowledge*. Minneapolis: University of Minnesota Press.

Machlup, Fritz. 1962. *The Production and Distribution of Knowledge in the United States*. Princeton: Princeton University Press.

———. 1994. Are the Social Sciences Really Inferior? In *Readings in the Philosophy of Social Science*, edited by Michael Martin, Michael. Cambridge, Mass.: MIT Press.

MacIntyre, Alisdair. 1984. *After Virtue*, 2d ed. Notre Dame, Ind.: Notre Dame University Press.

Macleod, R. B. 1970. Newtonian and Darwinian Conceptions of Man and Some Alternatives. *Journal of the History of the Behavioral Sciences* 6: 207-18.

Madison, Gary Brent. 1981. *The Phenomenology of Merleau-Ponty*. Athens: Ohio University Press.

Malone, Michael E. 1993. Kuhn Reconstructed: Incommensurability Without Relativism. *Studies in History and Philosophy of Science* 24 (March): 69-93.

Maritain, Jacques. 1995. *Distinguish to Unite or the Degrees of Knowledge*. Notre Dame, Ind.: University of Notre Dame Press.

Marx, Karl. 1956. *Karl Marx: Selected Writings in Sociology and Social Philosophy*. New York: McGraw-Hill.

Masterman, Margaret. 1970. The Nature of a Paradigm. In *Criticism and the Growth of Knowledge*, edited by Imre Lakatos and Alan Musgrave. Cambridge: Cambridge University Press.

Mazlish, Bruce. 1998. *The Uncertain Sciences*. New Haven: Yale University Press.

McCarthy, E. Doyle. 1996. *Knowledge as Culture*. London: Routledge.

McCloskey, Donald N. 1989. Why I Am No Longer a Positivist. *Review of Social Economy* 67 (Fall): 225-38.

McMullin, Ernan. 1984. A Case for Scientific Realism. In *Scientific Realism*, edited by Jarrett Leplin. Berkeley: University of California Press.

Merleau-Ponty, Maurice. 1962. *Phenomenology of Perception*, translated by Colin Smith. London: Routledge.

Merton, Robert K. 1967. *On Theoretical Sociology*. New York: Free Press.

Metz, Paul. 1990. Bibliometrics: Library Use and Citation Studies. In *Academic Libraries: Research Perspectives*, edited by Mary Jo Lynch and Arthur Young. Chicago: American Library Association.

Meyer, Susan Sauve. 1992. Aristotle, Teleology, and Reduction. *Philosophical Review* 101 (October): 791-825.

Miksa, Francis L. 1998. *The DDC, the Universe of Knowledge, and the Post-Modern Library*. Albany, N. Y.: Forest Press.

Mill, John Stuart. 1852. *System of Logic*. New York: Harper & Brothers.

———. 1961. *Auguste Comte and Positivism*. Ann Arbor: University of Michigan Press.

Miller, Richard W. 1987. *Fact and Method: Explanation, Confirmation, and Reality in the Natural and Social Sciences*. Princeton: Princeton University Press.

Mohanty, J. N. 1997. *Phenomenology: Between Essentialism and Transcendental Philosophy*. Evanston: Northwestern University Press.

Moser, Paul K., and J. D. Trout. 1995. *Contemporary Materialism: A Reader*. London: Routledge.

Munz, Peter. 1987. Philosophy and the Mirror of Rorty. In *Evolutionary Epistemology, Rationality, and the Sociology of Knowledge*, edited by Gerard Radnitzky and W. W. Bartley III. La Salle, Ill.: Open Court.

Natanson, Maurice. 1973. *Edmund Husserl: Philosopher of Infinite Tasks*. Evanston: Northwestern University Press.

Neill, S. D. 1992. *Dilemmas in the Study of Information: Exploring the Boundaries of Information Science*. Westport, Conn.: Greenwood Press.

Nelson, Lynn Hankinson. 1995. The Very Idea of Feminist Epistemology. *Hypatia* 10 (Summer): 31-49.

Neurath, Otto. 1959. Sociology and Physicalism. In *Logical Positivism*, edited by A. J. Ayer. New York: Free Press.

Newton-Smith, W. H. 1981. *The Rationality of Science*. London: Routledge.

Norris, Christopher. 1996. *Reclaiming Truth: Contributions to a Critique of Cultural Relativism*. Durham: Duke University Press.

Novick, Peter. 1988. *That Noble Dream: The Objectivity Question and the American Historical Profession*. Cambridge: Cambridge University Press.

Nowakowa, Izabella, and Lesek Nowak. 1978, Marxism and Positivism: The Idea of a Scientific Philosophy. *Poznan Studies in the Philosophy of the Sciences and the Humanities* 4: 210-32.

Owens, Joseph. 1992. *Cognition: An Epistemological Inquiry*. Houston: Center for Thomistic Studies.

Palmer, Richard E. 1969. *Hermeneutics*. Evanston: Northwestern University Press.

Park, Taemin Kim. 1993. The Nature of Relevance in Information Retrieval: An Empirical Study. *Library Quarterly* 63 (July): 318-51.

————. 1994. Toward a Theory of User-Based Relevance: A Call for a New Paradigm of Inquiry. *Journal of the American Society for Information Science* 45 (April): 135-41.

Phillips, D. C. 1983. After the Wake: Postpositivistic Educational Thought. *Educational Researcher* 12 (May): 4-12.

Pickering, Andrew. 1995. *The Mangle of Practice: Time, Agency, and Science.* Chicago: University of Chicago Press.

————. 1994. Objectivity and the Mangle of Practice. In *Rethinking Objectivity*, edited by Allan Megill. Durham, N.C.: Duke University Press.

Pickering, Mary. 1993. *Auguste Comte: An Intellectual Biography.* Cambridge: Cambridge University Press.

Piele, Colin. 1993. Determinism versus Creativity: Which Way for Social Work? *Social Work* 38 (March): 127-34.

Popper, Karl R. 1965. *The Logic of Scientific Discovery.* New York: Harper Torchbooks.

————. 1979. *Objective Knowledge: An Evolutionary Approach.* Oxford: Oxford University Press.

————. 1982. *The Open Universe: An Argument for Indeterminism.* London: Routledge.

————. 1957. *The Poverty of Historicism.* New York: Harper & Row.

————. 1983. *Realism and the Aim of Science.* London: Routledge.

————. 1989. *Conjectures and Refutations: The Growth of Scientific Knowledge.* London: Routledge.

————. 1994. *The Myth of the Framework: In Defense of Science and Rationality.* London: Routledge.

Porter, Theodore M. 1995. *Trust in Numbers: The Pursuit of Objectivity in Science and Public Life.* Princeton: Princeton University Press.

Prado, C. G. 1988. Imagination and Justification. *Monist* 71 (July): 377-88.

Prigogine, Ilya, and Isabelle Stengers. 1984. *Order Out of Chaos: Man's Dialogue with Nature.* New York: Bantam Books.

Putnam, Hilary. 1981. *Reason, Truth and History.* Cambridge: Cambridge University Press.

————. 1987. *The Many Faces of Realism.* LaSalle, Ill.: Open Court.

Quine, Willard Van Orman. 1980. *From a Logical Point of View.* Cambridge, Mass.: Harvard University Press.

Radford, Gary P. 1992. Positivism, Foucault, and the Fantasia of the Library: Conceptions of Knowledge and the Modern Library Experience. *Library Quarterly* 62 (October): 408-24.

Reedy, W. Jay. 1994. The Historical Imaginary of Social Science in Post-Revolutionary France: Bonald, Saint-Simon, Comte. *History of the Human Sciences* 7 (February): 1-26.

Ricoeur, Paul. 1967. *Husserl: An Analysis of His Phenomenology*. Evanston: Northwestern University Press.

———. 1976. *Interpretation Theory: Discourse and the Surplus of Meaning*. Fort Worth: Texas Christian University Press.

———. 1991. *From Text to Action: Essays in Hermeneutics, II*. Evanston: Northwestern University Press.

Roberts, Clayton. 1996. *The Logic of Historical Explanation*. University Park, Penn.: Pennsylvania State University Press.

Rorty, Richard. 1982 *Consequences of Pragmatism*. Minneapolis: University of Minnesota Press.

———. *Contingency, Irony, and Solidarity*. Cambridge: Cambridge University Press.

———. 1979. *Philosophy and the Mirror of Nature*. Princeton: Princeton University Press.

Rosenberg, Alexander. 1995. *Philosophy of Social Science*. Boulder, Colo.: Westview.

Rouse, Joseph. 1987. *Knowledge and Power: Toward a Political Philosophy of Science*. Ithaca: Cornell University Press.

———. 1996. *Engaging Science: How to Understand Its Practices Philosophically*. Ithaca, N. Y.: Cornell University Press.

Ruelle, David. 1991. *Chance and Chaos*. Princeton: Princeton University Press.

Saint-Simon, Henri de. 1975. *Henri Saint-Simon (1760-1825): Selected Writings on Science, Industry, and Social Organisation*. New York: Holmes and Meier.

Saussure, Ferdinand de. 1966. *Course in General Linguistics*. New York: McGraw-Hill.

Sayer, Andrew. 1992. *Method in Social Science: A Realist Approach*. London: Routledge.

Schamber, Linda. 1994. Relevance and Information Behavior. *Annual Review of Information Science and Technology* 29: 3-48.

Scharff, Robert C. 1989. Positivism, Philosophy of Science, and Self-Understanding in Comte and Mill. *American Philosophical Quarterly* 26 (October): 253-68.

Scheler, Max. 1973. *Selected Philosophical Essays*. Evanston: Northwestern University Press.

Scheman, Naomi. 1995. Feminist Epistemology. *Metaphilosophy* 26 (July): 177-90.

Schleiermacher, Friedrich. 1998. *Hermeneutics and Criticism and Other Writings*. Cambridge: Cambridge University Press.

Schmitt, Frederick F. 1992. *Knowledge and Belief*. London: Routledge.

———. 1995. *Truth: A Primer*. Boulder, CO: Westview.

Schneider, Susan M. 1992. Can This Marriage Be Saved? *American Psychologist* 47 (August): 1055-57.

Schutz, Alfred. 1967. *The Phenomenology of the Social World*. Evanston: Northwestern University Press.

Schwartz, Barry, and Hugh Lacey. 1982. *Behaviorism, Science, and Human Nature*. New York: Norton.

Scriven, Michael. 1966. *Value Claims in the Social Sciences*. Lafayette, Ind.: Social Science Education Consortium.

Searle, John R. 1995. *The Construction of Social Reality*. New York: Free Press.

———. 1992. *The Rediscovery of the Mind*. Cambridge, Mass.: MIT Press.

Shapin, Steven. 1996. *The Scientific Revolution*. Chicago: University of Chicago Press.

Shapin, Steven, and Simon Schaffer. 1985. *Leviathan and the Air-Pump*. Princeton: Princeton University Press.

Shelley, Mary. 1993. *Frankenstein, or The Modern Prometheus*. Hertfordshire, England: Wordsworth Classics.

Shera, Jesse H. 1970. *Sociological Foundations of Librarianship*. Bombay: Asia Publishing House.

———. 1972. *The Foundations of Education for Librarianship*. New York: Becker and Hayes.

Simon, Walter M. 1956. History for Utopia: Saint-Simon and the Idea of Progress. *Journal of the History of Ideas* 17 (January): 311-19.

———. 1963. *European Positivism in the Nineteenth Century: An Essay in Intellectual History*. Ithaca, N.Y.: Cornell University Press.

Skinner, B. F. 1965. *Science and Human Nature*. New York: Free Press.

Slezak, Peter. 1994. A Second Look at David Bloor's *Knowledge and Social Imagery*. *Philosophy of the Social Sciences* 24 (September): 336-61.

Smith, David. 1987. The Limits of Positivism in Social Work Research. *British Journal of Social Work* 17 (August): 401-16.

Smith, Laurence D. 1986. *Behaviorism and Logical Positivism: A Reassessment of the Alliance*. Stanford: Stanford University Press.

Snider, Alvin. 1991. Bacon, Legitimation, and the 'Origins' of Restoration Science. *Eighteenth Century* 32 (Summer): 119-38.

Sorrel, Tom. 1988. Descartes, Hobbes and the Body of Natural Science. *Monist* 71 (October): 515-25.

————. 1991 *Scientism: Philosophy and the Infatuation with Science*. London: Routledge.

Spencer, Herbert. 1971. *Herbert Spencer: Structure, Function, and Evolution*. New York: Scribner's.

Sperber, Dan, and Deirdre Wilson. 1988. *Relevance: Communication and Cognition*. Cambridge, Mass.: Harvard University Press.

Spiegelberg, Herbert. 1975. *Doing Phenomenology: Essays on and in Phenomenology*. The Hague: Martinus Nijhoff.

Staats, Arthur W. 1991. Unified Positivism and Unification Psychology: Fad or New Field? *American Psychologist* 46(September): 899-912.

Stewart, David, and Algis Mickunas. *Exploring Phenomenology: A Guide to the Field and Its Literature*. Athens: Ohio University Press.

Stich, Stephen P. 1990. Autonomous Psychology and the Belief-Desire Thesis. In *Mind and Cognition: A Reader*, edited by William G. Lycan. Oxford: Basil Blackwell.

Su, Louise T. 1994. The Relevance of Recall and Precision in User Evaluation. *Journal of the American Society for Information Science* 45 (April): 207-17.

Taylor, Charles. 1985. *Philosophy and the Human Sciences: Philosophical Papers 2*. Cambridge: Cambridge University Press.

Thomas, Brook. 1991. *The New Historicism and Other Old-Fashioned Ideas*. Princeton: Princeton University Press.

Tibbetts, Paul. 1982. The Positivism-Humanism Debate in Sociology: A Reconsideration. *Sociological Inquiry* 52 (Summer): 184-99.

Todorov, Tzvetan. 1984. *Mikhail Bakhtin: The Dialogical Principle*. Minneapolis: University of Minnesota Press.

————. 1998. The Surrender to Nature. *New Republic* 218 (April 27): 29-33.

Toulmin, Stephen. 1990. *Cosmopolis: The Hidden Agenda of Modernity*. Chicago: University of Chicago Press.

————. 1970. Does the Distinction between Normal and Revolutionary Science Hold Water? In *Criticism and the Growth of Knowledge*, edited by Imre Lakatos and Alan Musgrave. Cambridge: Cambridge University Press.

Trigg, Roger. 1985. *Understanding Social Science*. New York: Blackwell.

————. 1993. *Rationality and Science: Can Science Explain Everything?* Oxford: Blackwell.

Tuck, Richard. 1988. Hobbes and Descartes. In *Perspectives on Thomas Hobbes*, edited by G. A. J. Rogers. Oxford: Clarendon Press.

Tversky, Amos, Paul Slovin and Shmuel Sattuth. 1988. Contingent Weighting in Judgments and Choice. *Psychological Review* 95: 371-84.

Urbach, Peter. 1987. *Francis* Bacon's *Philosophy of Science: An Account and a Reappraisal.* La Salle,Ill.: Open Court.

Urmson, J. O. 1992. Berkeley. In *The British Empiricists.* Oxford: Oxford University Press.

van Fraassen, Bas C. 1980. *The Scientific Image.* Oxford: Oxford University Press.

Van House, Nancy A. 1991. Assessing the Quantity, Quality, and Impact of LIS Research. In *Library and Information Science Research: Perspectives and Strategies for Improvement,* edited by Charles R. McClure and Peter Hernon. Norwood, N.J.: Ablex.

Van House, Nancy A., and Thomas A. Childers. 1993. *The Public Library Effectiveness Study: The Complete Report.* Chicago: ALA.

Van House, Nancy A., Beth T. Weil and Charles R. McClure. 1990. *Measuring Academic Library Performance: A Practical Approach.* Chicago: ALA.

Visker, Rudi. 1995. *Michel Foucault: Genealogy as Critique.* London: Verso.

von Glasersfeld, Ernst. 1995. *Radical Constructivism: A Way of Knowing and Learning.* London: Falmer Press.

von Wright, Georg Henryk. 1971. *Explanation and Understanding.* Ithaca, N.Y.: Cornell University Press.

Wang, Peiling, and Marilyn Domas White. 1999. A Cognitive Model of Document Use During a Research Project. Study II. Decisions at the Reading and Citing Stages. *Journal of the American Society for Information Science* 50 (February): 98-114.

Wartenberg, Thomas E. 1992. Reason and the Practice of Science. In *The Cambridge Companion to Kant,* edited by Paul Guyer. Cambridge: Cambridge University Press.

Weber, Max. 1949. *The Methodology of the Social Sciences.* New York: Free Press.

———. 1992. *The Protestant Ethic and the Spirit of Capitalism.* London: Routledge.

Weingand, Darlene E. 1997. *Customer Service Excellence: A Concise Guide for Librarians.* Chicago: ALA.

Wilk, Richard. 1999. When Theory Is Everything, Scholarship Suffers. *Chronicle of Higher Education* 45 (July 9): A42.

Williams, Robert V. 1986. Public Library Development in the United States, 1850-1870: An Empirical Analysis. In *Libraries, Books, and Culture,* edited by Donald G. Davis Jr. Austin: Graduate School of Library and Information Science, University of Texas at Austin.

Wilson, Edward O. 1998. *Consilience: The Unity of Knowledge.* New York: Knopf.

Wilson, Patrick. 1977. *Public Knowledge, Private Ignorance: Toward a Library and Information Policy*. Westport, Conn.: Greenwood Press.

———. 1983. *Second-Hand Knowledge: An Inquiry into Cognitive Authority*. Westport, Conn.: Greenwood Press.

Winch, Peter. 1958. *The Idea of a Social Science and Its Relation to Philosophy*. London: Routledge.

Wittgenstein, Ludwig. 1990. *Tractatus Logico-Philosophicus*. London: Routledge.

Woolgar, Steve. 1988. *Science: The Very Idea*. Chichester: Ellis Horwood Limited.

Zabeeh, Farhang. 1960. *Hume: Precursor of Modern Empiricism*. The Hague: Martinus Nijhoff.

Ziegelmeyer, Edmund H. 1942. Auguste Comte and Positivism. *Modern Schoolman* 20 (November): 6-17.

Ziman, John. 1978. *Reliable Knowledge: An Exploration of the Grounds for Belief in Science*. Cambridge: Cambridge University Press.

Zimmerman, Jerome H. 1989. Determinism, Science, and Social Work. *Social Services Review* 63 (March): 52-62.

Žižek, Slavoj. 1989. *The Sublime Object of Ideology*. London: Verso.

Index

Adair, Douglas, 55
adaptationism, 97-98
Adorno, Theodor, 26, 83
Alston, William P., 212-13
Altman, Ellen, 195
American Revolution, 57
Andaleeb, Syed Saad, 198-99
Anderson, Elizabeth, 235-36
Andreski, Stanislav, 78
Appleby, Joyce, 99-100, 149,
    154-55
argumentation, 233
Armstrong, David M., 112-13,
    151-52
Atkinson, Ross, 306-08, 319
Audi, Robert, 210-11, 218
Ayer, A. J., 89, 91

Bacon, Francis, 24-31, 34, 36,
    38, 42, 48, 55, 76-77,
    93, 159
Baconianism, 25, 57-58, 67, 71,
    93, 107, 155

Bakhtin, Mikhail, 266, 283, 289,
    313-19
Baldus, Bernd, 92-93
Barnes, Barry, 126
Bauer, Henry H., 110
Bechtel, William, 89
Becker, Carl, 41
Becker, Gary S., 176-78, 187
behaviorism, 158-63
being and phenomenology, 252-
    55
Belensky, Mary Field, 236
Belkin, Nicholas J., 295
Benediktsson, Daniel, 285-86
Bennett, George E., 284-85
Berkeley, George, 42-45
Bernal, J. D., 33, 41-42
Bernard-Donals, Michael F., 317
Bernstein, Richard J., 142, 274-
    79
Bertman, Martin, 36
Betti, Emilio, 273-75, 277-78
Bhaskar, Roy, 118

353

bibliometrics, 199-200, 251
Bloor, David, 126, 130
Bocock, Robert, 322
Bohman, James, 177-79, 240
Bonetkoe, Ron, 276
BonJour, Laurence, 120, 212
Bourdieu, Pierre, 323-26
Boyce, Bert R., 145
Boyd, Richard N., 124
Boyle, Robert, 43
Brier, Soren, 312-13
Briskman, Larry, 162
Brooks, Terrence A., 115
Bryant, Christopher G. A., 82, 103-04
Buckland, Michael, 200, 222
Budd, John M., 192, 246, 255, 266, 311, 322
Burke, Edmund, 59-60
Burt, Cyril, 167-68
Butler, Pierce, 3, 6

capitalism, 53
Carnap, Rudolf, 87-88
Cassirer, Ernst, 54-55
causation, 18, 23, 27, 44, 48-50, 53
censorship, 324
Chabris, Christopher, 169-70
Chalmers, A. F., 125, 141, 146
Childers, Thomas A., 239
Churchland, Patricia Smith, 218
Churchland, Paul M., 217-18
Clarke, Desmond, 32-33
classification of information, 309-11
Clinchy, Blythe McVicker, 236
Cleverdon, Cyril W., 293-94
Coffman, Steve, 196-97
cognitive viewpoint in information science, 295-96

Cohen, I. B., 25-26
coherentism and knowledge, 211-14
Cole, Stephen, 136
commodification, 189-90, 222-23
communication. *See* information and communication
Comte, August, 64-71, 77, 80-81, 96, 101-02, 110, 200
Condorcet, marquis de, 58-61, 64-65, 69
constructivism, 128-31, 133, 135, 227-28, 230-31; in education, 184-86
consumerism, 322-23
Copernicus, Nicholas, 28
Corlett, J. Angelo, 227
Cornelius, Ian, 244-45, 286-87, 312
corpuscular theory, 43-44
cosmology, 22
Cranston, Maurice, 30
criteria for knowledge, 8, 206-11
Crosland, Maurice, 60
Culler, Jonathan, 84
customer and LIS, 192-93, 322-23

Dancy, Jonathan, 205-07, 210
Danford, John W., 47-48
Daniels, Michael, 164-65
Darwin, Charles, 78-79
Dasein (Heidegger), 254
Davidson, Donald, 113, 120, 124, 211-12
Davis, Charles H., 201, 203-04
de Certeau, Michel, 326
de Gramont, Patrick, 302-03
de Saussure, Ferdinand, 84-85
deduction, 110-11
Dervin, Brenda, 300-303

Descartes, René, 24, 31-35, 37-38, 40, 49, 79, 151, 262
determinism, 15-22, 51, 76, 78-79, 81-83, 160, 179-84, 206
deterministic scientism. *See* scientism
Devlin, Bernie, 164-65
Dewey, John, 3
Di Censo, James J., 277
dialogic communication, 314-19
Dick, Archie L., 14-15, 245-46
Dilthey, Wilhelm, 272
discursive practice, 266-67, 282-83
Donaldson, Lex, 182-84
Dreyfus, Hubert, 10
dualism, 32, 99, 151
Dunn, John, 40
Durbin, Paul T., 23
Durkheim, Emile, 79-84, 104

Eagelton, Terry, 320-21
Eco, Umberto, 85, 270
economics, 99, 176-78; and information, 187-91
Egan, Margaret, 222-23
eliminative materialism, 217-19
Ellis, David, 297-98
empiricism, 15, 32-34, 43-45, 53, 102, 261
Engerman, Stanley, 179-82
Enlightenment, 4, 28-29, 32-33, 40, 42, 54-57, 60, 154, 170-71
essence and phenomenology, 252, 255-58
ethics, 327-28
evaluation of services, 193-96
experience, 37-38, 46

Fay, Brian, 239, 241
Feenberg, Andrew, 322

feminism and knowledge, 138-39, 235-38
Feyerabend, Paul, 133-34, 136
Fodor, Jerry, 218-19
Fogel, Robert William, 179-82
folk psychology, 216-17
Force, James E., 50
Foucault, Michel, 9-12, 149, 171, 257-58
foundationalism and knowledge, 209-10, 214
French Revolution, 57-59, 63, 105
Friedman, Michael, 52-53
Frohmann, Bernd, 296
Fuller, Steve, 116, 226-27

Gadamer, Hans-Georg, 273-74, 276-81
Galgan, Gerald J., 24-25
Gardner, Howard, 165
Gassendi, Peter, 43
Gatten, Jeffrey N., 136
Gay, Peter, 55
genealogy, 9-13; defined, 9-10
Getz, Malcolm, 191-92
Gey, Frederic, 200
Giddens, Anthony, 82
Giere, Ronald N., 117, 125, 133, 144
Goldberger, Nancy Rule, 236
Goldhor, Herbert, 115
Goldman, Alvin I., 129-30, 204, 212-13, 221, 228-35, 237, 304
Goodman, Nelson, 230
Gould, Stephen J., 12, 169
Graduate Library School (Chicago), 104-05
Gramsci, Antonio, 76
Great Instauration, 25
Green, Donald P., 178

Greiner, Joy, 189
Grice, Paul, 301
Gross, Alan G., 129
Gross, Melissa, 308-09
Gross, Paul R., 237-38
Guerlac, Henry, 42

Haack, Susan, 16, 145-46, 212, 214
Habermas, Jurgen, 106, 109, 114, 281, 304-05
Hacking, Ian, 115-16, 129
Haines, Valerie A., 78
Hammond, Michael, 245, 260-61
Handlin, Oscar, 180-81
Hanfling, Oswald, 88
Harding, Sandra, 139, 237-38
Harré, Rom, 126-27
Harris, Michael, 14, 105, 109-10, 186
Hawkes, David, 192
Hawkesworth, Mary E., 138
Hawking, Stephen, 18
Hawkins, Richard, 71
Hayek, F. A., 15, 58-59, 66, 69
Hegel, G. W. F., 76-77, 247
Heidegger, Martin, 246, 254, 262, 291
Heineman, Martha Brunswick, 101-02
Hempel, Carl G., 91, 153-56
hermenutical phenomenology 246-47, 291, 329
hermeneutics, 6, 77, 252, 263, 269-73; and LIS, 284-87
Hernon, Peter, 2-3, 195
Herrnstein, Richard J., 163-70
Hirsch, E. D., Jr., 275-76, 281
historicism, 62-63, 79, 153-54
history, 99-100, 153-56, 179-82, 260

Hjørland, Birger, 244, 305, 311-12
Hobbes, Thomas, 35-37
Hofstadter, Richard, 79
Horkheimer, Max, 26
Houser, Lloyd, 115, 119
Howarth, Jane, 245, 260-61
Hoyningen-Huhne, Paul, 135
humanism, 27
Hume, David, 45-51
Hunt, Lynn, 99-100, 149, 154-55
Husserl, Edmund, 248, 250, 252-53, 255-57, 262-63, 271, 285, 288, 291

ideology, 76, 232, 319-22
Iggers, Georg, 61
imposed query (information seeking), 308-09
incommensurability, 134-37, 184
indeterminism, 21, 240
induction, 25-26, 28, 50, 71-72, 159
information and communication, 300-05
information retrieval, 124, 295
information seeking, 204, 264, 300-05
instrumentalism, 159-60, 184
intelligence, measurement, 163-70
intentionality and phenomenology, 252, 261, 301-02
interpretation. *See* hermenutics
intuition and phenomenology, 285-86

Jacob, Margaret, 99-100, 149, 154-55
Jacobs, Struan, 72

James, William, 3
Jardine, Lisa, 25, 27, 54
Jonas, Hans, 327-28
Journal des sçavans, 30
justification, 10, 122-24, 204-08, 213-16, 220

Kafatos, Menas, 116-17
Kamin, Leon, 168, 173, 175
Kanekar, Suresh, 159, 162
Kant, Immanuel, 51-53, 120, 151
Kaplan, Abraham, 114-15
Keat, Russell, 245, 260-61
Keller, Evelyn Fox, 139-40
Kincaid, Harold, 113
King, Joyce E., 169
Kingma, Bruce R., 143, 187-91
Kitcher, Philip, 121-22, 228
Knorr-Cetina, Karen, 128
Kockelmans, Joseph J., 253
Kornblith, Hilary, 228
Koyré, Alexander, 39
Kraft, Donald H., 145
Krausz, Michael, 126-27
Kraynak, Robert P., 28-29, 36
Kühlewind, Georg, 24
Kuhlthau, Carol C., 303-05
Kuhn, Thomas S., 98, 131-37
Kvanvig, Jonathan L., 204

Lacey, Hugh, 161-62
Lakatos, Imre, 136-37
language and knowledge, 84-91, 120-21, 240, 266-67, 282-84, 323-24
Laplace, Marquis de, 17-18, 20
Latour, Bruno, 128
Laudan, Larry, 66-67, 131, 142
Lehmann, Jennifer, 81
Lehrer, Keith, 204-09, 211, 214

Lenski, Gerhard, 92
Leplin, Jarrett, 119
Lesk, M. E., 292-93
Levinas, Emmanuel, 285-86
Levitt, Norman, 237-38
Lewontin, R. C., 173, 175
Library Bill of Rights (ALA), 324
lifeworld and phenomenology, 253, 277, 304
Little, Daniel, 75
Livingston, Paisley, 245
Llobera, Josep, 46
Locke, John, 38-44, 55
logical positivism, 45, 85-93, 102-06, 209-10
logos, 24
Longino, Helen, 140-41, 143
Lorenz, Edward, 19
Lukacs, Georg, 189
Lumsden, Charles J., 108
Luntley, Michael, 143
Lynn, Richard, 168
Lyon, Peyton V., 62
Lyotard, Jean-Francois, 195, 197

Mach, Ernst, 117, 159
Machlup, Fritz, 152, 224
MacIntyre, Alisdair, 154-55
Macleod, R. B., 40
Malone, Michael E., 135
management, LIS, 191-92
Maritain, Jacques, 204, 208
Marx, Karl, 74-76
mass media and social epistemology, 233-34
Masterman, Margaret, 132
materialism, 112-14, 151-52, 171
Mazlish, Bruce, 25, 32
McCarthy, E. Doyle, 136
McCloskey, Donald N., 99

McClure, Charles R., 194-96
McCombs, Gillian M., 189-91
McMullin, Ernan, 123-24
Merleau-Ponty, Maurice, 258-61, 267-68
Merton, Robert K., 157
methodological idealism, 110-11
Metoyer-Duran, Cheryl, 2-3
Metz, Paul, 136
Meyer, Susan Sauve, 24
Mickunas, Algis, 251, 264
Miksa, Francis L., 79, 309-11
Mill, John Stuart, 70-74, 77
Miller, Richard W., 101, 107
modernisn, 34, 36
Mohanty, J. N., 250, 253
Morris, Pam, 318
Moser, Paul K., 112
Murray, Charles, 163-70
Munz, Peter, 220

Nadeau, Robert, 115-16
Natanson, Maurice, 257
naturalism, 16
Neill, S. D., 225
Nelson, Lynn Hankinson, 236-37
Neurath, Otto, 88
Newton, Isaac, 41-42, 50, 55, 67, 71, 77, 155
Newton-Smith, W. H., 134
nomological, 70, 111
Norris, Christopher, 118-19
Novick, Peter, 154, 181
Nowak, Leszek, 75
Nowakowa, Izabella, 75

objectivism, 30-31, 82, 115, 117, 155-56, 267, 294
operations research in LIS, 145
organizational theory, 182-84

Owens, Joseph, 204

paradigm, 132-33, 136
Palmer, Richard E., 272, 274, 276, 280
Park, Taemin Kim, 214-16
Peirce, Charles Sanders, 3, 85
perception and phenomenology, 252, 258-61
phenomenalism, 78, 108-09, 111
phenomenology, 5-6, 246-69, 282-83, 316-19
Phillips, D. C., 96
Philosophical Transactions of the Royal Society of London, 30
phronesis, 279-81, 327
physicalism, 207-08, 216-18, 292, 297
Pickering, Andrew, 128, 146
Pickering, Mary, 64-65, 69
Piele, Colin, 17, 21-2
polysemy, 285
Popper, Karl R., 20-21, 26-27, 89-91, 110-11, 121, 125-26, 141, 153-54, 209-10, 243
Porter, Theodore, 172-73
positivism, 4, 14-15, 25, 32, 59-62, 66-70, 80-83, 96-106; in LIS, 104-06, 109-10
Prado, C. G., 221
pragmatism, 3, 5, 219-21
praxis and LIS, 3, 5, 279-81, 286-87
precision and information retrieval, 294
Prigogine, Ilya, 18-19
progress, 1-2, 42, 156-58
psychologism, 271, 273
public libraries as businesses, 196-97

Putnam, Hilary, 122-23

Quine, W. V. O., 16, 90, 210

Rabinow, Paul, 10
race, measurement, 163-70
Radford, Gary P., 14, 257-58
rational choice, 59, 171-79
rationalism, 22, 32, 59, 116-17,
  190, 238-39
realism, 5, 18, 114-22, 144-47,
  207, 263-64
reason, 52-53; in LIS, 123-25
recall in information retrieval,
  294
reductionism, 34, 44, 73, 107-
  08, 111, 160, 207, 216-17
Reedy, W. Jay, 60-61
relativism, 125-31, 135, 142,
  144, 230, 268, 273
relevance in information
  retrieval, 292-300
reliabilism, 213, 229-35
Renaissance, 28-29, 32, 54-55
Restoration (England), 28
Ricoeur, Paul, 266, 268-69, 278,
  281-84, 286
Roberts, Clayton, 182
Roeder, Kathryn, 164-65
Rose, Steven, 173, 175
Rosenberg, Alexander, 156, 178
Rorty, Richard, 3, 5, 219-21
Rouse, Joseph, 139, 141, 143,
  145
Royal Society of London, 30
Rushton, Phillippe, 168-69

Saint-Simon, Henri de, 61-65,
  68, 74, 104
Salton, G., 292-93
Sayer, Andrew, 110, 157, 240-42
Schaffer, Simon, 128

Schamber, Linda, 294
Scharff, Robert C., 73
Scheler, Max, 250
Scheman, Naomi, 235
Schleiermacher, Friedrich, 270-
  72
Schmitt, Frederick F., 207, 213-
  14
Schneider, Susan M., 98-99
Schrader, Alvin, 115, 119
Schutz, Alfred, 264-65, 302
Schwartz, Barry, 161-62
scientism, 4, 15-16, 22-23, 31,
  34-36, 50-51, 54, 69-70, 74,
  78-79, 91, 95-97, 100-14,
  160, 209, 239, 267, 321,
  326; in LIS, 186-201
Scriven, Michael, 157
Searle, John, 117, 144-45, 230,
  299-300
self and other in phenomenology,
  252, 259, 265
semiotics, 85
sensory perception, 35-36, 46-
  47, 49, 256
Shapin, Steven, 126, 128
Shapiro, Ian, 178
Shelley, Mary, 62
Shera, Jesse H., 5, 222-25, 228-
  30
Simmonds, Patience L., 198-99
Simon, Walter M., 63, 73
Skinner, B. F., 158-63, 266
Slezak, Peter, 130
Smith, David, 99
Smith, Laurence D., 160
Snider, Alvin, 28-30
social constructivism. *See*
  constructivism
social Darwinism, 78-79, 146
social epistemology, 5, 222-35,
  268

sociobiology, 108
sociology, 77-78, 80-82, 157
sociology of knowledge, 130
Sorrel, Tom, 15, 23, 31, 37
Spencer, Herbert, 77-79
Sperber, Dan, 298-99
Spiegelberg, Herbert, 248-49, 289
Staats, Arthur, 97-98
Stengers, Isabelle, 18-19
Stewart, David, 251, 264
Stich, Stephen P., 216-17
Su, Louise, 200-01

Tarule, Jill Mattick, 236
Taylor, Charles, 287
technology, 8-9, 21
teleology, 23, 35
testimony in social epistemology, 232
theory and LIS, 244-45, 311-13
Tibbetts, Paul, 102-03
Todorov, Tzvetan, 173, 318
Toulmin, Stephen, 28, 54, 134
Trigg, Roger, 107-08, 110, 144
truth, 46, 122-24, 231
Tuck, Richard, 37
Tversky, Amos, 179

uncertainty principle, 18
understanding, 47-48, 253, 270, 272
unity of science, 88-89, 109-10, 112, 150-53
Urbach, Peter, 26, 28
Urmson, J. O., 43-44

value neutrality, 105, 155
van Frassen, Bas, 123
Van House, Nancy, 186-87, 194-96
verification, 88

veritism, 233-35
Vienna Circle, 86-91, 96, 102, 104
Visker, Rudi, 10
von Glasersfeld, Ernst, 184-86
von Wright, Georg Henryk, 100-01

Wang, Peiling, 296-97
Wartenberg, Thomas E., 53-54
Weber, Max, 55, 108-09, 240
Weil, Beth, 194-96
Weingand, Darlene, 192-93
White, Marilyn, 296-97
Wilk, Richard, 247
Williams, Robert V., 198
Wilson, Deirdre, 298-99
Wilson, Edward O., 170-75
Wilson, Patrick, 224-25
Winch, Peter, 240
Wittgenstein, Ludwig, 85, 209
Woolgar, Steve, 128-29

Zabeeh, Farhang, 46
Ziegelmeyer, Edmund H., 69
Ziman, John, 118
Zimmerman, Jerome H., 17, 19-20
Žižek, Slavoj, 323

About the Author

John M. Budd is an associate professor with the School of Information Science and Learning Technologies at the University of Missouri-Columbia. He earned his Ph.D. in library science from the University of North Carolina at Chapel Hill in 1985. Prior to joining the faculty of the University of Missouri, he taught at Louisiana State University and the University of Arizona. He also worked for several years at Southeastern Louisiana University.

He is the author of other books, including *The Academic Library: Its Context, Its Purpose, and Its Operation,* published by Libraries Unlimited, and *The Library and Its Users: The Communication Process,* published by Greenwood Press. He has also written several dozen journal articles. Most recently, he has been examining the intellectual and theoretical foundations of library and information science. This book is a product of that investigation.